CLOSING THE CIRCLE

IYNX PUBLISHING 2002

CLOSING THE CIRCLE

THOMAS HOWARTH, MACKINTOSH AND THE MODERN MOVEMENT

Timothy Neat and Gillian McDermott

To my family and friends for their love and support.
GILLIAN McDERMOTT

To John Berger – his words, his vision, his love.
TIMOTHY NEAT

Previous page. Dr Thomas Howarth (c. 1972),
Dean of the Faculty of Environmental Design
at The University of Toronto. *Robert Lansdale*

First published in 2002 Great Britain by
iynx publishing
Countess of Moray's House
Sands Place
Aberdour
Fife KY3 0SY

www.iynx.com

British Library Cataloguing in Publication Data
A catalogue record for this book is available
from the British Library

ISBN 0 95405 830 5

Book design by Mark Blackadder

Printed and bound by Bookcraft

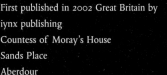

CONTENTS

Acknowledgements   vi

Preface   vii

Introduction   1

1.   Boyhood   13

2.   The University Years   43

3.   Glasgow and Discipleship   65

4.   The Mackintosh Years   84

5.   The Living Word   128

6.   Manchester and the United States   153

7.   Professorship   186

8.   The University of Toronto   203

9.   Architecture and Planning   238

10. April in the Fall   257

11. Closing the Circle   295

ACKNOWLEDGEMENTS

In writing this biography, it has been a privilege to have been drawn into the brilliant circles Thomas Howarth inhabited. As authors we first acknowledge our debt to Tom Howarth – a man who was a professional colleague, a difficult character, a dear friend, and a most stimulating companion. We also thank all those friends and associates who have provided us with letters, statements, thoughts, remembrances, insights, and ideas. Work on this book has proved a pleasure and we have been the recipients of much generosity. In particular we thank Liz and Tom Short, Aubrey Russell, and the Howarth family; Harry Ferguson, Leslie Rebanks, Olga Williams, Moses Znaimer, Marilyn Lightstone, Eb Zeibler, George and Milena Grenfell Baines, Sidney Tasker, John Berger, Hamish Henderson and Ian Hamilton Finlay. Also the exemplary custodians of the Howarth Archive in the Library of the University of Toronto, especially Harold Averill.

Gillian McDermott would also like to add personal thanks to all those friends and colleagues who professionally and personally helped her to maintain the promises she made to Tom Howarth, they include Mike Adams, Laurie Barker, Rob Brown, David Cochlin, Carlos, Daphne, Dr Russel Goldman, Daniel, Valerie Sinclair, Scott Gwilliams, Mel Kestenberg, Olga and Miro Klement, Max Kothe, Norma Macfarlane, Kim, Dr George Photopolous, Walter Putzer, Kammy Samarsand, David Scott, Barbara Solowan, John Sapsford, the administrative staff of Toronto Homecare Services, Helgie Tiernmann, Everel Waterman, Winsome and Marina Winters.

The publishers thank the following for permission to reproduce copyright material: Carcanet Press, Christie's Images and Faber and Faber. Extracts from 'Selected Poems of Rainer Maria Rilke', edited and translated by Robert Bly reprinted by permission of Harper Collins Publishers; extract from Selected Poems (New Edition) by W.H. Auden, edited by Edward Mendelson, copyright 1979 by Edward Mendelson, William Meredith and Monroe K. Spears, used by permission of Vintage Books, a division of Random House Inc.

All images are the property of the Thomas Howarth estate or the Thomas Howarth archive unless otherwise stated. Every effort has been made to trace and acknowledge copyright holders, but if any have inadvertently been overlooked the publishers will be pleased to make the necessary arrangements at the first opportunity.

PREFACE

This biography is based upon personal memoirs set down during the last decade of Dr Thomas Howarth's life. The original 700 close-typed pages have been much pruned and edited but they still provide long sections of first person narrative which give *Closing the Circle* a deliberate, autobiographical directness.

'Every force evolves its own form' is a Gaelic proverb that encapsulates a powerful truth and this biography has evolved through an unusual combination of processes to become a many-faceted account of a remarkable life. The aim has been to create an intimate personal portrait that is also an inquiry into the artistic, educational and cultural reality of Western society in the twentieth century. 'There is Hope in Honest Error, None in the Icy Perfections of the Mere Stylist', as Mackintosh once graphically put it.

During his lifetime, Thomas Howarth gained recognition as a scholar, a teacher and historian of international importance but it will be as an exemplary and obsessive Mackintosh enthusiast and collector of art that future generations will remember him. Most collecting has an aesthetic impulse and historical value but when Thomas Howarth started his great study of Mackintosh he set in train a sequence of events that have taken on revolutionary importance. The combination of Mackintosh's visionary creativity with Howarth's wish to evangelise has changed the direction of art in Scotland and profoundly influenced international culture. Like Freud Mackintosh has become, 'a whole climate of opinion'.

INTRODUCTION

TIMOTHY NEAT

JOHN BERGER | *Mackintosh: this is a man who,*
by himself, created a civilisation.

Howarth's magnum opus, *Mackintosh and the Modern Movement*, was published in 1952. It is a book that resurrected a lost reputation, and Howarth's perceptions have remained the measure of all subsequent studies of the architect who is now recognised as the most original visual artist that Scotland has produced. Howarth was a 'man o' pairts': a scholar, teacher, architect, planner, university administrator, pianist, poet, patron, and benefactor. In the 1940s he played a significant role in establishing all the major Mackintosh Collections: at the Hunterian Museum, at Glasgow School of Art, and in the City of Glasgow's own collection at Kelvingrove. In the 1990s he part sold, part bequeathed and part gave away the marvellous personal collection he had accumulated over a lifetime. In the year before his death he wrote the cheque that enabled the Mackintosh Society to buy its own premises, Mackintosh's Queen's Cross Church. Howarth was always a 'man with an eye'; he bought Mackintosh when Mackintosh was almost totally disregarded and he was gifted numerous 'priceless' objects by people who recognised the value of the work he was doing. This was a man who ploughed and sowed before reaping. This was a man dedicated to the idea of service; a man who inspired love, as well as irritation and envy.

Thomas Howarth died on 21 July 2000, in Toronto, Canada. It was a 'timely' death that he accepted with contentment – partly because he had enjoyed longevity, happiness and achievements that he had not dared hope for during the long years of his sickly boyhood, and partly because age had brought a return of his religious faith. *Dreams, Visions and Nightmares* was Howarth's original title for his *Memoirs* but, on reflection, he recognised that *Closing the Circle* was a better title for the book that we planned. There is, however, a real sense in which the trajectory of Howarth's personal life has complimented a century during which Western experience has embraced democracy, mass prosperity and sustained peace, the dream visions of Margaret Macdonald, and the nightmare realities of bombs and holocaust.

Berger's statement, 'this is a man who, by himself, created a civilisation' defines the Mackintosh achievement with revelatory force and it was with similar, instinctive insight

Howarth (1927) at
Blackpool Pleasure Beach.
Thomas Howarth

1

that Howarth, forty years earlier, recognised that Mackintosh and the small, brilliant circle around him, had, in a few short years around 1900, done something astounding. With what Jack Yeats liked to call the 'diffidence of the spear point' they nurtured values and created a style just as recognisable, useable and developable as those created, over centuries, in Ancient Egypt, in Classical Greece, in Renaissance Italy, and Aztec Mexico. Looking back today, few people are surprised to learn that the architects of Austria, on learning of Mackintosh's death, toasted 'Mackintosh – the Greatest since the Gothic', but such recognition was anathema seventy years ago. Then, except amongst tiny bands of 'cognoscenti', Mackintosh's reputation was at the bottom of a trough of wilful rejection; a non-comprehension aggravated by years of World War and Depression. It also remains a surprising and inspiring thought that when the young Thomas Howarth arrived in Glasgow in September 1939, exempt from war service because of chronic asthma, he should, almost immediately, decide to dedicate his life to the art and ideals of this rejected man – Charles Rennie Mackintosh. North Renfrew Street, where the Glasgow School of Art stood with its broken window panes shining in the evening sun, became for Howarth another road to Damascus; a place of vision in which he still exalted on his deathbed.

It is a fact of history that Charles Rennie Mackintosh died honoured by few. In January 1928, only six people attended his cremation at Golders Green in North London. Five years later, six people attended the cremation of Mackintosh's wife, Margaret Macdonald. Her assets were then valued at eighty-eight pounds. For a short while this marvellously creative two-person team, along with Margaret's sister, Frances, and her husband Herbert MacNair, generated admiration and love amongst avant-garde artists across Europe but, not surprisingly, their revolutionary clarity also generated antagonism. In 1914 the Mackintoshes left Scotland – Charles never to return. His career as an architect did not revive in wartime London and, long before his death, Mackintosh had become an almost invisible figure in British cultural life – an eccentric designer whose works were 'spooky' footnotes to a former age of unseemly, personal vision. The man who changed all this, and orchestrated Mackintosh's emergence onto the world stage as a great artist and one of the creators of the Modern Movement in architecture, was Thomas Howarth.

It was a great and genuine discovery. Few men, even of pre-eminent genius, make more than one such discovery in their lives; the potentialities of the greatest discoveries being so profound that they often preoccupy the lives of whole societies for generations and there can be no doubt that Howarth's decision to 'follow' Charles Rennie Mackintosh shaped and fuelled his life for the next sixty years. The fact that Mackintosh has now become an unavoidable cultural force in Scottish life, and a seminal influence on many artists, designers and architects round the world, is very much a consequence of Howarth's work. If the clarity of form and the spiritual energy that Mackintosh packed into his designs are now recognised as archetypes and facts of the language of contemporary international art, Thomas Howarth must be recognised as partly responsible. If, at the start of the third millennium, much of Mackintosh's work looks as pristine and modern as at the moment of its inception, Howarth must be given some of the credit. Of course Howarth was never alone in propagating the genius of the Mackintosh group, but, in the 1940s, after three decades of neglect, Howarth was instrumental in revealing Mackintosh to a world that remains hungry for the memes and values to which Mackintosh gave form.

If Thomas Howarth had not decided to become Mackintosh's champion there can be no doubt that these revolutionary designs would, slowly, have been reassessed and be well-honoured today but Howarth's espousal of the Mackintosh cause, at a time when remnants of his generation were still alive, bore wonderful fruit. Furthermore, it was his scholastic exactitude, his architectural knowledge, and his historical insights that established the standards by which Mackintosh's posthumous reputation has blossomed. Howarth's collation of the Mackintosh oeuvre and his seeding of the Mackintosh collections in Scotland, laid the foundations for the coherent preservation and study of the Glasgow style worldwide. Howarth's grit and determination to disseminate the 'word' of Mackintosh have provided a rock on which future generations will see, interpret and love what his 'Master' did. Howarth chose to become posthumous 'secretary' to a man of great genius: by doing so he has given us the opportunity of knowing who *he* was and what *his* genius will mean to mankind.

•   •   •

I first met Thomas Howarth in 1988, to ask his advice with regard to my research on 'meaning and symbolism' in the work of Mackintosh and the Glasgow Group. He was extremely encouraging and helpful; we became friends across the Atlantic. In July 2000, he phoned me in the middle of the night to say goodbye. His doctor had given him, he said, just three days to live. As we chatted, he suddenly interjected, 'Tim, you know I've been writing my memoirs? Now they'll never be completed, and they're not very good. I'd like you to turn them into a biography. What do you think? Can you come to Toronto – tomorrow? I'll pay your fare. There are things I'd like to tell you and decisions to be made face to face.' It was one o'clock on a Monday morning. I said, 'you know I'm in Scotland? It's the middle of the night.' 'Well,' he said, 'I'll try to stay alive – till Friday! You think about it and phone me tomorrow.' We then talked on, said our farewells and, later that week, I flew to Toronto.

Arriving in Howarth's handsome apartment I found a frail, bedridden old man. He was very weak but still able to talk, pleased to be talked to, and intellectually alert, occasionally, to the point of pedantry. On that first morning, we were discussing the problems that had beset Lord Norman Foster's Millennium Bridge in London (Foster being one of Howarth's many successful former students) when his eyes flashed and he changed the subject to tell me about a visit he had made to a clairvoyant a few years before. He took a draught of painkiller, then gathered his strength to speak. 'She didn't know me. She knew nothing about me, but when she saw me standing in the doorway she said, "I see you're a man of distinction and achievement." ' He assumed a quizzical look, then half-smiled and went on. 'She asked me to sit down, and as I did so, she said, "I see a man standing behind you, a young man, he's dark, he has dark hair, dark eyes..." It was Mackintosh; the young Mackintosh. And she was right. Mackintosh has always been with me, as I will be with you as you write this book... You know the painting by Caravaggio, of the Angel and St Matthew? The paintings I should say...' And so began the week of reminiscence, discussion, question and answer, that has resulted in this book.

Thomas Howarth was a surprising character: a middle-class, inhibited, rational north Englishman and a mystical half-Celt; a fundamentalist Methodist and libertarian hedonist; a studious introvert who also conducted massed choirs with theatrical enthusiasm. For forty years Howarth enjoyed the conventional trappings of being a distinguished university professor but once his lid was loosened out jumped a Lancashire showman and go-getter, like a jack-in-the box. Having listened to many hellfire and brimstone sermons and having long earned his living as a charismatic teacher, Howarth knew well how to impress and draw people to him. In childhood he was frequently confined to his bedroom and to the end of his life he used his ill health as a weapon in his battle for love and attention. Scholastic habit and administrative experience made him a fastidious note-taker with an accountant's concern about the Ps and Qs of every invoice passed to him, yet he always remained a man of great human generosity. It was this generosity that made him an artist, a poet, an inspiring teacher, a servant of beauty, a disciple of Mackintosh and, all his life, true to his contradictory self.

Was it chance, providence, or sheer will that led the lives of Howarth and Mackintosh to converge so decisively? Howarth himself believed it was destiny and, in retrospect, he saw himself drawn irresistibly towards Mackintosh through a series of coincidences. He became an architect, as the result of a 'draw' at a tennis tournament. Like Mackintosh, he won a scholarship to Italy at the age of twenty-three. Like Mackintosh, he felt an innate attraction towards pure, numinous forms: things black and white. Like Mackintosh, he found himself drawn into a circle of people inspired by Rosicrucian philosophy and, during his last weeks, he recurrently wondered why he had been invited out of the blue, to take up an architectural lectureship in Glasgow and why the Lord Provost had invited him to lecture on that war-torn city's 'lost genius'.

Chance and circumstance certainly played their parts in Howarth's career, but so too did planned ambition and it is easy to find 'significant' form in events after they have happened. In a similar way, many original achievements in the arts and sciences, in religion and philosophy, seem obvious once they have been made. Such achievements and developments are rarely easily won. Might they be predetermined? Many educated people today, totally dismiss the concept of 'fate', but few of even the fiercest rationalists would deny that the *idea* of 'destiny' has a place in the human psyche, even if it has no place in science. And it has to be accepted that the elderly Howarth believed that providence had, crucially, shaped his life and that some kind of 'destiny' had propelled him towards the goals and causes to which he gave himself. At various times in his life, when determining moments presented themselves, he believed he had always taken 'the new path and followed my calling. It was destiny, Tim, though I shaped what I desired.' Howarth was proud of the conventional success he achieved but more proud of his 'openness to the moment' and most proud of the fact that, he believed, he was leaving the world a better place for having lived the life he had. During late middle-age Howarth lost interest in his Christian faith, but in youth and age he was naturally religious and he accommodated 'destiny' in his understanding of life rather as Carl Jung accommodated the idea of God: 'It does not matter whether He exists or not – as long as we believe in Him.'

This biography holds up a mirror to the life of Tom Howarth and to the friends, associates, artists and ideas that encircled him. It asks questions of the man and the age in which he lived. In particular it asks what prepared Thomas Howarth to recognise and assume responsibility for the art and reputation of Charles Rennie Mackintosh. Howarth was a conviction teacher and a conviction collector - a lifelong idealist who enjoyed risk and the unknown. Just as Mackintosh liked to challenge his fellow architects, so Howarth liked to challenge his students: 'The man with no convictions – no ideals in art – no desire to do something personal, something his own, no longing to leave the world richer, his fellows happier – is no artist. The artist who sinks his personal convictions is no man.'

•   •   •

In his book *Bull Fever*, Kenneth Tynan describes the character of an eccentric, orphaned bullfighter, Miguel Baez, in words that throw surprising light on the personality and character of Thomas Howarth. Miguel Baez, Tynan writes, had 'an upbringing which could scarcely fail to produce abnormal results – he lived among women, with a mother twice bereaved, in a poor home where he was the only breadwinner. The qualities of over-mothered children, shyness, quick resentments, passionate cleanliness, guilt feelings, defiant independence, were early planted in him; his childhood friends remember him as being always 'absent' in his demeanour, moody and distant.' All those childhood characteristics apply strongly to Howarth and continued to colour his behaviour till the end of his life. Howarth's mother was not twice bereaved, nor ever poor, but her husband died suddenly in 1925, aged forty-one, and she remained a widow. At the time of the death of his father Howarth was nine years old, his brother, Joseph, three. It was a shocking blow to a boy who had already suffered years of chronic asthma, and the combination of orphaned status and permanent ill health must be prime reasons why Howarth remained, even in adulthood, physically and psychologically insecure. This insecurity encouraged his natural shyness, his resentments, his need for cleanliness, his wide-ranging guilt feelings and arbitrary sense of defiance. But, like many people with special gifts, Charles

Darwin, Emily Dickinson, John Keats, Florence Nightingale and Beethoven are classic examples, Howarth used his partial disability as a tool to concentrate his creative focus and make substantial his achievements. Too ill, for long periods, to attend school, it was his mother and grandfather who first recognised and channelled his intellect and musical gifts. Howarth was nurtured as an introvert; he became capable of sustained hard work at a very early age and remained fastidious, meticulous and orderly all his life. It was this conditioned privacy that made Howarth the collator, collector and omnivorous hoarder he became. He was also intensely competitive. He was proud that his archives, in the library of the University of Toronto, took up seventy metres of shelving. He hoarded against the world and his brother! He even enjoyed an ongoing struggle for 'spatial supremacy' in the archives with another fiercely driven Toronto 'achiever', his friend, the television mogul, Moses Znaimer. It's a struggle that 'No Pain, No Gain' Znaimer, a much younger man, looks set to win.

Amongst the tens of thousands of items that the Howarth Archive contains, is an obituary, carefully preserved by Howarth in 1948. It comes from *The Manchester Guardian* and refers to the life of Professor Randolph Schwabe, once principal of the Slade School of Art in London. Schwabe was, like Howarth, a Lancastrian; he was a painter and teacher who became a friend of the Mackintoshes during their stays in London between 1914 and 1928. Howarth, therefore, had a professional interest in Schwabe but he also seems to have recognised a philosophical, personal and physical kinship. The Schwabe obituary concludes, 'He was a walking example of how a man may dress picturesquely without looking as though he had dressed up. To meet him strolling in his debonair fashion, late at night into the Café Royal, with his dark cloak, well-shaped tall hat, and ivory knobbed cane, was to be brought face to face with a figure out of a Regency tale by Max. He will be sadly missed by the many friends who enjoyed his quiet, congenial after dinner talk, no less than by the young people at the Slade, where for nearly twenty years he imparted the methods and traditions of good drawing.'

Update that description to the 1990s, place that professorial Englishman in downtown Toronto, and you have Professor Thomas Howarth – almost to a T. The two men shared many similarities. Howarth was habitually well dressed and stylish and, despite the inheritance of a slightly bland set of North-English features, could look dashingly handsome. His mouth was relatively large and sensuous; his eyes grey, mischievous, and highly intelligent: they could be hard but would also flash, brilliantly lighted, as an idea or insight took hold in his mind. He was a loquacious dinner-guest with a strong, rather superior, sense of humour, which occasionally shot sideways into a wickedness that might be ironic, might be ribald but was always controlled. Ten days before his death he was visited by a lifelong friend and former student, the architect Leslie Rebanks, a handsome man of great style, wealth and gravitas. Howarth was lying half asleep, crumpled and small; his hair uncombed, wild and druidic. As Rebanks entered the bedroom he paused to call out from the doorway, 'Hullo, Tom! You're looking devastating!' Startled and disorientated, Howarth turned his head slowly, focussed his eyes, and challenged the intruder with headmasterial authority, 'What did you say?' Taken aback, Rebanks repeated himself, 'I said, "Tom, you're looking devastating."' 'Oh', said Howarth, suddenly modifying his gaze from quizzical glare to conciliatory smile, 'I thought you said I was looking devastated! That's what I feel.' Howarth liked to be recognised and always liked to wear something distinctive – his pink cravat, a brilliantly patterned tie, a great trilby hat, a greatcoat, a rose. Such a conscious sense of style identifies Howarth, like Schwabe, with an earlier age when 'class', the Music Hall and street-trader 'flash' really meant something. As the grandson of a mill owner, Howarth knew the importance of 'looking the part' and cutting a dash but he was also, throughout his life, propelled by a high seriousness, a 'personal force' and spiritual ambition.

Did he create enduring work? Time will tell. Who, today, remembers or cares anything about Randolph Schwabe? Very few. Schwabe's reputation has contracted into public invisibility, he has become another forgotten teacher, another very minor artist. Will the same happen to Thomas Howarth? It is most unlikely that Howarth will be recognised as a great man but his life tells us a great deal about twentieth-century Britain and his place in the still burgeoning story of Mackintosh is assured. After 500 years Michelangelo's biographer, Vasari, remains known and exemplary; might Howarth's documentation be judged equally important by future generations? Charles Rennie Mackintosh has become one of the world's big Modern artists and Howarth as his biographer, must share a little of his artistic immortality.

Despite his forty-two years in Canada, Howarth remained an archetypal, cultured, north Briton; a type that has left a very definite stamp on the second half of the twentieth century. Glimpsing Howarth in the street he might easily have been confused with the Lancastrian cricket correspondent Neville Cardus, one of the few journalists whose achievements are best described as the product of genius. He might also be facially confused with the Leeds playwright Alan Bennett, or the Bradford artist David Hockney, or Salford's L.S. Lowry, or the B.B.C.'s great American correspondent, Alistair Cooke. Alistair Cooke was a young Lancastrian who crossed the Atlantic to find fame and fortune two decades before Howarth. Today, Cooke is best known for his weekly *Letter from America* but, sixty-five years ago, his seminal folk series *I heard America Singing* was one of the things that first stirred the young Howarth to think about emigration.

From boyhood, however, Howarth was, psychologically, an unpredictable one-off: self-obsessed yet always willing to serve, wilful but always susceptible to persuasion by both strong men and strong women. One woman whom he got to know well whilst teaching architecture at the University of Manchester was Margaret H. Bulley, a curator at the Whitworth Museum. Over many years she exerted a powerful influence on Howarth's life and his practice as a teacher. Bulley was evangelically committed to 'advancing' the best contemporary artists and the education of 'good taste'. She was a Christian Scientist, married to a wealthy industrialist, G.W. Armitage, but the couple shared a cultural vision of the world – best described as Rosicrucian.

The Howarths lived next door to the Armitages for nine years and Miss Bulley was delighted to use the young architectural historian as a 'test bed' for the aesthetic ideas with which she was experimenting. The older, eccentric connoisseur and the ambitious Mackintosh scholar got on well and many of her ideas became subtly locked into Howarth's mind. Although Margaret Bulley did little serious work on Mackintosh, Fra Newbery or the Glasgow Four, the work of the Glasgow Group encapsulated many of the artistic values she championed in her various publications: *Art and Counterfeit, A Simple Guide to Pictures and Painting, Have You Good Taste?* and her magnum opus, *Art and Understanding,* published in 1937 by Batsford. In *Have You Good Taste?*, a didactic teaching tract, she enthuses about the functionality of the kitchen and against the pretensions of the drawing room in typically Modern style:

> Things delightful in themselves may not always join together to make a pleasant whole. Do you know a beautiful room? If so, notice the character of both room and furnishings and try to discover why they go so well together. Study the size and shape of the furniture in relationship to that of the room. Mark the fireplace, the mantelpiece, the electric light or gas fittings, the clock.
>
> Is the room full of light? Do effects of light and shadow play a part in the general effect? Do colours help? Are the walls light or dark, plain or patterned? Is the beauty of the room due in part to the objects seen against a clear and plain background? Or is the general effect rich and elaborate? Has use been sacrificed to beauty, or beauty to use? Do both combine?
>
> A room that is delightful will not be overcrowded. It will not be bare, but it will have a peaceful sense of unoccupied spaces. During the Victorian Age and on into this century, when taste was at a very low ebb, rooms were apt to be as full as junk shops. Now in reaction they are empty as barns. Beauty may spring from the balance and harmony of severe forms and empty spaces in combination with light and shadow. In the great periods of English interior decoration, rooms united richness with severity...

The aesthetic she outlines is very close to that pursued by Mackintosh and lauded by Howarth from 1936 onwards. In *Art and Understanding*, Bulley used, as her frontispiece, Donatello's *Amorino;* a naked androgynous boy with arms raised towards the sun. His pose is very similar to many created by Margaret and Frances Macdonald, and her extended introduction concludes with a poem by her husband, G.W.A., in which he sums up 'their' thinking about the nature of art and the role of the artist. The poem, entitled *The Artist,* is not great poetry, but it makes a powerful artistic statement very relevant to anyone interested in the Mackintosh phenomenon and Rosicrucian philosophy. These extracts present its gist:

You say the artist's queer. Of course!
That's what he's here for. Would you force
Him to be level, rational, steady?
As level as mud. Lord! How their mildness
Needs his dynamite, needs his wildness
To blast a hole in it, hammer it, slate it,
Pierce its stodge and illuminate it.

Follow the artist down the street
To a butcher's shop. What's in it? "Meat!"
Says the wall-eyed public, "Something to eat:
Sausages, kidneys, oh, the pets!"
That's all it sees, and all it gets,
And all it wants.
       The artist sees
Colours, volumes, substances:
The riddle of matter, the riddle of light
Throw down their challenge...

Look at that picture. There's a glass,
A bowl, some apples, and a knife.
Dull stuff. No, no! The thing has life!
Who bade it live? What eye, what hand
Selected, ordered, balanced, planned
Those petty nothings till they stand
Emblems of being, charged with force
Like thunderclouds? Why, his, of course,
The artist's. His the eye that sees
Beneath all beautiful surfaces
A subtler beauty darkly hidden...

    ...it's there, it's there
Though hard to find, though hard to share.
Ninety-nine painters in five score
Just paint life's surface and no more,
Its woods, its seas, the loveliness
Of man's inheritance. Oh yes,
All these are dear, all move the heart,
But untransformed they are not art...

> Art demands
> That nature's random loveliness
> Take from man's mind a deep impress:
> That rose and stone become design,
> And show in moulded mass and line
> An ordering spirit, every part
> Set to one measure. Then the heart
> Feels more than just a rose that's fair:
> A deeper loveliness is there:
> Spirit illumines matter: mind
> To stones and petals has assigned
> Its own immortal qualities.
> That's not a rose: it's life that dies,
> This is not stone: it is the face
> Of deathless time: in this small space
> Are beauty, death, eternity.

If one stands across the road from Glasgow School of Art and looks up at the sculpted relief above the entrance door one sees maidens, roses, and the rising sun; a field of symbolic imagery remarkably similar to that which G.W.A. sets out in the lines above. As Thomas Howarth lay waiting for his death in his Toronto apartment he knew he had enjoyed his life because of his 'openness to artistic vision'; and he became a man content to recognise death as a very small thing, in no way to be feared, just as the images in the poem suggest. Howarth was a creative intellectual rather than an impelled, self-sufficient artist but he honoured and fully understood the concepts with which G.W.A. continues his poem:

> Is all this present, consciously,
> To the artist? No, perhaps, but he
> Is the hand of the race: he must express
> Some part of all men's consciousness.
> If he does not, he fails. Unless
> His work is everyman's yet his,
> All time yet now, all things yet this,
> Unless the universal root
> Of being in his being fruit,
> He's just a shiny looking-glass
> Reflecting pretty shapes that pass…

> At last
> He wins. He does it. There has passed
> Onto the canvas something which
> Has made the sum of life more rich,
> Loveliness born of sacrifice.
> What of the man who paid the price?
> He sits there haggard, beaten, broke:
> He cannot paint another stroke:
> The empty tubes are cracked and curled,
> The palette's in the corner hurled:
> He has brought a manchild into the world.

Armitage uses mirrors as a powerful symbol in this poem and it is not surprising that mirrors played an important part in the oeuvre of the Mackintosh group: mirrors integrated into the design of clocks, mirrors decorated with the seeds of the honesty plant, mirrors surrounded by the head of Christ. The Glasgow Four wanted us to see ourselves as others see us, and in time, in context, and amidst the continuum of Nature. Like Christ, it proved the lot of the Mackintosh group to be beaten and broken but this wounding, was in a strange way, like a carapace, necessary and protective and it enabled them to produce art of sublime value outwith the power of death. And Howarth, in preparing for his death, knew that he had done a fair measure of all that he might ever have hoped to have done in the here and now, and achieved a sense of his own 'conscious immortality'. 'Immortal, Invisible, God only Wise' were amongst the last words he spoke on earth. Unspoken was his pride in knowing that he had revealed an extraordinary 'manchild' to the world – Mackintosh.

It might seem pretentious to suggest that Thomas Howarth consciously chose to become the disciple of Mackintosh, rather as the apostles Peter and Paul choose to carry the Testament of Jesus Christ, but the suggestion is neither groundless nor profane. Howarth's work was inspired, necessary and important. He took up a cause that transformed his life, and has since transformed the culture of Scotland. And, it is salutary to realise that, at the very moment Howarth took up the Mackintosh banner, Scotland's great radical, nationalist poet, Hugh MacDiarmid, was crying like a prophet in the same wilderness for the very transformation that Mackintosh/Howarth have now achieved. In his wartime poem *Glasgow*, MacDiarmid writes:

> A terrible shadow descends like dust over my thoughts,
> Almost like reading a Glasgow Herald leader
> Or any of our Anglo-Scottish daily papers,
> Smug class organs, standardized, superficial,
> Unfair in the presentation of news, and worse than useless
> As interpreters of the present scene or guides to the future...

Whenever the slightest promise, the slightest integrity,
Dares to show in any of the arts or thought or politics
At once the jealous senile jabber breaks out
Striking with sure instinct at everything with courage and integrity
(There's nothing too cowardly for Glasgow's spokesmen
To have the courage to do!)
'Confound it all! If once we let these young folk in
What is to become of us?'... But who knows in this broth-like fog
There may be greater artists yet by far than we,
Unheard of, even by us, condemned to be invisible...

Open Glasgow up! Open it up. It is time
It was made sun-conscious. Give every house
Ceilings and roofs of iridescent glass, windows for walls,
Let great steel-framed windows bring the blaze
Of the sky into every room; half-partitions
And low divisions of polished shining wood break up
The entire sweep of the main construction and give
A sense of space and air; waxed floors
Reflect the window vistas. Have chairs of chromium steel,
Let metal ornaments and glass shelves
Catch and multiply the flood of light everywhere...

And do not fear to use new materials too. I do not fear
So much black and white and shining steel will give
A chilly effect – colour will be everywhere,
Strange subtle colours hard to name,
– Schooner, terroco, graphite, matelot,
Sphinx-like fawn and putty, string and carbon blue –
The most utilitarian objects unrecognisable
But none the less useful, every room will be enlarged
To huge dimensions by the windows; the rippling foliage
Of the trees will dapple your tables...

Is that not Glasgow, and Mackintosh? Is that not the architectural and environmental vision to which Thomas Howarth dedicated his life?

1 BOYHOOD

THOMAS HOWARTH *My earliest recollections, from my perambulator,*
were of blue skies, red squirrels and ladies walking in summer dresses.

A caul covered the face of Thomas Howarth as he was born in a small terraced house at Wesham, near Kirkham, Lancashire on the 1 May 1914. This first day of summer and birth in a caul are recognised signs of good fortune and when Howarth died, on 21 July 2000, in a beautiful apartment in downtown Toronto he was a content and satisfied man. His mother preserved the caul and, after her death, Howarth meticulously added it to his archive – now gifted to the library of the University of Toronto. When asked why he should wish to keep such a thing, he answered by quoting the epitaph that Mackintosh carved on the gravestone of his friend Talwin Morris: 'Life is greater than we conceive, Death keeper of unknown redemptions.' Thomas Howarth was a continually surprising man: his life touched many countries and influenced many people, and it was consciously orchestrated like a work of art.

Howarth's family, on both sides, came from north-west England. His father, Lawrence Howarth, was the only son of Mary Alice and Thomas Howarth, of whom little is known. His mother was Agnes Cornall, daughter of Eliza Alice Ford and Joseph Cornall. The Cornalls were corn millers who, during the nineteenth century, prospered and it was this family, rather than the elusive Howarths, who shaped Tom's childhood. The family business was originally based at a picturesque windmill in the village of Weeton, five miles from Kirkham, halfway between Preston, one of the great cotton towns, and the famous seaside resort of Blackpool. When wind power was replaced by steam power the centre of the Cornalls milling business moved in to Kirkham, where, even today, the industrial brick streets sit hard amidst the splendid, rolling green countryside that links the Pennine mountains to the Irish Sea. This part of Lancashire is known as the Fylde, one of the most productive agricultural regions in the north of England; cattle, sheep and pigs all thrive, as do market gardens and arable farms. It is also good horse country, on the frontier where the English Shire meets the Scots Clydesdale. These two spectacular breeds of draught horse were memorable facts of Howarth's boyhood; annual shows and ploughing matches were popular attractions and, in an early demonstration of the

13

intellectual cast of his mind, the young Howarth contrasted these splendid creatures with the scruffy piebalds that delivered the milk to his door. In his *Memoirs,* Howarth describes his grandfather's mills with vivid pleasure:

> one of the corn mills had a splendid gas-engine with a great, polished-steel flywheel some six feet in diameter and a brass 'governor'. I would watch fascinated, observe the men working, enjoy the smells, the bustle, the energising feeling that here food was being prepared for the world. And I rode sometimes in the firm's lorry which collected corn from outlying farms, so I got to know the countryside and farming community. The lorry-driver was a handsome, slightly-built but strong young man, Bill Knapton, who was always kind to me. Dust and flour made him look like a sculpture.

Howarth's name and ancestry are, historically, strongly linked to the Kirkham area but the fact that he was born there was partly fortuitous because his parents had, in 1913, left Lancashire to work on the south coast of England. Lawrence Howarth, a trained and ambitious young scientist, was appointed civic inspector of Food and Drugs to the municipality of Bournemouth and, with his young bride, he bought a house in that prosperous, airy, holiday town. The couple quickly settled happily but Agnes Howarth decided it best to return north to give birth amongst her own people. However, it was in sunny, pre-war Bournemouth, not industrial Lancashire, that Howarth's early sensibilities were developed:

> my earliest recollections, from my perambulator, were of blue skies, red squirrels and ladies walking in summer dresses – a wind on my face.

It was all very proper, old fashioned and impressionist, and Bournemouth was to remain an attractive remnant of the Edwardian Age until after the outbreak of the Second World War.

Howarth's early experience of life on the Dorset coast is of some historical importance because it was from Dorset that Mackintosh's great headmaster and patron, Fra Newbery, came and to which he returned in retirement. The Mackintoshes also stayed in Dorset for extensive periods. In a letter to Fra and Jessie Newbery, written in 1925, Mackintosh's wife, Margaret Macdonald, describes the county as containing some of the most beautiful rural architecture in the world and she remarks on the great contentment she and her husband always experienced amidst that Neolithic landscape. Tom's time in Bournemouth, however, was brief; towards the end of 1915 his father was promoted Chief Inspector of Food and Drugs in Lowestoft, an ancient east-coast port which had boomed in the late nineteenth and early twentieth centuries as one of Britain's great herring centres. It then developed major sewerage problems that Lawrence Howarth was to play a leading role in correcting.

Unlike Bournemouth, Lowestoft was close to 'the frontline' of the war then ranging across Europe. The town suffered a series of 'hit and run' shellings from the German Navy, and bombing from airships, which, at that absolute beginning of aerial warfare, inspired awe out of all proportion to its military consequences. Howarth writes,

> I have a vivid recollection of a Zeppelin being shot down in flames over Lowestoft and I have no doubt that I was carried out of the house by my parents to witness the spectacle. And later, I remember the maids chasing me – pretending they were Zeppelins! For a hundred years after the Napoleonic Wars British children were terrified that 'Boney was coming!' But for me, aged two and three, it was always Zeppelins.

We had a succession of maids. They were smartly dressed in the accepted black uniform with a white starched collar. Their work consisted of serving at table, lighting coal fires, clearing out the ashes, keeping the house clean, and looking after me. First we lived at 8 Dene Road, then 24 Royal Avenue, which was a house that was a joy to live in. The garden seemed enormous with a tree in the corner. It was either a sycamore or a chestnut. I would climb out along its branches, stand on the wall, and imagine all that might go on in the neighbours' gardens – poetical, medieval things. One of the parks we walked in was called the Sparrow's Nest. I remember the passing shade of the trees, the flashes of sunlight; I took great delight in feeding the sparrows. The maid I especially remember is Gladys, with dark bobbed hair. She was an avid reader of the weekly magazine *Tit Bits*, which had a green cover. I suppose it was the green cover that made the lasting impression on my memory; she kept piles of these magazines in our kitchen cupboard...

That paragraph paints a clear picture of the formalised and middle-class environment within which Howarth grew up. Today, the idea of servants in a small family house sounds very grand but it was then a fact of life across most of Europe, even in wartime. It is interesting that Howarth makes such a definite point about the magazine *Tit Bits* having a green cover. Did the colour green really dominate his perception of the magazine? Does reference to the cover, camouflage his rather precocious interest in the half-naked ladies that bedecked this once *risqué* magazine? Or does Howarth, in retrospect, assert his allegiance to green as a life-symbol? Green was widely used and much discussed in the Mackintosh circle, and it is a colour favoured by Rosicrucian artists and thinkers. Certainly, despite his asthma, Thomas Howarth seems to have had, from an early age, a strongly sensual nature:

> I was surprised to find, many years later, when I travelled in North America, that the name *Tit Bits* was always discreetly changed to the rather ugly alternative of *Tid Bits*, presumably to satisfy the Victorian prejudices of Americans and Canadians. Sexual inhibitions hung on in Canada long after they had all but disappeared in Britain...

The history of erotic relationships between nannies and their charges is long and a number of the children so nurtured have grown up to become distinguished artists and poets – Lord Byron and John Ruskin are two classic examples.

It was in Lowestoft, at the age of about eight and after the birth of his brother, Joseph, that Howarth established his first close friendship with a boy. Ted Chambers was big, practical, and a year older than Howarth; this 'senior/junior' balance was to become the prototype for most of Howarth's male friendships until he reached middle age. Ted's father ran a garage that sold cars and motorcycles, and he owned several aeroplanes – bought cheaply at the end of the war. Father and son loved engines and Howarth looked on with admiration and wonder. The two boys used to go fishing from Lowestoft docks, and their families would picnic together; the two fathers each, proudly, driving the same make of car, GWKs.

This boyhood friendship lasted long after the Howarth family returned north to Lancashire in 1923. One day, when Howarth was a student of architecture in Manchester in the mid-thirties, Ted phoned to say he was flying to Blackpool on his way to the annual Round-the-Island Race on the Isle of Man and he was racing! Howarth, immediately, volunteered to design and paint a special 'logo and number' on the fuselage of his plane. Two days later, Tom was there, with his fiancée Edna, to greet the young aviator as he roared in to land, 'after a series of spectacular loop the loops!' Howarth set to work, designing and stencilling 'Ted's logo – in a Modern Chivalrous Style!' Each letter and number needed time to dry and because the plane was a biplane with two cockpits, one behind the other, Howarth's reward was to be taken up for practise spins after each letter was completed. It became a day he was to remember all his life. The serious, hardworking architecture student revelled in the exciting mechanised world of 'my friend Ted and those Magnificent Men in their Flying Machines'. It was not just Howarth who flew, Howarth's fiancée and his seventy-year-old grandfather, both had their turns. But Howarth writes in his *Memoirs,* with typical egocentricity, that whilst *their* flights were sedate and conventional, he 'hedgehopped, chased cows, banked, rolled and to my delight, looped the loop! I had total confidence in Ted's competence; I lived for the moment and gave no thought to the fact that that plane dated back twenty years to the War and had been found dust-clogged in an East-Anglian barn!'

Howarth concludes his vignette of Ted Chambers by proudly documenting the role Ted played in the Second World War, as a ferry pilot, bringing planes, manufactured in Canada and the U.S.A., across the North Atlantic to Britain. Despite lifetime ill-health there was always a bold, spontaneous, joyous, and theatrical side to Howarth and he was never ashamed of it. It was a characteristic he shared with his mother who, in her youth, was a notably beautiful woman.

> In 1919, to my mother's delight, I was asked to participate in the ceremonial surrounding our Chapel Bazaar. The affair was to be opened by Lowestoft's Lady Mayoress and, when the vote of thanks was given, it was my job to walk down the aisle of the crowded hall and present her with a large bouquet of flowers... I was carefully got up in my very best clothes and I remember slowly negotiating what seemed an interminably long distance, whilst hundreds of faces in the pews on each side looked round as, like a bride, I walked forward to the altar. Then, having

presented my flowers, I bowed and received the customary kiss from the mayoress. For my parents this was a very important occasion. And I enjoyed it too, more than I would have admitted, until recently.

Howarth's relationship with his father was a mixture of the close and the distant. He remembers his parents entertaining a wide circle of friends. Both sang in the Lowestoft Methodist choir and numerous musical and chapel-going people used to visit the house. Lawrence played the violin but not to his son's satisfaction; Howarth remembers him loudly announcing 'a practise', then hearing,

> excruciating noises coming from the bedroom, to which he retired on such occasions. I do not think he had any special aptitude for this instrument. I certainly have no recollection of him playing in public. But he practised and practised behind his locked door. And I remember special celebrations each St Valentine's Day. A party of friends and family would gather for a feast and games. During the evening there would be various knocks on the outside door. The children would rush to open it but the knocker would have vanished into the darkness, leaving on the doorstep a parcel addressed to one of the children. The mysterious donor was never seen but the knockings and disappearances would continue, intermittently, until all the children had received a present. It was like an early spring version of Halloween. Whether this was a St Valentine's custom we brought from Lancashire to Lowestoft, or a Lowestoft custom we picked up, or something my parents invented, I don't know.

Like many northerners the Howarth's made a point of enjoying the fresh air, picnicking in the Herring Fleet Woods, and on the Norfolk Broads where they rowed through the reed beds in search of that rarest of British birds, the bittern. Howarth was proud to say, 'I am a man who has heard the "boom of the bittern".' He went night sea-fishing with his father and scenes of the fishermen, spaced down the beach whirling their short bamboo rods, stuck in his mind 'like Constable's painting of the Bay at Weymouth'. Father and son also went out shooting rabbits.

> Rabbits, I learned, at that early age, have a habit of coming out of the woods to feed at sunset. My father and I would crawl very carefully, undercover, to watch these creatures. A long silent wait, then we selected the target, jointly aimed – then, he'd whisper, 'pull the trigger'. Explosion! The vicious recoil of the double-barrelled gun, the smell of gunpowder. We were both very good shots! I carried them home and we ate them.

In modern Britain, this would be an unusual sport for a scholarly, asthmatic boy but at that time the hunting of rabbits provided rare leisuretime entertainment, and food. Later, as a teenager, Howarth specialised in winning shooting prizes at fairground stalls.

The East-Anglian countryside is flat, like Holland, and a great place for cycling. The Howarth's all had bikes and weekend expeditions led to Howarth's first lessons in architecture. Although they were staunch Methodists, the family had no qualms about cycling to Norwich specifically to view the magnificent Anglican Cathedral, half Romanesque and half Gothic. And, before he was nine years old, Howarth had explored most of the best of the city's thirty-two pre-Reformation churches. Sunday teas would be taken in coastal villages like Alderburgh and Walberswick, where splendid half-timbered houses were accepted as a natural part of the landscape. The clear coastal light and great skies of Suffolk attracted many artists, musicians and writers and Tom drank in the space, the colours, the textures and he stored them away. Tom's young brother, Joseph, would ride mounted on his father's crossbar. For Tom these were heroic adventures and, rather as Thomas Hardy envisioned the meeting of the *Titanic* and the iceberg as preordained, so Howarth, in his old age, saw those rural bike rides as one of the many spokes of fate that drew his life towards art and the Mackintosh orbit:

> I now recognise that the forces that led me to Mackintosh were structured by something far more coherent than chance.
>
> After spending my first two years in Dorset, I moved to Suffolk. The Suffolk coast plays a distinctive part in the Mackintosh/Newbery/ Howarth story. Lowestoft being just a few miles from Walberswick, where Fra Newbery had a holiday cottage for many years and which the Mackintoshes regularly visited after their marriage in 1900. Walberswick was the place where Mackintosh painted many of his most original flower studies and where in 1916, walking on the beach in his great cape, he was arrested as a suspected German spy! This, at the very moment perhaps, when I was playing with wood bricks, and teddy bears up the road, in Lowestoft.

Thus, the young Thomas Howarth grew up in a stimulating and happy family environment but his asthma remained a nightmare that blighted the whole of his childhood. On the evening of Armistice Day, 11 November 1918, he remembers a severe attack:

> By ill-chance a friend had come round for tea, a lady who was a Christian Scientist. She persuaded my parents that I was not really ill; that my condition was spiritual, or of mental origin, and not a physical phenomenon at all. I should be taken out into the town to enjoy the fun

and the fireworks! She left a copy of Mary Baker Eddy's *Science and Health with a Key to the Scriptures*, which I still have in my library… My parents, having slowly despaired of finding a medical cure decided, on the spur of the moment, to take her advice. My father dressed me in warm clothes and carried me forth on his shoulders out into the night! We boarded a tramcar and rattled down Main Street. I saw the flags and the fireworks. I vividly remember the rejoicing and the dense throng of the crowd, then – breathless panic and being rushed home in pain and terror into unconsciousness…

Another equally horrible incident, again involving his father, remained etched in Howarth's memory.

Lowestoft built an open-air swimming pool in the sand dunes at about this time and my father, optimistically, took me there to teach me how to swim. He lifted me up high, told me to hold my nose, and plunged me underneath the cold salt water. I was terrified. I must have gasped for breath whilst still submerged; I inhaled a lot of water which brought on an immediate attack of asthma. I have never been able to rationalise my father's action. It was so uncharacteristic. He was a gentle, considerate and kindly individual and I do not remember any occasion on which he chastised me or inflicted any kind of punishment. Except that one! Perhaps, he wanted to test the theory of the caul – that children born wrapped in their caul will never drown!

At that time, asthma sufferers did not have the benefit of modern inhalers, or any effective drugs. The medical profession had been defeated by this common illness. All our family doctor did was, optimistically, tell my parents that I would grow out of it when I reached the age of seven. I didn't. He then ordered the removal of my adenoids and tonsils and told my parents that the age of fourteen would see me cured! Or, if not fourteen then I would be cured at twenty-one! He was a doctor who seems to have had huge faith in multiples of the magical digit seven! But neither he nor the number seven did me any permanent good. At the age of fifteen, an age I had often thought I would never reach, my mother decided to try new methods and a new doctor took a hand. He believed that adrenaline, administered intravenously, would stop attacks. It certainly accelerated my heartbeat but it did nothing to improve either my physical or my psychological health; all it did do was give me a lasting antipathy towards hypodermic needles! My twenty-first birthday also passed with no obvious signs of improvement so I phlegmatically decided asthma is a condition that I must live with – all my life. But I have been lucky; in adulthood, with various modern medicines, and a life in more equable climes, my asthma slowly became manageable and lost the terror it still brings to so many children.

For those who have not experienced a major asthma attack I should explain what happens. An attack is usually triggered by an infection or irritation, a chest cold, an allergy to an animal, to dust mites, to flower pollen, or undue stress. As the attack develops one has, literally, to fight for breath as the lungs refuse to expel the air already in them. The pulse-rate increases and one perspires freely, the face and lips turn blue because the supply of oxygen in the blood rapidly reduces; fear of suffocation then further inflames the problem. Physically and psychologically a bad attack is a very unpleasant experience not just for the patient but also for the family and any observers.

The only alleviation, in my childhood, came from patented herbal remedies. 'Potters Asthma Cure' was our standby, a fine green powder which one poured onto a fire resistant plate and then ignited. If I wasn't too desperate for air I always made a cone of the powder and lighted the top, creating my own miniature Vesuvius. Mount Vesuvius seen from the Bay of Naples! The powder burned slowly with a rich red glow, emitting clouds of white smoke which one inhaled. I became a secret alchemist! The whole house would fill with a pungent but bracing odour. If one could manage an attack, relief soon came but many a night I would lie for hours in my bed, struggling for breath, and strangely conscious of my mother and grandparents restlessly pacing downstairs, contemplating my demise. I would listen for their feet coming up the stairs. I remember seeing them standing in the doorway of my room, and sitting by my bed – so keen to help but totally frustrated by their inability to do anything to alleviate my intense distress.

Howarth did not attend school until he reached the age of seven. His mother taught him at home.

She was systematic; at a very early age she taught me reading, writing and arithmetic. She would sing to me, tell stories, and get me to draw. My parents gave me a love of the good things of life – books, art, music, and the beauty of close human friendship – long before I went to school.

When, at last, Howarth seemed fit for full days away from home, he was sent to a small private school in Lowestoft, run by a Miss Rose.

She was stern and kindly. She drifted amongst the children in flowing, dark, ankle-length, floral-patterned dresses. She was statuesque, with pince-nez high on her nose and grey hair piled high on her head, like a caryatid.

Tom did well under the benign 'Arts and Crafts' eye of Miss Rose. He won two prizes for drawing and within two years, still only nine years old, he was offered a place at Lowestoft Grammar School.

> The offer was not taken up because my father received a pressing invitation to return to Lancashire, to become a partner in my maternal grandfather's prospering business… I remember being taken to the railway station to wave goodbye as he set off for Preston, to discuss the situation with grandfather and my uncle Frederick Fleetwood. Goodbyes are often moving occasions and I still remember vividly the acute sense of loss I felt as my father, leaning out of the carriage window, waved to us as the train carried him away. Perhaps this was a premonition of forthcoming tragic events. He returned quite soon with the news that we were going home to Lancashire, a place I hardly knew and which he, I think, felt he had already left forever.

Howarth's description of his grandfather's business 'prospering' is, presumably, accurate but the use of the adjective suggests, perhaps, that something was not right: and Lawrence Howarth seems to have been dutiful, rather than enthusiastic, about his return to Lancashire. Initially, the family moved in with the grandparents and shared the terraced house at 37 Garstang Road, North Wesham in which Howarth had been born nine years before. A search began for a permanent home and, after some months, a three-bedroomed house, Jesmond Dene, in Ribby Road was selected. It, too, was part of a terrace but Agnes Howarth seems to have been pleased to be back with her parents and the friends of her girlhood. She was busy with plans for a new home and a toddler to care for, but Tom, like his father, suffered a culture shock. His playground, suddenly, became the terraced streets and his companions a group of rough Lancastrians who did not take kindly to the 'southern' accent and genteel manners taught by Miss Rose. Instead of going off as a select scholar to Lowestoft Grammar School, Tom now found himself a 'fish-out-of-water' at Kirkham and Wesham Council School – a school which catered for all local children aged between five and fourteen. Then, just before the family moved to their new house, Lawrence Howarth went down with septic pneumonia and, within a week, was dead. This loss was a defining moment for Howarth.

> My mother had come home to Lancashire; she had a new house but her husband was dead and she had the unenviable task of raising two children

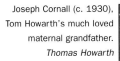

Joseph Cornall (c. 1930),
Tom Howarth's much loved
maternal grandfather.
Thomas Howarth

on her own. Fortunately, she was a strong, independent lady, with an unshakable religious faith. She was determined to survive and that her two boys would do well. It must have been devastating to have moved into Jesmond Dene, a large spacious family house, as a widow. For two or three years we lived there but, when her limited financial resources came close to exhaustion, it was decided that we should move back with my grandparents — not into their original terrace but into a large five-bedroomed house with garage, greenhouse, large garden and small field bought with their daughter and grandchildren in mind. Its name was Mayfield, Ribby Road. It was not an easy change for my mother since it represented a considerable loss of freedom and independence. It must also have brought her husband's death back to the forefront of her mind. To be a widow in the nineteen twenties was to be a widow indeed.

For my brother and I, however, Mayfield lived up to its name and it provided us with a new lease of life that dispelled the gloom associated with our move back north and the subsequent loss of our father. Mayfield had large well-lit rooms, space for games and corners to read in. The garden had raspberries, fruit trees and a splendid green lawn that was ideal for horseplay, batting and bowling. I was eleven. Street cricket now became 'net-practise' on grass! Our school friends were delighted to be invited to savour 'our square'. Mayfield provided us with a privileged, almost idyllic refuge amidst the grim streets close by.

Coming back, as an outsider to Lancashire, I was fascinated by the crowds of mill-workers who flooded onto the streets when the whistles blew at the end of a shift. Most of the workers were women. They dressed in long black skirts and dark drab blouses. They wore shawls around their heads and shoulders, and clogs on their feet — great wooden soles and leather uppers. The kind of feet and clogs Van Gogh had painted in the coalfields of Belgium forty years earlier! To increase their strength and length of wear iron strips, like those for shoeing horses, were nailed to the sole. The streets echoed to the ring of steel and when night fell those clogs produced showers of sparks like trains passing in the distance. The children made a game of it. I would have loved to join them, but my mother wouldn't hear of her son wearing clogs! She was a good and generous woman but, like most people then, very conscious of the divisions of class; for her the human realities of industrial manufacturing were a thing apart.

The artist who documented the spectacle of industrial Lancashire was, of course, L. S. Lowry. A great gallery has recently been opened in his name, The Lowry, in Salford. It's a major work of contemporary

Eliza Alice Ford (c. 1920), wife of Joseph Cornall and a rather severe grandmother to the young Howarth.

architecture like the Guggenheim Museum in Bilbao and is part of the long overdue rejuvenation of Salford and Manchester. After a lifetime as a provincial eccentric, Lowry has slowly emerged as a unique British artist; a man who documented a place and a people at a particular moment of history. He 'kept an eye' on that monochromatic, overbearing urban landscape I knew in my youth, as though he were a mad caretaker! He walked the streets as a rent collector, and he transformed that which was grey and plebeian into something visionary and beautiful, something tragic and comic. As an artist he is not a world-figure, like Charlie Chaplin or Mackintosh, but he was a genuinely important image-maker who did what nobody else did with amazing single-minded dedication. 'Facts are sacred' in the city of *The Manchester Guardian.*

One of my uncles, Edwin Willacy, was a maintenance engineer in the mills. One day he took me into what was known as the weaving shed. There were rows and rows of looms, hundreds of great machines, each tended by a woman whose job it was to detect and repair broken cotton threads, before the fault marred the fabric. The noise was a thunderous, soul-destroying clatter that was, to the visitor, unbearable but the factory women bounced about in the cacophony in abandoned good humour! Their fortitude struck me, even then as a boy, and looking back, with the hindsight of age, I see their phlegmatic gaiety in the face of adversity as truly remarkable. Uncle Edwin's job was to maintain the machinery and effect immediate repairs. He was known as the tackler. It's a marvellous description of what Uncle Edwin did and what he was. He was 'the tackler' and that word somehow carries in itself all the energy and vividness that makes English such a devastating and effective language. It is clear, hard and precise. It is easy to say and easy to hear. It describes the job and the man who does it. It carries, for the people of the North of England, strong associations with 'their' game, Rugby League. It also carries the sound of the clangourous clank of machinery, and a sense of the matter-of-factness with which 'the tackler' will sort out any, and all, mechanical problems. Short, sharp and to the point, 'tackler' is a word that grew out of visceral experience, practical knowledge, real sensibility and poetic imagination; its a word that captures the essence of the thing described.

Wesham and Kirkham were industrialised pockets on the edge of larger, more heavily industrialised areas but, like many Lancastrian towns, they continued to possess easy access to the countryside and the continuing rural tradition. Our local 'lords of the manor' were the Duckworths, who lived at Ribby Hall; a fine neo-Georgian house in those days but today, a grossly disfigured public building. I remember going one year, with my grandfather's male voice choir, to serenade the Duckworths and their Christmas guests. We stood in gently falling snow, with lamps and candles, outside the large drawing room windows. The curtains were undrawn and a distinguished company stood in dinner suits and black ties, the ladies in fine dresses, in front of a great log fire. Candles and lanterns made the room sumptuous and very orange as seen from our blue vantage point in the snow. They were drinking their aperitifs. Watching the people gathered in those lighted rooms, hearing our voices rising in the snow, I felt as though I was some character in a play, that I was part of some drama observed from a distance and that it had nothing to do with me... Then, we were invited into the hall and drinks were brought round. It was a scene from Charles Dickens. Most of us being Methodists, didn't accept any alcoholic drinks. I remember my grandfather, a strict teetotaller, graciously refusing offer after offer. For some reason I was offered nothing! Perhaps because I was the youngest person there. All I had to do was watch and witness an extraordinary scene – a scene that presaged the end of several great English traditions. It was 1925. Hundreds, nay thousands of years, came together for a moment, and for the last time then, at Ribby Hall.

In school I gradually learned to get on with my northern cousins, but tensions remained. I once invited home a squint-eyed boy whose name was Ben Nicholson (no relation to the great modern painter of that name!). He was a rough, tough boy: one of a very large family who lived on Railway

A Kirkham Methodist Sunday School outing (1924).

Kirkham Grammar School which Howarth attended intermittently from 1926 to 1932. The building shares various architectural features with works by Voysey and Mackintosh.

Terrace. He had great physical strength and for some reason he took a liking to me; he protected me from the bullying that my 'southern ways' invited; he appointed himself my 'bodyguard'. We established a strange allegiance. I hadn't prepared my mother for his coming to the house and when she saw him she was genuinely shocked by his ragged condition and dirty clothes. She always kept my brother and I meticulously clean. We wore good quality clothes and soft felt hats, whereas Nick wore a workers' neb cap, almost like a jockey cap, had filthy nails and carried that unmistakable odour of the great unwashed. She soon sent the two of us packing out into the street with a handful of sweets, but I learned and gained much from Nick, and we remained friends until I was transferred from the Council School to Kirkham Grammar School two years later. It was housed in a handsome, ivy-covered building and had a good local reputation. It modelled itself on the fee-paying public schools that had played such an important part in the development of nineteenth-century Imperial Britain. England in the twenties was certainly a contradictory place. It still is.

Kirkham Grammar School had eight masters. All had university degrees except for one, responsible for agricultural studies. These highly intellectual men instilled in Howarth principles of scholastic exactitude that profoundly influenced his career. It was not the School of Architecture in the University of Manchester that prepared Howarth for his success as a research academic, it was his old-fashioned grammar school. The headmaster was the Rev Cresswell Strange, a graduate of Trinity College, Oxford. He had been

ordained into the Church of England in 1909 and experienced extended war service as an education officer with the British Expeditionary Force in France. He was headmaster at Kirkham from 1919 until 1945. Howarth describes him as,

> a strong man dedicated to upholding and enhancing the reputation of the school. He was a martinet and at times an awe-inspiring figure. In school he always wore his black academic gown and carried his cane, just partially concealed. Punishment was administered in the assembly hall; the unfortunate miscreant had to join him on stage, bend over and take the traditional 'six of the best' on the backside...

Kirkham was run on very Victorian lines but the Rev Headmaster ran an excellent school and his authoritarianism allowed teachers and pupils to get on with their work. Corporal punishment seems to have found a level appropriate to circumstances. Those boys who 'wanted' the cane would get it: those, like Howarth, who didn't want it, rarely, or never did. As in most academic schools at that time, art and music had a minimal place in the curriculum. Howarth's cultural education proceeded through study of English, Latin, French and Carpentry:

> English was taught by an enthusiastic Welshman, E.J. Williams, known to the boys as 'Chinny Williams' because of his inordinately long chin. He also taught carpentry and had a great love of the beauties of smoothness produced by the plane and sandpaper. He taught boys to plane and sandpaper wood to a perfect flatness that he then liked to 'test' in a dark room with a light, shone close-up, from behind – absolute darkness was proof of a true 'straight-edge'!

It was not the kind of craftsmanship that would have thrilled William Morris, or Mackintosh, but it gave Howarth practical, hands-on experience of materials, tools and craftsmanship. It developed his hand, his eye and one aspect of his aesthetic judgment.

> 'Chinny' was a brilliant teacher who nurtured in his pupils a genuine understanding of poetry and literature. Certainly he did this for me and I will be eternally grateful. He also had a wonderfully short temper that verged on the apoplectic: it was a weakness that certain boys played on but he rose above them – at least his temper did!

Lionel Budden, the French Master, was not much of a teacher but he was a cricketer of some local stature and this endeared him to the more sporty boys – among whom Howarth was not.

Agnes and Jay Howarth (c. 1932) on Lake Windermere.
Thomas Howarth

Budden also taught 'Scripture', a subject about which he was honest enough to inform his pupils, 'I flounder like a poor player on a "sticky dog"!' Meaning he was unable to tackle this difficult subject with any more authority than a weak batsmen was able to deal with a good spin-bowler on a cricket pitch, turning viciously, after heavy rain!

Mr Budden was one of those teachers able to invite derision but who never became the object of derision, and he subtly nurtured a form of intellectual rebelliousness that the scholarly and well-mannered Howarth joined in with gusto. Always interested in questions touching sex, Howarth, on his deathbed, remembered raising with Mr Budden, the issue of foreskins:

We had been reading a chapter from the Bible about the martial exploits of Gideon, who, I believe, ordered his bloodthirsty followers to count the dead after a battle, by collecting, not scalps but foreskins. Pretending to be ignorant and hoping to brighten a boring lesson, I adopted an earnest expression and asked; 'Please sir, what IS a foreskin?' There was a tense silence in the classroom whilst a self-conscious Mr Budden tried to summon a suitable response. I then suggested a precise description must exist in the *O.E.D.* A dictionary was consulted but it, like Mr Budden, sought to avoid the point! An interesting and humorous debate then ensued and Mr Budden finally agreed to agree with the class that 'foreskin' was, probably, just a general term for a loose bit of skin that could be easily removed with the blunt edge of a Bronze-Age sword...

The most extraordinary member of staff was Cyril Kynaston Lee, a classicist from Exeter College, Oxford. He moved in a curious, slow mechanical way. He was a tall, slightly built man with a sallow complexion – as devoid of colour as he was of humour. He was nicknamed 'Nicky Bogey'. He appeared to live in a world of his own; he was always neatly dressed, almost never smiled, and seemed impervious to every kind of practical joke. Many were aimed at him but Nicky Bogey remained unstintingly courteous, and for those interested in the Classical World he was a delightful man who invited boys like myself to his family home for extra guidance. I was one of a group who explored, around his sitting room fire in Kirkham, the intricacies of Latin and the importance of virtue to the Romans. It was then that my love affair with Italy began. Mr Lee was a highly sensitive man and an excellent teacher. He opened up vistas through literature, Caesar, the mighty genius of Dante, the lyrical subtlety of Torquato Tasso. He taught me that great culture is indivisible – poetry, painting, sculpture, architecture, religious belief... Nicky Bogey provided

me with a marvellous introduction to the Latin world that I was to renew
when pursuing my doctorate at Glasgow University.

Whilst at Grammar School, Howarth remained a frequent victim of illness and it was
while he was locked in the isolation of his bedroom at Mayfield that Howarth's addiction
to 'collecting' was nurtured. He acquired a huge Meccano set with which he constructed
aircraft, bridges and great buildings.

> One day I realised that Sparklet soda-water siphon gas containers looked
> exactly like small torpedoes so I designed a Meccano biplane that could
> carry two 'siphon-torpedoes', one under each wing. By moving a lever, I
> could drop them one at a time. I also made parachutes of good quality
> handkerchiefs and, by weighting the parachutes with a small Meccano
> gearwheel, I managed to work and release them, out of doors, from kites
> flying at high altitudes!

With games like these Howarth determinedly entertained and sought to impress his
friends. He accumulated huge numbers of toy soldiers.

> My soldiers all represented action: Bengal lancers, machine-gunners,
> motorcycle squadrons, artillery batteries. I had a scale model howitzer that
> was capable of lobbing real lead shells across our living room; my mother
> sewed me sandbags (I would secretly object because they were usually
> hopelessly out of scale but I didn't complain) and I stacked them as
> defences in my many improvised battles.

Howarth was also an avid cigarette card collector. The best of these were beautifully
designed and vividly coloured. They came in sets of twenty-five or fifty, each enclosed
inside a packet of cigarettes – to encourage sales and carry advertising. They covered an
encyclopaedic range of subjects: architecture, heraldry, famous tennis players, sports of all
kinds, theatre, movie stars, astronomy, animals and birds.

> The information printed on the back of each card was usually remarkably
> accurate and these sets of cards were a simple and cheap educational tool
> of great benefit to deprived children in those pre-television days. At
> school we compared collections and exchanged cards to make up sets.
> Collecting proceeded on surprisingly sophisticated lines. Cards in prime
> condition were much sought after; rarity and quality were the two chief
> determinants with us – as in the antiques trade today. Because many boys
> played throwing games with the cards, many sets quickly lost their pristine

status. I remember two games. A row of cards was set against a wall; we took turns in spinning cards against them from a distance of about six feet. When one of the standing cards was knocked down, the thrower picked up all the thrown cards that had missed up to that point, plus the knocked down card. Then the game would continue till all the cards were down and claimed. 'Experts' soon detected cards that flew accurately and competition become surprisingly fierce. The other game required less skill. Cards were flipped against a wall and fell to the ground; if any falling card overlapped any card already on the ground the thrower would win all the cards lying about at that moment. In general, however, I was more interested in the cards than the games and I kept all my favourite sets in good condition. In time, I handed my collection to my son and he has now handed them on to his son. Recently I used some as the basis of a slide lecture entitled 'Collecting Cards'. That was in 1995 and, after eighty years, they still held a certain magic, for me, and the audience.

Howarth's great friend during his teenage years was John Appleton. He was six years older, had already left school, and was apprenticed to a pharmacist in Kirkham.

John and I were inseparable for several years, in fact until I went away to university in 1934. During my bouts of asthma he was a frequent visitor, he brought me books to read, we talked about everything that interested us: he kept my spirits up. He was a devout Roman Catholic who had thought of entering the priesthood. He was serious but far from stuffy. One Christmas, John told my mother not to worry about buying a Christmas tree, 'I will bring you one'. One dark night he got a saw, went down to the Catholic cemetery, climbed a young pine tree and cut off the top seven feet! This, he then presented to us without a word as to where it had come from. It fitted our living room to perfection and he helped my brother and I with the decorations. All went well until, after the festivities, when, without a thought, I flung the tree into the back lane for the dustmen to remove with the garbage. Within half an hour, a very large and irate cemetery gardener was hammering at our backdoor demanding to know who had ruined the great tree that grew in the sacred ground of the cemetery! He had hunted for the thief, without success until our discarded tree gave John Appleton's game away! Fortunately, the gardener's temper abated when he realised that 'the despoiler' was not some Methodist villain but a loyal member of his own Catholic flock! John, then, had to make apologies to the Monsignor and the incident was forgotten soon enough but that tree is still there to this day, still scarred by John Appleton's generosity.

On another occasion we went skating on a frozen pond. We had one old pair of skates between us, primitive things that were supposed to screw into the soles of leather boots. John tried them first. He skated away and I ran to have a slide, in my boots, beside him – I then remember nothing more. When I came too, I was in a darkened room. John had carried me home. I had severe concussion and the doctors thought I might lose my sight. I remember lying long days in the darkness. I also remember rising each evening to part the curtains when I heard the lamplighter coming down the street. Would I still be able to see him? He carried a long pole with which he turned on the gas of each streetlight as he passed. It was a strange, rather melancholy but beautiful process. However depressive and unhealthy the winters of industrial Lancashire may have been, they could also carry an eerie, foggy beauty – a low-light impressionism; – that wet, shimmering glimmer that the painter Atkinson Grimshaw captured so well.

Tom Howarth (1930) in the Photographic Shooting Gallery, Blackpool, triggering his own excellent photograph. *Thomas Howarth*

Tom and Jay Howarth (1932) on Lake Windermere. Tom's ill-health is clearly visible in his drawn and strained face.

Howarth left Kirkham Grammar School at the age of sixteen because of his incessant asthma attacks. He had, however, already acquired a considerable local reputation as a pianist and organist and his mother now encouraged him to become a professional musician, working from home. She also encouraged him to keep fit, playing tennis. Howarth's skills as a tennis player were average but his musical talent was very real. His grandfather had been choirmaster and organist at Wesham Methodist Church for fifty years and, at the age of fourteen, Howarth took over his grandfather's responsibilities with relish. In fact, when Howarth left school he was already teaching the piano to six private pupils and was in demand as an organist – far beyond his own chapel. He enjoyed playing, conducting, and the authority of his position as church organist. He also recognized that music would provide him with a means of enjoying life outwith the confines of home.

My mother had a pleasant contralto voice and she, occasionally, sang at church concerts. Her sister Edith was a good soprano, she played the piano and it was she who gave me my first lessons. Edith was a good teacher but the dominating musical personality in our family was, undoubtedly, my grandfather, Joseph Cornall. He was self-taught but he had great natural ability and a wonderful ability to get people to sing, and sing well. He had his own male-voice choir. It practised in the Methodist hall but was a genuinely inter-denominational choir with an excellent reputation. In those days Lancashire was famous for its music festivals and we attended religiously – not just as performers but also as listeners and judges. My grandfather made certain we got good tickets to most of the big events – at the Blackpool Music Festival, at Lytham St Anne's and at Morecombe. Sometimes we would attend – morning, noon and night – for a week! This meant that I had a wonderful opportunity to hear large numbers of choirs and soloists competing, singing the same piece over and over again. The experience of hearing say, twenty contraltos in succession, all singing the same song, was both an exercise in patience and a valuable experience in the development of my musical judgment. My ear was trained, over several crucial years, to detect imperfections in vocal achievement and breath control and, most important, to recognise artistic quality. My own 'estimations and judgments' were, immediately, tested by the official 'judgments' made by the various adjudicators, many of whom were leading composers. My artistic 'confidence' was born in those music halls and I became particularly interested in 'the poetic cadence of words in music;' the ability of a soloist to enunciate clearly and to convey the message of a song to the audience was rated highly at our music festivals. There was a general belief not just that the words of a song were important, but that the poetic value of the words were there to be sublimely enhanced by the music itself. This orchestration of all elements in the 'total' artistic experience is something that I later sought in the field of the visual arts; I sought and I found – for the greatest art works by its 'wholeness'. The best art shapes, and is shaped, by what T.S Elliot described as our 'unified sensibility'.

These Lancashire music festivals also taught me the importance of 'teamwork' in the field of the arts. The 'humble' accompanist, usually a pianist, was extremely important. The aim was to compliment, not to intrude or seek to dominate in any way. I also recognised how important it was for an accompanist to have a thorough understanding of the works being sung – so that he could respond immediately, and appropriately, to the technical and emotional demands of the soloist, or group, being accompanied, however unusual or idiosyncratic their performance might be.

These statements are of great interest when one considers how Howarth was to later 'orchestrate' his role as first the researcher – and then the advocate – of Charles Rennie Mackintosh. He became the perfect 'accompanist': his experience as a pianist, conductor and choirmaster helping him to become the ideal partner of the temperamental genius who was his 'master in art and in life'.

The Howarth *Memoirs* contain a glowing tribute to his favourite accompanist, John Daniels, who dominated events behind the scenes at the Blackpool Music Festival:

Daniels was a hunchback who received a great ovation at the end of every season. He sat askew at the piano, but he had magical hands and could coax the best response from the most nervous performers. And when my grandfather realised that the piano instruction I was getting from my aunt was geared too much towards theory and not enough towards performance, he decided to send me to have lessons with this man, John Daniels, who was performance personified. For several years I travelled weekly, when fit, to Blackpool to sit as apprentice to this extraordinary music-maker and I did my best to acquire some of his technique and his thrilling, humane response to whatever musical score was placed before him. He told me I had to unlearn many of the habits I had acquired and he set me a rigorous programme of scales and exercises that I followed for many hours every day. All this was very helpful to me as a teacher, as organist and as choirmaster of Kirkham Church.

My teenage years as a choirmaster were some of the most rewarding of my life. I seemed to have a gift, inherited, perhaps, from my grandfather, for making people sing, and make them sing I did. As a rather reserved and isolated individual, chapel singing provided me with communal therapy of a high order. The Welsh tune, *Cum Rhonda* sung to the words 'Guide me, O Thou Great Jehovah' was a great favourite with us. In Kirkham Church I was completely screened from the congregation by the solid back of the pulpit – these great pulpits dominated the architectural layout of all churches in which delivery of 'The Word' was the prime feature of services. Thus, I was only visible to members of the choir and I had my back to them! I observed them by means of a small mirror but was otherwise totally protected and totally in charge! In such circumstances I felt free to give myself utterly to the music, and I did this with a kind of abandon. This was just what the congregations wanted. It was thrilling. Some of the most moving experiences I have ever had were extended, ecstatic moments playing those rousing Methodist hymns to the large congregations that attended church in Kirkham in those far off days – those blue remembered hills of dream.

After the morning services, and during weekday evenings, I worked with the Sunday School children – particularly on cantatas and I produced many local concerts. These, frequently, proved major successes and they gave me a great deal of personal satisfaction. By having to encourage the children to overcome their inhibitions and shyness, I further overcame my own. Teaching seemed to be my natural vocation and, in retrospect, I realize that my early music-making gave me invaluable experience in the handling of young people – both in groups and as individuals. Chapel draws people together in heightened moments of experience and, at the

age of fifteen, I fell in love. Her name was Isabel Kent; she was very attractive. She, too, was a fervent churchgoer and, like me, a teacher. She taught voice-production and verse speaking. Fifty years later, on her birthday, the 15th of September, I woke very early and as day dawned I thought deeply about her and about my first and only visit to her home, and this poem formed itself in my head.

Isabel Kent (c. 1934), Tom Howarth's first serious girlfriend. A Licentiate of the Guildhall School of Music, London, Isabel advertised herself as receiving 'Pupils for Complete Practical and Artistic Tuition in Elocution.'

I saw her first
    On a hot summer's day
Reading in her garden tent.
    Exquisitely beautiful
With golden waist-long hair
    Blue eyes
And a perfect English complexion
    She taught verse-speaking classes
And poetry
    To adoring children

As we wandered through our leafy lanes
    And over green green meadows
Lost in the contemplation of an idyllic future
    She taught me to love my language even more
By exploring the richness and subtle cadences
    Of Shakespeare the Romantic poets and St Paul

(Corinthians 1:13 King James' Version was her favourite).

This was in truth a dream-time
    But her parents said 'No'
They had other ambitions so
    At our last dance
After assuring me that I was
    As steadfast as a mountain
She left me to marry a parson
    A parson indeed!

So ended in personal tragedy
    My first serious teenage love
And the fifteenth of September
    Was her birthday.

It is a rather awkward poem, too self-conscious to take wing as literature but of interest because it is so 'Thomas Howarth'. It succinctly conjures images and illuminates youthful, middle-class experience at a particular moment in English history but it also quickly, slips sideways into retrospective knowingness. A lifetime as a researcher, a teacher, and academic turns too many of Howarth's poems into 'conversation pieces'.

Howarth clearly suggests that it was Isabel Kent's *parents* who put the damper on a mutual love affair and that their action exemplifies a meaner aspect of the Methodist mindset, but Howarth was always a little over-eager to blame 'others'. Did he really presume to marry at the age of fifteen? Did her parents really arrange that she marry a parson at that age? No – Howarth concertinas time to suit his old man's grumbling. In fact both youngsters displayed striking boldness in their relationship and the *Memoirs* tell a much more compelling story than the poem.

> Isabel and I met on numerous occasions in Blackpool, where I was having piano lessons from John Daniels, and she was attending verse-speaking classes. So, together we took lessons in ballroom dancing, an activity at which we became very proficient. Speaking of the future, she believed I should go into the Methodist ministry – where my ill-health would not be a great handicap. I discussed the possibility with one of our senior ministers – who with great perception dissuaded me from doing so! Despite this our surreptitious meetings continued, irregularly, for some months. Then she was invited to give a performance of her verse-speaking choir at our church... Consequently, as choirmaster I was invited to the Kent home – I took with me my grandfather's beautiful black labrador retriever – to give me Dutch courage. I was shown into the garden where I was told Isabel was working. And there she was, sitting reading in an attractive green and white striped tent, with her waist-long, blond hair, blue eyes and all the other seductive aspects of teenage English femininity. And there we spent our 'allotted half-hour' discussing arrangements for the coming together of our two different choirs. I walked home with that shining black labrador, treading on air. However, almost immediately, Isabel's parents seem to have got wind of the fact that our relation was, potentially, something more than purely professional and, at the last moment, they refused her permission to conduct her choir in my church. She tearfully informed me of the situation, by phone, and asked if I could stand in as substitute and conduct her choir! As everything was arranged I felt impelled to accept the invitation. Fortunately, with my back to the audience and her 'script' in front of me, I managed much more satisfactorily than I could have imagined was possible – interweaving the upper and lower registers, drumming up dramatic emphasis here, controlling the

length of a silence there... The whole evening was a success. I was a success – but without Isabel success meant nothing! To crown my unhappiness Isabel wrote shortly afterwards to say she had left me. Man's inhumanity to man! Years later, I learned she had married a parson, according to her parents wishes. Perhaps they were the happiest of couples, but I doubt it. Perhaps all was for the best – I expect so – but the negative forces in Respectable Society are very powerful – and catching.

Howarth's diaries contain few mentions of Isabel Kent but it is clear that they spent a group holiday together in the Lake District and that the relationship continued for at least three years until Howarth went off to Manchester to begin his architecture studies. Lancastrian Methodism seems to have been remarkably less puritanical in its behavioural codes than convention would presume: Blackpool was enjoyed as a Methodist Mecca and Howarth remained, throughout his life, a Blackpool enthusiast.

As a pianist Howarth met many talented musical performers, amongst them a brilliant local tenor, Tommy Pickup, whom he describes as,

built like a cross between Caruso and Pavarotti, with a prodigious lung-capacity and a glorious voice. I always enjoyed accompanying him: he had a rare sense of humour as well as artistic understanding. He sang the ballads and light classics popular at the time, but born in another age, or another place, he would have been in opera. Foremost among the women I worked with was Agnes Wall, a contralto with an extraordinary voice – without a break she could range from the high to the low register with no noticeable change in the quality of tone. She used to practise with me at home, and these were always pleasant experiences. Of the instrumentalists, I remember most clearly a young saxophonist, Gerald Derbyshire, tall, dark, handsome, and 'very thirties' in every aspect of his demeanour. He handled that difficult instrument with verve and great elegance and he brought a draught of fresh air into my conservative repertoire; instead of three hours of systematic practise, or disciplined service to a singer, I extemporised in harmony with that lazy and most sensual of the new jazz instruments, the saxophone.

One weekend, Gerald Derbyshire's band had been commissioned to play at the local races. At the last moment his pianist was taken ill and he asked me to play as substitute. I was eighteen, I drove to the course in my grandfather's car, in a blazer and cravat, and there was the piano set out under a great chestnut tree with six or seven musicians lolling around, waiting for me! I was warmly greeted and sat down feeling if this is life, its very good! We started to play. I didn't do badly. The crowd was more interested in the races than in us, but our music was soon one with the shouts, the cheers and the thunder of hooves; beautiful ladies moved by in large hats, the sun shone, sheer pleasure embraced me. I became, as it were, part of a painting by Degas and I hammered those keys with happy abandon. Then it was time to go. Packing up I heard not a word of comment or a word of praise! The crowd was totally oblivious to the band and the band oblivious to their first-time pianist! For them it was just another engagement but for me it had been something much more. I wanted others to recognise the special nature of what had happened, I wanted acknowledgement of their pleasure and our creation. But nobody acknowledged anything and I came away from that race feeling strangely downcast: music, like love, often falls on deaf ears.

Looking back I can see that I brought critical judgements to every aspect of my life at a very early age. One person about whom I never had any doubts was Kathleen Ferrier. Like many people in Lancashire, I felt strangely and immediately drawn to her. It was like falling in love and I knew, from the moment I heard her, that here was a great artist. I attended numerous of her concerts and the voice of Kathleen Ferrier still lifts my heart and affirms my faith in the genius of the people of Lancashire.

Gracie Fields was another singer I greatly admired. She was assumed by many to be a mere *comedienne* but comedy only partly disguised her greatness as a singer. She would bring the house down singing *The Biggest Aspidistra in the World* in a broad Lancashire dialect, then switch to some sweet and romantic song that melted the heart. She was a consummate artist. Sadly, she later lost the support of much of her audience when she married a wealthy Italian and moved to Capri. Having visited that beautiful island on an architectural scholarship in 1937, I know well why she moved there and why those who called her 'a traitor' for doing so were wrong! She was another of those royal stags – marked out to be shot.

Howarth's first visit to the theatre had been in Lowestoft, when his father took him to see *Buffalo Bill's Travelling Circus.*

There was a log cabin on a stage of simulated trees, made of painted strips of canvas. Indians were attacking cowboys and there was a continuous exchange of gunfire. I was totally unimpressed by the whole show, I thought the canvas trees quite absurd, it was provincial theatre at its worst, but the theme song, *The Wild, Wild Women have made a Wild Man of Me* lodged in my mind and I've never forgotten it. Looking back I'm confident that my boyish judgement was entirely correct – that song had life, force, form and truth whereas the rest of the show was just an excuse for money-making.

Once settled in Lancashire my mother took me regularly to see Shakespeare and various serious plays. I remember watching Donald Wolfit playing in *The Bells*. My mother had carefully primed me for the appearance of the man whom she described as 'The Great Tragedian': he came on stage to a hushed expectation. He was carrying a lighted candle, he made an impassioned speech that greatly impressed me, but, as it ended, great guffaws and shouts rang out from the gallery above us. Wolfit was being ridiculed by some latter-day groundlings! He stood still, looked up at the gallery, hurled the candle across the stage and walked off – refusing to continue. The whole production came to a halt. After much confusion the theatre manager came on stage and made a public apology. It was twenty minutes before the trouble-makers were cleared out and Wolfit was persuaded to continue his performance. Finally he came back to resounding applause and I had had a genuine introduction to the dynamics of Shakespearean theatre – where the audience is an active participant in the totality of the drama! Recent research suggests that Shakespeare, as a young man, might have spent two crucial years as a tutor to one of the great Lancashire families and certainly the Lancashire of my youth was a multifaceted place still capable of fermenting the chaos, humour and tragedies out of which the great man created his plays in the Elizabethan period.

Howarth was omnivorous in his youthful cultural enthusiasms but the environment within which he grew up was deeply conservative and politically, he remained an old fashioned Tory till the end of his days. His grandfather's cars reflected his status as a mill-owner and capitalist; first a T Ford, then a khaki-coloured Humber Tourer which Howarth proudly described as having, 'a large fold-down hood, removable celluloid side screens and an ineffective glass windshield for the rear seats – in bad weather, passengers needed long coats and rugs to keep themselves dry, or warm.'

At the age of sixteen Tom obtained his own driving licence and he frequently chauffeured his grandfather to business meetings in Preston, 'in a Morris Isis, six cylinder saloon. It would cruise comfortably at 60 mph and on straight stretches of road surge forward at 80 or 90 mph – much to my grandfather's delight.' In 1934, however, this 'chariot' was replaced with a smaller, more luxurious Austin which Tom laments, 'was grossly underpowered, but suited my now increasingly elderly grandparents and reduced the risk of accident to their much-loved eldest grandson.'

Howarth had had a long and important friendship with John Appleton, the chemist shop worker, but, at the age of nineteen, he meet a young man who was to have a much greater influence on his life, George Grenfell Baines. Howarth describes their meeting as, 'The first great miracle in my life'.

As a member of Kirkham Tennis Club I entered a competition organised by the Preston Tennis Club to raise money for the Church Missionary Society. The fee was sixpence per person. I was drawn to play against a man whom I did not know – George Grenfell Baines. The match took place in Kirkham. I was introduced to a handsome young man several years older than myself. He beat me, but it was a good and enjoyable match. Afterwards I invited him home for supper, whereupon my mother established that he was related to an esteemed family of Methodist lay-preachers. Much more importantly, I learned he worked in an architect's office and was a part-time student at the University of Manchester. As we talked we found we had a great many common interests and immediately became firm friends. He was interested in my music; I was interested in his enthusiasm for art and architecture. I remember him quoting Mme de Stael's famous phrase that 'architecture is frozen music'. It struck me with tremendous force. George was an infectious optimist and his clear thinking was crucial in transforming me from being a jobbing music teacher to a dedicated student of architecture. After discussions with my mother and grandfather, I decided that what I wanted to do was to give my life to architecture – to leave the drawing room and help shape the world.

My grandfather then arranged a meeting with Professor Reginald A. Cordingley, head of the School of Architecture at the University of

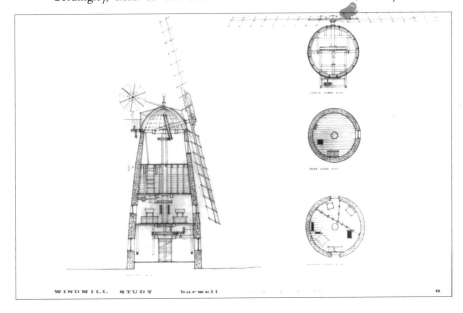

WINDMILL STUDY   burwell

Manchester. We drove together to the school's forbidding premises at 244 Oxford Road. It was a day I shall never forget. A steward occupied a scruffy office-cum-shop at the front of the building. We were conducted up an uncarpeted, domestic staircase to Professor Cordingley's office. No one seeking a new career in the field of Modern Architecture could have started from a darker or more depressing rung of the ladder but I was, immediately, impressed by the man who greeted us. Professor Cordingley had a quiet dignity, great gentleness and clear strength of character. He would have been, then, in his early forties but a shock of white hair created an effect of mature dignity, sharply contradicted by a mischievous twinkle in his eyes. He was a Lancashire man and immediately relaxed in the congenial company of my grandfather. I remember little of the actual interview but I know I enjoyed it and, there and then, it was agreed that I would be admitted to the five-year professional programme.

Two shore markers at Walberswick, Norfolk. These were the kinds of forms that fascinated Tom Howarth in boyhood and later as a designer and historian.
Thomas Howarth

A new and dramatic phase of Howarth's life was about to begin — as the result of his buying a sixpenny entrance to a tennis tournament. He manipulated chance to create his future. He embraced his 'destiny' and called it 'fate'.

2 THE UNIVERSITY YEARS

THOMAS HOWARTH

Professor Cordingley was an early advocate of the importance of Planning. He loved nature and encouraged us to consider the possibilities of a new architecture so closely integrated into the environment that it would become almost invisible – revealing itself as 'architecture' only from within.

Thomas Howarth commenced study at the School of Architecture in Manchester in the autumn of 1934. Like most architecture departments at that time it was small, catering for a total of only forty students but it offered several routes by which students might gain different qualifications. There was a Bachelors Degree for the academically qualified, a Diploma for those lacking the normal high school qualifications, and a Professional Certificate for candidates, like Howarth, whose education and experience defied categorisation. The degree students had to study a foreign language plus one other non-architectural subject. Diploma and professional certificate students concentrated all their attention on architecture. Howarth's course was thus predominantly practical and gave him the chance of immediately immersing himself in a subject entirely new to him. Howarth had a tremendous capacity for sustained hard work and very soon, in addition to long days in the studio, he was volunteering for extra courses in 'Aesthetics' and the 'History and Theory of Art'. After eighteen years under the wing of his mother and grandfather he found personal freedom and the prospect of any independent professional career hugely exhilarating.

He moved into digs with two medical students. It was a small student boarding house run by a kindly Mancunian lady noted for the traditional food she cooked for her 'boys' – black puddings, bacon, potatoes, greens, turnips, Lancashire hotpot, and plenty of bread and jam. The medical students were Norman Stansfield and Bill Ball, two Kirkham Grammar School boys with whom the Howarth family had connections. It seems to have been natural for the Howarths to tackle any new situation within a network of people and systems with which they were already familiar. This applied to personal and social contacts, to sport, to the church, and to business dealings. Whether this 'networking' was a by-product of a natural sociability, Methodist practice, traditional business procedures, or sheer opportunism, it is difficult to say but Howarth retained similar habits and impulses throughout his life. Much of the social, educational and cultural success he later enjoyed depended on 'networks of established connections'. The ethical issues raised by such attitudes are of little consequence today because 'everybody does it', but it was a real issue seventy years ago when civic virtue and Victorian rectitude were powerful realities. Even on a purely personal level, Tom Howarth consciously made use of friends and acquaintances: he would presume a bedroom and 'driver' were his for the asking long after he'd become a small-scale millionaire. In Manchester, however, the Kirkham connection provided no immediate returns; indeed, it proved something of a burden. Howarth's former schoolmates were a difficult and intimidating pair who enjoyed intellectually and physically taunting the asthmatic student architect.

> Norman Stansfield was a tall gangly young man with his hair already thinning; Bill Ball was a stocky individual with a pugnacious nature. I have never forgotten a day, in the quad at Kirkham Grammar, in which Bill featured strongly. There was a 'conker session' and I, having strengthened my conkers in vinegar and brine, was known to be having a good run of success. Well, Bill Ball sauntered over and watched me whilst I 'scat' another conker for six. Afterwards, he asked if he could see my winner, a niner! He held it up – turned it round – then bit it in two! Mean actions like that remain etched in the memory and are not easily eradicated. Bill Ball had that quick sense of practical action that distinguishes many a good doctor. He cut the Gordian knot. He had the Wisdom of Solomon! But there was also a callous hardness in him that I was always uncomfortable with. Both he and Norman Stansfield served in the Royal Navy through the Second World War and then both established separate, very successful, private practices. Another thing about those Manchester digs that sometimes returns to my mind was this student pair's enthusiasm for enemas. Following lectures on the subject, a French medical practice I believe, my companions became, for a short while, wild enema enthusiasts! They delighted in announcing enemas the panacea for this, that and the other. It was certainly a stimulus to clean living! Enemas became the order of the day at our lodgings – and before too long I moved out.

In the School of Architecture, Howarth was, initially, surprised by the lack of basic instruction and direct professional teaching given to the students.

> We were required to purchase all kinds of equipment but nobody bothered to teach us how to use it. I bought, and still have, a double-elephant

drawing board, an Imperial board, and a smaller one for sketching. I bought T-squares, set-squares, compasses, dividers, and the ruling pen, but my training in their best use was non-existent. We bought watercolour paints, tracing paper, and chinese stick-ink for rendering drawings, but as draughtsmen and painters, we had to sink or swim. Stick-ink made a delightful, sepia-like liquid which, overlaid in several washes, produced the exquisite transparent, monochromatic results greatly loved by the Beaux Art teachers of those days. As enthusiastic students we just got on with the job, we learned a great deal from each other but there is no doubt that direct instruction would have provided us with many a useful short-cut. Normally we found older colleagues the best source of instruction. George Grenfell Baines was three years ahead of me and he became one of several experienced students who provided me with help and encouragement.

I enjoyed learning about the different qualities of paper and the significance of watermarks – from the superbly textured Whatman, to cheap rolls of tracing paper which we used for rough sketching and preliminary design work. We *were* taught how to stretch a sheet of Whatman – soak it in water, secure the edges by glue or brown adhesive tape; then we would watch with trepidation as the paper dried. Would it spring from its moorings, split apart, or slowly grow tight as a drum – perfect for the application of a design or the laying-down of a colour? We also still used tracing linen. The smallest things could bring pleasure and fundamentally alter the quality of the work one was doing; I learned to sharpen pencils to a wedge shape, or needle point, and the difference between H, HB, B, and 6B pencils. I began to enjoy drawing and, through drawing, to see more and more. There is a splendid quote from John Ruskin: 'Unless the minds of men are particularly directed at the impressions of sight, objects pass perpetually before our eyes without conveying any impression to the

brain at all, and so pass actually unseen, not merely unnoticed but in the full clear sense of the word unseen.' Drawing is a marvellous discipline and often leads on to more than we imagine.

Our studio desks were flat, crudely made tables. We had to use bricks or piles of books to tilt our drawing boards to the appropriate angle. In the gloom of industrial Manchester, artificial illumination was almost always necessary; we rigged up the most extraordinary devices to bring the various ceiling lights down close to our boards. We suffered hardships and handicaps but we had enthusiasm and commitment, we didn't grumble, rather, we overcame each problem as it presented itself. Excellent work came out of those Manchester studios and the best work of earlier generations, displayed on the stairs and brought out occasionally, I judged to be exquisite. The work of Emil Scherrar and Leslie Martin (both of whom I later got to know) was outstanding. Leslie Martin's wife, Sadie Spaight, another Manchester graduate, had produced an important book on modern design called *The Flat Book* and it provide me with crucial insights into contemporary developments. It carried many illustrations of modern interiors, furniture and furnishings – complete with prices and addresses from where they might be obtained.

The lack of professional guidance at Manchester had clear disadvantages but it was a dynamic and prestigious place to be and students were forced to develop their own thinking and espouse new ideas. From year one, Howarth was thrust straight into the revolutionary orbit of the great Modernist architects who were, at that moment, fundamentally reshaping the art and practice of building: Walter Gropius, Alvar Aalto, Le Corbusier, Mies van der Rohe, Marcel Breuer, and Richard Neutra.

Howarth got involved in student politics and played a leading part in bringing several internationally celebrated figures to speak in Manchester. Eric Mendelsohn made a powerful impact and, after his talk, Mendelsohn gave the young enthusiast a copy of a book of his lectures. Gropius was another of 'the great ones' who visited Manchester. He made a point of giving free lectures to student groups whilst he discouraged invitations from well-heeled sections of society by demanding substantial fees. From the beginning Howarth seems to have had an instinct for the significant in art and architecture and was naturally drawn to those contemporary artists who were creating lasting work. He 'knew' what was genuinely original. He went to the 'sources', honoured 'the masters', and kept himself at a healthy distance from all those secondary artists who imitated others or merely picked-up 'styles'. He admired the simple functionalism of the new Scandinavian designers. Amongst the British designers he made heroes of were Maxwell Fry, Robin Day, Gordon Russell and Ernest Race. He visited London Zoo to study Lubetkin's brilliant Penguin Pool, with its sculptured spiralling ramp. He 'followed' design developments in the contemporary arts magazines and collected the catalogues of Modernist firms like Liberty, Heals, and Hilles. One building that particularly struck Howarth's student imagination was the Bexhill Pavilion in Brighton, jointly designed by Mendlesohn and Chermayeff:

> It really captured our attention with its functional plan, long horizontal lines, large glass areas and the circular staircase-hall flooded with light. This was a work that, we believed, surely pointed the way ahead! Working amidst the grime and darkness of Manchester we applauded as heroes those architects who advocated a new world, a hygienic world of clean white surfaces, steel and glass.

The prime influence upon Howarth as a student, however, was not a foreign architect, not a book, not a fashion, not a style but a teacher – the man who had selected him as a student and dominated the School of Architecture at Manchester, Professor Cordingley. Howarth was always susceptible to dominant and brilliant men and in no way ashamed. Recurrent periods of committed discipleship illumined and shaped his life. On his deathbed, having described his meeting with George Grenfell Baines as the first miracle in his life, he went on, 'and the second miracle was my meeting with Professor Cordingley.' Grenfell Baines introduced Howarth to architecture; Professor Cordingley inspired and masterminded his life as a designer, scholar, and teacher.

Cordingley was a recent appointee at Manchester. He was a contemporary architect of substantial achievement but, more importantly, he genuinely loved teaching. Once in post, he gave himself to his school, and his students, with utter dedication. His wife had died in childbirth some years before; he had an only son who lived abroad with relations, and the School of Architecture at Manchester quickly soon became the centre of his life. He gave himself unremittingly to the well being of 'his' students, often working late into the night with them. His home was a large Victorian house in Cheshire, which he shared with his sister. He seems to have established his paternal relationship with Howarth during the first year and it became a personal friendship that lasted a lifetime. Cordingley was a powerful thinker, with a highly personal vision. Howarth greatly admired his designs for the Rising Sun Colliery at Wallsend in the north east of England.

> The Rising Sun Colliery was a powerful modern building of clean rectangular forms which had been well received in the architectural press. In social, industrial and architectural terms it was seen to embody the future, yet Cordingley was also an Italian Renaissance scholar and consultant to the fabric of Durham Cathedral: he was one of those exciting teachers who combined great respect for the past with a practical vision of the different needs of a new age. He encouraged us to recognise that we were on the cusp of a new age. It was an exciting time to be a student. With the rise of Hitler many of Europe's leading architects were fleeing westwards to Britain and America, and the thrust towards a new vision of architecture was greatly stimulated by their presence and ideas.

Cordingley was open to all this. He was also an early advocate of the importance of Planning. He loved nature and encouraged us to consider the possibilities of a new architecture so closely integrated into the environment that it would become almost invisible – only revealing itself from within. Such vision and foresight was necessary; during the twenties British architecture in particular had reached a low ebb, our Victorian, industrial hegemony had imploded into a mechanised obsolescence, the Arts and Crafts movement was an irrelevance after World War and Depression, Mackintosh's heroic achievements at the turn of the century had been forgotten. It was during the thirties that new architectural ideas began to circulate again and Cordingley embraced the new initiatives emanating from the Bauhaus, from Berlin and Paris. He enthused about Maxwell Fry's project for 'A City of the Future', full of light and space and exciting new forms dependent on new structural possibilities... As students, we became deeply committed to the idea of embracing this brave new world; we wanted to be in there at the moment of a new architecture's take-off, an architecture based on new technologies, health, fitness and beauty...

Because of Cordingley, Manchester University's School of Architecture was much more than the sum of its parts. There were some inept and lazy teachers there.

Jimmy Nunn taught structures with a cheerful competence but the one lecture I remember involved him turning from the blackboard to say to the class, of a calculation he couldn't complete, 'I haven't had time to work this one out, so you'll have to do it yourselves'! That statement was made not to exercise the minds of the students but because the lecturer did not know the answer to question he had raised! The factor of safety for structural steel had been recently changed. This meant that the formulas he had long worked with no longer applied... He was out of his depth and he thrust the responsibility onto his students. I was not amused!

The 'Building Construction' man was John Willy. He had been gassed during the First World War and could only speak in a whisper. He lived at Matlock, high in the Derbyshire Peak District, partly for his health, partly for its beauty and partly for its distance from Manchester. He drove an old Austin 7 that was unreliable and in winter his attendance at the university was less than dependable. A whole series of lectures never happened. Because these lectures were part of final examinations we sent John Willy an ultimatum, 'The class will refuse to answer any questions that would have been covered in the cancelled lectures.' The examinations went ahead as normal. Many students, including myself, refused to answer all questions dealing with subjects not covered by the lecturer. Unfortunately, several students failed to honour our ultimatum and attempted the banned questions. John Willy, giving them credit for their boldness and support, passed them all, whilst almost all the 'rebels' failed the exam! We fiercely opposed his action and were very unhappy with the disloyalty in our ranks! We decided to take the whole problem forward to Professor Cordingley. As usual, he sorted the matter out with minimum fuss – to the proper advantage of those students who had been marked down and no one was seen to be the obvious loser.

Edward Cahill taught 'Studio Design'. He was well read and intelligent but never lost an opportunity of pressing these facts upon us. He had a predictable mind. Our first year essay on the theory of architecture was entitled, 'What is Beauty, What is truth?' Our first studio problem was to design a telephone kiosk. This, when most of us had not learned to use our drawing equipment, and those that had, believed Sir Edwin Lutyens had already solved the telephone kiosk problem very satisfactorily!

My favourite member of staff was Reginald Edge, a small man, a hunchback with a badly deformed right hand. It was shaped like a claw, but it could still hold and control a pencil, or brush, with marvellous skill. He taught 'Colour Theory', 'Calligraphy', and a subject euphemistically called 'Decoration'. This consisted of 'interior design', 'furniture', the 'crafts' and 'heraldry'; these subjects immediately appealed to me and Mr Edge's teaching served me well in Glasgow, years later, both as a Mackintosh researcher, and a teacher. Edge was always very kind to me and he stimulated my lifelong enthusiasm for the Arts and Crafts movement. From that time forward I always sought to integrate appropriate works of art and the highest standards of craftsmanship into the architecture of all the buildings and institutions I became in any way responsible for. He encouraged me to broaden my horizons and my taste. Be architecture ever so pure and technological it can still benefit hugely from good craftsmanship, and that unified sensibility within which mind, eye and hand all feed each other. As a non-degree student, I got no 'credit' for attendance on other university courses, but Edge encouraged me in my enthusiasm for 'volunteer' courses and lectures across the university. Two courses I vividly remember were run by the distinguished art historian R.H. Wilenski – one on 'Early Italian Painting', one on 'Indian Art'. My knowledge and cultural vocabulary was greatly extended under Wilenski's inspiring guidance. He was a stocky man with an awful cough. He talked incessantly, parading up and down the lecture room brandishing a long pointer, coughing away. He showed us a wide range of slides. He analysed each composition, explaining the themes and special relationships of form and colour. From time to time he put up a blank slide and asked us to draw, diagrammatically, the composition of the last slide we had seen and indicate, by shading, the main colour arrangements. This I found to be an exacting but extremely valuable device for determining (and remembering) the essentials of a painting.

This method of honing the visual memory was part of an academic tradition that Wilenski introduced to Manchester from Central Europe, where the method is used not only to sharpen the process of 'critical viewing' but as an important factor in the practice of drawing. For example, anatomical and life models were frequently drawn not 'in line' with the drawing board but at, at least, ninety degrees to one side; thus, students were forced to hold the image of the model in their 'mind's eye' before representing it on paper. It is a method that trains and sharpens both perception and visual recall. Howarth, naturally, had a good eye and precise, retentive memory but Wilenski honed his aesthetic skills and sowed art historical ambition. Howarth spent many pleasurable hours in the Whitworth Museum and the visual arts now began to give him the kind of pleasure music had given since his early childhood.

It was, however, 'Studio Design' that dominated architectural education in Manchester, as it dominated the teaching of architecture in all British schools of architecture.

A subject is chosen by the teaching staff and a programme (a definition of spatial and 'user' requirements) is prepared, printed and circulated to the class. It usually includes a site plan. The brief is then discussed, evaluated and research of various kinds undertaken. Students then prepare and submit a preliminary design for formal criticism. This may involve one or more staff or, maybe, a general 'crit' involving the whole class. As a student I enjoyed this process and as a teacher I have always found it an efficient and practical learning discipline. Students, prompted by the drawings before them, soon gain confidence in presenting and describing their proposals verbally – even to a highly critical audience. Clarity of thought and expression are developed and these things are crucial to success in architectural practice: as is courage.

After this initial criticism, it's 'back to the drawing board' for all students, and the design is further developed in the light of the comments – critical, constructive, praiseful, destructive – from staff and fellow students. Depending on the project, final presentation varies but usually takes the form of attractively rendered and mounted drawings; plans, sections, elevations, locational drawings and site plans with road access, landscaping proposals etc. There may also be models, rendered perspective drawings, and working drawings. These were usually meticulously detailed sheets of constructional information, drawn to a specific scale with, perhaps, full-sized details of important or special features. Working drawings were often drawn on tracing paper or linen: from these, 'blue prints' could be inexpensively made (photocopying had not been invented in the thirties). The amount of time, effort and practical skill needed to fulfil demanding briefs, without the reprographic and computerised aids we take for granted today, is now difficult to imagine! It could be exhausting; at certain times of the year students would work all through the night. One thing such hard work ensured was that 'ideas' didn't run away with you. Designs advanced within a physical framework of making and understanding.

To effect a change of pace and stimulate the imagination, students were also set 'sketch' designs which were to be realised within twelve or twenty-four hours. Subjects might range from a grand building to a single object of craftsmanship. I remember a casino, an island resort, a park shelter, a stained glass window, a poster, and a 'best-actor' trophy in silver. Some students produced beautiful and imaginative work, while others struggled. To develop our sensibilities and our executant skills, life drawing was an occasional part of our studio programme. These classes were taught by an artist called Jack Malpass. They were, at first, anticipated with pleasure but turned out, in the end, to be rather boring. Malpass was an excellent water colourist but not a good teacher. Certainly he failed to inspire me. He gave no adequate technical instruction in the use of pencil or crayon. We just sat down before an unattractive, undraped man or woman and were expected to draw whilst Malpass drifted round, making occasional comments on our efforts. This lazy and largely useless method of teaching is, unfortunately, still common in many art schools. Certainly I have always regretted that life drawing was not taken more seriously in our programme.

Years later, Howarth learned to regret the fact that Manchester did not provide the genuinely wide-ranging 'art' education that Fra Newbery orchestrated so superbly at Glasgow School of Art in the 1890s. There, Newbery inspired a truly 'Mediterranean' approach to art as the formalised 'essence of life' in which 'body and soul' and all the arts fed each other. Neither Howarth, nor any of his Manchester contemporaries seem to have luxuriated in the naked human body as a source of architectural inspiration as Mackintosh and his compatriots did in Glasgow. Surprisingly, Victorian prurience was more destructively alive in the 1930s than it was in the 1890s, and Howarth's enforced discourses on 'medical enemas' were a poor substitute for the Macdonald sisters' pleasure in their study of 'live human sperm' down microscopes. Everything coming out of the Glasgow School, at that time, was imbued with the authority of youngsters in love with life and art; independent spirits who were not going to be put down. If the newspapers labelled them 'The Spook School', they exalted in the label. They had an extraordinary confidence in their burgeoning powers, and they sought affirmation, not from the authority of teachers, but from the well-heads of their own energies and idealism. It was their teachers who nurtured this confidence and vision. They recognised and embraced the uniqueness of 'their' moment. Fra Newbery married one of his most talented students, and in contributing to his own students' magazine completed a poem with a line that encapsulates what he and the Glasgow Group were about: 'The moment is, the living is.'

Beyond all this, Glasgow in the nineties was a city brimming with ferment and antagonisms. Alive with money and ideas, Glasgow was building ships, trains, turbines and Utopian hopes: it was one of those great modern cities that stimulated the imagination of the Italian Futurists. For an extraordinary generation Western culture was in a creative, tumescent and wonderfully proponent state, a state that finally dissipated itself in the First World War. The desperate consequences of that war were still everywhere apparent in the mid-nineteen thirties when Thomas Howarth began his architectural studies. What was 'new' tended to be frivolous or treated with contempt; whole sections of British cultural activity had degenerated, the once vital Victorian/Edwardian tradition had become a poisoned chalice that needed not only to be emptied but washed clean. The second Georgian Age was proving disastrous to design. Consequently by 1937, Howarth was a convinced architectural Modernist ambitiously exploring new aesthetic and technological possibilities and he began planning his escape as a political and artistic émigré. He knew things had to change and he began planning to move, physically and ideologically, somewhere else. To his great satisfaction, at the end of his third year in Manchester, he was awarded a travelling scholarship to spend six weeks in Italy. It was another defining, magical, moment in his life; it was not the money, a mere sixty pounds, but the recognition he was being given; it was the idea of a journey, the chance to tread fresh ground.

Howarth was twenty-three – exactly the same age that Charles Rennie Mackintosh had been when he won a similar scholarship to spend three months in Italy in 1889. Each scholarship was to have a profound artistic influence on the recipient. Mackintosh returned hugely stimulated by direct contact with magnificent architectural forms articulated in strong sunlight and with his skills as a watercolourist greatly increased. Howarth returned 'blooded' by wine and creatively primed to 'meet' Mackintosh.

> One day, shortly after my return to Manchester, I was browsing through a consignment of new books in the university library when I picked up a small, illustrated volume, *Pioneers of the Modern Movement from William*

Morris to Walter Gropius. As I flipped through the book, one photograph leapt out at me – an image of the entrance to the Glasgow School of Art. Its form, its strange beauty, its poetic force came out at me, and amazed me. The author was Nikolaus Pevsner, a man of whom I then knew nothing. Was it chance drew me to that shelf at that moment? Was it Italy that prepared me to 'see' Mackintosh? I have never forgotten that image and that moment – and there is no doubt it played a part in my decision to leave Manchester for Glasgow, two years later.

Thus I have to admit it was Pevsner who introduced me to Mackintosh but, whilst the more I learned about Mackintosh the more I loved him, the more I learned about Pevsner the more I disliked him and I quickly began to see his work as a challenge. He was wrong about so many things that his 'misreading' became a great stimulus to me. He stated that the School of Art was rigidly symmetrical which it isn't; that Mackintosh was born in 1867 which he wasn't; that he died in 1933, which he didn't. The fact that youth, frequently, likes to pull down age is not a seemly process but Pevsner's mistakes were the tip of an iceberg of misinformation about Mackintosh which I became determined to correct as soon as I began serious research in Glasgow 1940. But, all that was in the future then.

Howarth travelled to Italy with a fellow prize-winner, Charles Hilton and, once more, his old tennis opponent, George Grenfell Baines, enters the equation. Baines was now a fully-fledged architect, working in Preston.

George was greatly pleased when he heard I had won the scholarship, it seemed to confirm his faith in his protégé. He invited me to visit his office and, Tom Hargreaves, one of the senior members of the Grenfell Baines group, lent me his Rolliflex camera, a very fine instrument that took high-resolution pictures. This enabled me to bring back many excellent photographs.

Neither Charles Hilton nor I had been out of the country before and we very systematically planned our itinerary with the help of Thomas Cook, the travel agency. We went by rail, each of us limiting our luggage to a small handbag and a rucksack. The fact that Mussolini was deeply involved militarily in Abyssinia, and Anglo-Italian relations were at a low ebb, did not deter us. Having crossed the channel, our first destination was Switzerland, where we spent the night at Brunnen. We arrived after dark and found accommodation in a hostel with immaculate beds of a kind I hadn't seen before. No sheets, blankets or heavy eiderdowns but a simple, very thick, extremely light 'duvet' – a new word to add to our expanding

Tom Howarth (1939), Blackpool.

vocabulary. The next day was beautifully clear and on emerging from our hostel, we had our first glimpse of real mountains, rising high above early-morning clouds. Unbelievable! Awe-inspiring! Exquisite! During the afternoon we explored Brunnen, the old capital of Switzerland, and were intrigued by the timber-framed houses... Rendered in plaster with large colourful frescoes of historical events; a form of exterior decoration inconceivable in the rainy, grey, polluted atmosphere at home... The train took us on its spectacular route through the Alps, dashing through tunnels and slowly climbing steep gradients before rolling us downhill into Italy.

At this time, Howarth already knew the writings of John Ruskin well, and it is interesting to compare Howarth's responses, to those set down by John Ruskin almost exactly 100 years earlier. 'Suddenly – beyond – beyond! There was no thought in any of us of their being clouds. They were clear as crystal, sharp on the pure horizon sky, and already tinged with rose by the sinking sun. Infinitely beyond all that we had ever thought or dreamed – the seen walls of lost Eden could not have been more beautiful to us; not more awful, round heaven, the walls of sacred Death.' That passage, from *Praeterita*, illustrates the gap between student effort and genius, but the literary connection is made more clear in the following extract from *Modern Painters, Vol. IV*. During a description of the countryside around Fribourg, Ruskin states, 'I believe, for general development of human intelligence and sensibility, country of this kind is about the most perfect that exists. A richer landscape, as that of Italy, enervates, or causes wantonness; a poorer contracts the conceptions, and hardens the temperament of both mind and body; and one more curiously or prominently beautiful deadens the sense of beauty. Even what is here of attractiveness – far exceeding, as it does, that of most of the thickly peopled districts of the temperate zone, – seems to act harmfully on the poetical character of the Swiss; but take its inhabitants all in all, as with deep love and stern penetration they are painted in the works of their principal writer, Gotthelf, and I believe we shall not easily find a peasantry which would completely sustain comparison with them'. Howarth writes,

Charles proved an admirable companion for a trip of this kind. He was a quiet, intellectual individual, who looked the part. He was very pale, bespectacled, of slight build and always neatly dressed. But he had a rich sense of humour and was a good conversationalist... We found Naples indescribably dirty and our meagre financial resources limited us here, as elsewhere, to very modest accommodation. Our bedroom, some three floors up in a dingy apartment block, looked out on a narrow alley with laundry strung across it on several levels. During our first night I got out of bed, picked up a shoe and killed a scorpion that was scuttling about beneath the window. I was in bare feet! We made the usual tourist visit to

Vesuvius. We had to walk on black lava and we could see, only a few inches below the deeply cracked surface, the red glow of the molten rock; a number of men were scooping out red-hot lava and they asked us for a coin. Then they pressed the coin into the lava and sold it, and the cooling rock, back to us as 'uno momento'!

For the equivalent of nine pence we boarded a boat to Capri carrying goats and a group of young and very arrogant Nazi cyclists. The crossing to the island was windy and rough and both Charles and I were sick. To our disgust, coming from a seafaring race, we had to watch the Germans as they boldly enjoyed the sunshine and the heaving of the boat. When we recovered we went out to the Blue Grotto. Our rower had been recently wounded in the Abyssinian war and was glad to be home in his paradisal surroundings. In stilted English he described how the sunlight at certain times of day was refracted to create an unequalled blue translucence in the water. It was clear to a great depth and the oars, or one's arms, when plunged beneath the surface, assumed an almost hallucinatory luminosity. It was a magical and deeply sensuous experience.

During each summer vacation the architecture students at Manchester were expected to complete a 'measured drawing assignment'. Charles and I decided to measure the *Ospedali degli Innocenti*, Brunelleshchi's early masterpiece in Florence, and famous for its della Robbia 'putti'. We persuaded a friendly priest to find a ladder that enabled us to climb all over the façade and to reach relatively inaccessible places. It was a rewarding experience to examine, at close range, the wonderful modelling of della Robbia's ceramic blue and white plaques, and to get the dust of Italy on our hands as we measured and sketched. Small, entirely original expeditions like this were the logical, architectural extension of our human intercourse with the vibrant Italian crowds, the glorious sunshine of the market places, the forum of Rome in the midday sun. Florence was very hot and sticky and we took one afternoon off to visit the attractive village of Fiesole, a funicular ride away. We enjoyed this cooler, hilltop environment and the intimate spaces and decided to have some refreshment in the tiny garden of a café. Charles ordered red wine for both of us but, being a teetotaller, I was reluctant to drink. After some time he persuaded me to try a taste – which I did – and which I didn't like at all!

Thus, it was with a host of new experiences and a small loss of 'virginity' that Howarth returned to Manchester in the autumn of 1937. The idea of being an architect and master of his own destiny now began to take on substantial reality. In his first year, Howarth had produced mandatory drawings of the Orders of Architecture and lettering based on

Trajan's column, now he knew these great forms first-hand. His first year exercise in 'classical composition' had been a front elevation of Brunelleschi's Pazzi Chapel in Florence, 'my design surrounded by drawings of details of columns, cornices and sculptural details'. Now he was a veteran – having scrambled over Brunelleschi's roofs and sipped wine within sight of Brunelleschi's dome! In our age of televisual communication, when foreign holidays have become the norm for most British children, it is difficult to comprehend the innocence of even the best-educated students during the pre-war period. Thomas Howarth was amongst the most innocent. At the age of twenty-three he was still very much 'a late developer', but innocence gave Howarth a purity of vision that was one of his great strengths and which informs all his best work, insights, and enthusiasms. But it is also true that Howarth's physical and social inhibitions left him with an experiential debt that was to haunt him and which he, consciously, sought to repay himself in later life when wine, worldly pleasures, and intellectual authority replaced youthful innocence, organ music, and teetotal abstinence.

In his fourth year as a student, Howarth enrolled for a part-time course in 'Town and Regional Planning'.

> This included aspects of landscape design, highways and transportation. I delighted in the calculation of Lemniscate curves, to accommodate high-speed traffic around corners, a complex problem in pre-computer days. As a result of these planning studies my major project in the fourth year was the design of a small town hall in a landscape setting. It was to be built of brick and was a fairly formal, symmetrical building of little consequence but it established my lifelong interest in civic architecture. I constructed a model of my design. I enjoyed this process and developed a permanent interest in architectural models. I continue to find them one of the very best ways of demonstrating the reality of a building – to examiners, students, clients and builders – indeed I have found models an extremely useful tool throughout my career as a scholar and historian, as a teacher and as an architect/planner. It presumably goes back to my childhood enthusiasm for Meccano and miniature model-making of all kinds.
>
> Fifth year students were allowed to choose their own subject for a final year thesis. I chose to design a new town hall for Blackpool – a place I knew well from my teenage years.
>
> I remember, as a boy, standing in adolescent awe in the mysterious green half-light of the aquarium and, in the zoo, watching with sadness the eternal pacing of the great carnivores in their tiny indoor cages. My best design in the second year had been a project entitled 'An Aquarium'. I conceived mine as a great new feature for Blackpool – a circular building in concrete, with a large central 'swamp' surrounded by a pedestrian

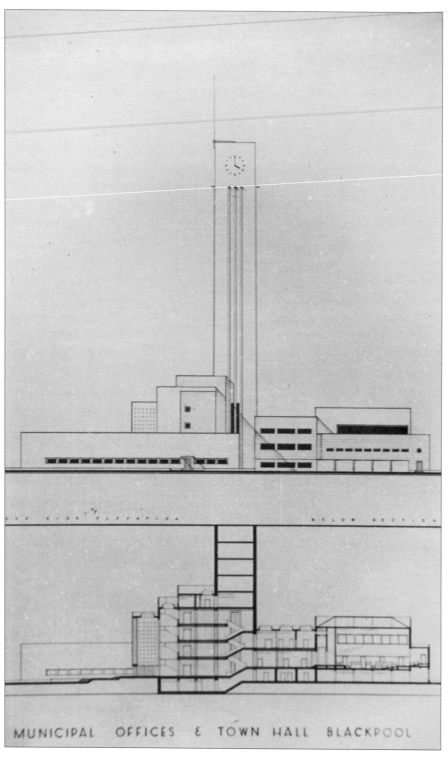

A New Town Hall and
Municipal Offices for
Blackpool (c. 1938–39);
part of Howarth's thesis
presentation at the University
of Manchester.

MUNICIPAL OFFICES & TOWN HALL BLACKPOOL

Thomas Howarth, student,
design for a public house
(c. 1935).

walkway and, around its periphery, the great glass-fronted tanks in which the aquatic creatures could be observed close-up.

My thesis proposal for a new Town hall was radical but symmetrical, as the site seemed to require. Observation of existing buildings made it clear to me that, because of the salt sea air, commonly used materials such as brick and stone tended to deteriorate quickly. To remedy this, various builders and architects in Blackpool had used glazed faïence since the nineteenth century. These tiles were largely impervious to atmospheric pollution, had a long life, and cleaned easily. I decided therefore that my town hall would be faced with white faïence set in regular rows but cemented in on end. This gave a subtle mosaic-like effect and, since there were few horizontal joints, encouraged the rapid run-off of rain and windborne sea-spray.

The pristine whiteness of Howarth's building was very 'seaside' and avant-garde. Its form seems to have echoed various features of the main British Empire Exhibition Pavilion built in Glasgow in the same year, 1938. Although Howarth's town hall was never built, there may be some link between it and the extraordinary headquarters built to house Scottish Television, in Glasgow, around 1960. This building, originally, depended on the orchestration of horizontal and vertical forms faced with white tiles, very much along the lines Howarth proposed for his Blackpool Town Hall. Did Howarth, during his eight years as a young lecturer in architecture in Glasgow, plant his vision of a Modernist town hall in the consciousness of students who later designed the Scottish Television building?

The composition of my town hall was dominated by a tall clock tower, in the tradition of several modern town halls but I made mine very tall – to allow it to compete successfully with the Blackpool Tower, which is over 700 feet high. I have, since, thought that my tower was too tall, and my corridors too long – but the examiners were pleased and I gained an eighty percent mark. The principal examiner was Professor Lionel Budden of Liverpool University. As usual, I constructed a large model of my design and submitted it with an impressive array of drawings, plans, sections, and elevations in fine black ink on Whatman paper, mounted on broad grey borders. Since the building was intended to be white I used no colour whatever on any of the sheets – so that the impression was of pristine clarity and everything was easy to read.

There was considerable competition between the Liverpool and Manchester University Schools of Architecture. I remember when a group of Liverpool students raided us and carried off a portrait of Professor Cordingley. Our students then went to Liverpool and brought back a

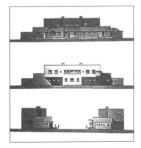

portrait of Professor Reilly, head of the Liverpool School. I was not involved but poetic justice was – because whereas Cordingley's portrait was a small cartoon, drawn by one of our more gifted students, Reilly's portrait was a large oil, painted by a distinguished artist – and considered very valuable! The portraits were later exchanged but the escapade returned to my mind, years later, when I learned that Mackintosh believed it was Reilly who stymied his competition submission for the new Anglican Cathedral for Liverpool, eased MacNair out of his teaching post in Liverpool and later worked to ensure that Mackintosh got no major commissions in London… The enmity between the two men was savage and it is worth quoting from one of the letters Mackintosh wrote to Margaret Macdonald, from Port Vendre in France, in 1927:

If Mr Christian Barman is really coming to see you before he goes to Glasgow – it's very amusing – at least I hope it will amuse you, being interviewed. He wants to write some articles on English (present day) architecture. I have written [to him] to say that I can't write about present day architecture in England because it doesn't exist – nor will there be any daylight until it is made impossible for pompous bounders like a well-known (at least well advertised) professor at Liverpool to have any say in architectural education. He is teaching efficiency – but even then he is only a twenty-third rater because they do it already better in America… I did not mention Reilly by name – I simply said (certain pompous bounders), like a certain 'loud speaker' at Liverpool who knew as much about what he was professing as the mechanical instrument of that name, knows what it is shouting. I have waited patiently for twenty years to get one back on Reilly – and during that twenty years I have never said one word about him to any outsider. Now I can get a few nails in his nasty stinking cheap coffin! I am not vindictive – far from it – you know how much I want to paint well – (but) I think I have one stronger passion and that is to make Reilly a really discredited outsider before I am finished with him. When I get him on the run I will drive him like a fiend until he is a raving lunatic. Sweet idea? But true. I know where to get the nails and by God, if I drive [live?], I will drive them home...

Mackintosh was a man of passion and it seems extraordinary that the correspondence between Mackintosh and Margaret Macdonald was so long withheld from public gaze; first by William Davidson, and later the University of Glasgow. Although sections from the letters have been published and pirate editions have circulated widely since 1968, the world has had to wait until 2001 to see the whole correspondence published. Now, at last, a complete and handsome book of the letters has been edited by Pamela Robertson, curator of the Mackintosh Collection at the Hunterian Museum, Glasgow and it makes available a great deal of the material for the first time.

Unlike Mackintosh, Howarth could never, easily, be described as a man of passion; whilst his fellow students raided Liverpool, he remained 'the good swot' in Manchester. There is no record of him ever being involved in any kind of student prank or staff room rowdiness; however, when the Cordingley portrait was returned, it was Howarth who saw that it was conserved, rehung and protected.

Rag Day occasionally produced highly imaginative events. One year a group of mature students, dressed as workmen, dug a hole in a city street and started charging drivers to be allowed to pass. When it was known that the police had been informed, other students told the 'workmen' that a rival group of students was coming from the Technical College – dressed as policemen – to evict them! The result was a violent mêlée that lived long in the folk-memory of Manchester's students. Battles with water-bombs and hosepipes were regular occurrences, and one year all the statues in the main hallway of the Technical College were whitewashed. Such high jinks provided release for students who, in general, worked very hard and within very tight social and educational restraints. That said, a fair number of students in the School of Architecture were quite wealthy young men – of a kind I hadn't met before – tough, self-possessed and independent. Many had a car, some had sports cars, and whilst most were extremely well educated, many treated their architectural studies with a nonchalance that I found disconcerting.

The 'star-turn' in our year was Denis Thornley, a brilliant, handsome, fair-haired young man who quickly established himself as an outstanding practitioner. He later became a Fleet Air-arm pilot. And, after marriage to a beautiful young Rhodesian, he followed me north to Scotland where he became a landscape architect working with the Hydro Board. He was centrally involved in landscaping many of their great reservoir projects in the Highlands and Islands. Later, at Rhu, near Helensburgh, his wife, Jean, created one of Europe's great rhododendron gardens. It is open to the public and when I travelled to Scotland from Canada they usually provided me with great hospitality. Helensburgh is a place that retains strong Mackintosh connections; it was there Mackintosh designed his domestic masterpiece, The Hill House, for Mr Blackie the publisher. Thus Denis and Jean became part of the strange web my life has become – the strange web all our lives become.

There were only two girls in our year but I established close friendships with both Barbara W. Waterhouse and Prudence Bennington. Prudence was a studious and attractive brunette. Her brother, a plump, be-spectacled ex-Manchester Grammar school boy, was also a student, and I got invited

several times to join them for Easter holidays at their seaside holiday
cottage at Little Haven in Pembrokeshire. It had a beautiful situation
overlooking St Bride's Bay, where red rocks stretch out into the Atlantic.
The country lanes were full of thousands upon thousands of primroses.
We used to send boxes full to friends and relations – in those days the
Royal Mail delivered packages anywhere in England, or Wales, next day.
Prudence's mother was a large and charming lady who had once been an
opera singer; her husband, a distinguished doctor, did not usually join us.
Mrs Bennington presided over the household with a benign 'Bloomsbury'
dignity; everything she did she did with a clear sense of purpose. She was
always taking us out in the car to explore places of historical and
architectural interest. On one occasion I climbed a dangerous cliff to find
an osprey's nest, and I took one egg from the clutch for my boyhood
collection. I have now given it to the Royal Ontario Museum. It must have
been one of the last osprey nests in Britain. The species then became
extinct in the British Isles for about forty years. Fortunately, however, it is
now thriving again, in the Highlands of Scotland.

Two other students whom I admired greatly were the Armenian
brothers, Archie [Leo] and Arthur Arschavir. Little Archie and Big Archie.
They were men of deep culture, spoke various languages and perfect
English, indeed they spoke with remarkable 'upper crust' accents. They
were not pretentious and the accents seemed to suit them. Big Archie later
became Head of the School of Architecture in Hull, and Little Archie
specialised as a designer of hospitals. They played tennis and I frequently
joined them, and so did their sister Kitty. As I moved into my mid-twenties
my asthma and my general health improved considerably. And, it was

Tennis party with Thomas
Howarth and Edna Marland,
(1939).

Thomas Howarth
and his bride to be,
Edna Marland, Kirkham,
Wesham, 1939.

whilst playing a rather formidable mixed tennis team at Ribbleton, near Preston, that I met the girl who was to become my wife. Her name was Edna Marland. My abiding memory of her was standing, racket high, legs apart, on the other side of the net. She was strong and athletic; I had a good opportunity to observe her in action, and both she and that image stayed with me.

Lawn tennis is a very English sport and it still carries an idyllic, Impressionist undercurrent of romance; it was a sexually mixed activity and before the Second World War acted, like chapel and the dance hall, as a form of respectable marriage bureau. Tom Howarth's first meeting with Edna Marland embodies to perfection John Betjeman's delightful thirties poem, *Miss Joan Hunter Dunn.* For the next thirty years, Edna Marland was to play a crucial role in Howarth's life and achievements.

3 GLASGOW AND DISCIPLESHIP

THOMAS HOWARTH

The dining room was furnished in eighteenth-century style and the table, set with glass and silver, was exquisite. Professor Hughes sat at the head of the table with, on his left in the bay window, a large white cockatoo, and, during the meal Hughes would, occasionally, rise in a very dignified fashion, take a piece of food from his mouth and feed the creature – with a few appropriate words of endearment.

In 1939 Howarth was in his final year in Manchester and, like the other students, he discussed his future with senior staff. Professor Cordingley advised Howarth to pursue a career in the academic field rather than enter an architectural practice. With another European war imminent, Cordingley believed that the outlook for creative architects was likely to be limited, but that the demand for good teachers would remain. He asked Howarth whether he would like to be recommended for a position in Glasgow, as a lecturer in architecture at the Royal Technical School. Howarth affirmed strong interest and quite quickly, without an interview, the appointment was confirmed.

As Howarth prepared to set off north to Glasgow, Hitler invaded Poland and, on 3 September, Britain declared war on Germany. That afternoon Howarth went down, with a cheerful group of fellow students, to one of the Manchester recruiting stations.

I volunteered for the Navy, the Royal Air Force, and the Army – in that order. Each service, in turn, rejected me because of my history of asthma and the continuing weakness of my lungs. Thus, unfit to fight, I packed my bags and set off for Glasgow to start a teaching career that would last fifty years. I said farewell to my mother, grandparents, to my fiancée Edna, and, feeling very much alone, boarded the train for Scotland. The journey, despite wonderful views of the countryside – Morecambe Bay, the Lake District, the Border hills – seemed interminable. It was four or five hours. Approaching Glasgow I stood at an open window to view the city that

Edna Howarth (1940) in the Howarth's first home, No. 73 Waverley Gardens, Glasgow. *Thomas Howarth* would now become my home. At first I was depressed by the grey sprawl of another industrial metropolis but then I saw dozens of barrage balloons, floating high amongst small white clouds scudding over the city – they were at once surreal and reassuring – they embellished and articulated the city – they brought the actuality of war to the front of my consciousness. With their tangle of ropes hanging below them they protected the docks and shipbuilding areas from low-level air attack. I suddenly felt part of an operation beyond me and directly involved in events important to the history of the world. My heart soared as the train chugged its way in to Glasgow Central where I was met by Bill Haddow, brother of our family doctor at Kirkham.

Bill Haddow was a rotund businessman whose company manufactured margarine. His wife was a tall, elegant lady of French background. They gave me board and lodging and made me welcome in an old fashioned, very conservative way. They lived in one of Glasgow's best residential areas, Kelvinside. Their apartment looked out over splendid wooded parkland and the river Kelvin. They had a son, Ian, and a daughter, Roma who made it discreetly apparent, to me, that she was determined to marry well! And before long she did. All rooms in Haddow's apartment were heavily furnished in a very traditional Scottish-French manner and Mrs Haddow was proud to tell me that she bought most of the furniture, rugs and pictures at auction from the Glasgow salesrooms – at 'very reasonable prices'. It was one of many things that opened my eyes to other ways of doing things in Scotland. In Kirkham, my family would not have had second-hand furniture in the house, and certainly not floor coverings! The Haddows were wealthy, yet they did this. I didn't much like what they bought but I liked the idea of collecting from auctions and, even before I married, I began to drift into salesrooms on the hunt – not for Victorian tables and sofas but in the hope of finding a good drawing board lamp or a Mackintosh chair! I didn't stay with the Haddows long, but they eased me into the life of the city and introduced me to a lifelong habit of bargain-hunting – the pursuit of beautiful objects in the most unlikely places, grubby salesrooms, dank cellars, down the backs of long-disregarded chests of drawers. This hunting was to become very important to my life as a scholar and collector.

The School of Architecture was situated on an upper floor of the Royal Technical College and overlooked St George Street. Student hours were strictly nine to five. Each evening everything, design work and equipment, had to be locked away in vertical lockers stacked around the walls of large en suite studio-rooms. This was to allow the night-class students to pursue their separate courses. War had put a clamp on the city but Howarth was shocked by the atmosphere and practices he found in Glasgow – all aspects of organisation and teaching seemed rigid and mechanical compared to the informality and sophistication of the 'round-the-clock' studio life he had experienced in Manchester. The head of school was a Welshman, Professor T. Harold Hughes. Despite the fact that Hughes, via Professor Cordingley, had sought out and appointed Howarth, he made little effort to integrate the totally inexperienced new lecturer into his new post.

T. Harold Hughes had an office in the school, complete with a secretary but, as far as I could judge, he spent little time there. The prime reason being that he also had an architectural office in Oxford and shared a practice in Glasgow, with David Waugh. Both men were, at that time, deeply involved in completing a new library for the University of Glasgow – a circular, modern neo-Georgian essay in dark grey brick (a sound functional building of modest architectural merit but it has lasted and now harmonises well with the older buildings around it). These external architectural commitments meant that Hughes rarely had any contact with either students or staff at the Royal Technical College, however, as time went by, I gradually became quite fond of him. He was a handsome, eccentric character – tall, grey-haired and very active. He was always impeccably dressed, with the manners and many of the qualities of an eighteenth-century gentleman but, always 'on the run' and it was extremely difficult to pin him down with regard to the taking of important educational decisions, let alone get him involved in conversation or ideas! Fortunately, the school was held together by W. J. Smith, his right-hand man. Smith was a genuine 'power behind the throne'.

Administrative structures were minimal but Smith, successfully, oversaw all day-to-day arrangements in the school. We never had formal staff meetings and in all my years at the Royal Technical College I never learned what the management system was except that Hughes was finally responsible to the Principal of the College, Sir Arthur Huddleston. He was a large and awe-inspiring figure whom I met just once! With a war on, neither staff nor students were politically orientated, nationally or departmentally, nor was there much interest in cultural ideas or the practice of design education. This was understandable but frustrated me a good deal. By the time I completed my architectural studies in Manchester I was deeply interested in modern architecture and the theory and practice of design education – and, I knew, the students in Glasgow were being denied access to much of the best architectural thinking of the twentieth century. For example, Professor Hughes adamantly refused to allow the work of Le Corbusier, or any of the great Bauhaus designers, to be discussed within school classes. He considered them to be subversive influences liable to destroy the great traditions of British and European architecture. This seemed to me monstrous. Frank Lloyd Wright was acceptable, as were Wilelm Dudok and Eliel Saarinen, but I remember thinking 'Hughes isn't paid to peddle private prejudices, nor to run a 'private' practice; his responsibility is to educate a new generation of architects, twentieth-century architects!' It was, however, a difficult time and I do thank Professor Hughes for one thing of the greatest importance – it was he who asked me to begin serious work on Mackintosh. And looking back, despite his limitations, he was a man of considerable distinction and his school actually produced highly satisfactory results or, perhaps I should say, his staff did.

Professor Hughes was married to Edith Burnet, daughter of the distinguished Scottish architect Sir John Burnet and, when Edna Marland joined Howarth in Glasgow, the newlyweds were invited for a weekend at the Hughes home at Dunblane, Stirlingshire. This gave Howarth an opportunity that he jumped at. He left Glasgow by train, encumbered with several changes of clothes and a large portfolio of photographic prints of all his best student work – with which he was determined to impress his new professor.

During the morning, before our visit to Dunblane, I spent four hours in the dark room, making large new prints of my design thesis, 'A Town Hall for Blackpool'. Many of these prints were still damp when we arrived in Dunblane and I asked if I might lay them out in some inconspicuous place. Hughes told me to go ahead and suggested I lay them out in the hallway. I set them out – on the floor and round the walls – and they became an unavoidable and very conspicuous fact within the house – this ensured they were carefully studied. Despite the fact that my design owed something to Le Corbusier, both Hughes and his wife were cautiously complimentary. This led on to a discussion of my architectural ideas and, perhaps more importantly, my hopes re the future of architectural teaching in his school. It was inconceivable that any Glasgow student, at that time, would have been allowed to tackle 'my subject' as the basis of their final year thesis and I was keen to show him the kind of standards that could be achieved. We talked a great deal. I know my actions were close to the mark but I don't think I overstepped it.

The weekend was a pleasure and a professional success. The Hughes had two teenage daughters. One played the cello, the other played the violin; they gave an accomplished performance, then I was invited to join in on the piano.

The marriage of Edna Marland and Thomas Howarth (1940).

> I remember especially our first family dinner. The dining room was furnished in eighteenth-century style and the table, set with glass and silver, was exquisite. Professor Hughes sat at the head of the table with, on his left, in the bay window, a large white cockatoo, and, during the meal Hughes would, occasionally, rise in a very dignified fashion, take a piece of food from his mouth and feed the creature – with a few appropriate words of endearment…

Hospitality, formality and eccentricity are three constants in Scottish life and, since the early eighteenth-century have nurtured a gracious and formalised lifestyle in most well-to-do households. D.Y. Cameron, the painter and etcher, lived just up the road from Dunblane, at Dun Eaglais, Kippen, and his guests were treated to rigorous aesthetic experiences: 'Dun Eaglais was the acme of hospitality. Everything was conducted with proper laws and ceremonies – no slipshod hours, nor vague arrangements! Guests were expected to appear for prayers at a quarter to eight and for breakfast at the hour! First the family, the guests and the servants were summoned to the library, and then the master read a chosen portion of Scripture, and offered a prayer for the day. Many of the prayers were specially chosen, and edited by Cameron himself!' That extract comes from Florence Robertson Cameron, writing in *The British Weekly*. D.Y. Cameron, in his youth had been a close friend of the Mackintoshes and he contributed to the Glasgow School of Art 'Magazine', in which the Macdonald sisters and Mackintosh presented some of their earliest original artistic sketches. And it was D.Y. Cameron who gave Mackintosh one of his earliest 'independent' commissions – for a new studio at 12 Ruskin Terrace, Glasgow, in 1897. Thus, Professor Hughes and his wife began to introduce Howarth to various individuals who had known the Mackintoshes and, perhaps even more importantly, Hughes gave him direct access to a living continuance of the cultural milieu within which the Mackintosh achievement had blossomed fifty years before. For all their originality, idealism and genius, the Mackintoshes achievements were a response, on the deepest existential level, to time and place, and the particular demands of particular patrons at a particular moment in history. Mackintosh gave sublime expression to his own highly personal vision but he also gave architectural form to the aspiration of patrons who sought functional buildings, appropriate to their needs and station. People like D.Y. Cameron who knew what they wanted, a 'sensuous austerity' that gave expression to deep cultural convictions; an architecture at once ancient and modern, stylish and spiritually dynamic. The resultant 'collaborations' produced a rare combination of ascetic minimalism and aesthetic flamboyance and created what is now known as the Mackintosh style. And it is not surprising that, shortly after the visit to Dunblane, Professor Hughes asked Howarth to prepare a lecture for the leading citizens of Glasgow, on Charles Rennie Mackintosh.

Professor Hughes also asked Howarth to teach a new course entitled 'Descriptive

Geometry'. This necessitated, 'research into the structure of Gothic vaulting, the design of individual vaulting ribs, the evaluation of the shape of *voussoirs* in a skew bridge...' These things were still integral parts of basic architectural training in Glasgow, where stone building and almost mediaeval traditions of craftsmanship continued up till this time. Howarth's natural diligence and scholastic temperament were prime reasons why Hughes had chosen to appoint him; he was willing to research and master a range of 'boring' subjects with which most practically minded architects refused to bother themselves. Despite the fact that technical knowledge of Gothic construction was, essentially, obsolete information in terms of twentieth-century building, Howarth's knowledge of stone technology was to prove useful to his research into the construction of Mackintosh's buildings and he became one of the very small band of architects who carried practical knowledge of traditional stone building into the twenty-first century. He knew a great deal about something that most modern art and architectural historians know nothing; educated in the lecture theatre, the seminar room and the library, contemporary historians have become almost completely 'non-literate' with regard to the technologies and mechanics of their subjects – and it shows. Howarth was never merely a documentary historian, an art connoisseur or sociological observer; he was a trained architect, a theoretical specialist in construction, and a heraldic draughtsman with personal knowledge of the craftsmen upon whom so much of 'the quality of buildings' has depended. One of his great strengths as a modernist historian is the fact that his knowledge was gathered directly and his sensibility nurtured slowly, in direct contact with the craftsmen, as well as the best artists and cultural thinkers, of his time. Such breadth makes him an 'amateur' in the eyes of many trained academic historians, but it gave him a 'measure' that was as much beyond narrow academicism as it is beyond academic praise.

Howarth (back right) with a group of architecture students on the roof of the Royal Technical College, Glasgow (1942).

Architectural education at the Royal Technical College was, like that at Manchester University, strongly studio based; a small team of lecturers circulated through the studios looking at the work of every student in term. Participation in this process was Howarth's prime teaching responsibility.

Our intercessions were made methodically, quietly and without pressure. It was a continuous process affecting all five years and was only occasionally interrupted – by my lectures on descriptive geometry, by history lectures from Willie Smith, and lectures on structures and construction by Archie Maclean – though most of his knowledge was passed on directly in the studio. When staff had completed one circuit of the studios we would go back to the beginning and start again. We were like the painters on the Forth Bridge! One advantage of this method, for the students, was that they knew exactly where staff were at all times. They could collar them with questions, or time the development of their projects to harmonise with the imminent arrival of the appropriate specialist. This direct and economical form of staff/student contact is now rare in all too many schools of architecture and much time is wasted whilst students hang about waiting for 'missing' members of staff. They're always at meetings! Or they say they're at meetings! Meetings are the last refuge of a scoundrel! Things were not like that in Glasgow in 1940.

Willie Smith, the historian, immediately struck me as a marvellous teacher, humane, well-informed, kindly and highly respected. Archie Maclean was a detached individual who gave of his time and practical knowledge without stint. David Waugh, Professor Hughes' architectural

partner, was not an easy man to work with and, like Hughes, primarily committed to work outwith the college. I got on best with our two young 'instructors', Clunie Rowell and John Murray, each was even younger than I was. Clunie was tall, blonde, strongly built and very handsome. We became close friends. He was an outstanding draughtsman, a good designer and a great admirer of Charles Rennie Mackintosh. He had a tremendous enthusiasm for Scottish architecture and was most helpful during the months of my first serious work on Mackintosh. He was also an outstanding teacher, sitting for long periods at each student's drawing board. In a deep slow voice he would discuss all the possibilities of each project with brilliant perception. We became close friends and used to share all-night fire-watching duties on the roof of the college. Many a night, to pass the time, I would go inside to play the college organ, whilst he kept watch, or 'conducted' the moon, on the rooftop. Sometimes he would rush down to request Tchaikovsky's *1812 Overture* when a raid was starting! And back he would go hoping to orchestrate the distant thumping and flashing of the bombs! Clunie Rowell, unfortunately, soon went off to join the army. And, before being posted overseas, he married a very attractive young lady whose name was Dorin. He asked me if I would play at their wedding, which I did, and a wonderful wedding it was. They wanted lively modern melodies as well as the traditional Scottish pieces and I obliged with great pleasure. I remember how splendid Clunie looked in his officer's uniform and the special magic with which he pronounced his bride's name, Dorin, in his lilting Scottish brogue.

Inverary, Argyllshire (c. 1945). Photograph taken as part of a student project to measure and document the village for the National Trust for Scotland. *Thomas Howarth*

Despite several years as a fire-watcher, Howarth was not involved in any serious fire-fighting, though he did witness both the great raid on Clydebank on 13 March 1941, and the burning of Alexander Greek Thomson's church at Queen's Park, 'the most serious architectural loss suffered by Glasgow during the war'. The long nights hanging about gave him an opportunity to read widely and also establish an important new friendship with a young research chemist, Geoffrey Muir. Muir was a member of the Association of Scientific Workers, a left-wing group which worked under the wing of the eminent scientist P.M.S. Blackett. Geoffrey Muir was a Communist. Howarth was, and was always to remain, a staunch old-fashioned Conservative but the two men got on extremely well and Muir drew Howarth into his work on developing hydroelectric power in the Highlands. He encouraged Howarth to bring his architectural and planning skills to an A.S.W. committee doing research into new ecological sources of power and Howarth, in turn, co-opted one of his old architectural colleagues from Manchester, Gordon Dearden. Dearden was also strongly left-wing and, bored by his military service in Glasgow, delighted to work on the Hydro project. The three men went out on various research expeditions together, notably to the new aluminium works at Kinlochleven, by Fort William.

> We were horrified by the conditions under which the workers were living and the desecration of the natural environment. I managed to get some telling photographs and reported back to the A.S.W. It decided to bring out a publication looking at the current situation and future possibilities. Gordon Dearden and I wrote the chapter on architecture and planning and I designed the booklet, including its cover, diagrams and illustrations. It was not much more than a pamphlet but it was published in Glasgow and won commendations from Blackett and the A.S.W. headquarters. The wartime situation, unfortunately, diminished its impact but it presented imaginative long-term proposals that I like to think might have had huge impact like President Roosevelt's Tennessee Valley Authority. Of course, the Scottish Hydro Electric Board became a major force in the Highlands after the war – but how much or how little they referred to our work I have no idea. In retrospect I can see that this work nurtured my later interest in the importance of planning and a unified, ecological approach to environmental needs.

Another voluntary task Howarth undertook at this time was research work for the National Trust for Scotland. As the war moved to its close, Professor Hughes suggested that Howarth take students out to do measured drawings of various National Trust properties – to provide future records for the Trust and practical experience for the students. Howarth took matters further, suggesting that rather than documenting particular buildings, for which plans often already existed, he would document whole villages and set all the important buildings in their environmental context. Eaglesham in Ayrshire and Inverary in Argyll were selected – two fine examples of traditional Scottish design and planning.

> I believe these 'environmental studies' to have been the first of their kind in Scotland… Each village was planned in the late eighteenth century and consisted of mainly white-painted, two-storey, terraced cottages and houses. Both were planned around a large rectangular 'village green', which at Inverary also had an axially planned church. The spatial relationship of buildings to open spaces was excellent and the human scale admirable. My students created not only a plan of each village but elevations of each aspect of all dwellings, with cross-sections through each site, to show the relationship between the vertical height of buildings and the spaces between them. The students did a first-class job and produced excellent drawings. We also gathered old postcards and photographs which would be likely to help future reconstructions and repairs: then everything was lodged with the National Trust officials. In 1999 I checked with the present custodians of the National Trust as to where our submissions were and how they had been used over the last half century. They informed me that they had no knowledge and no record of any such plans. C'est la vie!

Howarth's wartime workload in Glasgow was heavy. After teaching all day at the Technical College he would go on to the Glasgow School of Art, where he worked as a tutor at evening classes. The students there were young architectural draughtsmen who had worked full-time in architectural offices for some years but still needed 'the diploma in architecture' that would enable them to apply for membership of the Royal Incorporation of Architects in Scotland, R.I.A.S. Membership of this body was the key to professional advancement. Howarth enjoyed this work greatly, partly because he was able to use his time in the School of Art to advance his research on the building's designer. As if this was not enough, Howarth also became deeply involved in the life of the local Methodist community, playing the organ at least once a week and attending St John's Church in Sauchiehall Street every Sunday.

> The great square tower of St John's church was a noted city landmark – until it was demolished! Although not designed by Greek Thomson I saw it as a splendid example of the way Thomson's influence left a permanent imprint upon the architecture of the whole city of Glasgow. Inside, it had a great four-manual organ, an elevated pulpit, balconies on three sides and fine windows that created a spectacular space flooded with light; the

epitome of a great 'preaching house'. The resident minister, John Brazier
Greene, had a wonderful resonant voice encased in a body very like that
of the film actor Charles Laughton – famous for his portrayals of the
reprobate Rembrandt and the heretical Galileo! John Brazier Greene was
renown for his long sermons – which were highly intelligent and held
huge congregations spellbound. I played the organ at his Wednesday
lunchtime services throughout the war. The church also had a large choir,
and Sunday services at St Johns were always memorable and stirring events
– nurturing human as well as spiritual experiences. One fine summer
morning a young man in R.A.F. uniform sat down beside me. As soon as
we started the first hymn I noted that he had a beautiful, rich, baritone
voice and afterwards I introduced myself. He immediately impressed me
and I urged him to join the choir. He said he would join if I introduced
him not just to the choirmaster but, also, to 'his very attractive daughter'.
I had already noticed his enthusiasm for this girl and said I'd be delighted
to make a double introduction. His name was John Allegro. After a few
moments chat with the choirmaster, he agreed to join both our congregation and the choir. Then I introduced him to the daughter. It wasn't long
before they were married.

The name John Allegro will not mean a great deal to many people
today. He's been dead for many years, but John Allegro briefly gained
considerable fame; he had a genius for languages, he became, first, a
brilliant Hebraic scholar, then one of the leaders of the intellectual revolts
that swept America in the sixties and seventies. During the war, however,
John Allegro was just another R.A.F. conscript at a loose end in Glasgow.
He was a little like Lawrence of Arabia. He had exceptional intellect, great
energy, imaginative insight and a great capacity for enthusiastic
commitment whilst, at the same time, being socially and psychologically,
somewhat disturbed. We became close friends and I encouraged him to
make use of his tremendous natural gifts. On his demobilization, in 1945,
I helped him gain a place at the University of Manchester, where he went
to study Semitic languages. He also decided to become a Methodist
minister and so shared his time between linguistic studies at the university
and theological studies at Didsbury College (directly adjacent to the house
in which Edna and I set up home when we returned to Manchester in
1947). John did so well in both his Semitic and Religious studies that,
when the Dead Sea Scrolls were discovered, he was one of those sent out
to the Middle East to assist in their translation and interpretation. The
head of his department in Manchester was responsible for overseeing
developments and, very methodically, he set about gathering all the

information necessary for publication of this red-hot material – it seemed then to have the potential to reshape our understanding of early Christian history. The timetable that emerged seemed to many people unnecessarily, slow. Thus, John, on the spot, and hugely excited by what the scrolls were revealing decided, or was persuaded, to steal a march on his colleagues and, in league with Penguin books, published his translation of *The Dead Sea Scrolls*. Publication caused a sensation and John Allegro became a celebrity overnight. I remember him coming round to our house and presenting us with a copy of the book – still warm from the press! I can still see his excitement as he told us the whole story in vivid detail. His eyes shone. Some aspects of his translations were later critically disputed but there is no doubt that his book was an important and timely document.

Following this, John was funded to return to the Middle East to investigate another remarkable discovery – a collection of inscribed copper scrolls. The problem this time was technical as well as linguistic; the scrolls were corroded, heavily oxidised and couldn't be unrolled. But, once more, John Allegro cut the Gordian knot. He knew that the Watch Making Department at Manchester Technical College had an extremely sensitive machine for precisely cutting metal into thin strips and, he believed, that by carefully cutting the rolls of encrusted copper into thin strips – it would be possible to unroll each strip, secured by an adhesive, onto paper or fabric… John convinced the relevant authorities this was the best solution and the scrolls were sent to Manchester. His experimental procedure worked remarkably well and John told us that he was then asked to translate the text. Once more he was responsible for the publication of a unique historical document, *The Treasure of the Copper Scroll*. It was an inventory of treasure hidden in the Qumran area at about the time of Christ, by a little known sect called the Essenes. Naturally, John then went off to find the treasure! He didn't. For the first time one of his great plans failed. He returned to Manchester somewhat chastened, then left for the Isle of Man. It was, and remains, an international, offshore tax haven – so, perhaps, he did find the treasure!

Up until 1958, Edna and I continued to see a lot of the Allegros but, when we moved to Canada, we lost touch with them. He, at sometime, went off to the United States where, he lost his religious faith and got sidetracked into the drugs culture of the 1960s. He was, however, a man of the most exceptional intelligence and imagination and even when he went 'over the top', he continued to produce work that was highly original and boldly challenging. His last major book was *The Sacred Mushroom and the Cross*, published in 1970. It remains one of the classic, controversial works of modern religious literature. It provoked a marvellous review in *The Times*, 23 May 1970, by the television dramatist Dennis Potter. He too came from a Methodist background.

John Allegro was once a Methodist parson, spooning out the grey salvation of his church to shuffling villagers. He was until recently a theological lecturer, and is a philologist skilled at excavating obsolete languages which have been preserved in more modern tongues like fossils in buckling rock. A scholarly, perceptive, quirkily talented man who somewhere along the way – and while immersed in the language and the teeming quarries of faith – has developed an intense antipathy to the whole edifice of Christianity. An apostate who uses all his formidable equipment not to shift, soften, adjust or hone down his old belief, but to destroy it once and for all.

The Sacred Mushroom and the Cross attempts by plucking out the root meaning of words in the oldest written language known to us – to reveal the explicit, sometimes beautiful sexual images of early religious experience. God is understood as a gigantic penis fertilising female earth. Rain is God's spermatozoa, spouting out in a mighty orgasm which at its most forceful shakes the heavens with its thunder. After the rain, after the thunder, sprouts up the puzzlingly swift mushroom.

The phallic shape of this weird fungus contained a drug which, logically, was the purest possible form of God's own spermatozoa. The red-capped Amanita Muscaria was God made manifest on earth. A mushroom containing a powerful hallucinogen with which the ancients blew their minds and walked with God.

Allegro boldly sketches in the origins of the primitive fertility cult with an exciting plunge into the catacombs of antiquity where mythology and mycology mingle in a poetic, hallucinatory haze of credible speculation. It is a dazzling foray into the obscure hinterlands of comparative philology. But this, of course, is no mere linguistic frolic: the full thrust of this thesis is directed head-on against the figure of Christ.

Reading Dennis Potter's review one is reminded that certain of the ancient, pagan ideas he discusses are quite similar to some of the mystical ideas explored by Mackintosh, the Macdonald sisters, and the circle around them. Howarth, too, had a long interest in spiritualism and it is interesting that at about the time of his meeting with Allegro his diary documents his attendance at a series of religious meetings in which the lives of Salome and Mary Magdalene were the centre of serious study.

ıst OCTOBER 1941 – Zebedee – Salome, his wife, asks for his sons to be placed in Kingdom – intense ambition – she was there at confirmation.

Probably sister of Mary. 5 OCTOBER – Sunday – Induction. 8 OCTOBER – Dead Sea, 1,400 feet below sea level. Jerusalem – Bethel = 6 miles. Dead Sea now where Sodom and Gomorrah were. 15 OCTOBER – Mary Magdalene – not an immoral character – not poor – friend of James – wife of high civil servant at court of Herod Antipas. Mary – Bold and Unconventional. Love (last) story at the tomb.

Thomas Howarth had married Edna Marland, at Ribbleton Parish Church, Preston, on 6 July 1940. It was a modest, wartime, purely family event. After a short honeymoon at Keswick in the English Lake District, the Howarth's settled in a rented, furnished apartment at Waverley Gardens, Shawlands, Glasgow. Howarth writes, 'Edna, my wife, had a charm and natural dignity that was immediately recognised and respected'. It is a precise, minimal compliment but the grandest he makes in all his *Memoirs*. Howarth's tight-chested reticence about close personal relationships is typical of a reticence then endemic across Britain. In northern England the 'idea' of romance was 'manfully' reduced *absurdam*. Even Neville Cardus, music critic and cricket correspondent of *The Manchester Guardian* in its golden age, and one of the most poetical and romantic writers of the inter-war years, describes his wedding as an 'interruption'. The following extract comes from his autobiography:

Left. Edna Howarth with her grandfather, Joseph Cornall, on a Loch Lomond steamer. (c. 1943) *Thomas Howarth*

Right. Waverley Gardens, Glasgow; the top floor was the Howarths' home from 1940 to 1946. *Thomas Howarth*

> There are many things about cricket, apart from the skill and the score. There is, first of all, the leisure to do something else. Cricket, like music, has its slow movements, especially when my native county, Lancashire, is batting. I married the good companion who is my wife during a Lancashire innings. The event occurred in June, 1921. I went as usual to Old Trafford (the Cricket Ground), stayed for a while and saw Hallows and Makepeace come forth to bat. As usual they opened with care. Then I had to leave, had to take a taxi to Manchester, there to be joined in wedlock at a registry office. Then I – that is, we – returned to Old Trafford. While I had been away from the match and committed the most responsible and irrevocable act in a mortal man's life, Lancashire had increased their total by exactly seventeen – Makepeace 5, Hallows 11, and one leg-bye.

That is written tongue-in-cheek but it epitomises an attitude that Howarth carried into marriage nineteen years later. Like Cardus, Howarth was committed to an ethos of work, work and more work. Leisure was there to be enjoyed but must be clearly focussed and purposeful. Consequently, for various reasons, a new life in Glasgow was no easy option for Edna Howarth. She was a stranger in a city pinned down by war and enforced austerity. There was a vibrant camaraderie abroad but with a workaholic husband, dark streets and a louring climate she felt, frequently, very much alone. She kept house, did voluntary work, supported her husband's wide-ranging lecturing and acted as his unpaid research secretary. She overcame difficulties with remarkable energy and fortitude including a miscarriage at home. Howarth phoned for the doctor. When the doctor learned that the baby was stillborn but the mother had stopped bleeding, he calmly stated that Howarth should incinerate the foetus in their domestic range. He would visit when time allowed. It was a shocking event but Edna recovered and Howarth put the incident aside for sixty years. Both partners stoically accepted their experience as ill fortune and a product of the strictures of war. Both were buttressed by their religious faith. Howarth immersed himself ever deeper in his Mackintosh research, Edna worked ever harder to be the good wife and citizen.

Howarth's formal introduction to Mackintosh came, out of the blue, in the spring of 1940. Late one afternoon, Professor Hughes made one of his highly infrequent visits to the architecture studios where Howarth was now lecturer-in-charge. Suddenly, in front of the students, Hughes asked Howarth whether he would like to give one of the Lord Provost's lectures, next year. Whether the request was premeditated, or spur of the moment, it was to prove a monumental turning point in Howarth professional life. He notes, 'that sort of request from T. Harold Hughes was a command!' And, with his usual mixture of youthful diffidence and ambition, he replied, 'Yes of course – but on what should I lecture?' Hughes, immediately, said, 'Why not Charles Rennie Mackintosh? You've almost a year to prepare.' And he left the room. A great discovery, a career, success and a new life lay ahead.

In conversation Howarth remembered the incident as another of 'the small miracles that articulated my life', but he was not to be drawn on the question as to whether the miracle was divine, self-engendered, effected by outsiders, or a purely accidental occurrence. He was happy to remember it as a moment of felicity, like the alignment of planets, like the sight of a green oasis arising out of the desert.

Once commissioned to do his lecture, Howarth approached the task with dedication and systematic enthusiasm. The two men who helped Howarth most, at this time, were his fellow lecturers, Willie Smith, the historian, and James Clunie Rowell. Clunie Rowell had a seasoned love for Mackintosh's work, he knew the Glasgow School of Art inside out and he took great pleasure in showing Howarth round.

Margaret Macdonald and Charles Rennie Mackintosh

Glasgow School of Art.

The building, during those war years, was forbidding, depressing, and much neglected: the great library window frames were cracking, numerous panes were broken, the iron railings on the north side of the school had been vandalized, and the bells on the iron coats-of-arms on the roof, had been stolen… My initial reaction was somewhat guarded but later, when I was teaching regularly in the school, I came to love the building; the hen-run with its splendid views across the city, the great studios with their north lighting, the spatial magic of the small entrance vestibule and the great roof-lit staircase hall above it. I began to enjoy, at leisure, the rich detailing of glass, tiles, and metal, and – in the sombre, brooding, forest-

like stillness of the library – to know what it was to be Mackintosh, and a scholar-scribe of the mediaeval period.

As I prepared my lecture I decided to present Mackintosh to his fellow Glaswegians as a great genius, and with all the *gravitas* I could muster. Willie Smith informed me that numerous hidden treasures existed in Glasgow and he suggested I should incorporate them in my lecture. I remember him taking me home to his own house, where he showed me a set of high-backed, Mackintosh dining chairs he had acquired. He had decided they were too tall for comfort and cut the backs down! It seemed like sacrilege but I kept mum. Indeed I kept quiet for forty years until, one day, Roger Billcliffe, of Billcliffe Fine Art, wrote to query a set of Mackintosh chairs he'd come across – with strangely low backs! He couldn't find any documentation about them. I told him of William Smith's modifications and we, jointly, concluded that the chairs in question must once have been his…

In the summer of 1940 Howarth was introduced to William Davidson, who had commissioned Windyhill in 1901, the second grandest of all the houses Mackintosh designed, and who, on the death of Margaret Macdonald in 1933, had become trustee of the Mackintosh estate. Davidson was circumspect in all discussions but, generously, gave Howarth free range of his Glasgow warehouse:

I spent many hours sorting through a vast number of drawings and documents stored in dusty, brown paper packages. It was an exciting experience and I quickly became concerned about the well-being of these precious objects. As I got to know William Davidson better I broached him about the future of his collection. He was an old man. He told me that neither the University of Glasgow, the School of Art, nor the City Art Gallery had shown any serious interest and that neither would guarantee a permanent display of a 'Mackintosh exhibition'. This kind of information was very depressing.

By now Howarth was absolutely confident of Mackintosh's greatness and he was angry that such a man should be becalmed in the doldrums of general non-comprehension and ignorance. In certain quarters he saw Mackintosh's reputation being sullied by ill-disguised contempt, and he determined that he would put matters right. He had discovered a cause and he had a master.

Howarth prepared his lecture with great care. He assembled an excellent collection of slides and he psychologically prepared himself – like an actor given a first major theatrical opportunity. The Lord Provost's audience was large, distinguished, and knowledgeable, and it received Howarth's lecture with rapturous applause. The evening was chaired by Sir William Hutchinson, Director of the Glasgow School of Art. Obviously inspired, Hutchinson immediately suggested, publicly, that Howarth should continue his research and turn it into a book for publication. Within weeks, Professor Cordingley had been drawn into the equation and he arranged a deal whereby Howarth would continue his Mackintosh research as a PhD. student supported by both the University of Manchester, and the University of Glasgow.

Thus, in the summer of 1941, at the age of twenty-seven, Thomas Howarth launched himself into his life's work – as the first scholar/disciple of Charles Rennie Mackintosh. From the beginning he quite consciously planned his work as an attack on four fronts. First, he would study and document everything he could find out about Mackintosh, his work and his associates. That would provide the basis of his PhD. Second, he would create a book that would present Mackintosh to the world as a great modern architect. This would provide him with the *intellectual capital* that would fund his professional career. Third, he would work to see that Mackintosh's work was preserved, collected, collated, and properly exhibited within his native city of Glasgow. Fourth, he would start his own Mackintosh collection.

The idea of a collection satisfied something fundamental in Howarth's character but, more importantly, it gave him hands-on, direct, personal contact with his subject – Mackintosh, a man who was always an artist and craftsman as well as an architect. Howarth began to live with Mackintosh; he became familiar with every aspect of Mackintosh's creative imagination; he saw, he held, he conquered. Looking further ahead, he knew a major personal collection would provide him with superb teaching tools for use with his future students. Howarth loved collecting; he wanted to be surrounded by beautiful things and he knew that these unique, historic creations would become increasingly valuable. He felt himself to be walking in step with high genius. Despite the war, overwork, and impoverished surroundings, he knew he had been drawn into the company of a group of the most exceptional artists; men and women who would bring joy, beauty and happiness into his life and that of cultured people around the globe. It was his acceptance of discipleship that gave him his freedom.

THE MACKINTOSH YEARS ④

Endurance was to him the crowning quality of Building. | WILLIAM MOYES
When I left Glasgow (c. 1907) the prospects for Mr Mackintosh
were bright. His heart was in his work and in the
beauty of the flowers he rejoiced.

The request by Professor T. Harold Hughes that Howarth give a major public lecture on Charles Rennie Mackintosh came as a shock but Howarth quickly recognised that Hughes had given him a golden opportunity to acquire his reputation. The lecture was scheduled as one of four prestigious explorations of Scottish culture delivered to the Provand's Lordship Society of Glasgow in the spring of 1941. His date was 17 March. The title Howarth chose was the most straightforward he could think of – 'Charles Rennie Mackintosh: Architect'.

First, he set out to systematically establish the facts and familiarise himself with all known Mackintosh buildings in the Glasgow area. This was no easy task. All of Mackintosh's major commissions in Scotland had been designed within the firm of Honeyman and Keppie and it was normal practice that the heads of such firms were named as the architects of all projects carried out – even when established architectural draughtsmen (and architects), like Mackintosh, took complete control of large commissions. No one knew exactly which buildings were Mackintosh's, which were joint projects, or which were designed entirely by other architects within the firm – except, of course, John Keppie, who was still alive but unwilling to discuss the matter. Accordingly when Keppie died in 1944, it came as no surprise to Howarth that press obituaries acknowledged him as 'architect of the Glasgow School of Art'. Howarth became even more determined to set the record straight: he knew that Keppie had played a part in the design commission but he was not the architect – the School of Art was Mackintosh's 'masterpiece', in the true and original meaning of the word.

It was during his summer holiday in 1940 that Howarth began the long task of establishing what the oeuvre of Mackintosh actually was. He soon began to make real discoveries but his conclusions, when he delivered his lecture that autumn, were tentative

84

and extremely conservative. The problem was a 'crossword puzzle' that he, and others, worked on for years and, even today, the Mackintosh oeuvre continues to grow – particularly in the fields of furniture, architectural drawings and small artefacts. The reasons for this 'slow burn' are fourfold, and it was Howarth who first recognized them. One, Mackintosh was a far more productive designer than many people had assumed and his enemies wanted to believe or let on. Two, his work was much more varied than generally assumed and his genius of the kind that only reveals itself over time (as new generations learn to read his personal vocabulary of forms). Three, a good deal of his non-architectural work was actually 'lost' and awaited 'archaeological' finding. Four, Howarth's researches were savagely constricted by the wartime emergency, by the demands of full-time teaching, by a lack of money, and the non-existence of those reprographic technologies that modern academics take for granted. Even paper was hard to come by during the war years and much of Howarth's correspondence was conducted on scraps used two or three times.

From the beginning, Howarth wanted to set Mackintosh in a wide historical, international and cultural framework. To this end he became a bold correspondent and a compulsive sleuth, seeking information and help from wherever it might be found. Commendably, he did this without preconceptions and without national, class, or ideological bias. A letter he sent on the 25 November 1940 to the distinguished art historian, Professor Wilenski, one of his lecturers at the University of Manchester, sets the tone. Howarth's letters were always polite, very respectful, sometimes diffident, always personal, and always accompanied by a stamped and addressed envelope. He begins by informing Wilenski of his research into the work of Charles Rennie Mackintosh then continues,

> *For several years I had the pleasure of attending your lectures at Manchester University. I was the bespectacled contemporary of Frank Fielden; perhaps you remember me? Though I have not commenced serious research at the moment I understand that in addition to his architectural aspirations Mackintosh was a keen water colourist, his subject usually being wild flowers… I should appreciate your opinion and shall cover as much ground as possible… In closing I would like to say how invaluable I have found the knowledge gained at your lectures in Manchester both in criticising and guiding the students under your care. This lecture of mine in March is a great opportunity for me to become a little better known in a foreign country and I shall be really glad of your advice...*

Almost by return, on 28 November, Wilenski sent an extended, encouraging and helpful reply. Howarth was away to a flying start and he never looked back.

The more Howarth delved into the activities of the Mackintosh circle the more excited and committed he became. He identified himself, personally, with many aspects of Mackintosh's life, architecture and ideals. And, with inspired perception, he seemed to

discover exactly the right armature on which to build his research – a set of principles,
ideas and procedures that successfully guided the project forward over many years. This
armature also provided him with an intellectual refuge when things went wrong or times
were hard. In 1994 Mrs Mhairi Fraser Monteith Sinclair of St Andrews, who attended the
Lord Provost's lecture series in 1941, recalled being physically thrilled by the lecture
delivered by the young Thomas Howarth: 'It was not just Mackintosh, and the slides of
his work, it was the sheer committed enthusiasm of the lecturer! Here was a man with
something to say and a transparent love for his subject. My brother, Bremner Monteith,
was one of his most devoted students.' As a lecturer, Howarth used skills learned from the
pulpit, sometimes revealing facts and advancing his ideas in something close to reverie,
almost an ecstasy. This un-English enthusiasm immediately endeared Howarth to many in
his Scottish audiences, as did his recognition that Mackintosh's originality owed a great
deal to a particularly Scottish and Celtic tradition.

As a north-Englishman, Howarth was well placed to see and evaluate the ways in
which Mackintosh transformed mediaeval and Scottish baronial forms into modern forms.
He also saw how Mackintosh made use of the Arts and Crafts movement as a platform
for his own highly personal art. Howarth began study of Mackintosh as a historian but
he was a trained Modernist architect and he, naturally, viewed the Mackintosh
achievement through Modernist spectacles: there can be no doubt that he *wanted* to draw
Mackintosh into the Modernist fold. This was, in academic terms, a dangerous preconception to carry, but it was a preconception founded in reality. It illumined the direction
his research took and the material he gathered. To his great satisfaction, Howarth soon
began to realise that the work of the Mackintosh group was far more Modernist and
internationally influential than even he had conceived. The profound impact that he
discovered the Mackintoshes had had on the Secessionist artists in Vienna alone validated

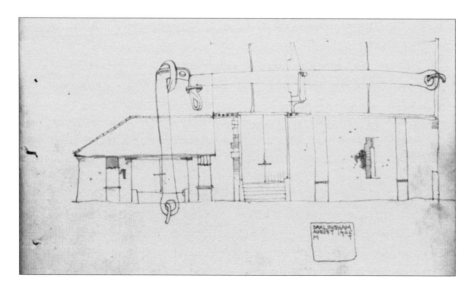

Chair (c. 1906), ascribed
to Joseph Hoffmann.

and justified the line he was taking. Indeed, Howarth quickly understood that his confirmation of the Modernist connection between Glasgow and Vienna was of such
importance that it was best kept secret until his thesis was complete and publication of
his ideas under his name assured. He wanted credit where, credit was due, and he decided
the book he would write should be entitled *Mackintosh – and the Modern Movement.*

Another important and largely unrecognised component Howarth brought to his
researches was his religious faith. As an evangelical Methodist, Howarth was well placed
to recognise the spiritual and religious energies that fuelled the art of the Mackintosh
group. Whilst this recognition of the 'Mackintosh Vision' played only a subterranean role
in Howarth's PhD thesis, there can be no doubt that his awareness that Mackintosh was
deeply involved in the idea of a 'spiritual quest' informed, inspired, and sustained him as
he struggled to have his 'revelations' recognised and his 'great book' published. Howarth
was not, by nature, courageous; he could be a churlish individual and a pernickety scholar
but Mackintosh's fearless example helped make Howarth bold. From 1941 onwards,
spiritual enthusiasm and raw courage informed Howarth's research just as surely as it
illumines every object Mackintosh created.

Such courage was necessary because considerable antipathy towards Mackintosh was
still firmly ensconced in certain sections of Glasgow's architectural community. There was
a fashionable will to perpetuate his memory as a drunkard; a weakling reduced by an
overbearing wife; a bad egg who stained the grand circles he might have been part of.
These residues of prejudice caused Howarth continuing difficulties but despite this and
despite his youthful Englishness, Howarth was given remarkable support by the great
majority of the people he contacted in Glasgow and, later, across Scotland. This encouragement increased the sense of responsibility Howarth felt for his subject and the work
he was doing. As his network of contacts expanded, personal reminiscences blossomed
into hard information; lost paintings and lost letters appeared; mouldering furniture was
dusted and brought out into the open; cutlery polished and jewellery remembered.
Howarth had entered a gold mine.

Howarth recognised that his scholarly endeavours were likely to become part of the
cultural history of mankind and, quite consciously, he strove to become much more than
an academic historian and scholar: he became an archivist, a cultural agitator, and a
philosophical interpreter. Howarth became a kind of documentary folklorist, taking unto
himself the responsibility of harvesting all relevant remembrances, ideas and facts about
Mackintosh and his circle, and their role in the world. Partly because he knew he was
prone to 'evangelical' proselytising, he became ultra systematic in his collation, collection,
and preservation of information and objects, buildings, artefacts, paintings and drawings.
Thus, the establishment of appropriate and coherent museum collections of work by
Mackintosh became part of Howarth's 'grand plan' from 1942 onwards. This was
ambition and vision of a high order.

It may be surprising that, twelve years after his death, Mackintosh still had vociferous enemies in Glasgow but it would be entirely wrong to assume that he had no admirers or followers, that he was totally ignored in the country from which he'd fled, never to return, in 1914. Most people of genius invoke deep love amongst their close friends and death often reinforces the allegiance of adherents. This was true of Mackintosh and although his circle of friends had contracted by the time of his final illness in 1927, Mackintosh still had loyal friends and patrons. His cancer surgeon refused to accept payment from 'the great Scottish architect'. Major Chapman Huston gave the Mackintoshes free accommodation in his Hampstead house with its garden and a tree. In 1928, Mackintosh was the subject of generous obituaries in *The Glasgow Herald* and *The Times* and, after the final exhibition and sale of art works from the Mackintoshs' estate in Glasgow in 1933, an extremely perceptive critique of Mackintosh's achievement appeared in the B.B.C. magazine, *The Listener*. It was written by Professor Allan D. Moinds and brilliantly sets the scene into which Howarth moved eight years later. Allan Moinds should have an honoured place in the Mackintosh story:

> The new School of Art stands as a monument to [Mackintosh's] vision and genius on Garnethill, Glasgow. To those of us who had the privilege of watching this building grow from its foundations and who have since seen the development on the continent and in these islands – of the new order of architecture, the Glasgow School of Art is recognized as a landmark in the history of architecture and Mackintosh is recognized as a pioneer. That his work has been misunderstood by many and derided by not a few is not to be wondered at; had it been universally understood and accepted at its inception it would not have been worthy to take its place in the new world order that it foreshadowed… Fra Newbery, the then director of the Glasgow School of Art was outstanding; a man of virility, force and understanding, he saw to it that Mackintosh was not hindered in his work.
>
> In order to grasp the significance of Mackintosh and the Glasgow artists who worked with him, in order to understand his position as one of the founders of the Modern style, it would be necessary to review the situation from the time when William Morris undertook the reformation of the domestic arts in the teeth of violent opposition from his contemporaries. Here, it must suffice to indicate briefly in what ways the Scottish and Continental movement differed from the English School in general principles, and attempt to show today that it is towards Glasgow and the Continent rather than to England that one must look for the new order of architecture which is sweeping over the world and changing the character of our homes and our cities…

Professor Moind's article was, almost certainly, the trigger that encouraged Nikolaus Pevsner to give Mackintosh an important place in his book *Pioneers of the Modern Movement*, published two years later. With broad strokes Moind, a Glaswegian patriot to his fingertips, brilliantly anticipates what Howarth, with scholastic precision, was to make substantial in his doctoral thesis. Moind articulated what a small but select band of perceptive Scots were also deeply aware of – that Mackintosh was truly exceptional. Howarth set out to find them and with exemplary care and dedication, he sought to draw-in everybody, and everything, that might contribute to his Mackintosh enquiry. Nothing and no one was too mean or lowly to be pursued.

One invaluable source of information was the letters page of *The Glasgow Herald*. It provided the stage for a long collaboration between Howarth and a marvellous cross-section of Scotland's thrawn, argumentative, hugely diverse newspaper readership; over the years this newspaper, above all others, has served Mackintosh proud. Howarth asked for information and a steady flow of letters came back to him; all were answered, and many were extremely useful. The majority were kept, catalogued and stored in his archive. The most important led to personal visits and some created lasting friendships. Two letters from Mr D. Cross of Limekilns, Fife, are brilliantly insightful. Describing his remembrance of what he calls 'the small façade in Sauchiehall Street now forming part of Daly's shop', Cross wrote, on 6 March 1944,

> *It seemed to me then – its seems to me now – one of the most extraordinary achievements in architecture: a minor achievement doubtless, nevertheless a feat of design difficult to parallel; the work of a born artist, masterly, subtle, original, almost flabbergasting in its revelation of a vivid and profoundly unusual personality. I felt that interior stir with which we all recognise a transforming experience...*

A friendship began and Howarth printed and framed a photograph of the facade of the Willow Street Tearooms for Mr Cross. He charged two pounds for this service and Mr Cross wrote back,

> *I must thank you again for your assistance. I do not mind a little expense in this sacred cause... By the way, I showed my new-framed picture to a local architect: after a few minutes he said 'I can do that!' I nearly said 'Oh! Can you!' But instead, nothing. I reckon he was entitled to his opinion – and to my silence... Although of unorthodox appearance, Mackintosh's work was unmistakably Scottish in character. This point [made by Howarth in a B.B.C. broadcast] is good; it confirms what anyone with critical faculties can see and cannot be emphasised too much... Mackintosh's art was a delicate plant. But not a plant in a pot. Its roots were deep.*

Mr Cross recognises four profoundly important facts about Mackintosh's work: that it is frequently 'flabbergasting' (what Mackintosh liked to describe as art of 'hallucinatory quality'); that the work is, in some way 'sacred', perhaps, part of 'a cause'; that the work is unmistakably Scottish; and that the work is not synthetic but natural, deep-rooted and delicate. Mr Cross observes facts but writes from a position of knowledge that seems to be, specifically, Rosicrucian. Cross, however, was only one of several Scots who affirmed 'the Scottishness' of Mackintosh's highly personal art. In February 1944, Captain Sidney W. Cruickshank wrote to Howarth referring to an article in the German magazine *Dekorative Kunst* of 1905, which illustrates a Mackintosh house, 'with a façade akin to a rather severe two-storey Scottish farmhouse of the early nineteenth century'. Captain Cruickshank then goes on to ridicule contemporary understanding of Mackintosh:

> *I read, recently, a popular book* The Story of English (!) Architects, *by one Talmadge, published in America. His references to Mackintosh's work are definitely derogatory, and the only Mackintosh works he mentions are 'Reggiori's Restaurant' at Kings Cross and 'The Famous Wilton Tearooms'! I visited Reggiori's recently – a travesty of cauliflower tilework, brass hat racks and heavy plush. I only trust that in his lifetime Mackintosh was spared the agony of visiting this orgy of tile-makers exhibitionism. 'The Famous Wilton Tearooms' I have looked for in vain, but suspect that they, too, were decorated when Mackintosh was in his cradle. I have found that the Talmadge opus teems with inaccuracies, and I suspect that the author has never set foot in the British Isles... May I say how relieved and delighted I am to hear that, at last, someone has undertaken the too long delayed task of compiling a complete record of Mackintosh's life and work? It would have been nothing short of a tragedy had it been delayed much longer. I wish you all success...*

Captain Cruickshank's letter was posted in Colchester and his address was given as c/o Messrs Pringle and Clay, W.S., 7 Alleyn Place, Edinburgh 2.

A letter from Alfred Longden, Director of Fine Art at the British Council in London, written in January 1945 shows him to be one of Mackintosh's English enthusiasts.

> *In a recent conversation I had with Allan Walton, I mentioned an interesting fact about our old friend Charles Mackintosh, which Walton then asked me to add to your store of knowledge about this unquestionable genius... I kept in touch with him after he went to France. In 1929 I received a letter from a group of Vienna architects saying they had searched for his address in vain and, as they wished to invite him as their guest to Vienna and honour him for his remarkable influence on their country – upon the architecture and arts of the time – could I supply it! Alas, I had to write and say they were too late for he had passed away only the year before in the Pyrenees.*

Mackintosh died in London, not the Pyrenees, but Longden's recollections are just one of many first-hand confirmations of Mackintosh's high status in Vienna. Whether this invitation from the Austrian architects predated the famous toast, 'Mackintosh, the

Greatest since the Gothic', is not clear, but the icing on the cake, with regard to the reality of the Mackintosh's Viennese connections is provided by Joseph Hoffman, one of the outstanding leaders of the Viennese Secession, in a beautiful unpublished letter to Howarth dated 20 December 1947.

> *It is a pleasure to tell you something about my adventure with Mackintosh. At the turn of the century the Morris Movement was of very great interest to us of England's efforts in the subject of Industrial Arts. We were well informed about the experiments and successes through the publication. The Studio, and some could recognise and admire the activities of Carl MacIntosh [sic]. We had to appreciate especially his extraordinary feeling for architecture, his new dreaming colour symphonies in grey, light pink and light violet. His strange furniture, light fittings, and his interior decoration was very impressive to us.*
>
> *In spite of all these new ideas his home feeling [His highly personal style? The homeliness of his domestic style?] was easy to recognise. In 1901 we arranged, in the newly erected building of the Sezession, an exhibition of Mackintosh's works, his furniture etc. There we had also set up the Vienna Workshops and we had the pleasure to greet Mackintosh and his wife.*
>
> *Fritz Waldorfer, one of the founders of our workshops, lived some years in London and knew the English Movement and Mackintosh personally. He seemed to us a deliverer from dead styles – a founder of new forms and an impressive renovator of Scottish peculiarities. We liked both the artists very much – and stood a long time in stimulated thought.*
>
> *Of course we didn't want to imitate his personal peculiarity and style in Vienna, but we could take power and courage from his standards. Up until his death we followed his work with the same interest but we had often to regret that his artistry was not appreciated enough. His noble and reserved character certainly was the reason for it. What you, Professor, will publish about our unforgetable friend is certainly very important – and now his efforts will find recognition.*
>
> *I send Mrs Newbery many greetings. I shall be pleased to hear more about her. I can assure you that inspite of the terrible war we have made some progress in craftsmanship, which would be interesting to you. So our situation is still very confused and not very hopeful. I lost almost everything through bombs and looters and have little consolation in anything. I have lost my studio and flat and my belongings and my sketches, and am faced with my 77 years to start again.*
>
> *It is time that the artist should reform politics. Humanity must again – will back the good life for itself...*

It is a great letter. And it was obviously partly a reply, forty-five years late, to the marvellous letter that Mackintosh had written to Joseph Hoffman in 1902, when their initial collaboration was at its height, and which Howarth was to publish as one of the revelations of his book in 1952. Mackintosh wrote to Hoffmann:

> *If your programme is to achieve artistic success (and artistic success must be your first aim) then every object you produce must have a strong mark of individuality, beauty and outstanding workmanship. Your aim, from the beginning, must be that every object is created for a specific purpose and a specific place... Many years of hard work, earnest hard work – by the leaders of the Modern Movement will be required before all obstacles are removed... For a beginning the 'artistic detractors' (excuse the term) must be subdued and those who allow themselves to be influenced by them must be convinced through continuous effort and through the gradual success of the Modern Movement that the Movement is no silly hobby for a few who try to achieve fame comfortably through their eccentricity but that the Modern Movement is something living, something good and the only possible art for all – the highest achievement of our time.*

It is important to note the references in Hoffman's letter to Margaret Macdonald Mackintosh and Jessie Newbery, wife of Fra Newbery the Headmaster of Glasgow School of Art. Hoffman knew that their work, ideas, support, and championship were integral to the Mackintosh's achievement and the international success of the Glasgow Group.

Howarth's researches also unearthed information about the Mackintoshes influence on Russia and, by implication, on the Suprematist and Constructivist Movements. In *Art Work, No. 21*, (1930) he found an article by the Mackintosh's Rosicrucian friend, Major Desmond Chapman Houston: 'The Grand Duke Serge of Russia visited the Turin Exhibition (1902) and was so enamoured of the work of the Mackintoshes that he became one of their most ardent admirers and invited them to give an exhibition in Moscow, under Imperial Patronage. This they did in 1913. Their work was received with acclamation by the Russian public: it secured an instant success. Everything was sold but the carpet, designed by Mackintosh...' No serious work has been done tracing Mackintosh's influence on Russian and early Soviet artistic developments but the abstract and spiritual thrust evident in the work of Kandinski and Malevitch, in Suprematism and Constructivism were nurtured first by Modernist developments in Germany, Austria and Glasgow *c.*1900, and secondly by Cubism and Futurism. All these movements owe some debt to Mackintosh and *The Studio* magazine.

Over the years, the more Howarth travelled and felt at home in Scotland, the more he understood the contribution Scottish vernacular architecture had made to Mackintosh's version of 'Modernism'. As his confidence in his interpretation of Mackintosh's sources gathered momentum various people offered new insights and supplied him with new leads. A letter from Dr G.P. Insh of Bothwell, Lanarkshire, illustrates the 'national dialogue' Howarth had stimulated in Scotland.

Top. Windyhill,
Kilmacolm.
(Mackintosh 1900)

Bottom. Model of
Haus eine Kunstfreund
[house of an art-lover].
(Mackintosh 1901)

The inspiration of the Glasgow painters came from the French Impressionists. That of Mackintosh, as you so effectively demonstrate, came from his native Scottish tradition… It is in a way analogous to the policy of our younger Scottish poets and their effort to get back to Dunbar and this great mediaeval tradition, but whilst their efforts are at best tentative, Mackintosh made of his venture a triumphant success… [though] the welcome accorded to his craftwork emphasises the old, old lesson of the little regards paid in Scotland to pioneering work.

Left. The Hill House gateway.

Below Left and right.
The Hill House, Helensburgh.
(Mackintosh 1901–03)

This linkage of Mackintosh's revitalisation of Scottish architectural traditions with the Scots Literary Renaissance orchestrated, a generation later, by the poet Hugh MacDiarmid and the composer F.G. Scott is very interesting. It was not a field of enquiry that Howarth chose to enter, but study of certain poems being written by MacDiarmid, and others, during the 1940s, show remarkable parallels with Mackintosh's particular vision. MacDiarmid's poem, *Glasgow*, quoted in the introduction to this book, suggests extraordinary parallels. The particular mixture of the ancient, the libertarian, the austere, the sensuous, and revolutionary that distinguishes the work of Mackintosh, and Scottish national culture, is brilliantly encapsulated in the prologue to Hamish Henderson's *Elegies to the Dead in Cyrenaica*, published in 1948.

> Let my words knit what now we lack
> The demon and the heritage
> And fancy strapped to logic's rock.
> A chastened wantonness, a bit
> That sets on song a discipline,
> A sensuous austerity.

Those words, written during the very years Howarth was embracing the art of Charles Rennie Mackintosh can be seen, in retrospect, as giving classic expression to a new Zeitgeist in Scotland; as a nation, terribly wounded by war and industrial depression, sought to resurrect herself – and has. But, new ideas and new art also, always bring old antagonisms and professional resentment to the surface. A letter to Howarth from the Glasgow architect Alexander Paterson, dated 1946, deliberately casts more shade than light: 'I have no means to account for the particular character of Mackintosh's work or that of George Walton but consider the latter the finer artist and believe that much of his tableware and decoration was wrongly attributed to the former.'

In June 1944 Mrs Gordon Millar of Cairnsaigh, 79 South Beach, Troon, wrote to Howarth:

> *Thank you for your letter of the 6th inst. Re Charles Rennie Mackintosh. I am very sorry I cannot help you with any more data, except that the mantelpiece in the book* [Dekorative Kunst] *was at my late house, 34 Kingsborough Gardens, Glasgow W.2, off Hyndland Road. It is now, as far as I know, a boarding house and access easily obtained. There might be some other bits and pieces around, I cannot remember. Only interior stuff anyway... Personally I dislike the furniture, which seems to me to have nothing to do with architecture! Fra Newbery is eighty-six and has just fallen downstairs. Mrs N. is eighty. When Mr and Mrs Mackintosh went on their honeymoon to Vienna, they took all their furniture with them, sold it, made a home, and stayed to make houses... I think he had no sense of*

*colour – it was all dull. The medium was always oak. Even if it was painted or
stained – Good luck to your endeavours...*

Mrs Gordon Millar was obviously a powerful personality! Her letter provides us with a
telling glimpse of the great strengths and weaknesses of the Scottish bourgeoisie: she
snappily dismisses Mackintosh as an artist but, with commendable disinterest, supplies
Howarth with a lead that helped lay the foundations of his Mackintosh collection.

England could be equally dismissive of Mackintosh. In the summer of 1946 the
following letter was published in the R.I.B.A. Journal:

> *In the Journal of Sept.1946 appear two pages of illustrations of furniture
> designed by the late C.R. Mackintosh. While I disclaim any desire whatever to
> belittle the work of one who certainly did not lack originality, it seems to me that
> most of the designs are impractical in the extreme and in very doubtful taste. I
> question whether it is desirable to publish these photographs at all and particularly
> at the present time when many students are entering the profession.*
> *Yours faithfully,*
>
> *E. C. Francis. Taunton.*

Mr Francis may have been right about educational needs but his letter exemplifies the poor
historical and artistic judgement endemic amongst many professional architects, and Howarth
must have been pleased when he unearthed Mackintosh's lecture 'On Architecture', delivered
in 1890. 'The greatest writers on architecture are not architects. Ferguson, the historian, was
trained as an indigo planter, Rickman the authority on English work, was a Quaker merchant
and Professor Willis, a clergyman.' Over the years, Howarth found his relationship with most
of Glasgow's architectural establishment an uphill battle but one of his great 'finds' was an
ex-Glaswegian architect, William Moyes. As a young man, Moyes worked in the office of
Honeyman and Keppie. He was a draughtsman and artist, and had acted as Mackintosh's
'right-hand man' throughout the great creative years. Moyes emigrated to Australia around
1907. It took Howarth years to track him down but, when he did, he was rewarded with
crucial first-hand information that has helped shape all subsequent Mackintosh studies. Their
correspondence is worth quoting at length. It begins on 1 April 1947 when Howarth writes:

> *To my delight I recently obtained your address from the secretary of the RAIA
> after many fruitless enquiries in Scotland... I am writing a biography of the late
> Charles Rennie Mackintosh whom, I believe, you knew well many years ago and I
> shall be extremely grateful for any help you may be able to give me in settling one
> or two important points. The most trivial detail is often of value in work of this
> nature. I might add that I have been collecting information for over six years and*

am well aware of Mackintosh's failings as well as his good points... To simplify matters I have appended a list of questions to which you, better than anyone, can provide the answers. I should be particularly glad to have your personal opinion of Mackintosh – his work, his ideals, his character, and also an account of the role you played in the Keppie office – amusing anecdotes are also very useful. I seem to be asking a great deal of you but I would appreciate your co-operation and only regret that we cannot meet personally...

1. To what extent did Keppie control the Competition Design of the School of Art, (1896)?

2. Do you know anything about the unusual design of the School of Art Board Room (the room with the curious ionic pilasters)?

3. What influence had Mackintosh on designs prior to the School of Art, e.g., Glasgow Herald Offices, Martyr's School, Pettigrew's Dome?

4. From what sources did Mackintosh draw inspiration – can you name architects whom he particularly admired?

5. Did you know George Walton – if so do you agree that he influenced Mackintosh?

6. Did Mackintosh visit the Continent between 1896 and 1900?

7. Can you give me any information about his Continental visits? Were any of his designs ever executed abroad?

On 29 April 1947 William Moyes replied:

In reply to your letter of April 1st re questions about the life and work of the late C.R. Mackintosh. I can only answer several in this letter, others require more consideration. 1. not able to say; 2. not able to say; 3. perspective drawing by Mackintosh of Glasgow Herald Buildings appeared in 'Academy Arch.', Queen Margaret College in 1895 and Martyr's School in 1896 under the firm's name but the design and detail was the work of Mackintosh. (I was not in the office when they were being erected but the late J B Fulton referred to Mackintosh as having designed them both.) Compare the proportion of staircase windows at Queen Margaret College in 1895, Martyr's School, and first floor windows of The Herald buildings with the windows of Staircase, Windyhill, Kilmacolm – plan and design entirely by Mack. (Not one of the various buildings designed by Mr Keppie has any resemblance to above – e.g. Annan's Building Sauchiehall St; or Pettigrew & Stephens, Paisley Library, or Patients Building South Side Glasgow – or residence for Beattie, Milngavie.) As far as I can remember the dome at Pettigrew & Stephens building was the work of Mr Keppie, and Mackintosh had no influence on the design (but some internal show cases were designed and detailed by Mack., also some internal wall decoration).

4. From a leek seeding to a cow standing in a pool of water. I am serious – for he had several blocks of sketches made during several trips in England — from various counties, Devon, Dorset, Norfolk and Suffolk. One sheet had a drawing of a leek seeding and another a sketch of a cow standing in a pool of water. The sketch of the cow was seen from its rear and as its hindquarters were reflected in the water the effect was striking. As for the drawing of the leek going to seed, I have cultivated several and allowed them to seed and it is wonderful what decorative effects are suggested.

In these blocks were two sketches of Lindisfarne Castle, Holy Island, restored by Lutyens (I have copies but am not able to find them at present). I am unable to say if they influenced Mackintosh in the design of the residence of F.J. Shand at Killearn, Stirlingshire (so different from the designs for Windyhill and the Hill House at Helensburgh). It is possible Mr Shand asked for the mullioned windows.

Mr Mackintosh was in Italy early in his career — for in the Bath St office was a measured drawing in pencil and coloured of The Certosa, Pavia. He was well acquainted with the palaces, castles and other buildings in Scotland and made an interesting drawing of the front of the restored entrance to Falkland Palace, Fifeshire. He was a genius with a brush and his studies of flowers were superb. I have a drawing by Mackintosh of a solitary violet in which he demonstrated his idea of the flower, but he was in merry mood at the time and it would hardly do him justice to reproduce it.

The influence of various works in Scotland is very pronounced in the relieving arches over lintels — the bell-shaped roof of the staircase at Queen Margaret College and in the roof of the water tower of the Herald buildings. The balusters and spacing at Queen Margaret and Martyr's Schools may have been influenced by work at Stirling Castle. The mouldings at windows and doorways are similar to what one can see at Aberdour, Fifeshire. The corbelled courses of the water tower of the Herald Buildings is similar to work in many an old castle. In a small building at St Fillans (Comrie), Perthshire, he designed a crow-stepped gable — and I have one preliminary sketch design of his with a crow-stepped gable... To be continued...

Postal services were largely by sea at that time and it was not till 30 May that Howarth penned this response to Moyes:

Many thanks for your informative letter about Charles Mackintosh. You will be interested to hear that I have in my possession a fine collection of his Italian sketches — and also the drawing of the cow!

I was surprised that you considered the Martyr's School, Queen Margaret's College, and Herald buildings so predominantly Mackintosh — surely the detail has more in common with Keppie's work e.g. the affected pediments and abundance of classical elements which also occur at Annan's and Pettigrew's! Admittedly the buildings have a curious character which I'm inclined to ascribe to Mackintosh's influence, no doubt he worked on them as a draughtsman, but I hardly think he could have been entirely responsible for their ultimate form – they bear little resemblance to his later designs.

I should like to have your opinion on Keppie and his influence in the office and particularly on the business relationship between the two men prior to their quarrel and the unfortunate events which led to Mackintosh's dismissal...

On 22 July 1947, Moyes makes another spirited and brilliantly informative reply:

I was pleased to have your letter of 30th May and learn that you had a fine collection of Mr Mackintosh's Italian sketches, also notes made by him in England. I was desirous that you should see his sketches of Lindisfarne Castle, Holy Isle, restored by Lutyens as it may or may not have influenced Mr Mackintosh in his design for the residence at Killearn. The Killearn residence was designed entirely by Mackintosh yet it is very different to Windyhill and the Hill House – both earlier examples of his domestic work. Had you expressed surprise at Mackintosh being responsible for the Killearn residence after Windyhill and the Hill House you would have been quite justified in doing so but I was in the office when the three above residences were erected. Personally I think the Killearn residence alien to the climate and the country even though designed by Mackintosh, yet to me there is as much difference between the Killearn residence designed by Mac and the Milngavie residence for Beattie, designed by Mr Keppie as there is between the Herald building and Pettigrew's or Annan's in Sauchiehall Street... Note also the type of roof construction in the lecture theatre of Queen Margaret's College and the roof at Queen's Cross Church designed by Mackintosh. Note also the type of roof in the hall at Martyr's School and the roof above the staircase in the School of Art. Note the detail of mouldings, the type of carving at the semi-circular window in the Herald Building. And where will you see, in Mr Keppie's work, the well-designed metalwork of entrance gates?

Wishing you every success in the work Mr Howarth and a good sale of the publication when issued, and may it be followed by one on Sir John J Burnett.

That is a brilliant letter. Howarth is delicately but firmly put in his place by a close colleague of Mackintosh's. He is also subtly 'warned' against his acquisitive instincts by a grand old man with knowledge, values and a superbly critical 'eye'. The reprimands implicit in Moyes letter were just, and for Howarth, any slight he felt was more than outweighed by the ideas and information Moyes so generously gave. Howarth replied to Moyes on 17 July 1947:

*Your second and third air letters have reached me safely in Glasgow where I shall
be spending the next six or eight weeks. I found them most interesting and full of
useful information. During the time I've collected data about M. I've been surprised
at the lack of enthusiasm shown by his contemporaries and their unwillingness to
discuss him: his artist friends have been communicative enough but I'm afraid the
architects very reticent, however, your letters have been a veritable mine of
information and filled in numerous gaps in my research. I wonder if you know the
curious house he designed at Kilmacolm for Major Collins – it was named
'Mosside' and was built at about the same time as Shand's house at Killearn. It is a
peculiar building, T-shaped plan, constructed in ramble rubble. Frank Burnet,
whom you may know, re-roofed one arm of the T during the war with green slates
and red ridge tiles: the corresponding arm is covered with variegated stone slates
and the third with red tiles, so you can imagine the cumulative effect!*

*Graham Henderson, who has taken over Keppie's practice, informed me that
you were M's draughtsman on the G.S.A. boardroom, hence my query about the
neo-ionic capitals. He also claimed you executed the excellent perspective of
Scotland Street School which has always been ascribed to Mackintosh and which I
consider to be one of his best drawings in this media (ink). However, I am already
indebted to you for all the information you have sent me and must restrain my
enthusiasm. Thank you once again – I hope the illustrations you have posted arrive
safely – and of course I shall be glad to hear from you at any time if further points
occur to you.*

On the 30 July, Moyes wrote again,

*Received your airmail of 22/07/47 for which I thank you. Regarding perspective
of Scotland Street School – I may have set up the perspective in pencil for Mr
Mackintosh but he would have completed it in ink and added the master-touches.
You are quite correct in ascribing it to Mackintosh. I have a feeling that some
individuals, instead of helping you in your work, may be trying to pull your leg –
as the saying is. So far as I remember, Mr Mackintosh did all the design and details
in connection with the School of Art building, and I was not the draughtsman, as
Graham Henderson mentioned, in connection with the boardroom. And I only just
remember the residence at Kilmacolm for Major Collins, by Mac.*

*With regards to business relations between Mr Keppie and Mackintosh before
the rupture. I had left the office several years before it occurred. Pardon me for
suggesting that I think you should refer to the partnership being dissolved; rather
than refer to Mackintosh's dismissal.*

Part of this third letter from William Moyes seems to be missing but it concludes with what appears to be a description of Mackintosh's or, more probably, Margaret Macdonald's method of working gesso:

> *Pinned with ordinary pins through the centre of twine on to plaster groundwork,*
> *in order to obtain the required relief, and covered with gesso… He had no hobby as*
> *far as I know and limped when he walked. He appeared to get on well with his*
> *clients and the various contractors who carried out his designs. In connection with*
> *the building of Queen's Cross Church, slow progress was being made with the work*
> *and the contractor was asked to expedite the work. I remember Mr Mackintosh*
> *being highly amused on the contractor replying, he was building for eternity.*
> *Endurance was to him (Mackintosh) the crowning quality of building.*
>
> *When I left Glasgow the prospects for Mr Mackintosh were bright. His heart*
> *was in his work and in the beauty of the flowers he rejoiced. As for the part I*
> *played in the office – at one time or another I worked for each of the partners, and*
> *was very interested in the work of Mr Mackintosh, and am forwarding by*
> *ordinary mail a few illustrations which may be of some slight assistance to you.*

Again Moyes provides us with vivid insights and facts. The single sentence, 'His heart was in his work and in the beauty of the flowers he rejoiced' is an extremely economical way of placing poetic sensibility at the core of the Mackintosh's achievement. And the little story about endurance and 'building for eternity' says a great a deal about Scotland and the tradition out of which Mackintosh came. It was a tradition Mackintosh had thought about deeply:

> the history of nations is written in stone… Much of Assyrian life and manners and the source of their descent are known from their ruins – the actual buildings themselves are history. While of many other races now wholly extinct, nothing but their architecture remains, such as those mysterious peoples of N. and S. America – especially the Aztecs – our sole knowledge is confined to their buildings… So much is this the case that Ferguson considers that inquirers into the science of Ethnology, by, hitherto, neglecting the study of ancient architecture – has overlooked their surest guide… (Lecture on Architecture, 1890)

'Endurance' is not the word most Mackintosh enthusiasts would use to describe the master's work but the concept was crucial to him – as Moyes asserts. And it was an understanding of architectural reality that came to Mackintosh with his mother's milk: he was born of a people nurtured amidst rock and wind and rain. The poetry of Hamish Henderson, again, provides a precise link between Mackintosh's architectural vision and the common experience of the Scottish people. In the fourth of his *Elegies for the Dead in Cyrenaica* he concludes:

> Endure, endure. There is as yet no solution
> And no short cut, no escape and no remedy
> But our human iron.
> And this Egypt teaches us
> That mankind, put to the torment, can bear
> On their breast the stone tomb of immolation
> For millennia. The wind. We can build our cairn.

It is in this historical context and this harsh environment that the seeds of Mackintosh's ecstatic art were planted, as he sought the antithesis of cold and death in a lifelong search for sun, beauty, gentleness, feminine grace; the flowers of nature and the joy of living.

On 7 August 1947 Howarth wrote what appears to be the last letter of this Australian correspondence.

Dear Mr Moyes,

Thank you very much for sending me the drawings, illustrations and articles on Mackintosh. Two packets have arrived safely, the cardboard containing the house with the crow-stepped gable and Liverpool Cathedral, and also a flat packet containing Dekorative Kunst, *1902,* The Studio *1933 etc.*

*I am particularly glad to have the sketches of the house with the crow-stepped gables – is this the building at St Fillans you mentioned in your first letter?...
Again one of the most interesting items was the Conversazione programme dated 1894 – one of the earliest Mackintosh designs in this style that I have come across and a most important contribution to my record...*

Your views on the three buildings – the Medical School, the Herald, the Martyr's School – have persuaded me to reconsider my first thesis, which was influenced by Graham Henderson, that they were essentially Keppie and I shall examine them again more carefully in the light of your comments and probably rewrite the chapter.

You'll be interested to hear that I've been trying for some years to persuade the powers that be to provide a Mackintosh museum in the city. This objective has more or less been achieved: in 1945 the University responded to my suggestion to purchase the architect's house, No. 78 Southpark Avenue. It is now occupied by a senior member of the university staff and is in fine condition. Last summer the governors of the School of Art were prevailed upon to open a Mackintosh room and the Deputy Director and I were responsible for its decoration and furnishing – we secured a good collection of furniture, watercolours and the like and the room, incidentally the old Board Room in the east wing, is now open for inspection...

P.S. Your letter dated 22 July arrived today and I've noted your further comments.

*Did you by any chance come across Mrs Mackintosh? Did she, in your opinion,
influence her husband to any great extent?*

There can be no doubt that William Moyes played a seminal role in helping Howarth
establish Mackintosh's oeuvre and the characteristics of his methods of working. The
excellence of Moyes' information, and generosity, deserve more recognition than has
been, publicly, given – by Howarth or anyone else. Howarth's insistence on his personal
role in establishing the Mackintosh collections in Glasgow is fair but is, also, partly a
justification of his increasingly acquisitive habits (Howarth reassures Moyes that the
drawings, plans and memorabilia he has so generously sent are in good hands). Beyond
this, however, Moyes must have been delighted to learn the facts of Mackintosh's
improved status in Glasgow and Howarth's role in establishing the various Glasgow
collections. Such facts, concerning Howarth's contribution in this field, are worth
clarifying here because, in recent years, there have been concerted attempts to diminish
Howarth's pioneering role in what is now the highly competitive field of 'Mackintosh
studies'.

Various letters, predating those from Moyes, confirm Howarth's early involvement in
the conservation and display of Mackintosh's work. In September 1946 Howarth wrote
to the editor of the RIBA Journal in London,

> *As you may know, I have been advocating the establishment of a Mackintosh
> Museum in the city for some years – the University's acquisition of two
> watercolours from the collection of the Mackintosh's great friend Major Chapman
> Huston, was a great step forward and now at last, a room has been set aside at the
> School of Art. To my great satisfaction the project has the enthusiastic support of
> the new director, Mr Douglas Percy Bliss, M.A., A.R.C.A., and we hope to acquire
> a representative collection of furniture and drawings from Mackintosh admirers, on
> extended loan or by donation.*

Another small but important discovery made by Howarth, early in his research inquiries,
was that Mackintosh's youngest and favourite sister, Nancy Mackintosh, was still alive.
Indeed she lived almost next door to the Howarth's flat in Shawlands, Glasgow. She
stayed with her widowed sister, Mrs Gibb.

> Nancy was a lively, delightful person who idolised her brother and was quite
> thrilled at the prospect of my writing his life story, but Mrs Gibb was an
> introverted and rather suspicious lady whom I never really got to know well.
> Nancy was very happy to talk and tell me about life in the family, and all she
> could remember about Charles. There were eleven children, Charles was the
> second and she was the last – so a number of years separated them. Her

apartment was undistinguished except for a number of pieces of furniture designed by her brother. She had gone to the sale of 1933 and acquired one of the white oval tables inlaid with ivory rose symbols, a watercolour painting from East Anglia, some candlesticks and other items. As time passed I came to know Nancy intimately and she said she would leave her collection of pieces by Charles to me, in her will, as a token of her thanks for my writing about her brother (and drawing him [and her] back into the Glasgow scene). Unfortunately, Nancy's death preceded that of Mrs Gibb, and the gift she had planned was not part of her will. Regrettably no one informed me of Nancy's death but, by chance, I was in Glasgow some years later and learned that Mrs Gibb was in hospital at Kelvinside with severe arthritis and not expected to recover. I went to see her and she was delighted to have a visitor. She recognised me and we had a pleasant conversation. When I was leaving, she whispered that she had not forgotten her sister's promise to leave me her brother's paintings and furniture etc. in her will.

However, when Mrs Gibb died the various pieces went to the Hunterian Museum in the University of Glasgow. My friend Andrew McLaren Young was Dean of the Faculty of Arts and knew of the promise Nancy had made, and he arranged for me to purchase several items of which they already had similar items. One of these was the oval table with inlaid roses of white ivory, which had been Mackintosh's own. I also acquired two watercolours, *A Hill Town* and *A Garden Bouquet*.

In Glasgow, the women were, in general, more generous to Howarth than the men. Several provided him with invaluable help. Amy Malcolm, a teacher, wrote on 23 March 1946:

> It is a long time since I heard your long-looked-forward-to talk on Charles Rennie Mackintosh in the G.S.A. lecture theatre – but have always wanted to say – thank you. The friend who was with me shocked me by saying that she just never thought to mention Mackintosh to her pupils! Somehow I never thought of not doing so… During my G.S.A. days, the staff spoke of his work with such enthusiasm – I always remember being told that all the G.S.A. woodwork is resin side out – in accordance with Mackintosh's ideas – and how intrigued I was. Apart from the sheer enjoyment of your lecture you corrected several wrong impressions…

Mrs K McNeil of 32 Kerrishead Avenue, Thornliebank, sent a card saying, 'you may be interested to know that I have some of Charles Rennie Mackintosh's furniture and have seen some of his work in Finland. I am an admirer of his work.'

Another helpful informant was Mrs Dodo Dunderdale, owner of Dunglass Castle, once home to the parents of Margaret and Frances Macdonald. On 9 March 1948, she writes,

Mrs Macdonald (Mrs E. J. Macdonald, wife of Margaret Macdonald's brother, then living at 'Dunglass', Steyning, Sussex) is up staying with me just now, and she is delighted to let you keep the stencilled canvas and the frieze, and she says next time you are in the North, and want anything else in that box, you are just to collect it... The weather here is glorious and the spring flowers are far too far advanced – and will get an awful shock if we get frost now. We even have a plum tree in blossom.

Ann MacBeth, the painter wrote,

I only knew Mr Mackintosh very slightly as he and his wife were about two generations ahead of me as students. I went to Glasgow about 1897. I used to occasionally meet them at the Newbery Sunday evenings. I hope his delightful watercolours, especially of flowers, may be noticed in any record of his doings. His work was distinguished by his delightful use of unexpected materials – as for instance – a fireplace faced, instead of with tiles, a façade of plate glass – broken not cut – and their edges outward – looking like a beautiful effect of water seen in an aquarium...

This is one of many references to the Newberys' habit of inviting students and artists to meet at social events outside normal school of art hours. It was a policy that had long-term cultural and artistic consequences in Glasgow, and it became a custom that Tom Howarth, on a smaller scale, continued as a professor and faculty dean in Canada.

Ann Macbeth's information about Mackintosh's fireplace seems to be the only known description of a very interesting creation, presumably long since destroyed. With the continuing boom in Mackintosh reproductions, this brilliantly original fireplace surround would seem to be an excellent candidate for future production. From the description it is not clear whether the glass tiles were square, rectangular, or round. They are described as plate glass but are more likely to have been crown glass (the name given to the large roundels of hand-spun glass from which window panes were traditionally cut) and thus of any shape but, it is interesting to speculate as to whether Mackintosh chose to use the 'useless' centre of the plate-roundel, where the pontil mark, made by the glassblower's iron, left this section of glass useless for normal windows... Ann Macbeth describes the glass as 'broken not cut – and their edges outward' and it may be that Mackintosh found dramatic domestic use for glass which was normally recycled, or used decoratively in the windows of 'olde worlde shoppes' and pubs. If Mackintosh was doing this he was, once again, putting his own inimitable stamp on a traditional Scottish practice that continued up till the end of the First World War – it being normal practice that toasts 'to the ladies', and Jacobite toasts, were followed by the ceremonial shattering of glasses. The bowls and stems normally disintegrated but the 'foot' of the glasses often remained unbroken. Thus, the morning after major festivals (Burns Night, Hogmany, Empire Day, Regimental and Masonic dinners), the glaziers of Edinburgh and Glasgow would send carters round to gather up the broken bases of the smashed glasses for use in over-door fanlights, in church windows and cellar lights. Mackintosh exulted in the architectural use of glass; for example, in the great windows of Scotland Street School he used a great deal of superb hand-coloured glass and it is typical of his associative mind that he should recognise the possibilities of glass illumined by the flickering light of a fire.

Howarth makes no mention of Ann MacBeth's 'fireplace' in his book. Presumably he felt impelled to deal with fundamental issues and not to be sidetracked into speculation about the form of lost fireplaces; however, by throwing nothing away and archiving everything, Howarth consciously provided future generations with corn.

The Howarth archive also contains two unpublished letters from Jessie Keppie, youngest sister of Mackintosh's boss, John Keppie – the young woman to whom Mackintosh was engaged before meeting Margaret Mempes Macdonald. They shed interesting light on a slightly mysterious affair. For some years John Keppie and Mackintosh were friends as well as colleagues but, when Mackintosh's relationship with Jessie fell apart, their friendship collapsed and all sorts of professional differences emerged. To break an engagement in grand society in Glasgow in the 1890s was a very serious step and it was, probably, only because the senior partner in the firm, John Honeyman, recognised Mackintosh's great potential as an architect that he continued to work within the practice. When Mackintosh and Margaret Macdonald fell in love they quickly established one of the great partnerships in the history of art and Margaret's artistic vision seems to have helped expose John Keppie's artistic barrenness.

Jessie Keppie is known to have been deeply hurt by the termination of her relationship with Mackintosh; she never married and always retained a loyal affection for her former fiancé. It seems certain that she attended Howarth's first lecture on Mackintosh but it was not until after her brother, for whom she kept house had died, that she contacted Howarth, in 1946. She sent him some photographs of Mackintosh, herself, and various friends, including the Macdonald sisters, for use in the exhibition he was setting up at the Glasgow School of Art. Howarth decided not to use them and they remained unknown until recently unearthed in the library of the school. Jessie Keppie writes,

> *The photographs arrived safely today. I am sorry you are not having them for the Mackintosh room at the School, as I think they are particularly good of him at that period. However I daresay your space is limited. The photographs were at a much earlier period than Mr Newbery's portrait – of course, it is splendid having it... I hope to see the exhibition when it is completed. Is it to be a permanency? I am glad if I have been able to help you in any way...*

Howarth arranged that Nancy Mackintosh open the exhibition and although he describes her as shy and reclusive, she was proud to perform the opening and she did it with style. And, having done so, she turned to sharply, publicly criticise Howarth for decorating the room with Mackintosh tartan! Howarth had swathed the room in the traditional red tartan of Clan Mackintosh; Nancy declared, 'Charles would not have been seen dead in a room decorated with this!' She told him that he MUST use the black and white, chequered tartan her brother had invented and made his own. As soon as he could, Howarth changed the tartan.

Three years later Jessie Keppie writes, in response to another of Howarth's letters in *The Herald*,

> *I have read with great interest your letter on Charles Rennie Mackintosh in*
> *yesterday's Herald. I knew him so well in his early days and always felt that*
> *architecture was to him the most important thing in his life. I could never understand*
> *how Glasgow got the name of not appreciating his work as I think no young*
> *architect ever got so many of his own ideas carried out – or was so much admired –*
> *by so many clients: with the war intervening while he was still at the zenith of his*
> *work he had to be content with the lighter phase of his capabilities, otherwise we*
> *might have had many more of his beautiful buildings. I think your letter was most*
> *enlightening and very fair. And I am sure his work will live long and be appreciated*
> *by many. I am waiting with interest to see your book. Believe me.*

On the top right-hand corner of this letter, in pencil, Howarth wrote. 'Reply by hand – thanking – and stating cost of research (£300) and difficulties re publishing.' When approached, in Canada, about this apparent request for money from Jessie Keppie, Howarth bridled and said, 'It can't be correct, I would never have considered it.' But, a few moments later he qualified his initial response by stating, 'If I did make that note I certainly never acted upon it...' It seems strange that he should have been so defensive. In 1949, Howarth was undoubtedly short of money and his researches had proved very costly. Why shouldn't he ask a wealthy old lady who loved Mackintosh, for financial help with his work?

One of the great strengths of Thomas Howarth as a researcher was his determination to seek the opinions of 'anybody' who knew anything about the Mackintosh circle: from some of the most humble, came illuminating replies. Mrs Hettie Swaisland, a waitress, wrote from Wandsworth Common, London, on Burns Night 1946,

> *I am unable to give you much news of Mr Mackintosh. He was a customer for*
> *nine years, always at the same table, and would be very annoyed if he was unable to*
> *have it. He was a very distinguished looking gentleman. In spite of his club foot*
> *and defective eye, Mr Mackintosh and his wife gave quite an air to the shop and*
> *were greatly missed when they left. He was most kind to me and was liked by*

everybody. He only signed his name in my book. When they went away they always
sent cards. Mr Mackintosh was known as one of SOUL CHELSEA.

Howarth was the first person to study and bring into focus Mackintosh's work in England. He travelled to London, to Suffolk, Dorset and Northampton and, whilst the Second World War raged, succeeded in placing the work Mackintosh did during the First World War into context. There is no doubt that Mackintosh's English work is secondary to the great Scottish achievements but it is historically important and it embraced new forms at the forefront of new developments – Cubist, Vorticist, and proto-Art Deco. Howarth studied the designs and made direct contact with acquaintances, friends, patrons and colleagues. Requesting information from Harold Squire, a wealthy patron of the Mackintoshes in their Chelsea days (1916–22), Howarth, on 21 October 1946, set out the following questions:

> *1. How did you first meet the Mackintoshes and when did you lose touch with them?*
> *2. What were your impressions of Mackintosh as a man – as an architect? Was he difficult to deal with, e.g. in regard of your studio in Glebe Place?*
> *3. Professor Schwabe tells me that the studio was haunted by the spectre of a man on horseback – I sincerely hope this is true – can you corroborate the story and give details?*
> *4. Was the building satisfactory, and how long did you stay there?*
> *5. Why did the project for Derwent Wood's and A. Blunt's studios fall through – who was A. Blunt?*
> *6. What had Archdeacon Bevan and the Earl of Cardogan's agent to do with the design of your studio?*

This is a surprising and interesting list. Few people, today, would need to ask who this A. Blunt was; this was Anthony Blunt, Soviet spy and informer, distinguished art historian, and Keeper of the Queen's Pictures! Harold Squires replied from The Hundred, Henfield, Sussex, with a letter that is 'a stream of consciousness' out-pouring very typical of the twenties and of 'mystical', Yeatsian society.

> *You must excuse pencil – I have been ill for some time. I was interested in your letter on Mackintosh and will do my best to answer your questions.*
> *1. I met the Mackintoshes through the League of Arts Service which sprang up in Chelsea. I think M. disappeared about eighteen months after he finished my studio.*
> *2. He was an intelligent man but I fancy he drank too much – which accounted for his strange manner at times. As architect I cannot judge – the studio had a magnif-icence that no other studio in London possessed. I never had any difficulties with him though I could imagine there well might be with some clients.*
> *3. The studio was haunted. I distinctly saw a portion of a man and horse sail*

across the room in the middle of the afternoon and a good deal higher than a horse would naturally be expected. A well-known medium of the time gave me details without anyone giving her previous information. The land was a queer spot – a Dr Phene had a strange crazy house on the Oakley St corner and at Upper Cheyne Row corner stood a black, neglected little house where the wedding breakfast was still laid out – the bride had died on her wedding morn. There was about an acre of land and scattered all over it bits of church demolitions and what appeared to be alters of sorts. Phene was supposed to indulge in strange rites, including snake worship. There were two altars of sorts on the site I bought.

4. The studio was too expensive to run – the heating alone was a very big item. I don't think I was there longer than two years. I forget now.

5. I forget your questions – Schwabe would surely know. There certainly was a studio built to the west but Derwent Wood was directly across the street. Cadogan's Agent had nothing to do at all with my studio.

The whole thing was a queer exciting incident but it was certainly a rich man's place (even if he saw ghosts – which were not at all frightening except to servants). I never heard of anybody else seeing one.

I hope this will meet your requirements – I really feel too ill to collect my wits.

At the same time as seeking information from ageing waitresses and eccentric, occult millionaires, Howarth was also writing letters to many of the world's great Modernist architects. What did they know of Mackintosh? When did they first become acquainted with his work? Did his forms and ideas influence them? The questions to each man were slightly different and, almost to a man, his letters were answered; perhaps, after six years of war and no serious architectural commissions, these architects were pleased and flattered to be asked questions about their Scottish colleague and his influence on their Movement. Their letters are interesting, generous and historically important.

On 17 July 1944, Eric Mendelsohn wrote,

I heartily welcome your thesis on Mackintosh. My first acquaintance with his work occurred after I left Munich for Berlin. The Viennese Olbrich and the Belgian Henry van der Velde seemed to be, then, my only forerunners. Studying their work at the library of the Berlin College of Arts and Crafts I found a folder of Mackintosh's drawings. This was at the beginning of 1915. You may see from Arnold Whittick's biography, figs 1–25, that my ideas of an architecture of steel and concrete were, then, firmly established. Thus, Mackintosh's influence on my work was more confirmative than incentive. His work proved that the movement was not merely restricted to continental Europe (but) by including England (Britain) it was bound to become worldwide – the logical expression of the

Chapelle de Notre Dame at Ronchamp (Le Corbusier 1952). *Timothy Neat*

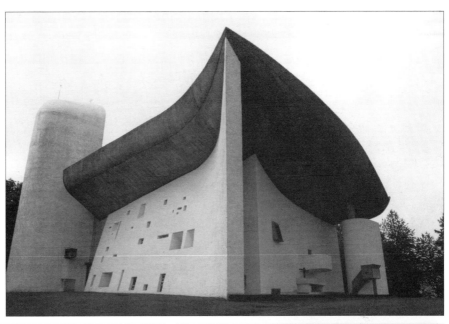

world's new needs and desires. I feel that Mackintosh's work was an important contribution to the genesis of contemporary architecture, a courageous and original venture amidst the timid atmosphere of a still 'traditional England'... I am now working on 'A Contemporary Philosophy of Architecture' which I hope will be finished before this ghastly and fateful war will call all hands.

Mendelsohn's letter encouraged Howarth to seek out Henry van der Velde, Mackintosh's great Art Nouveau contemporary from Belgium. This line of enquiry, however, was terminated when he received a note, in October 1945, from Mr E. Carter at the RIBA: 'Henry van der Velde is a very old man. One correspondent told me he is somewhat implicated with collaborationist groups...'

On 16 December 1945 Howarth received much better news from Le Corbusier, the great French Modernist.

In answer to your letter dated the 3rd of December, related to Mackintosh, I can give the following thoughts. In 1904 or 1905, in my school library at Chaux-de-Fonds, I came upon and was surprised by the works of Mackintosh — some, probably, in The Studio *of London, and some in the well-known magazine* Deutsche Kunst Dekoration *— related to the Vienna Secession.*

My personal thoughts? Well, Mackintosh was an extraordinary, individual and inventive man — when I was just fifteen or sixteen years old. As far as I remember there was also another man — who wasn't as well-known as Mackintosh was, who also surprised me by way of his exceptional architectural capacities — an amateur architect, of course, because he was a painter — and the house happened to be the house he built for himself. His name? Fernand Koppf. Or was it someone else? I guess he was a Belgian.

In the same period, Auguste Perret, began his career in Paris. He didn't have real plastic imagination, or plastic sensibility, but he was the first to set architecture on a solid new base — using reinforced concrete — by giving it a structure, a frame and constructive reality. It is by great effort that I have now reached the point where I am, and it is because I am a plastician, and a very sensitive person by the way, and also because I believe in the necessity of the Aesthetics of Period, that I have the feeling of being engaged at this time, and able to produce architectural developments within which everything fits — from the inside to the outside, from biology towards character, in one word, an architecture that grows like life itself.

I am sure Mackintosh was a sensitive man, original and inventive. I wish you the best in your studies.

As a great architect, champing at the bit, desperate to start building after years of World War, it was marvellous that Le Corbusier should reply to Howarth, and write more about himself than about Mackintosh! His phrase 'de la biologie vers la caractere' was originally written as 'detail vers l'ensemble' and Le Corbusier seems to have instinctively allied himself to Mackintosh with regard to his 'overall' vision of what constitutes architectural achievement: various of Le Corbusier's late buildings display certain features that might be described as 'Mackintosh'. Certainly his great chapel at Ronchamp is worth analysis in terms of the Mackintosh aesthetic. Did Howarth's letter help reawaken Le Corbusier's interest in Mackintosh, at a seminal post-war moment, when he was redeveloping his architectural language and forging new ideas for an organic, sculptural, concrete architecture? In general, historians and critics have undervalued the plastic, three-dimensional force of Mackintosh's work – the values which so dominate Le Corbusier's later creations. But there are 'sculptural' connections between the work of the two men and Le Corbusier's use of harling (roughcast concrete), at Ronchamp, is a common and dramatic feature of Scottish architecture much used by Mackintosh. Le Corbusier's use of small, asymmetrically placed windows, ovaloid towers, and split circular forms at Ronchamp also have clear parallels in the Mackintosh oeuvre. Of course many sources, other than Mackintosh, fed Le Corbusier in his inspired design for the Chapelle de Notre Dame at Ronchamp; the building is a unique and highly personal creation but the trace of Mackintosh is there, as are traces of the Rosicrucian mysticism with which both men, and Fernand Koppf, were associated.

Le Corbusier's enthusiasm for Mackintosh can also be contrasted with his lack of interest in the architects of the English Arts and Crafts movement. On a visit to London, Le Corbusier was asked, 'What do you think of the work of Edward Lutyens?' He replied, 'Qui est-il?' Lutyens was a marvellous domestic architect who made a telling contribution to the continuum of English architecture at a crucial historical moment but he was never a Modernist and Le Corbusier, as a self-declared Modernist and a spiritual revolutionary, had good reason to ignore Lutyens, whilst recognizing Mackintosh as a man of similar mettle to himself. That the young Howarth should have established a clear artistic relationship between these two architects, so early, suggests critical insight of a high order and, from 1945 onwards, Howarth advanced the theory that 'his' Scotsman and the flamboyant Frenchman were the twin piers of organic international Modernism. Robert Furneaux Jordon developed the connection further in his book, *Le Corbusier* published in 1972.

> For him [Le Corbusier] architecture would always be the massing of great volumes in sunlight, within the rules of structure. And nowhere in the whole of Art Nouveau could he ever have found *that*, except just possibly in the Glasgow buildings of Charles Rennie Mackintosh... Horta, Sullivan, Guimard were all ornamental... That leaves only Mackintosh's Glasgow School of Art, Scottish, dour and hardly stylistic at all – the 'first modern building' – and Gaudi's marvellous pseudo-Gothic extravaganzas in Barcelona, probably the first revelation to Le Corbusier of the potentiality, of the sheer plasticity of concrete.

> Mackintosh and Gaudi, the two poles of Art Nouveau, the stern functionalist and the magnificent lunatic – neither of them quite conforming to Le Corbusier's definition of an architect...

Jordon's suggestion that Mackintosh lacked 'style' and was merely a 'stern functionalist' serves his dialectic rather than experiential reality. And it is interesting that just as Le Corbusier was always comfortable with the Mackintosh vision, he was never comfortable with the Functionalist aesthetic, 'Functionalist – the word was born under other skies than those I have always loved – those where the sun reigns supreme...' And although Le Corbusier knew that Mackintosh came from one of Europe's great 'sunless' cities he also knew Mackintosh to have been a man obsessed by the architectural possibilities of 'light' – a man bewitched by the image and symbol of the sun. In one of his letters to Margaret Macdonald, from Port Vendres in the South of France in 1927, Mackintosh writes, 'even in the brightest sunshine my pictures are still very sombre – and I want to get more and more light.' As a young man he wrote of his dream of a new architecture: 'All will be sweetness, simplicity, freedom, confidence, *and light*: the other is past – and well it is – for its aim was to crush life. The new, the future, is to aid life – and train it 'so that beauty may flow into the soul like a breeze.'

When Le Corbusier wrote to the Archbishop of Besanson, on the completion of his 'pilgrim chapel' at Ronchamp, he used very similar language to that used, recurrently, by Mackintosh.

> *In building this Chapel, I wished to create a place of silence, of prayer, of peace, of spiritual joy. A sense of what was sacred inspired our efforts. Some things are sacred; others are not, whether they be outwardly religious or otherwise... It was a project difficult, meticulous, primitive, made strong by the resources brought into play – but sensitive and informed by all embracing mathematics which is the creator of the space that cannot be described in words.*
>
> *A few scattered symbols, a few written words singing the praises of the Virgin.*
>
> *The cross – the true cross of suffering – is raised up in this space; the drama of Christianity has taken possession of this place, now and forever.*
>
> *Excellency: I give you this chapel of dear, faithful concrete, shaped, perhaps with temerity, but certainly with courage, in the hope that it will seek out in you (as in those who will climb the hill) an echo of what we have drawn into it.*

Le Corbusier exalts in his creation of a building of just the kind he seems to have 'imagined' when writing to Howarth in 1945 – 'an architecture that grows like life itself'. Howarth, naturally, was hugely encouraged by Le Corbusier's letter. For many years he kept a drawing of Ronchamp, by his friend the English architect Tom Mellor, on his apartment wall next to a sketch for a geodesic dome by Buckminster Fuller. Howarth himself made several pilgrimages to Ronchamp and, until the day he died, kept a small blue glass-pane, from one of Perret's ruined churches, on his windowsill.

Howarth also wrote to various of the Modernists who had emigrated to the United States, where the war hardly effected architecture and lines of communication were much easier to establish. On 13 February 1946, Mies van der Rohe wrote:

> *To answer your letter, I should say that not only in my opinion but also in that of my friends, Charles Rennie Mackintosh was in his time one of the leading architects in Europe. I do not know enough about his association with the Vienna Secession, but I truly believe that his greatest influence was as a purifier of architectural forms, and I believe those active in the field were influenced by him...*

On 18 March 1946, Walter Gropius wrote

> *Thank you very much for your letter of February 21, asking me about the late Charles Rennie Mackintosh. Of course I know his work and I remember that, in my youth, I have seen quite a lot of illustrations in* The Studio. *I don't think I have been much influenced by him. The greatest impression I had was the work of Peter Behrens, in Germany, with whom I worked for years, and also that of Frank Lloyd Wright in this country. They have both definitely influenced my own approach.*
>
> *Mackintosh's work has been published also in German books, particularly his interior work, and I remember a large volume that was published in Munich, containing quite a lot of furniture made by him. But generally I should say that he has not been very well known in Germany – not as much as he deserved. I know that he had some influence on the architects in the Darmstadt colony, particularly on Olbrich; and the Jugenstijl Movement, which started there, is definitely related to Mackintosh.*

A letter from the Finnish/American architect Eliel Saarinen is dated 27 April 1946: 'Your note about Mackintosh interests me very much. Mackintosh's work was well known to me in the early years of 1900. In fact I have just finished a manuscript where I, in speaking retrospectively, mention Mackintosh as the front page representative of Scotland in those early years.'

Howarth tried to gather the opinions of Frank Lloyd Wright but he got no replies to his letters and he had to wait until personal meetings in 1956 before learning what Wright thought of Mackintosh.

Architectural historians also became targets of Howarth's enquiries. His contacts with two in particular are illuminating – Edgar Kauffmann Jnr and Professor Nikolaus Pevsner. Kaufmann was director of the Department of Industrial Design at the Museum of Modern Art in New York. It was his father, Edgar Kaufmann, who had commissioned Frank Lloyd Wright to create one of his finest houses, cantilevered out from the rocks, at

Falling Water. Howarth, immediately, established a good two-way relationship with Kaufman and he sought his views on Mackintosh, on the Viennese connection, on Mackintosh's relationship with Wright and United States architecture. He also, openly, sounded Kaufmann out about the possibilities of himself teaching in America. In return Kaufmann sought information, photos and Mackintosh artefacts and the two men pooled a good deal of mutually beneficial knowledge. In a letter dated 16 July 1946 Howarth writes,

Drawing for Wärndorfer Music Salon, Vienna. *Howarth collection*

> *Many thanks for your kind reply to my letter in the* Architectural Review *concerning Charles Rennie Mackintosh. I am delighted with the photographs, letters and information about Mrs Warndorfer... I have had great difficulty in obtaining accurate information about Mackintosh's continental visits and was particularly interested in your statement that his work was first shown in Vienna in 1898 – according to my record his work did not appear in the Austrian capital until the Secessionist Exhibition of 1900, as a result of which he received the Waldorfer commission...*
>
> *You ask what use I intend to make of my material. In the first instance it forms the basis of a PhD thesis which I hope to submit this year to Glasgow University. If and when the paper situation in this country improves I intend to recast and publish it in book form. I have another objective too, the foundation of a permanent Mackintosh collection in Glasgow and this has, to a certain extent, been achieved already as you will probably see from next month's issue of the* Architectural Review. *The School of Art has also agreed to cooperate and has allocated a large room as a Mackintosh museum for which I am trying to secure a collection of drawings and furniture. If these plans materialise Mackintosh should at last be given a worthy place in his native city – where so much of his best work has been destroyed during recent years...*

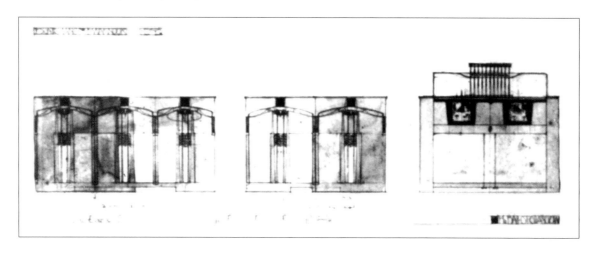

Kaufmann put Howarth in contact with Mrs Fritz Warndorfer when she visited London in October 1947 and she provided direct confirmation of the high regard Vienna had for the Mackintoshes. She wrote on 11 September 1947,

> *I have some photographs of the room; which he [Mackintosh] designed and executed for my husband's house in Vienna and I should be glad for you to see these if you care to do so, among these photos is one of the artist and his wife who were both in Vienna at the invitation of my husband. But the photos, I must warn you are not very large, though still clear and give a good idea of the type of work (as well).*

In September 1949 Howarth sent three Mackintosh sketches to Kaufmann in New York and wrote,

> *At last I have despatched to you by surface mail the three promised original sketches by Mackintosh, from my collection. These were executed in 1891 when, as a student, he made a scholarship tour of the Italian cathedral cities. Though they may not possess great artistic merit, I thought you might like to have them because of their artistic associations. Would you then accept them for the Museum with my compliments?*
>
> *I believe you know that the future of the Ingram Street restaurant is in the balance – I have been in close contact with those concerned in the affair for some time but nothing is settled yet. I shall keep in mind your request for furniture and if the premises come on the market it should be possible to secure some pieces for the museum.*
>
> *You may like to know that my work on Mackintosh has been approved by Glasgow University and the degree of PhD conferred… Now, a request, will you kindly give me the addresses of about six of the most progressive schools of architecture in the United States (excluding Harvard)?*

Many years were to pass before Howarth's first tentative enquiries about a future career in America were to bear fruit but his gift to the New York Museum of Modern Art solicited an immediate reply from one of the United States leading architects, Philip C. Johnston who was at that time Director of the Department of Architecture and Design at M.O.M.A. Johnston writes,

> *I know that Mr Kaufmann has already written to thank you personally for your generous donation of the three Mackintosh sketches to the Museum… I should like to add my expression of appreciation for your gift. As you say the value of the sketches lies in their associations, and it is a pleasure and an honour to receive these works by the pencil of a man whom we all esteem so highly.*

It was a generous gift but Howarth was presuming he would get something in return and a few months later Howarth, needing comparative imagery for his book on Mackintosh, writes to Kaufmann,

> *I am having difficulty in obtaining several photographs of domestic work by Frank*
> *Lloyd Wright, c.1900, to contrast with designs by Mackintosh of the same period.*
> *Do you have a library of pictures at the museum and if so would you kindly send*
> *me prints? I require a characteristic interior and an exterior view. The dining room*
> *at Waller House, River Forest, Ill. (1899) that you used in your article on*
> *'Modern Rooms' (*Interiors *February 1947) would do admirably...*

The relationship of Howarth and Kaufmann was undoubtedly one of a professional and scholarly equality, conducted in friendship and it proved to be productive, long term and beneficial to all concerned. The relationship between Howarth and Professor Nikolaus Pevsner was, however, quite different and opens up an uglier side to academic study – scholastic rivalry, professional jealousy, issues of intellectual property and copyright law, seniority and prestige, and the perennial conflict between youth and authority. Howarth and Pevsner had an extended confrontation over their linked but separate work on Mackintosh.

There is no doubt that Nikolaus Pevsner had an established reputation in the field of Mackintosh studies before Thomas Howarth. Mackintosh plays a significant part in Pevsner's book *Pioneers of the Modern Movement* published in 1936, three years before Howarth moved to Glasgow and four years before his research into Mackintosh began. But, by the mid forties, Howarth's knowledge of Mackintosh and his Glasgow contemporaries was much greater than Pevsner's. And, it was Howarth's papers and articles and, in particular, a series of letters Howarth wrote to Dr Saxl at the Warburg Institute in London where Pevsner was working, that reawakened Pevsner's interest in Mackintosh in 1947. It was a dangerous moment for Howarth; most of his pioneering research had been done, but his book was not published and his feet remained firmly on the bottom rung of the ladder of both fame and academic success. Dr Pevsner was twelve years older, and already famous and a recognised historian of world stature.

Even before he left Germany to settle in England, in 1933, Pevsner had a significant reputation as an architectural historian having worked as an assistant gallery keeper at the Dresden Museum and a university lecturer in Gottingen. In England, Pevsner was soon recognised as the leading Modernist architectural historian and a man who moved in highly influential circles. For example, he played an important part in undercover operations that aimed to bring Jews out of Germany. The Scottish poet Hamish Henderson was just one of many selected young men, questioned, primed and informed at secret meetings with Pevsner before being sent into Germany to bring back young Jews threatened by the Nazi regime. Thus, at a time when Howarth was an asthmatic undergraduate, Pevsner was an esteemed academic and 'private' spymaster, with a powerful metropolitan base and in the autumn of 1947, Howarth was seriously worried that his 'thunder' was about to be stolen. On 24 November he wrote to Professor Walton, custodian of the University of Glasgow's new Mackintosh collection, to say,

> *I enclose the first draft of the catalogue to the Mackintosh Collection –*
> *incidentally, I hope that this catalogue will not be published for the time being as it*
> *contains evidence of particular importance to my work. This applies especially to*
> *Mackintosh's lecture notes, and I should be greatly relieved to know that these were*
> *not available for study meantime. This sounds rather selfish, I know, but I've had*
> *several enquiries from Americans and others who, largely as a result of my articles*
> *are taking a keen interest in Mackintosh and I feel it would be a pity if any work*
> *on the subject appeared at this crucial point. Perhaps I am taking too narrow a*
> *view, however, I shall be glad to leave the matter in your hands.*

Sometime during 1948 Howarth learned not only that Pevsner was to become Slade Professor of Fine Art at Cambridge but that he was also planning publication of a major monograph on Mackintosh. He had already given Pevsner far more information than he now deemed wise and he decided to send Pevsner nothing more until he knew what was going on. The two men, very politely, locked horns. On 10 January 1949, Pevsner replied to a letter from Howarth:

> *Many thanks for your letter of 3rd January. I am very much looking forward to*
> *seeing your article – and when is your book coming out? This also I am looking*
> *forward to… What I have signed up to do is a little book on Mackintosh with*
> *only about four or five thousand words and about thirty or forty pictures. It is for*
> *an Italian publisher. As regards England it is not certain yet whether the same*
> *material will be made use of, but it is just possible. In any case I would really*
> *prefer your book to be out first, because you have no doubt, done very much more*
> *research than was possible for me in 1934…*

Howarth replied on 14 January 1949,

> *Here at last is the promised article: I must apologise for the delay. Unfortunately I*
> *cannot give you any information at the moment about the publication of my work*
> *on Mackintosh. You can assume, however, that it will not appear in 1949. The vast*
> *amount of material collected during some nine years of research has taken far more*
> *arranging than I had anticipated. Will you kindly tell me when your book is to be*
> *expected? I rely upon you to acknowledge the source of any material you might use*
> *from this or any of my published articles – a compliment which of course I shall*
> *reciprocate…*

On 16 February Pevsner wrote back,

> *Many thanks for your article, which I am returning herewith, after having read it*
> *with great interest. It certainly is a very good thing to show in pictures the*
> *connections between Mackintosh and the Scottish Middle Ages… You ask about my*
> *book. This is, of course, a long story. I had prepared a good deal for a Mackintosh*
> *book, chiefly from interviews with people who had known him, from the building*
> *papers of the period and work in Glasgow from 1935 and the following years. My*
> *suggestion in the end was that Mr Blackie should publish a proper big monograph.*
> *This, however, fell through and during the war I lost a good many of my records.*
> *Now all that I intend to do is to add to a minimum of factual information, dates*
> *etc., my views on Mackintosh's style and significance. It will, I think, not be more*
> *than a matter of 6,000 words and I shall not write it before the summer.*
>
> *I am, of course, disappointed to hear that your book is not going to come out*
> *this year because, mine being reduced to a much smaller affair, I want very strongly*
> *to advise people to go to yours for a much fuller account. Can that not be done*
> *now? It really depends on whether your monograph is to be then safely at the*
> *printers…*

Pevsner's letter looks innocuous enough but, reading between the lines, professional tensions are evident and, behind the scenes, very strong pressure was being brought on Howarth to 'give up' his plan to publish a major book on Mackintosh. Various figures within the educational establishment in Glasgow suggested he offer his research material to Pevsner. He was 'the big man' in the field and it seemed best, to officials at both Glasgow University and the Glasgow School of Art, that Howarth join in some kind of partnership with Pevsner. A distinguished German professor at Cambridge offered a prestige by association that the young Mancunian asthmatic would never muster. Douglas Percy Bliss, Director at G.S.A. wrote to Howarth about the offer Pevsner had made: 'He agrees that your book is your capital and that he cannot ask to see it before offering to cooperate. From what he has heard, however, he is prepared to pledge his cooperation, without seeing the quality of your work…' Another powerful figure at G.S.A., Harry Barnes, then added his weight to the Pevsner camp in a letter that Howarth interpreted as an insult. He immediately sent back this impassioned retort in June 1949:

> *Thank you for your letter. I fully appreciate the difficulty you had in composing it*
> *and I send you my condolences. I should have been in the same boat had, say,*
> *Michael Ayrton or Sir Alfred Munnings offered to touch up a picture on which*
> *you had been working for eight years – in order to make it more marketable, and*
> *had asked me to put the proposition to you. A reasonable analogy I think, though it*
> *is not easy to find a parallel with Pevsner in the world of painting!*

Pevsner's scheme is not unattractive nevertheless and if, as you seem to believe,
he is sincere, his offer is very generous, though I find all this a little difficult to
reconcile with Bliss's remarks at our last meeting, and the fact that he [Pevsner] has
studiously avoided direct contact with me despite the fact that he knew my interest
in Mackintosh perfectly well.

Should an opportunity present itself I shall most certainly see him, in fact I had
every intention of doing so before your letter provided an added incentive. As my
manuscript is in the hands of a publisher, however, I can hardly take positive
action at the moment – at least until I have news of acceptance or otherwise...

In a crossed-out P.S. on his original draught Howarth continued, 'I was *not* furious at your letter: but I *should* have enjoyed listening in to the conversations that took place in Glasgow and its environs a fortnight ago – they would have been *most* illuminating I'm sure.' Cooling down, between his writing and Edna's typing of the letter, Howarth decided not to send this evidence of his anger – but having, almost, stood his ground, things suddenly turned to Howarth's advantage. Douglas Percy Bliss became a solicitous 'go-between' and Pevsner's attempt at collaboration – well-meaning or otherwise – came to nothing. The rest is history.

In retrospect one can see that for Pevsner, Mackintosh was 'a thing apart', just one segment in the great field of his intellectual enquiry, whereas, for Howarth, Mackintosh was his 'whole existence'. Put to the test, Howarth showed grit and a Mackintosh-like courage. He risked a good deal by standing alone, but he had confidence in the originality, quality and importance of his work, and confidence in Mackintosh. He had nurtured, in himself, a vision of Mackintosh's contribution to world civilisation that he believed himself, personally, responsible for. Howarth did not describe his escape from the 'overwhelming embrace' of Professor Pevsner as either a victory, or a miracle, but it was, undoubtedly, another decisive turning point in his life.

After protracted battles with various publishers, Howarth's magnus opus finally came out in 1952. It was very well received – winning two prizes in America. Meantime, Pevsner's book had appeared two years before and grown to double the size first suggested... Thus Howarth's suspicions were fully justified and although Pevsner's publication only minimally diminished the impact of Howarth's, some animosity stayed with Howarth till the end of his life. In May 1950 he returned draught proofs of Pevsner's book with the following guarded words:

I have few comments to make on the text proper. There are some statements that
could be revised according to my findings, but as they are of little consequence in
the brief Italian edition, they are not worth mentioning here. Three important
errors should be corrected however.
p.36. The Chelsea Studios were designed in 1920 – not 1914 – they and not Bassett

Lowke's house constituted l'ultimo lavoro importanto!

p. 43. Although the memorial stone of the school was laid in 1898, work commenced on the building late in 1897. Mackintosh might as well have another year to his credit.

p. 46. He did not live in Spain but in France. St. Matthews Church should read 'Queen's Cross Church of Scotland' — the caption on the photograph is incorrect...

In addition to these corrections I have revised some spellings and several dates. I think you have made a fair general assessment of Mackintosh and his work. It is evident that you too have found that many of the published articles are inaccurate and unreliable — and, of course, the reminiscences of contemporaries more so. Did you get much help from Macauley Stephenson for example? When I began serious work on Mackintosh ten years ago his personal friends were few and far between — they are the people colla luce vero negli occhi. *Now, of course, the slightest acquaintance with the architect or his work is sufficient to kindle a veritable bonfire — which can be most misleading as, no doubt, you have discovered.*

I enjoyed reading your text and was interested to see that you have followed much the same path as myself — for example in regard to the 'Glasgow Boys'. I hope my notes will be of use and I look forward to seeing the book published. I wish you success.

P.S. A further point does occur to me. Unless you have indisputable evidence regarding the dates of the tearooms...I would suggest you do not attempt to arrange them in order. The sequence is difficult to establish without complicated explanations.

In that letter one feels the tables turned. The young lecturer is treating the learned Cambridge don with all the respect he would offer any undergraduate essayist. And he, cheekily, attempts to lay Pevsner a false trail — by suggesting he needs to make contact with Macauley Stevenson, a Glasgow landscape painter, whom the Mackintoshes knew and had visited at Etaples in Northern France, in 1925, but who is, architecturally, a totally insignificant character in the Mackintosh story. Howarth's new-found confidence is well illustrated by a letter to *The Glasgow Herald* on 14 November 1949. A letter from Pevsner, about the conservation of Mackintosh buildings in Glasgow, had appeared ten days before; it gave Howarth just the opportunity he wanted, to see off this now unwanted 'outsider', and he used his letter to present himself as the pre-eminent authority on The Glasgow Four.

As author of the 'monumental' work on Charles Rennie Mackintosh and his contemporaries mentioned by Dr Pevsner in his timely letter to The Herald *(4th November), would you kindly permit me to make a few observations?*

Though it is often difficult to persuade the layman that a building erected later than say 1850 can possibly have any architectural significance, fears for the survival of the buildings designed by Mackintosh are surely unfounded.

What in fact is the position? All his buildings of any consequence are much as he left them. By far the most important historically are the Glasgow School of Art, Scotland Street School and the best of his country houses. Queen's Cross Church does not belong to this category, but nevertheless is of considerable interest. It is most unlikely that any of these will fail to survive. The real and ever present danger is that their character will be changed by ill-considered alteration, or by well-intentioned but misguided 'restoration' at the hands of someone out of sympathy with the architect's work. It would seem that the Municipal Authorities now are aware of this danger: the governing body at the School of Art, and the Church of Scotland have been fully alive to it for a long time. The future of the country house is of course uncertain, but one cannot believe that this building, so carefully preserved by its owner – himself one of the first to recognise Mackintosh's peculiar genius – would be allowed to fall into alien hands.

The impermanent nature of decorative schemes and furniture however, make them subject to the vagaries of fashion to a far greater degree, and much of the architect's work in this sphere has been destroyed. But even here, the picture is by no means dark. Two excellent collections of furniture and several interior schemes survive, and though we must deplore the destruction of the exquisite Willow Restaurant in Sauchiehall Street, it is surely remarkable that even one of Miss Cranston's tearooms has remained to all intents and purposes intact, despite two world wars and the commercial changes of the past forty years. Messrs Coopers, the present owners, have indeed honoured their pledge to retain the original character of the premises as far as possible.

Taken by and large then, Glasgow is extremely fortunate in possessing so many fine examples of Mackintosh's work (and that of his wife Margaret Macdonald, who should not be forgotten), and there is little cause for recrimination – unless of course the last tearoom is permitted to disappear.

This brings me to another point. I had another letter from Glasgow last week reiterating a widely held fallacy which should be disposed of once and for all; I refer to the belief that few people in Scotland are aware of Mackintosh's importance, and that he has never been recognised in his native city. Here, perhaps, a personal reference may be forgiven. During the seven years or so I devoted to the study in Scotland of his life and work, it became more and more apparent that interest in him was growing rapidly, an interest stimulated in part no doubt by the necessarily protracted and searching nature of my investigation, but largely due to the wide recognition afforded to him in recent books and periodicals, and, I am glad to say, by the Scottish press whenever opportunity offered. In fact, Mackintosh has been news in his own country for a long time. Furthermore, it is often forgotten

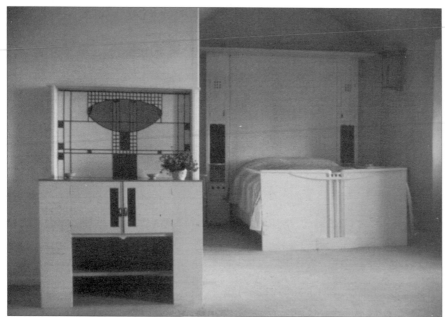

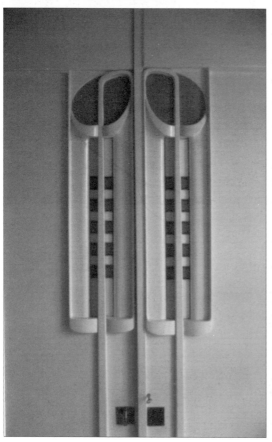

The Hill House, interiors
(Mackintosh 1902–03).

Opposite.
The Manageress's chair,
Willow Street tea-rooms,
1904.

that there are in Scotland a number of writers, many artists and a veritable host of admirers – of whom many are known to me personally – who have long championed the Mackintosh cause. How else could we have assembled the collections of furniture and drawings? How otherwise would the Ingram Street Restaurant have survived? How indeed, without the generous help of such people, could the broken and scattered fragments of the Mackintosh story have been reassembled?

And in Glasgow? Admittedly there has been some antipathy towards the architect in his native city, an antipathy born, I think, of misunderstanding and caution rather than antagonism. The revolutionary is seldom a comfortable bedfellow, and his activities are often least comprehensible to those among whom he has been brought up. The old antipathies however, are quickly dying and I cannot imagine anyone so uncharitable as to wish them revived.

Official recognition of course has been slow in coming, but then it usually is! Some time must necessarily elapse before an artist's contribution can be seen in true perspective and his influence assessed with any degree of confidence. The 'authority' must be sure of his ground before committing himself, and, exasperating as this may be for anyone seeking to preserve his work for posterity, it is by no means an unusual phenomenon in the world of art.

I submit therefore, that the struggle to establish Mackintosh's reputation in Scotland is not beginning – it is practically ended. In a few years, the fact that a struggle ever took place will be forgotten, and it is better so. The final issue as far as Glasgow is concerned – the preservation of the last of Miss Cranston's tearooms – is now joined. This incidentally, is not a sudden crisis in the cultural life of the city; the premises were advertised for sale many months ago and the problem of preventing their destruction has caused no little concern. If the civic authorities agree to take a hand in the matter, and surely they cannot do otherwise, it will be a fitting and logical conclusion to the Mackintosh story. The credit for this, the last act, will belong to Glasgow's 'cognoscenti' and all that remains to be done will be to consolidate the ground won. If at last the prophet finds honour in his own country, what other fields remain to be conquered?

That is a great letter. It has messianic fervour. Howarth lets Pevsner and the world know that it is he who speaks for Mackintosh in Glasgow, rather as St Peter spoke for Christ in Roman Italy. His assertion about 'the end of the Mackintosh story' has rhetorical force, not historical truth, but this letter is full of insights and passion and we must thank Professor Pevsner and Douglas Percy Bliss for bringing Howarth to the boil. The last two paragraphs refer specifically to Pevsner: he is the 'authority' from 'the world of art' that Howarth seeks to scorn. And his reference to 'prophets finding honour in their own country' is a 'knowing' reference to Francis Bacon, his four followers, and Rosicrucian tradition in the Jacobean period. It was an entirely appropriate reference and it carries resonant authority.

The 'last word' in this vignette of a classic, academic mini-feud, goes to one of Howarth's loyal Clydeside informants, Dodo Dunderdale of Bowling Castle. Howarth had written, warning her of the arrival of a new 'hunter' in the Mackintosh field and suggested she be wary of a certain Professor Pevsner. Drawing one of her splendid letters to a conclusion and offering Howarth more Mackintosh memorabilia, Dodo Dunderdale, writes, 'No, your Pro. Pevsner hasn't turned up here and in any case I don't think I'd have much interest in him...'

Finally, an article published in the C.R.M. Society Newsletter, No. 73, in 1997, throws new light on the combative relationship that existed between Howarth and Pevsner (and Harry Barnes and Douglas Percy Bliss). The article was written by Clare McGread, archivist at G.S.A. and concerns the battle fought to preserve the Ingram Street Tearooms in 1949. She commends the campaign conducted by Bliss/Barnes/Pevsner to preserve these rooms. She makes absolutely no mention of Howarth, although he was centrally involved, over several years, in attempts at preservation of these tearooms. When she quotes Bliss, writing to Pevsner, fawningly expressing himself in the following words: 'to correct your writing would be an impertinence – like correcting a drawing by Augustus John' we know Bliss is making unacknowledged use of Howarth – because these words are clearly a minor modification of the simile Howarth had angrily used in his letter to Barnes/Bliss just two months previously when he described the suggestion that Pevsner should help sort out his research as equivalent to him suggesting that Michael Ayrton or Sir Alfred Munning touch up a picture on which Glasgow's Head of Painting had been working for eight years! Whether Ms McGread's ignorance of Howarth was wilful, or unknowing, there can be little doubt that Howarth, recurrently, felt himself – like Mackintosh – in danger of being written out of history, undeservedly.

THE LIVING WORD 5

I think Mackintosh felt the tyranny of the 'dead land',
especially in the field of architecture. He spoke little of the then
prevailing lack of understanding and appreciation of his own work
by his own contemporaries, especially in his own country
but I believe he felt and resented it very strongly.

ALICE
TALWIN MORRIS

Historically, one unique product of Howarth's Mackintosh research was the firsthand information he gleaned from that decreasing band of friends, patrons and artists who had known Mackintosh well and were still alive in the 1940s. Prime amongst these were Herbert MacNair, the last surviving member of The Four; Fra and Jessie Newbery and their daughter Mary Sturrock; and Alice Morris (wife of Mackintosh's great friend Talwin Morris, the book designer).

Despite the difficulties of travelling long distances in wartime, Howarth first made contact with the Newberys in 1941. He quickly gained the trust of the man who had overseen Mackintosh's higher education, nurtured his artistic ideology, commissioned the Glasgow School of Art and 'orchestrated' the development of his protégé's reputation. Newbery was known to his friends and admirers as either 'The Fra' or 'Mr Newbery'; both were terms of respect and endearment. Newbery was a Dorset man who, after a short but notable career as a painter and lecturer in London, moved north to become headmaster of the Glasgow School of Art, in the mid 1880s. He quickly transformed the school into a leading European art institute. Newbery's closeness to his students was legendary, he married one of them, Jessie Rowatt, and they remained in close contact with many of their outstanding pupils until the end of their lives. If such a great and responsible teacher could be said to have had favourites, Newbery's favourites were the Macdonald sisters and the two men who became their husbands, Herbert MacNair and Charles Rennie Mackintosh.

In retirement the Newberys lived in a beautiful old house at Corfe Castle in Dorset and, between 1941 and 1947, Howarth visited several times. After The Fra's death, Jessie

Left. Mackintosh with
boy at the Hill House.

Right. Mackintosh
photographed by the
Rosicrucion photographer,
E.O. Hoppe, (c.1920)

Newbery decided to sell their much loved house and their daughter, Mary Sturrock, gave Howarth a variety of paintings, memorabilia, letters, books and magazines that were crucial research tools and invaluable additions to his collection. Most of the letters the Newberys gave Howarth remain unknown and unpublished. For example, on 27 December 1925 Mackintosh wrote from the Hôtel du Commerce in Port Vendres, France;

We had a very welcome letter from Jessie the day before yesterday but we both missed a small enclosure that had somehow become to us something expected and something hoped for. I refer to your supplementary sheet – small it may be and often was, but it had always some joyful words, some message of hope and comfort – sometimes you write in prose and sometimes in verse – but whether in verse or prose your single sheet enclosure always conveyed to us something of your own special personality and something of your own wide human understanding.

We both hope you will not forget to enclose your small sheet the next time Jessie writes. This really means that we shall be pleased to get a small sheet or a big sheet at any time.

I am glad to know that you enjoyed the Romanesque churches around Barcelona. I don't know whether they are better or worse than those we have seen in Rousillon. Personally I have been what they say 'struck dumb' – Elne, Arles-sûr-Tech, Prate-de Mollo and many others are surprising stone structures – of course built to hear the spoken word and not to follow the service by reading the printed

word. The artistic problem of lighting the interior of a church for these two conditions is one of – faith – or visibility. Of course we have the advantage over you of having stayed in this country longer and in thus having the chance of seeing some of the more inaccessible and most delicious small churches such as Montalba, Montbolo, Marion, Jugols, Canavels, Palalda etc. These are all simple stone structures with the most gorgeous altarpieces in carved and gilded wood – wood that is not carved but cut, showing every mark of the tool and not gilded but clothed in gold leaf (thick) – the first brought from America to Spain. Very rococo but very beautiful in the simple stone churches with no competing element but the sympathetic crystal chandeliers.

I hope your work goes well. I am struggling to paint in watercolours – soon I shall start in oils – but I find I have a great lot to learn, or unlearn. I seem to know far too much and this knowledge obscures the really significant facts – but I am getting on.

With love to both, yours always, Toshie.

P.S. I found Florence just as artificial in a stupid way as I did twenty-five years ago when I went as a small lad.

Conversazione programme for the Glasgow Architectural Association (Mackintosh 1893). ©Christie's Images, Ltd. 2002

It was thirty-four years since Mackintosh had been awarded the architectural scholarship, and first travelled, studied and sketched in Italy. Always rebellious and wary of the aridity of academic architecture, Mackintosh's Italian sketchbooks show how his interest was captured by the vernacular, the Gothic, the unsung, rather than the great renaissance set

pieces. His description, in the letter, of provincial French and Spanish churches shows how little his taste changed over his adult life. The letter is at once deferential and strangely paternal – it cajoles Newbery not to forget to write, not to be lazy or think his notes less than deeply important to the recipients. It is also, self-evidently, part of a long correspondence between equals in which major ideas are deliberately raised for serious discussion, and even more things are left unsaid. The touches of humour are typical of Mackintosh, as is his search for spiritual reinforcement and the honour he bestows on his master – 'always some joyful words, some message of hope and vitality'.

Mackintosh's brief thoughts about the ways in which the forms of church architecture are determined either by the needs of the spoken word (faith), or the written word (the need for the light that will make texts legible) are very interesting. They affirm Mackintosh's architectural adherence to plastic, enduring Romanesque-type forms, as opposed to the more linear, brittle forms of Gothic architecture and its Protestant derivatives where the needs of the 'written word' have, tended to undermine the haptic realities of stone and sculptural space. Mackintosh's preference for an architecture responsive to the spoken word is doubly interesting because it springs from something particular in his own psyche and cultural heredity. The pre-eminence of the spoken and sung word is rooted very deep in Celtic and Scottish culture, and over millennia, this pre-eminence has had architectural consequences. Growing from a lifestyle nurtured round the fire, and the need to shelter long months against cold and rain, living space tends to be articulated like a smithy; dark, illumined, mysterious, black and white – part byre, part kitchen, part monastic cell.

Jessie Newbery also gave Howarth what is probably the last letter Mackintosh wrote. It was written from hospital, after he had become ill with the throat cancer that was to kill him. It is fluently written in pencil.

Dear Jessie R.,

As Margaret is coming to see you I am taking the opportunity to write you a short note and tell you that as far as I can gather from the small scraps of information that the various doctors let grudgingly fall, I am making quite good progress. I had a good sleep last night and that is an event so unusual that it stands out as an event something very much out of the common.

I do not know when they will be finished with me here but I must be getting better because I am now longing to be out – the days are passing very slowly.

Thank you very much for the little garden posy – it lasted me quite a week and looked nice and cheerie on my locker. Love to you both.

Yours always, Toshie

The joy and the melancholy in Mackintosh's character are beautifully expressed. Long letters from Margaret are equally interesting, though much more factual. On 18 December 1924 she wrote:

My dear Jessie,

Here we are – back again in our beloved Pyrenees. We went back to London in September – intending to stay in London, perhaps till January and then return here – but strange to say – the studios this year let almost at once – and each tenant wanted to get in at once – so we just had a very short stay in Chelsea of five weeks. Last year we had such a difficulty letting the studios that I thought it better to take the chance whilst we had it – for altho' we find we cannot let them – so as to make

Left. Nomad Art Club design (Margaret Macdonald c.1896). Published in *The Studio*, 1897.

Right. *Peacock and Eye of Thoth*, Candle sconce designed by Margaret and Frances Macdonald (c. 1895) for Alice and Talwyn Morris.

anything off them – which seems rather strange – still – we get the rent we pay for them so we do not need to worry.

We like life here so much and Toshie is as happy as a sandboy – tremendously interested in his painting and, of course, doing some remarkable work. I hope he will have a show sometime – but that remains to be seen about – when he has got enough work together. In the meantime he is absorbed in this landscape – since we got here on 22nd November he has been able to work outside every day but two – from 9.30 till 3.00 – in brilliant sunshine. I don't work outside – but it is warm enough to sit in-doors without a fire. We intend to stay in Ille till the end of March anyway. It is a charming place and the little hotel most comfortable. We live – the two of us for 8/- a day, wine included.

We left London on Nov. 2 ; Folkestone-Boulogne and then to Montreuil-sûr-Mer to see the little town and the Macauley-Stevensons. Slausmole got us lodging with the mother of her servant and we were most comfortable. We spent most of our time with the Macauleys and had a very good time. They were most kind to us and they have made a charming dwelling for themselves and both seemed very happy and contented. Macauley has hardly altered at all and Slausmole is only a little plumper. There is no doubt she is a perfect wife to Macauley and she has a wonderful influence over him – just in the way in which he perhaps needs it a little – but there is no doubt he is a charming person, very entertaining and stimulating. He seems to do a lot of work and has some pictures in the studio which are very beautiful. We did not like the climate of Montreuil though. It is like Winchelsea – a little hilltown in a marshy plain and much too damp for our taste. When we left the Stevensons, an American painter – one of the colony at Etables – came to Paris with us to see the Autumn Salon, which we found very interesting. I liked especially the work of a man called Grotti – he seemed to be doing what I have been trying to do all my life – but Macauley would not look at it, he disliked it so much – which shows what an Ishmael I am! – Then we came on here – to this lovely rose coloured land and we were glad to be back again in its warmth and sun. We find that prices are going up a little here – but they still take us at this hotel for 8/- a day – both of us – wine included as we are going to stay some time. So there is not much to grumble about yet. London I found dearer than ever — everything costs more and rents are getting absurd.

I heard from Gladys Owen – she tells me that the eldest Alexander girl and the eldest Priestman girl are engaged. I was very sorry to see about Mrs Smiler's death. I know it would be a great grief to you… I hope you are both well and happy. We both send our best love and every best wish.

Margaret M. Mackintosh

P.S. You saw, of course, that Revel of Chelsea Poly. has got Glasgow. Schwabe thought Walter Bayes would get it. There seem to have been a lot in for it – including, to our amusement Stuart Park and David Gauld. (I think Macauley said – that was private – so not to mention it – I can't see it matters tho'!) We feel it does not matter much who gets it – no one will ever again know how to run it like Fra H. Newbery. That's our opinion and we know – perhaps better than anyone!

detail from *Mother and Children*, repoussé panel (Margaret Macdonald c. 1899). Hunterian Art Gallery.

Another letter from Margaret Mackintosh to Jessie Newbery is undated but addressed from La Petite Maison Bouix, Amelie-les-Bins, Pyrenees-Orientales, South France.

Dear Jessie,

This is our address just now – and will be for the next two months – I expect you will have heard from the Hutchies that we were intending to come. We should so much like to have seen you and Mr Newbery but I expect you were very much rushed. We were so glad to hear you were looking so well. It would have been nice to have heard about all your experiences in Spain. I suppose it was very lovely – we are more like Spain here than France – the people are quite a Spanish type and all wear dead black and speak Catalan amongst themselves, although they understand French. We have taken this tiny house, it has just two rooms – one on top of the other (I think it must have been the old Toll house), for studios, and we are living at the little hotel just across the bridge, at one end of which this house stands. The hotel is simple but beautifully clean and the cooking amazing. It is very cheap so that suits us.

I have let my studio furnished but Toshie has not yet let his – we have left it in

the hands of an agent – so I expect it will be let – though there is evidently not such a demand for studios as there was. Artists are demanding more comfort and a lot prefer to take floors in big houses, where they get big rooms and a bathroom – rather than put up with the discomforts of studios like ours even though very picturesque, however, the rents are now doubled and are really too high for such studios. I have been thinking for some time that we were foolish to go on with them. However, till we return and decide what is best to do – it is better to let them furnished.

This is quite a beautiful spot. In the valley of the Tech – so we are protected from the Tramontane – but we get the snow-wind off Canigou if the wind is from that direction. This, in spite of the sun, always gives a sharpness to the air which is rather exhilarating. Later on, in the spring, we think of going down to Collioure – we went to see how we liked it and think it is one of the most wonderful places we have ever seen. It is only a fishing village and it will be difficult to find accommodation – and there is no hotel – but I expect we shall manage somehow.

It seems so far from here to North Matravers – but so far we always say we have not yet seen anything quite so perfect – I suppose you often walk out. The only thing that tempts one abroad (besides the exchange rate) is the certainty of fine weather – it does make such a difference to know it will be fine. Of course there is the other side of the picture. At Collioure they have not had rain for two years – so water is rather precious. Here there is no lack – both drinking and boiling sulphur water – the latter simply flows down the street gutter and one can always get a can of beautiful hot water without the trouble of heating. It is lovely for washing – especially one's hair. Well, as I shall not write again before Christmas – I just wanted you to know where we were – we send you all our good wishes for a Merry Christmas and a very Happy New Year.

With best love – yours affectionately,

Margaret M. Mackintosh.

On 23 January 1925, Margaret writes from the Hôtel du Midi, Ille-sûr-Tet, Pyrenees-Oriental

My dear Jessie,

I am hastening to write – because I am afraid you may be uneasy not hearing. Your letter must have been held up in Amelie-les-Bains, while the dear people thought matters over. You directed it to Hôtel du Midi, Amelie-les-Bains – we, when we left Amelie, asked the post office to forward letters for Mackintosh, Hôtel Pujade to – Hôtel du Midi, Ille-sûr-Tet. This was of course too much for the dear Catalans to decide about quickly, they never do anything in a hurry, so they have evidently pondered it for four or five days before sending it on. So – that is why you have not heard from me before. Now – of course – you really should not send us such a parcel – it is far too kind of you. However – we know you love to do it – even, as I always say, to the giving away of your head – if anyone you loved wanted it! So we thank you very, very much indeed for it. Toshie instantly decided upon his present – he has been longing to get a pair of, what they call mountain boots – ever since he saw them here. They are made of a lovely soft natural-coloured leather – so now he is going to treat himself to a pair. I cannot yet particularly think of anything I want – just at the moment – but there is something sure to turn up and I shall buy it when it does.

Just now – I am enjoying influenza – Toshie has just finished his and passed it on to me. It is very prevalent just now – they say the winter has been too warm. It has certainly been amazing. Since we came here at the end of November we have had continual sunshine – except for two days tropical rain – we have not even had the winds that usually blow at this time. One day after another has been still – sunny – and blue. One cannot believe it when one reads of the weather in England. However – we may get it yet – the gardeners all live in hope of a little frost. They say it makes the worms do something to the earth which makes the salads good.

It will be very exciting to be building. I think you are very wise to put in a bathroom. Quite apart from the joy of a hot bath – I believe it averts many an illness. Macauley had put in a most generous bathroom in his house with a large sort of kettle heated by gas. Jean, we did not see – because she had gone for a year, I think, to travel about with some friends who are now in Corsica. They pay all her expenses and she lends a hand with the children when required. They seem to be charming people – I forget their name – but they came sometime ago to Etaples and bought a house there, which they tired of – so they have let it and are now wandering about just as fancy takes them. Slausmole thinks it will be very jolly for Jean as they are bright young people, always making friends, and the children are delightful, and Jean writes of all the jolly times she's having.

You think, as we do, about Dorset. It is quite the best in every way. This comes very near it and the buildings here are a perpetual joy to us. Toshie is going to paint some of the 'Maas' as they call them – farmhouses really – so you will see what they are like someday – I hope. When we come again to Corfe we must make an excursion to see the panels at Bridport The Fra is doing. You are both, evidently, very well and enjoying life which is the best thing in the world, isn't it?

Best love to you both from us both and many, many, thanks – Yours affectionately –

Margaret M. Macdonald

Isolated in wartime Dorset the Newberys were delighted to entertain Howarth and, on occasion, Edna. They were deeply grateful that somebody, at last, was seriously documenting the history of Glasgow in the Newbery years. They knew that their reputations had been undermined – like those of The Four. A letter to Mackintosh from John Keppie written shortly after Mackintosh left Scotland in 1914, gives an indication of the kind of contempt to which the whole group was exposed:

> ...I had almost given up hope of hearing from you and must confess you are not distin-
> guished as a correspondent. I heard from Newbery that you were in Suffolk. He has
> been very unwell with nerves and is not likely to be back to the school for sometime.

In contrast, on Tuesday 19 October 1947, Mary Sturrock writes to Howarth with the love, generosity and quick energy she displayed throughout her life,

> I think it would have been barely worth your visit for the Ver Sacrum alone – but it
> was here waiting for you – as it didn't turn up till after the book people had cleared up
> and gone. (And no one would have paid it any attention but me.) It is now parcelled
> up – two vols, with one Mackintosh frame, and two MacNair panels – keep them
> all. They will go with the beds – (though) I'm having difficulty in getting the beds
> lifted. Bournemouth firms seem all booked but I will try Carter Paterson...
>
> Carter Paterson is now booked. Enclosed are one or two letters I put away for
> you in April and should have sent. Please return them to me in Edinburgh, when
> you have done with them. One more thought – I have retained [an] immensely
> heavy, bound J.M. King – Le Reve and Emile Zola illustrated by Marcel
> Schwabe – mother considered that these illustrations had an influence on M.
> Mackintosh and the MacNairs. My sister didn't think the book men would lift the
> Kunst and Studios – but didn't think of you (she said they had reproductions of
> Daddy and Mother's work and a little Mackintosh, so they were obviously contem-
> porary and all bought with some purpose, as they were regular subscribers). I hope
> you get something out of them – and that you get them all right – but the
> transaction has largely gone through. You have been lucky to have had me [around],
> as my sister and husband don't have this stern conscience! While wanting to help
> you, I am probably really impelled by my personal friendship with Toshie
> himself... This letter has been very interrupted –

16 February 1949, Mary Sturrock writes again:

> It is a great pleasure to be able to congratulate both of you on the safe arrival of
> your son. Glad to hear he sounds full of vitality – and I will send a wish that he
> grows up to be healthy, strong and a good architect – consider all those pre-natal

influences – as I'm sure Mrs Howarth has had plenty to do also with your Mackintosh book. What a relief it must be to have it completed.

Your troubles are still to seek – as there seem to be long delays in the publishing world – a friend said – nearly a year's delay in the cloth-binding part, alone. We met Prof. John Walton and his wife lately and she was asking about the book. Huan and his wife are now settled in Edinburgh and another of these babies coming along. We haven't met Waterhouse yet – he seems very busy opening shows so far – but daresay we shall meet him through the Haswell Millers. They like him very much – in fact Haswell looks happier already than he did in Cursiter's days.

Would you return me the Mackintosh letter I sent you about the Roussillon little churches? It has long been a cherished scheme of my sister's and mine that we should go to the Roussillon – not imagining that Toshie had lived there and could give us this list. My sister is such a good grandmother, it will be difficult to uproot her – but sometime we'll manage it. I do hope Mrs Howarth will gain in real robustness with the coming spring days…

Howarth returned the original letter to Mary Sturrock but kept a copy for himself. Mary lived on into the 1990s and was to become the last person with direct memories of the Mackintoshes. She had, as a small girl, carried the key to ceremonially open, the Glasgow School of Art in 1900. In the 1960s, she wrote to Howarth to fiercely denounce Glasgow University's plans to demolish the Mackintosh's house in Glasgow.

I never know how many faithful correspondents you have in Glasgow to send on this sort of thing to you… There seems to be some sort of plan to re-erect one or two rooms of the Mackintosh house – in the University? One thought at the time that the University had bought the house to preserve it – but we – in Edinburgh certainly – know better now (George Square is in course of demolition)!

Its odd that newspaper articles are always a bit incorrect – but surely any Glasgow journalist might realise that there aren't any stucco terraces in Glasgow. Margaret used to paint – in the good light beside the long west window. It was Toshie who had his big black desk in the back bit – which was well-curtained and very dark.

Even Margaret, though she was so clean and tidy while painting, wouldn't have done metalwork on the white sitting room carpet! Her tools were upstairs in the attic.

I have been in S. Italy and Sicily this year… and in Rome, looking at early Christian mosaics and Etruscan tombs. The more one sees, the more interesting it gets. And there was a very good Edinburgh Festival this year – culminating in the Leningrad Orchestra which was truly thrilling – it made one's skin crackle – and we went floating out into the night, everyone with rosy cheeks and sparkling eyes –

Left. Menu designed by
Herbert MacNair (1908)
before his enforced
departure from Liverpool.

Right. Book cover for
Blackie and Son, Glasgow
(Talwyn Morris c. 1900).

elated with lovely sincere music-making. They must take a lot of trouble to get things so good.

Now things feel a bit dull and tame – but its time to get down to Work. The Cowans write glowing accounts of the interesting time they are having in America. They have been keen for some time to see America and it's living up to their expectations. Ralph's lectures at Cornell are only in the afternoon – so he has his own time to look around. There is an Art Nouveau Exhibition of British Art in Paris in October and I have lent two pieces of jewellery – one brooch you know – and another pendant, turned up in an old tea caddy. I think it got put away because the pendant pearls – raindrops – kept getting pulled off – so you haven't seen it.

An architect – English – was staying with me and maintains there is a Mackintosh designed house in Henley-on-Thames (where this man used to live). It's remained in my curiosity – so will probably write and ask him for some details. Tait [the architect] used the Art-lovers' House designs as a free quarry for a while?

I hope you are all well and have had a good summer – and are quite settled in Canada. Yours sincerely, Mary Sturrock.

Howarth's crucial contact with Herbert MacNair, the last survivor of The Glasgow Four, was arranged by Miss Helen L.A. Bell and Miss D.C.L. Dewar of the Hotel Creggandarroch, Blairmore, by Dunoon. In a letter, dated 12 May 1944, Miss Bell writes, with great warmth and generosity of spirit,

*Miss D.C.L. Dewar has asked me to send you the address of Mr MacNair, as you
wish to get in touch with him. His lodging is: c/o Mrs Muir, 'Monzie', Blairmore,
and if you are to write to him, would it not be more satisfactory if you could come
and see him? A steamer is due at Strone pier at 12.20p.m. and if you arranged
beforehand by phoning or writing here, you could have dinner with us at 1 p.m.
Then go along to see Mr MacNair. A steamer leaves Blairmore pier at 4 p.m. and
5 p.m., and the last one at 5.25 p.m. If the day is wet, Mr Burnett the Proprietor
could meet you with his car at Strone pier; but if fine you could easily walk here in
time for one o'clock dinner. Trusting that Mr MacNair may be able to give you
some information about his brother-in-law which you do not already know...*

That letter embodies a great deal of Scots nineteenth-century gentility. Howarth's
consequent contact with MacNair was to be fundamentally important to the biographical
jigsaw puzzle he was assembling. For example, when MacNair informed Howarth that in
the art of The Four, 'not a line was drawn without a purpose, and rarely was a single motif
employed that had not some allegorical meaning', he gave him something truly surprising
and crucial to the completion of his research. It, authoritatively, re-established The Four's
link with European Symbolism and gave Howarth the confidence to pursue lines of
enquiry about which he had, hitherto, been diffident. In fact, MacNair's information was
so important that many readers of Howarth's *Mackintosh* have wondered why he did not
develop MacNair's suggestions about meaning, allegory and symbolism much further.
MacNair, however, was a secretive individual and Howarth knew his book was already
'big enough'! Also, he was determined not to lose his focus on architecture and the
Modernist aspects of Mackintosh's work. He intuitively, understood that more 'time and
distance' was needed before the subterranean forces latent in the symbolism created by
The Four could be properly evaluated, because, as his archive makes clear, Howarth had
information in the forties that he deliberately set aside for later generations.

Over several years Howarth got to know Herbert MacNair well and the period is
punctuated by four splendid letters. They are at once informative and allusive, but the
moment they begin to touch on a subject of importance they slip away into silence. Like
a primitive tribesman, as soon as MacNair knows he has revealed himself, he steps back
into the bush. The letters display a sense of historical hurt, knowing privacy and great
charm. On the 3 June 1944, three days before the Allied invasion of Normandy, MacNair
writes from Monzie, Blairmore, Argyll, c/o Mrs Muir,

*Thank you for your kind letter and offer to call and see me, but I am very, very
sorry to say that such a visit would be quite useless – I have absolutely no data and
no works of my great friend, Chas R. Mackintosh to which I could refer you.*

*Two of my sisters died within a year of each other, an unmarried sister whose
home had been my home for some years, and a married sister, whose two daughters*

are now in the W.A.A.F. The house here was sold, and anything I particularly treasured, – such as the works of Chas. R. Mackintosh, went to my niece's house in England, which has since been let on a long lease. Other pictures and designs I gave to friends, whilst portfolios of old sketches, and, unfortunately, art magazines and cuttings, Home and Foreign, re Exhibitions with reference to Chas. R. Mackintosh and our little group – all went to Salvage. These references might have served you.

In the meantime I am in rooms with nothing *of art about me, and only a deplorable memory which would be of no use to you. A letter written by Margaret M. Mackintosh, shortly after her husband's death, told me how they were 'writing up' her husband and she was busy collecting all the data she could – of course all I had, she had, but now I have none. Thus you see a visit to me would be quite useless, a waste of time to you, and, under the circumstances, embarrassing to me. It is with much regret and apology that I write to you in this vein.*

I always looked upon my friend Chas R. Mackintosh as one of the greatest Architects and Artists. We were not very much together at the School of Art, but we often took trips into the country at weekends and made sketches of interesting buildings etc. And of course we made designs for the monthly competitions at the School of Art. I am afraid that is about all I can say, and I am very sorry I cannot oblige you further. His wonderful delight in all things beautiful, large or small, and the charm of his enthusiasm are beyond words.

Yours sincerely, J. Herbert MacNair

That is a marvellous, elliptical letter. It carries the sadness of a truly original artist brought, by time and circumstance, into isolation and rejection and it flashes with insight and illuminated thought. MacNair's point about Margaret Macdonald collating information about The Four, for 'writing up' is of great interest with regard to the University of Glasgow's subsequent refusal to allow publication of the letters that Mackintosh wrote to Margaret from Port Vendres in 1927. She wanted things known.

On 25 July 1945 MacNair wrote again:

Thank you for sending me your interesting extract from your draught article on the School of Art. I think you have summed up and put things very well indeed. With regard to your allusions to sketches by J.B. Fulton I am quite at sea, for I fear I have never heard either of him or his sketches. He certainly was not at Honeyman and Keppie's in my time. Fullerton the painter, I knew slightly, but then he was an Impressionist.

Again, I find it impossible to say to what extent Mackintosh controlled the competition design for the School of Art. He and Keppie worked it out between them, and, when two are working together in consort, it is hard to say how much is the suggestion or influence of one and how much that of the other. As for transitions from orthodox to unorthodox – the extent to which such could be made would depend greatly on the client. Miss Cranston gave Mackintosh an absolutely free hand and delighted in all he did. Others might demur at what they considered too bizarre. I mean that the various tastes or daring *of different clients would prevent any rigid line taking place between orthodox and unorthodox. Then again, Keppie was always spoken of as Sellars' right-hand man, and when he came into partnership with Honeyman after the death of the great James Sellars, he brought the work in hand at Sellars' office with him. This was in the beautiful but quite orthodox style used so well by Sellars. With the work he would bring the clients, and if these clients and their friends came with further orders they would probably wish for work in the same style rather than strange things which might be emanating from (elsewhere) in the office. But, at the same time, there were others who saw much of beauty and promise in these strange things and were only too pleased to get away from the beaten track, and to have such a man as Chas R. Mackintosh to take them off it.*

I am afraid that is all I can say and fear it will not be of any use to you. Of course, J.B. Fulton may have been in Mackintosh's office without me knowing… Thank you for so kindly inviting me to call on you and Mrs Howarth in Glasgow, however, I am pretty well 'put' at Blairmore – I had a nice break though, a fortnight ago when two nieces who are ambulance drivers, School of Artillery, Larkhall, Wiltshire spent part of their leave here. The weather was good and we spent one delightful day at Bute visiting old friends and relations. The Queen Mary, outward bound, passed close by our steamer...

In public estimation MacNair is tarred with the same drunkard's brush as Mackintosh, but his letters, even as an old man in his eighties, are clear and sharp and show no sign of the drunken incompetence many still assume he lived in. There are however definite hints of the combative strength of character that made him a difficult character. MacNair worked for several years, with Mackintosh, at Honeyman and Keppie's but he found the atmosphere and work increasingly restrictive and set up an independent design practice in the mid 1890s. It never really prospered. Although, in his second letter, MacNair introduces Keppie with generosity, he immediately tacks round to suggest that Keppie's success as an architect was heavily dependent on the work, and the clients, he brought to the Honeyman practice as a consequence of the death of James Sellars. In doing this, MacNair is resolutely defending Mackintosh; it being well-known that the prime reason for Mackintosh's removal from the firm of Honeyman, Keppie, Mackintosh, in 1913–14, was the financial inequality of the contributions made by the two partners. The imbalance is statistically documented in papers unearthed by Howarth in the forties. During Mackintosh's great years, from 1901 to 1912, the work he introduced into the firm was valued at £4,934: the work introduced by John Keppie was valued at £16,303. During that period profits were divided £5,467 to Mackintosh and £7,069 to Keppie; expenses divided £6141 to Mackintosh and £7172 to Keppie. These accounts clearly provided Keppie with financial reasons for questioning Mackintosh's role within the firm. If, in addition, Mackintosh was drinking 'too much' and being 'difficult' with clients it is easy to understand how tensions, between Keppie the competent practitioner, and Mackintosh, the wayward genius, led to the rupture that drove the Mackintoshes out of Scotland.

It must have been hugely frustrating for Mackintosh, having been recognised as one of the great artists of one of the great phases of European history, to find himself being treated like a delinquent in his own office whilst John Keppie was being elevated to chairmanships and governorships and basking in the glory of being 'long-distance golf-drive champion of Glasgow'. Whilst former friends, like D.Y. Cameron, were buying great houses in London and extending their country estates, Mackintosh and MacNair were struggling for their very existences. When the MacNairs returned from Liverpool to shared accommodation with the Mackintoshes, it was as though these four outstanding artists were students again! MacNair then emigrated to Canada to find work on the railways. In such circumstances it is amazing how sane, unresentful and normal MacNair remained.

On 6 August 1945, MacNair wrote a third letter, after obvious prompting:

> I haven't answered your letter because, alas! I cannot answer it. I know so little about the doings of Chas R. Mackintosh during the later period of his life – as exemplified by my knowing nothing about J.B. Fulton. I was quite out of touch with him and the Art World generally. Great misfortune had befallen my family, – and I had to banish all thought of Art. I went to Canada and found employment in the Grand Trunk Railway. I came back to Britain just before the Great War, and I was at the G.P.O. during the war. Shortly after that my dear little wife died. I then started a motor hiring business with my son (Sylvan MacNair). After some years we wound up the business, as my son had got promise of a post in South Africa; and as private affairs had changed a little in my favour, and my sisters wished me to live with them, I came to Blairmore. So except for the early years of his career, I know little of the doings of Chas R. Mackintosh.
>
> When I first had the pleasure of meeting you I told you that I feared I would be of no use to you. Even during those happy years long ago, it was only on holiday that the Mackintoshes and my wife and I were together – and though the Mackintoshes would show us beautiful things they had executed, and designs they were engaged on – we gave little thought to else than their beauty – and certainly none to 'influences'. Though we delighted in visiting all places of architectural beauty, old or new, and, perhaps, wherever there is admiration there is influence in some way. As for 'motif' – such one finds in Nature – and I think we all sought it there.
>
> I think it was very shortly after Mackintosh's return from his scholarship tour

that he joined Honeyman and Keppie. Outside office hours long before that — all along — one might say — he and I had both been doing work in furniture, glass, mural decorations, metal — anything, quite freely on our own individual lines. These mostly for our own families, relations and friends. Not for remuneration to ourselves, we were just too delighted if they gave us the chance and paid the tradesmen. Also we were doing designs for subjects set by the School of Art Sketch Club, but these of course weren't executed. At that time Margaret and Frances Macdonald — afterwards his and my respective wives — were also exhibiting.

I am very sorry not to be able to help you for your second question as to whether the School of Art, as built, differs to any great extent from the competition design. I do not know. Altogether I fear you will find this a most unsatisfactory letter, — but I trust you may be able to glean some really valuable clues in Chelsea...

MacNair's dismissal of Howarth's probing about 'influence' clearly marks him as a passionately creative artist. His concern is with the making of things and the beauty and resonance of these things; he is not interested in historical origins and influences — these are processes beside the point of making art! Howarth was a scholar, attempting to establish facts and place things in a historical and cultural framework. This, MacNair recognised as a valid pursuit, but MacNair lets Howarth know how differently artists pursue their vision of the world. And MacNair's point exposes a major fault of modern scholarship in the field of the arts; historians have become far too interested in where things come from and what they led to, to the detriment of the study of the objects themselves. Everything is period, style, influence, and documentary proof — whilst the art and the artists are almost irrelevant. This, as MacNair brilliantly recognises, is monstrous and destroys the essence of what all art, as art, actually is. And, today, state sponsored art teaching and scholarship have become, in themselves, self-justifying processes; the process of education so institutionalised and all pervasive that it is in danger of destroying the very things it presumes to be nurturing — the minds of the students being trained. They are not taught to see, to be informed, to love and be moved *by art*: they are taught to categorise, to document and 'lock things off' as though art is only another commodity, an example of this style, that movement, this sequence of events. Such things are examinable but beside the wider human point as MacNair was hinting sixty years ago.

His last letter to Howarth is dated 27 September 1947.

Thank you very much for your most kind letter enclosing the interesting photo of 'Toshie's Cats', which I now, at long last, return — I must indeed apologise for such delay — but, I am sorry to say, I have been again laid up. I caught a bad chill which brought back my old troubles and have had a pretty tough time. However, I am once more on the mend. You are quite right about the 'Cat' frieze — it was for Toshie's bedroom at Denniston, also the cabinet, and the fender with tall candle-

sticks which I remember so well. The Mackintoshes are a branch of Clan Chattan and he used their crest as his 'motif'. At the same time I made a frieze of mermaids – the mermaid being the MacNair crest. I also designed a cabinet. I was in 'digs' in Glasgow at the time, and my frieze was in water-colour, juicily floated on, and on ingrain paper, my landlady allowed me to fix it on the wall with drawing pins. I think Toshie's frieze was also in watercolour. It is a great pity the photograph has faded so badly as the cats were very cleverly and amusingly used. Later, my little wife to be, Frances, and her sister Margaret Macdonald were on a visit to my people at Skelmorlie, and the three of us adapted the Mermaid 'motif' to decorate the main staircase there.

I thought it very good of you and Mrs Howarth to call on me. Mrs Muir has remarked several times on what a nice young couple you were and I hope too that I may have the pleasure of seeing you both again soon.

With all good wishes, yours sincerely,

J. Herbert MacNair

Although MacNair lived on until 1953, this remarkably warm and informative correspondence ends there. The letters are clearly the product of a man of high intellect, sensibility and a vital, crusty good humour. They confirm MacNair, the least acknowledged member of The Glasgow Four, as a worthy player in the quartet. Little of his art has survived but he was a powerful and uninhibited image-maker and, for a short while, a genuinely original artist of European stature. Circumstances conspired against him – his art throve on rebellious self-expression but, in the end, his Highland temper and need for total independence proved his undoing – at least in conventional terms.

Of equal importance to Howarth's contact with MacNair was his correspondence with Mrs Alice Talwin Morris, wife of the great book designer Talwin Morris. Talwin Morris, like Fra Newbery, was an Englishman who came north in his early thirties to work in the booming cultural environment of late nineteenth-century Glasgow. He was chief designer at Blackie's, the renowned publishing house. Howarth, almost certainly encouraged by MacNair, wrote to Alice Morris at Greenhays, Braunton, North Devon, on 25 September 1944:

You may be interested to know that I am writing a life of Charles Rennie Mackintosh, 1868–1928, the Glagow architect, and I shall be pleased if you can help me in any way. I understand that you knew him well during the early part of his career in Glasgow. Can you, by recalling incidents or conversations, assist me to enlarge my survey of his life at that time – anything related to his manner of working, his attitude to life generally and to his work in particular, his hobbies or social activities? Do you think he was influenced by his contemporaries – by your late husband; by George Walton?

I am trying to arrange for a permanent exhibition of his work, after the war, and with this in view I am anxious to trace any examples of his furniture, drawings or paintings that are in existence. I shall be glad if you will give me particulars of any such work that you still possess...

Alice Morris replied by return,

I have your letter of the 28th Sept. And am much interested to hear of your intention to write a life of Charles Rennie Mackintosh. He was a valued friend of my husband and myself and we saw a good deal of him in the early days of his career. I hope to send you some notes of impressions that remain with one and of our intercourse in those long ago days – after I have thought back. I hope they may be of some small help to you, if only by confirming the information you have. As, at the moment, I am doubly handicapped by failing sight and an accident to my reading glasses you may not hear from me again before next week.

11th October 1944. I am at long last sending a few reminiscences of my long ago intercourse with my husband's – and my – friend Charles Rennie Mackintosh. Please remember that my remarks are those of a very interested observer, not an understanding artist... We saw most of C.R.M., in our home, between the years 1899, when our friends the Macdonalds moved from Glasgow to Bowling where we were living, and 1911 when my husband died. I also visited them in their Glasgow homes, and in later years, occasionally, saw them in London. I can remember well the sadness of the last months of C.R.M.'s life, after he had been stricken with fatal illness. His courage in trying to talk with cheerfulness, and to argue, after an operation which had almost destroyed his power of articulation, is an unforgettable memory...

Left. Cover of *The Natural History of Animals* for the Gresham Publishing Company (Talwyn Morris c. 1900).

Middle and right. Book covers for Blackie and Son, Glasgow (Mackintosh c. 1922).

He was a very warm-hearted, kindly, genial man to his friends, simple in his tastes and pleased with simple things. At that time he was rather reserved – even aloof in manner – with strangers, especially of the conventional sort but warm at once towards a sympathetic mind, and sprang at once to eager defence of any workman or principle which he thought was unfairly assailed. He was a tremendous tireless talker. Talks in which he was a partaker would often go on far into the night. I cannot now recall special conversations but can give you some idea of their general tenor.

He was intensely individual and sincere. To him an artist's creative idea was the one element of absolute and eternal value in him – and in life too, I think. He constantly spoke of it, urging its tremendous importance. Another subject much on his mind was – the prevalent opinion of the time that the productions of artists from the past – their strong and beautiful work – should be looked upon as models for imitation, or reproduction, in later years. This he felt was to trammel and clog the creative spirit. He said each successive age developed its own spirit in art – and this should be encouraged to express itself with freedom – in its own way. But he revered work of the past for its historical, educational, aesthetic and moral values. I think he felt the tyranny of the 'dead land' especially in the field of architecture.

He spoke little of the then prevailing lack of understanding and appreciation of his own work by his own contemporaries, especially in his own country but I believe he felt and resented it very strongly. And the appreciation which came to him from other lands, especially Sweden but also Holland and Italy was of real comfort to him.

I do not think he was influenced much by other artists of his time. He seemed too original and individual for that – almost fiercely individual. But he was quick and generous in his appreciation of the work of others, quick also to condemn anything which seemed to him to lack beauty or rightness.

He and his wife, M.M.M. worked and thought so much together, that I have often thought that I recognised in the work of one – some impress of the spirit of the other. I am grieved to hear that so much of the work they did together in Glasgow has now disappeared.

I do not remember if C.R.M. had any hobbies beyond his work and talk *in early days… He loved out-of-doors life but took up no form of sport – perhaps on account of his slight lameness. He used to listen to music, apparently in much contentment, puffing away at his pipe meanwhile, but I do not know that he felt more than its soothing or stimulating influence. I never heard him play or sing.*

We possessed very few examples of his work – a beautiful drawing partly in colour, Part Seen, Imagined Part, *and some posters. I think that was all. These in the early days of the war I gave to the Glasgow Art Galleries, as I feared they might be destroyed in London. (My fear was justified. Most of my possessions now lie in a damaged state in a warehouse store that was bombed and burned.)*

I sent also to the Art Galleries some work of Margaret Macdonald Mackintosh, in collaboration with her sister, Frances Macdonald MacNair. This was a set of delicate watercolours, The Seasons, *set in frames of beaten aluminium — the designs of which were carved out the subjects of the pictures: I possess more of Margaret's work but it may be damaged now.*

In writing to me at that time, Dr Honeyman told me that the directors of the Art Galleries intended to open a special section for the Mackintosh work after the war. This you doubtless know.

You will also, I expect, have seen the work of C.R.M. which Mr Walter Blackie of Helensburgh possesses. He was always a strong admirer of his art: this house — the Hill House — was designed by Mackintosh — who was introduced to Mr Blackie by my husband for that purpose.

I trust these notes may be of some help to you for your book. I shall look forward to seeing it (hoping for eyes again) when it comes out. I'm sure it will be of great interest to many who would like to know C.R.M. not only as a genius but also as a lovable man, warm-hearted, brave, an intensely sincere and honest man.

Yours sincerely, Alice Talwin Morris

In May 1948 in response to new requests by Howarth, Alice Morris sent a factual record of Talwin Morris' life and career — it is another document of real historical significance ushered into the world under Howarth's wing.

Memorial design for the grave of Talwyn Morris (Mackintosh 1911). The symbolism is very Rosicrucion. The words to be inscribed on the gravestone are: *Life is greater than we concieve and Death keeper of unknown Redemptions*

Talwin Morris was born in Winchester in June 1865. He was the same age as Margaret Macdonald and three years older than Mackintosh. The Morrises are an old Quaker family but his branch of it had adopted the tenets and customs of the Anglican Church in his grandfather's time. His mother died at his birth, and his father died suddenly a few years later. In his early years he was brought up principally by a spinster sister of his father – Emily Morris – a lady of very strong Anglican feeling and of many philanthropic activities. Her desire was that he should enter the church, and he was therefore educated at Lancing and was to have gone thence to Oxford, but his own artistic and literary taste and decision of character made him refuse to continue his theological studies, so instead of going to university he was articled to his uncle, Joseph Morris, an architect (principally I think of churches) practising at Reading. I do not think he had any 'art' training beyond that given at Lancing College, which was very good. He did well with Joseph Morris, I understand, and entered in various competitions for church drawings – winning some of them as far as I remember.

At the end of his course in Joseph Morris' office he went to a firm of church architects (Martin-Brooks, I think, the name). He did not attend any of the London Art Schools. He always had a strong feeling against anything set or rigid in thought or in life. He was interested in the work of Shannon, Rickets, Aubrey Beardsley and William Blake, and in the early black and white drawings of Lawrence Housman in All Fellows *and his fairy books, also in some French artists whose names I've forgotten (one of them did* A Dance of Death*).*

Music was a major interest with him, and a good deal of his leisure time during these days in London was given to concert going. He also took up study of the cello and in time became a good player.

In 1888 he became engaged to be married and soon afterwards, as there seemed to be a slump in church building, he left the Brooks firm and took a post as a sub-art editor under M.H. Spielman of the recently started illustrated paper Black and White, *edited by C.N. Williamson. He did a great many drawings (decorative design, headings and page frames) for this paper, which later amalgamated with* The Graphic.

He was married in 1892 and we lived for a year in Field Court, Grays Inn. Early in 1893 he answered a Times *advertisement for an Art Director to a Scottish publisher (Messrs Blackie). He was chosen for the post and in May of that year we moved north to Dunglass (we did not use the magnificent word 'Castle' in our address) which my father and I had discovered on a house-hunting expedition. My husband took up his work with Messrs Blackie immediately and remained there until his death in 1911. He was never either a student or a teacher at the Glasgow School of Art, but we soon became acquainted with Fra Newbery and his wife and the Macdonald family, then living in Glasgow, and saw much of them thereafter. Mr*

Charles Macdonald (brother to Margaret and Frances), the lawyer, became my husband's closest friend. Margaret and Frances Macdonald had by then finished their studies at the Glasgow School of Art and had taken a studio in Glasgow where they were already doing a good deal of beautiful work – painting and decorative metal-work. My husband was greatly attracted by their work and by themselves, and they were equally attracted, I believe, to him and his ideas. In this way, I dare say, each influenced each to some extent, but each kept, his – or her – individuality.

My husband began to work in metal at this time to a small extent but his main work remained – as always – drawing. He did much of this for Messrs. Blackie's publications, and gained some notoriety for his book cover designs; he also did drawings for art periodicals on the Continent, and – I believe – in England, and wrote a few articles on Arts subjects.

We were frequently at the Macdonalds' studio and met there many interesting people – including, of course, Charles Rennie Mackintosh, and also the young John Buchan – then a student – and his sister, subsequently known for her literary work as 'O. Douglas'. At the Newbery house we met many of the older artists and writers of the time who happened to be in Glasgow. I mention these details merely to show you the various influences which, to some extent, must have influenced the character and work of C.R.M. and his contemporary associates.

We left Dunglass in July 1899. By this time both my husband and I were finding the work and time needed for the upkeep of a large house and garden too much to be carried on – with our increasing outside work and interests. We took a small house (Torwood) on the same estate (Auchentorlie) on the hills above Bowling, and passed Dunglass on to the Macdonald family who had for years desired to live there. We remained at Dunglass to receive the Macdonald family: we never shared the house with them, but we were in constant contact, and before his marriage to Margaret, C.R.M. frequently stayed with us at Torwood.

While living at Dunglass I do not think the Macdonald sisters did much of their artwork. Frances was soon married to Herbert MacNair and not very long afterwards C.R.M. was engaged, and then married Margaret Macdonald and both couples removed to flats in Glasgow where again Margaret did much work. Frances already had a small son and was not able to give much time to any but domestic affairs.

In reviewing impressions (set down) over these last few days I decided that the influence of Talwin Morris on the work of the Macdonald sisters and of their work on him – if it ever existed – was due to the stimulation and encouragement given by each to each in sympathy and admiration. Their work appeared to me to show essential differences. Talwin Morris's general line *always struck me as forceful and uprising: theirs seemed to me a drooping* line *expressing of understanding and resignation to the inevitability of Fate and Fact. Perhaps you*

Below and overleaf.
Four postcards sent
by Mackintosh to the
Newbery family between
1908 and 1909. Each
says a great deal about
Mackintosh and his
sensibility as an artist
and designer.
Private Collection

would say the difference is that between the virile and the feminine.

I have written far more than I expected to do when I set out — more, doubtless, than you need — but the subject is naturally of great interest to me and I believe that a long and close comradeship with similar inherited instincts, faiths and outlook (I too am of the Morris clan) enable me to show you something of the roots of my husband's work, which would, I believe, have gone on to greater results had he lived longer. 'I have done so little yet', he said to me shortly before he died.

Yours sincerely, Alice Morris

P.S. Do you know that the figure in the picture Part Seen, Imagined Part, *by C.R.M., which I sent the Glasgow Corporation Art Galleries, was that of his wife?*

6 MANCHESTER AND THE UNITED STATES

THOMAS HOWARTH

Falling Water is one of my favourite buildings and we arrived at a marvellous moment – the waterfall beneath the house was frozen and spectacular.

Although Thomas Howarth's name is so strongly linked to Mackintosh and the city of Glasgow, he only resided in Scotland for seven years from 1939 till 1946. With the war over and the bulk of his Mackintosh research completed Howarth began to find his teaching commitments in Glasgow heavy and predictable; in 1946, he accepted an invitation from Professor Cordingley to return to Manchester as a lecturer in the School of Architecture. The academic reputation of the University of Manchester was at a high point, especially in the new field of computing, and the city itself was still buoyed up by the great liberal tradition that it had espoused in the previous century. The School of Architecture provided Howarth with an exciting new situation and it wasn't long before he was promoted to senior lecturer and Cordingley's deputy. He moved into a comfortable university flat at 1 Didsbury Park and both Edna and Howarth enjoyed settling back into their Lancastrian milieu. It was to be the birthplace of their two children, John and Katharine.

From Manchester, Howarth made frequent visits to Glasgow – organising exhibitions, following up new research leads, and endeavouring to persuade various Scottish publishing houses to publish his doctoral thesis as the 'definitive book' he believed it to be. The moment, however, was far from propitious; money was scarce, paper was in short supply, popular interest in Mackintosh non-existent. Publishers did not believe such a book would sell. In addition, Howarth found himself stretched between English and Scottish stools; a letter from Howarth to the London publishers, Allen and Unwin, illustrates his frustration. Dated 20th January 1950, it reads, 'Mr Hurd indicated that the Saltire Society would be delighted to publish my work for me *in Scotland* but doubted the willingness of his committee to cooperate with an English publisher – such is the nationalist fervour of our northern neighbours at the moment...'

In the end, after four years of struggle, Routledge, Kegan and Paul agreed to publish the book and it appeared as a substantial well-illustrated hardback, in 1952. It was well-received and won important prizes in America, but it was to be another generation before the book's importance and classic status was widely recognised.

In 1953 Howarth organised the first major exhibition of Mackintosh's work – for the Edinburgh International Festival. It was housed at Inverleith House in Edinburgh's Botanical Gardens and proved to be a huge success, later moving south to several venues in England. Howarth got his students to build models of various of Mackintosh's unbuilt designs and his own collection provided a significant proportion of exhibits. It was the combined impact of this exhibition and the publication of Howarth's book that set the Mackintosh bandwagon slowly rolling.

With the publication of *Mackintosh and the Modern Movement*, Howarth acquired 'scholastic capital' and he was delighted to begin to seriously plan his long-term career. He had three basic choices: one, to pursue scholastic research and architectural history and forsake design practice for academia; two, to join a major architectural firm and become a working architect like his mentor George Grenfell Baines; or three, to climb the university ladder as a teacher of architecture and an administrator. Ideally, he would like to have combined all three but, at that moment, with his customary self-awareness and realism, Howarth chose the safe option and decided to make his career in university teaching. He loved architecture but he knew his intellect was stronger than his creative instinct: he never felt impelled to be an artist like Mackintosh, his compulsion was to enquire, measure, analyse, interpret and make aesthetic judgements *about* art and architecture. In addition, Howarth was a natural teacher. He enjoyed teaching and was determined to become a systematic and efficient administrator. He understood that his creativity was best employed in the nurturing of others and in the revelation of genius.

Howarth's decision to commit himself to university teaching was, historically, timely. With the institutionalisation of architectural education within higher educational structures there was a greatly increased need for historians, theorists, technical specialists and administrators – and Howarth was perfectly prepared for the new situation. Before the Second World War, architectural education was essentially a practical subject, but after the war the history of architecture, and the history and theory of art began to become hugely important both as independent subjects and as subjects relevant to the practice of architecture. Post Modernism was to later arrive very much as a consequence of the teaching of these historians.

As early as the late 1940s, various of Howarth's letters, notably to Edgar Kauffman in New York and to Moyes in Australia, show that he was already searching out lecturing opportunities in the 'colonies' and the United States. His vision of a new architecture was a personal quest; but his desire for a new life in a 'new world' was nurtured by his medical problems. His physical health had improved with maturity, financial independence and marriage, but he still had chronic chest problems which he knew would be aggravated if he stayed in Britain. Each winter he suffered debilitating asthma attacks, made worse by

Thomas Howarth (back centre) with staff at the Manchester School of Architecture (1947).

the cold, wet, polluted atmospheres of Glasgow and Manchester. He knew emigration would be a wrench but felt a strong need to shape his future somewhere far from industrialised west Britain. He was interviewed for a post at the University of Hull. When he learned that Jessie Newbery was selling her home at Corfe Castle, Howarth enquired about buying it as a retirement home for his mother and a base for himself in southern England. Only the big discrepancy in house prices between the north and south deterred him. After that, he quietly immersed himself in work whilst he awaited 'opportunities – or for destiny to show its hand'. Several students report on how much he enjoy playing the martinet as 'over-master' of the first-year students. He was to become inordinately proud of the work produced by several of Manchester's outstanding young designers, particularly his prodigy Norman Foster. One girl student remembers how close she and Howarth became and how, during a study trip to York, he 'almost' decided that they should run away together. Back in Manchester, Howarth delighted in his enduring closeness to Professor Cordingley:

> He was my mentor and my friend and, without question, one of the main influences on my life. Most evenings we shared a bus stop and talked about ideas and the future as we battled with the inhuman climate of that great metropolis. Cordingley always dressed in an old raincoat and a very large hat which was famous amongst his students; a peculiar pork-pie hat with a large brim – partially detaching itself from the crown. Young and old needed hats because, at that time, Manchester was plagued every winter by dense, acrid fog and extraordinary levels of atmospheric pollution. Domestic heating was by open coal fires and we used to estimate the number of inhabited rooms in a building by counting the chimney pots,

smoking, on the roof. Fog, in the countryside, is white and relatively bright, but it turns yellow, dark and poisonous in cramped urban and industrial spaces. To make one's way home in such conditions was a genuine and depressing struggle – it burnt my lungs, made heavy my legs, and inhibited clear thinking. I remember the day Princess Margaret came to the city, one July. The day dawned fresh and clear but at about ten o'clock the sky darkened and turned almost black. Cars had to use headlights, the street lamps were switched on; it was like an eclipse of the sun – or the hours that followed the crucifixion. In the centre of Manchester we had no means of knowing whether the birds stopped singing but it was an event that left one appalled – the thought of what we were doing to ourselves suddenly struck home. Things have now hugely improved but such events encouraged further my plans for emigration.

We lived at 1 Didsbury Park. It was a dignified semi-detached brick

First-year students of Architecture at Manchester University (1948).
Thomas Howarth

house of Edwardian vintage with a large garden, mature raspberry canes and an aged pear tree. The adjacent house was owned by Mr and Mrs Armitage. Mrs Armitage being the distinguished art historian, Margaret Bulley. At that time she was deeply involved in writing *The Seeing Eye*. Her husband, Geoffrey Armitage, was a man of some wealth, his family having close connections with Armitage and Rigby, one of the companies that had dominated the Lancashire cotton industry at the turn of the century. The Armitages had no children. Their house was large and served by a cook and a daily maid. We were frequent visitors to the house and royally entertained – as were numerous immigrants and refugees from all over Europe. One young man I got to know there was a very bright teenager called John Polanyi; his parents had recently escaped from Hungary. We became friends and many years later, we found ourselves teaching at the same university in Canada and, on one occasion, sharing adjacent rooms

A typical page from Margaret Bulley's book *Art and Understanding*, showing her approach to 'comparative analysis' and 'good taste' across time and space.

Left. Wells Cathedral and Market Place

Below left. Augsburg, Almshouses, 1519.

Below right. Backyards, Stuttgart, 1920.

in a hospital recovering from the same surgical operation! He was at that time a renowned research chemist and, a little later, won the Nobel Prize for Chemistry. He reminisced about our days in Manchester and how Margaret Bulley had used him as one of the 'guinea pigs' she needed for her research into taste and perception. She had used me, I told him, as both a guinea pig and a consultant! Perhaps it was she who first excited Polanyi about the possibilities of 'research'.

Margaret Bulley's aim was to show that everyone, educated or uneducated, has an inborn ability to distinguish what, she believed, were 'true' works of art from 'counterfeit' works. Most of her books explore that one basic idea in different ways. She set out to prove her theory by publishing pairs of photographs – of paintings, sculptures, pots, buildings – and showing that everybody could be trained to distinguish the 'true' from the 'false'. She believed in 'the judgement' of the human eye. Her thinking owed something to Gestalt theory but she was not a scientist, she liked to be provocative and relied heavily on subjective responses. She had close contacts with the Bloomsbury group and knew many leading figures associated with contemporary English art – Duncan Grant, Roger Fry, Sir Herbert Read. Working for the B.B.C., she became a friend of Cyril Burt – the now discredited authority on heredity and the behaviour of twins. Her work, like his, has now become suspect but she, undoubtedly, helped educate my eye and sharpen my awareness as a critic of the visual arts. She encouraged me. She publicly challenged me to get my book on Mackintosh published before her *The Seeing Eye* rolled off the press. She would appear on our doorstep, at 8 o'clock in the morning, with new sets of paired photographs – wanting answers: 'Dr Howarth' she would say, 'I know you're rushing off to the university, but please – first tell me – which of these photos is the good one, and why you think so.' And often enough she would be back in the evening to argue the toss about 'truth' and the 'quality' of this, that and the other. Her taste was very catholic, ranging from Child Art to the most sophisticated products from China and Italy.

Over the years our two families became quite close. Margaret was always kind and gracious. She wore long, floral Edwardian dresses and superb but unpretentious jewellery – I remember a long necklace with exquisite unmatched pearls of various shapes and sizes and I have, subsequently, never enjoyed cultured, or matched pearls, since she showed me those wonderful products of wild nature. Her husband, Geoffrey, was always formal – always dressed in a dark, waistcoated suit – always polite and very genteel. He seemed to watch his wife's activities with a bemused affection. At dinner he always officiated, ceremonially, with the wine – like a cup-bearer – and he, very formally, carved the roast with marvellous skill. Whenever art was discussed, however, he quietly and unobtrusively withdrew to his study – only reappearing to say good night to his guests. It was the same kind of 'withdrawal from chatter' that MacNair would make in conversation and in letters.

Howarth found within the Armitage house an ambience very like that which, he assumed, had existed in the Mackintosh house and which he found in the Newberys. All three households had 'Rosicrucian qualities', and Geoffrey Armitage's silence on all matters of art can be quite precisely related to Rosicrucian codes of secrecy and the stylised mysticism practiced, for example, by the Yeats brothers in Ireland. After painting his *Roman de la Rose* in 1936, Jack Yeats decided never again to explain his art or its symbolism and glorified in the phenomenon of 'the passing world'. He would not reduce the irreducible; he recognised that, 'one can plan an event but if it turns out as planned – it won't be an event.' And, in his *Memoirs*, Howarth contrasts the elegant, cultural society of the Armitage house with the punctilious goings on in his own, immediate vicinity.

The other two apartments in No.1 Didsbury Park were inhabited by other university couples. We had mathematicians, the Camms, on the floor above us, and on the top floor, two social scientists, the McLeans and their only child. Much to our surprise, very considerable tensions would rise between these two families over the most mundane of issues – such as the harvesting of the raspberry crop and the picking and distribution of the large quantity of pears our 'shared' pear tree produced each year. Even Edna and I were drawn into the melees! At the time I thought such trivia were a product of the intellectual gulf that separated those who work in the sciences and those who work in the more varied fields of the arts and architecture – but, after a lifetime in art education, I now don't believe it!

Thankfully, in 1954, with Cordingley's strong support, I won a Rockefeller Travel Grant to study architectural education and practice in the United States. In the July of the following year, we crossed the Atlantic *en famille*, and set off on a 17,000-mile tour that was to prove the most memorable adventure of my life. In retrospect it seems we just packed our bags and took off – sailing from Liverpool to Montreal, one of the classic emigrant routes. But, in reality, I planned the itinerary carefully so that we could follow the sun and enjoy the best of the weather from Canada to Mexico – meeting all the best architects and visiting all the important schools en route. Edna took responsibility for all domestic arrangements – settling our affairs in Manchester, selecting, sorting and packing the many things we had to take, and ensuring the safety of those we left at home.

With her usual quiet competence, she did a faultless job. I only packed my 'Mackintosh Museum'.

We sailed on the Cunarder *Saxonia*, and soon ran into the tail of a hurricane. All of us were sick and a lot of damage was done to the vessel. On arrival we took accommodation in the Railway Hotel, Montreal and I, immediately, started work with a visit to McGill University, which had a very good school of architecture. The Head of School was John Bland; we got on well and established a friendship that was to last for many years. However, it was Orson Wheeler, who had come by car to pick me up at the Railway Hotel, who most stimulated my thinking. He was an artist and member of Bland's staff who had taken it upon himself to make scale models of most of 'the great buildings of the world' – the Parthenon, various of the Romanesque and Gothic cathedrals, St Peter's in Rome, St Paul's in London. These models were made in a plaster that had the plasticity of plasticine and which was capable of producing remarkable detail. The educational and historical importance of what he was doing was crucially enhanced by the fact that all models were made to the same scale and included significant aspects of the local environment. Thus, his model of the Parthenon included the whole Acropolis and the viewer was made very aware of the whole complex of buildings – the spaces between them and their scale in relation to the promontory on which they all stand… Placed amongst his other models it, suddenly, amazed me to see that, volumetrically, the Athenian mountain was about the same size as St Peter's in Rome! It was an astonishing revelation! I had always been interested in model-making – as a student, as an architect, and as a teacher – now Orson Wheeler reinforced every aspect of my prejudice. We spent a long time discussing his creations and their potential uses in architectural education – as well as the wider importance of model-making re educating the public, clients, city-planners etc.

The School of Architecture at the Massachusetts Institute of Technology was run by the distinguished American architect, Pietro Belluschi. Because I was staying sometime, I was given an office which I shared with a brilliant young architect, Marvin Goodie. He was working on the design of a prefabricated house – to be built entirely of plastic. His research was supported by the Monsanto Company of the United States, now deeply committed to the development of genetically modified foods. Goodie believed his design could help resolve the problem of the worldwide shortage of good, low-cost housing. His design was an ingenious T-shaped building – the living and sleeping areas being raised above a central column which contained all the services. It was certainly futuristic. Unfortunately, it seems not to have got beyond its prototype stage – as an exhibit at Disneyland in California – a rather ignominious end to a genuinely pioneering project.

Marvin Goodie's work was of special interest to me because beside the lectures I gave on Mackintosh, at each of the universities I visited, I also lectured on 'Low Cost Housing and School Design in England'. I had an interesting collection of slides of the most appalling slums, and nineteenth-century row houses – and the New Town developments with which both were being replaced. At that time, local authorities across Britain, were knocking down slums and row houses with equal abandon. I believed this to be wrong and, both at home and abroad, I pointed out the good qualities of certain aspects of nineteenth-century urban housing. It had become fashionable to condemn all aspects of our Victorian heritage; the combination of industrial decay and war damage had given local councillors, planners and architects, *carte blanche* to demolish great swathes of inner city areas – and they were doing great damage. The idea was, 'everything must go!' The theory was that new buildings on new estates would provide citizens with sound, pleasant and hygienic environments – worthy of a new, socialist society. The great drive was for quantity, not quality. The vision was political and sociological, not architectural or cultural, and tight financial restrictions meant that 'ideal' new estates ended up, within a very few years, as inhuman, concrete jungles. Perhaps, some deep psychological antipathy towards the 'lower orders' ensured that what was provided was aesthetically and socially unpleasant. But I'm proud to say that, I believe, I was the first British architect to show America the best of Britain's new, post-war, domestic architecture.

Tradition and experience are frequently better guides to what is humanly sustainable than the ideological plantation of new solutions – final or otherwise. For example, there were real merits in the old row houses of Manchester and the great tenements of Glasgow and I pointed out this, now fashionable theory, at M.I.T., in 1955. With various groups of my Manchester students I had made detailed studies of the humble brick row houses that surrounded the university, and we were pleasantly surprised to find that most of them, on a very small scale, made use of the same formal elements, the same layouts as those used in many of the great houses of the past. Some were only fourteen feet wide but they had a front door, a cellar, a *piano nobile*, several bedrooms, and even attic quarters in the roof. They were tiny compact houses of three storeys, but the better quality ones had beautifully proportioned windows with handmade glass, some had elegant fanlights above the front doors... Today, almost fifty years later, the remnants of these houses are being restored and many new houses are being built along similar lines.

As a counter to the unsatisfactory nature of most British post-war housing developments I was pleased to commend the new architectural thinking that was transforming Britain's schools. The best of these new schools, largely centred on the Home Counties around London, were becoming internationally famous. They were part of a 'new' educational philosophy and were beautifully designed – well-lit, clean, functional. One innovation that appealed to me was the integral provision of art works. Money for 'art' was included as part of the building contract. The art of this post-war period has become unfashionable but numerous excellent artists, working closely with architects, produced deeply humanist and significant works – they included Henry Moore, Barbara Hepworth, Victor Pasmore, F.E. McWilliam. Before setting off for America I toured the best of these schools and took a large number of slides that provided the basis of informative and interesting lectures. Unfortunately, over the longer term, ignorant committees and lesser artists did not deliver what we, with our youthful idealism, had hoped for. And in the sixties the nation's attention moved from schools to universities – new universities sprang up in Norwich, Colchester, Warwick, York, Lancaster, Stirling... All these reaped the benefits of the earlier experiments in the Hertfordshire schools, but perhaps only the University of East Anglia did all it might for the arts.

At the University of Harvard I lectured not just to undergraduate and postgraduate students, but also to senior staff in the School of Architecture. This was to prove the pattern right across America. Jose Sert was head of the school; Jacqueline Tyrwhitt was there as a visiting critic; and Welles Coates, a Canadian architect who had made a major reputation in England. Since my student days I had been interested in the use of tiles, faïence and mosaics in contemporary architecture – and Welles Coates was a designer who had made outstanding use of them. Thus, I was pleased when he came up to me and warmly congratulated me on my lecture. As he did so I remembered something unsavoury about him. A few years previously I had won an R.I.B.A. fellowship to study the use of tiles in European architecture and Welles Coates was one of several architects from whom I sought information! All had been helpful but for the man now standing before me – Mr Welles Coates! He had sent me the curtest of notes telling me that, he thought, my time and the R.I.B.A's money was being wasted! And he wasn't going to waste his! So, I reminded him of our correspondence and I told him that such letters were disconcerting to a young researcher. He more or less apologised, but said he had no recollection of the correspondence. If I had been Mackintosh, I would have told him that I had travelled to America to find him – and root out his abominable hubris!

Altogether, however, I felt highly privileged to be associated with one of the world's leading universities at a vital time in its history and I was pleasantly surprised to find that the quality of work by graduating classes at Harvard and M.I.T. was no better than that of similar students at the University of Manchester. There was the same proportion of excellent, good, average, and poor performers. But, one thing I would not have got in Manchester were personal introductions to Walter Gropius and Mies van der Rohe, both then resident in Boston.

My meeting with Gropius was memorable. We spoke at length about Mackintosh, about the early days of the Bauhaus in Germany, about emerging trends in Modern Architecture and contemporary architectural education. For Gropius, however, Mackintosh was neither a personal contemporary, nor a clearly defined historical figure. It was a moving experience to speak with this hugely influential modern architect but I gained no new architectural insights and it soon became apparent that most of what Gropius knew of Mackintosh had been gathered, second-hand from Nikolaus Pevsner, whom Gropius knew well, because he had been the central character in Pevsner's original PhD thesis, *Pioneers of the Modern Movement from William Morris to Walter Gropius*, submitted in Berlin around 1930.

From Boston we went south to New Haven, Connecticut where I met a younger master of the Modern movement, Mr Philip Johnson. We had a relaxed and enjoyable lunch in his famous 'glass house'. One of the issues I raised with him was the question of privacy. What do you do in a glasshouse at night? Was there a security problem? The property *was* relatively isolated but Johnson moved the argument sideward by telling me how *he* had been irritated, on first moving into the property, by a light on the other side of valley which disrupted his contemplation of the night's darkness. He decided to investigate the source of this light. It came from a lamp hanging in the porch of an elderly lady. He persuaded her to extinguish it so that it wouldn't trouble him any further. Having asserted this, he went on to inform me that he had illuminated the exterior of his house in such a way that all lights pointed away from the building, thus making it difficult for intruders on his property to see what was going on inside the house. There was some logic in this but a lot of questions remained unanswered. For example, what did the old lady across the valley

The entrance to Falling
Water, Pennsylvania
(Frank Lloyd Wright 1939).

think of his lights interrupting her night-time contemplation of the stars? As a guest, however, I felt unable to press my points too far, or ask to stay on till after nightfall. But – Mr Johnson was a charming host. He had invited me to bring Edna and the children, and he gave them free range to play in the house and the gardens. We talked about education, about new developments in architecture and I came away having had a truly memorable afternoon. Like a Mackintosh chair, his house was a poetical statement – an exploration of beauty and possibilities – not a purely functional or utilitarian object.

Another important connection I made at Yale University was Vincent Scully. He was then a young architectural historian, absolutely dedicated to his subject; today he is widely recognised as pre-eminent in his field. I arrived at his office just before he was due to give a lecture. I asked if I could attend. He said he would be pleased and I was ushered to a seat in the front row. He was a delightful man and as a lecturer he could hardly contain his enthusiasm, marching up and down the lecture room, sweeping his pointer to right and left. It is a style that always goes down well with students and, like them, I was swept along by the fluency of his rhetoric. Suddenly, he stopped and looked towards a door that had been left open. A dog appeared, and trotted across the aisle, mounted the podium steps, walked slowly to the middle of the platform, stopped briefly to survey the assembled audience, then trotted off whence it came – to thunderous applause and hilarious laughter. Scully's lectures were often so intense as

to demand release of this kind but as to whether he got the dog to perform in each week I forgot to ask.

Over many years we remained recurrently acquainted and, in the 1980s, when he was recommended as a candidate for the Gold Medal of the R.I.B.A. in London, I was one of those asked to write a recommendation. This I did with pleasure, and he was subsequently awarded this distinction.

I had long been a friend of Edgar Kaufmann Jr, in his role as a curator at the Museum of Modern Art in New York and from New Haven we travelled to Pittsburgh to see Frank Lloyd Wright's famous house at Falling Water, designed for Kaufmann's father. Edgar was there to meet us. Falling Water is one of my favourite buildings and we arrived at a marvellous moment – the waterfall beneath the house was frozen and spectacular. Great stalactites of ice shone in the sun, whilst small trickles of water tinkled like jewels. Here was that 'frozen music' Madame de Stael and George Grenfell Baines had talked about all those years before – here was sublime architecture at one with nature. It was January and the leaves from the surrounding trees had long since fallen so we could see the entire building quite clearly. In summer it is largely obscured by foliage and although this can add mystery and a gentleness to the building – we arrived at a revelatory moment.

First Edgar offered us lunch, and we sat down to find ourselves being waited on by a very dour, very tall servant – a Charles Adams figure who unnerved the children. Conversation was constrained but the meal was good and Edgar a solicitous host. We talked of the relationship between Mackintosh and Wright and the Celtic contribution to Modern architecture. For three millennia 'Celtic' architecture was a minor force in world architecture but, in the late nineteenth and early twentieth centuries Celtic imagination – personified by Mackintosh and Wright – suddenly made a profound impact and must now be accepted as a fundamental component of International Modernism. Abstraction, rhythm, sensibility, austerity of form, endurance in the face of nature – these are some of its characteristics. After lunch, Edgar took us on a conducted tour of the house. I was most impressed by the wonderful living space cantilevered over the falls, and Wright's use of materials – especially natural stone and reinforced concrete. A face to face meeting with Frank Lloyd Wright had been one of the high priorities I had set myself in planning the itinerary of my tour – having embraced his genius at Falling Water, I felt properly prepared to meet the great man.

At Princeton, by chance, I met two outstanding men: Buckminster

Fuller, inventor of the geodesic dome and the brilliant Italian architect, Peresutti. Fuller was there to supervise the thesis design of one of the fifth year students who was designing a 'new stadium' for the New York Yankees, the American football team. As far as I remember, Fuller got so excited by the project that with some help from the students, he designed an enormous geodesic dome that enclosed the whole stadium and the football field within it. Models were built and the whole thing costed and presented to the New York Yankees as a serious proposal for real development! Politicians got involved and the project seemed about to be realised but – just as suddenly as the scheme was invented – it collapsed. That kind of initiative and go-getting was typical of America and it was a genuine eye-opener to me. It showed me how much we, in Britain, needed to open up, including myself. Fuller and I became close friends. He gave me a drawing which I have now sent on to the R.I.B.A. in London.

Peresutti was a visiting lecturer and he confirmed my faith in the educational importance of student 'site visits' – the stimulation of mind by physical displacement. Coming from Italy, with its thousands of archaeological and architectural sites, Peresutti knew the value of on-site experience and at Princeton he set his students the task of designing an archaeological museum for Chinchinitza in Mexico. He informed the Dean of Architecture that the students would need to visit the site, if they were to approach their task intelligently and, in no time, the funds were in place – gifted by the local architectural profession. A class of twenty to thirty students then upped-sticks and went down to Mexico. I had been taking my Manchester students to York, a distance of about eighty miles – this was like setting off for Sicily! It was obvious when the group returned two weeks later that the students were not only precisely prepared to design their museum but refreshed and enthusiastic. They were actually in love with the course they were on – and the possibilities of architecture! Later in Toronto, field camps and far-flung visits became vital components of my own students' courses.

Another innovator I met at this time was Paul Rudolph, then emerging as a significant new figure in American architecture. He had a studio office in Florida but he enjoyed lecturing and he travelled around North America trying to establish his 'voice' in the architectural profession. He was keen to explore the architectural use of paper, cardboard and, most importantly, plywood. The climate and architectural demands he encountered in Florida had stimulated his thinking and when I visited his studio I was greatly impressed by his use of preformed plywood as a roofing material. He was a habitual experimenter. Many years later I was invited to the opening of the new School of Architecture building at Yale, which he had designed. As usual he had made experimental use of materials and the best apartment was the guest bedroom on the top floor of the building! It was beautifully furnished to Rudolph's own designs, with splendid views from windows – which went right down to the floor – dangerous – but very attractive. The building as a whole was a powerful massing of reinforced concrete, finished by hammered and chiselled surface striations that gave the exterior a rugged, almost barbaric appearance. The use of space was splendid but, as time passed, the students found the permanent hard greyness of the concrete unsympathetic, aesthetically. To brush your hand against the walls was to skin your knuckles for a fortnight. Eventually the building became very unpopular with those for whom it was designed. It was an experiment that did not work. During the years of student protest it was deliberately set on fire and very badly damaged. C'est la vie.

Travelling south to Florida, as the spring gathered pace, we stayed with my brother who had married an American and established a successful practice there as a neurosurgeon. Now, slowly coming to terms with the vastness of America, and adapting to the American way of life, we bought a Dodge station wagon for 500 dollars. It was 3 years old, heavy, low-powered, had a top speed of 55 miles-per-hour, and tended to stall going up hill – but it was capacious and was to safely carry us 17,000 miles in luxurious, suspended animation. It had a bench seat at the front as well as

Left. John Howarth (1956) at Taliesin West.
Thomas Howarth

Right. Sculpture at Taliesin West (Frank Lloyd Wright).
Thomas Howarth

The studios of Frank Lloyd
Wright at Taliesin West,
Thomas Howarth

the back and, for most of the tour, all four of us sat on the front seat, cruising along highways like trucksters. It was exhilarating. The children studied books they had brought from school. They did their homework as I drove. Katharine would recite her tables and Edna would run John through the rudiments of grammar. Poems would be read and discussed whilst the geography of the United States was studied out of the window. Like me, John and Katharine were instinctive collectors, and the back of the Dodge gradually filled up with boxes of drawings, butterflies, snakeskins and tree-barks – found objects of every description. We had two air-mattresses for the children to sleep on when tired. They stretched out above two layers of luggage and my precious Mackintosh collection! Overnight we stopped in various hotels and motels and boarding houses – marrying the Old World and the New. Looking back it is difficult to exaggerate the pleasure we experienced. It was a different world. The world of James Dean and Marilyn Monroe. A world of the open road and endless possibilities. We crossed and recrossed the Wild West with hardly a thought of crime, or insurance, or deranged hitchhikers. There we were in a station wagon, with two young children and a precious collection of original works by one of the Europe's great artists – and not a care in the world! It was the New World at one of its prime moments. Nothing serious went wrong during those 17,000 miles – my own education advanced as fast as that of the children – it came at us – like a warm breeze off the desert.

The Deep South fascinated us; the wonderfully rich accents of the people, their kindness, the spicy heat of the food, the red landscape of Georgia. Two schools of architecture particularly impressed me: South Carolina where Harlan McClure was head; and the school at Raleigh in North Carolina, directed by Henry Kamphorfer. Whilst I was there, the young Argentinean, Eduardo Catalano was *in situ*, developing the hyperbolic parabaloid as an important structural element. He had already used this complex geometric form for the roof of his own house. It had an eighty-foot span and a beautiful saddle-like form, of timber. The house appeared out of a forest clearing and was quite spectacular – the hyperbolic paraboloid anchored by concrete slabs at the two points where the roof descended to the ground. It was covered in a white plastic membrane and sat like some alien visitor from a science fiction movie – splendid amidst the trees. Catalano later moved to M.I.T. where he designed several impressive buildings before fading into obscurity – but I was deeply impressed by him as an architect, as an educator, and as a man. He was one of several young architects whom Kamphorfer 'discovered', only to see them 'seduced' away to the Ivy League schools where they frequently failed to find patronage, or ideological support, equal to his own. In a way it was the old story of Fra Newbery and Mackintosh. The best students, like dogs, find it difficult to love more than one master and lucky is the genius loved by more than one patron!

At the University of Berkeley we found accommodation in a cheap Oakland motel and I hurried off for my meeting with William Wurster, Dean of the School of Architecture and a Mr Allen, whose wife was Scottish and very interested in my work on Mackintosh. We got on very well with the Allens. They were embarrassed by our humble accommodation and, immediately, offered us a cottage he had designed at Carmel,

Student residence at Taliesin West. (Frank Lloyd Wright). *Thomas Howarth*

Left. The Walker House,
Carmel, California
(Frank Lloyd Wright 1948).
Thomas Howarth

Right. View from the
Walker House.
Thomas Howarth

a renowned West Coast beauty spot. The cottage was very close to the beach and we stayed for five weeks. It was another unforgettable 'extended moment' in our lives – not least because the cottage had been designed around a great tree, the trunk of which came in through the bedroom and out through the roof! Ants and other small insects made similar exits and entrances and you needed to watch where and how you sat down but the tree-cottage was exciting and Carmel was beautiful – the sands so white; the sea otters playing in the surf. We watched them cracking shells open on their chests with stones held in their paws. The water was too cold for comfortable bathing but for five weeks we tasted Paradise. I would rise in the morning and look across to the promontory on which Frank Lloyd Wright had recently built the Walker House. It stretched out along the rocks like a great chameleon. It had a blue-grey tiled roof – not normal tiles – they were made of enamelled steel and made to last, Wright hoped, forever. I made contact with the owners and they kindly showed us round. The house was surprisingly small but entirely suited to the needs of the occupants and superbly part of the ground on which it stood. The plan of the house was rather like a boat, with its prow pointing out to sea. Perhaps it is one of the buildings that helped inspire Miralles' design for Scotland's new parliament – whatever, it perfectly matches its site, looking out over that great ocean I remember thinking of Keats:

> Then felt I like some watcher of the skies
>> When a new planet swims into his ken;
> Or like stout Cortès when with eagle eyes
>> He stared at the Pacific – and all his men
> Looked at each other with a wild surmise –
>> Silent, upon a peak in Darien.

Two things impressed me at Berkeley: first, the department of architecture was part of a school of environmental studies; and second, a lecture given by Mies van der Rohe, one of my heroes. Fifty years ago, the idea of 'environmental studies' was anathema to most architects and to university senates, but it seemed to me then, and it seems to me now, that schools of environmental are the obvious and best frameworks within which architecture should be taught. Architecture exists in its human, social and environmental context or it is nothing. Thus, I felt that Berkeley was showing a lead in architectural education, as it was in so many other fields and later, when I became a professor in Toronto, I tried to get the university to adopt the Berkeley practice and, in the longer term, I succeeded.

Bill Wurster epitomised American informality but he was a teacher brilliantly in control of his school, a highly respected practising architect and a stimulating educational thinker. Mies van der Rohe was just one of dozens of distinguished visiting speakers whom Wurster invited to Berkeley and I have total recall of the seminar he gave Mies in 'The Ark', the old timber-framed building that then dominated the school. The weather was perfect and I can see him in that handsome courtyard, surrounded by admiring students and most of the staff. I was introduced and I reminded him of the letter he had written me, ten years earlier, about Mackintosh and his influence on the Modern movement. The acclamation he received was very moving, and I remember thinking what a shame it was that Mackintosh, in his maturity, was never invited to speak to similar groups of students or be lifted by such recognition in his lifetime. For six weeks, at the age of thirty-four he was lauded in Vienna, but in public, after that – nothing, or next to.

Whilst ensconced in our tree-house at Carmel I was invited to attend the annual convention of the American Institute of Architects, in Los Angeles. It was an overwhelming event – so many papers on so many subjects! Concentration was difficult, focus impossible, and no specific theme was followed through to, what I considered, a satisfactory conclusion. The convention was, however, a grand meeting place, and it introduced me to an important American innovation – the working breakfast, something unknown in the Britain of the fifties. One breakfast stint I found particularly useful tackled issues related to the preservation of historic buildings. I made points and asked questions and was, later, approached by a white-haired gentleman called Allan Siple. He was involved in conservation in the United States but, as a great Anglophile, was very interested in how we, with our much older and richer tradition, were approaching this huge subject in Britain. He invited me to his home in Mandeville Canyon, north of Los Angeles and a productive working friendship began.

I was also delighted to meet Charles Eames. I had long admired his work as a designer – his extraordinary fibreglass and steel furniture, his glass and steel house at Santa Monica – but I found his conference performance a great disappointment. He was a member of a panel that meandered around various confused issues in a very confused manner. I honestly didn't understand what they were talking about and afterwards I told him my problem. He might have dismissed me as a pretentious English academic but he didn't, he was charming, and immediately invited me out to his house in Pacific Palisades. Some days later I arrived for dinner and was introduced to his wife and design partner Ray Eames. I was shown my bed – in the guest room – part of a balcony that overlooked his studio. He showed me round and there, on the walls, were the original drawings for his swivel chair and ottoman – now, frequently, described as the most comfortable chair ever designed. It had just gone into commercial production and was being acclaimed by critics and the international architectural press. He spoke about its inception and development and showed me various new work he had in progress. We had dinner. Afterwards he spoke with great enthusiasm about his latest interest – making movies! We then watched his new film *Baroque Churches* and spent the night discussing it. He had filmed and photographed many of Europe's great baroque churches, then combined these 'moving images' with filmed still photographs – all to the accompaniment of the dramatic and magical music of Johann Sebastian Bach, played on the organ. There was also commentary. I told Charles that I played the organ myself, that I loved the music, but whilst the magnificent imagery we had seen and the great music we had heard were both marvellous – in combination I found them very unsatisfactory. Maybe it was my puritanical English nature but I told him I liked to listen to music and see the pictures as separate experiences. He seemed happy to let everything rip. I told him I liked the order and clarity he put into chairs but thought his film-experiment needed more of both! We argued, and got on very well.

Eames was an artist of overflowing energies and, as the evening went on, he brought out film after film. He had made many notable documentaries – all were short, ingeniously worked out, and beautifully photographed. I remember especially *The Day of the Dead*, a record of the well-known Mexican rituals conducted in celebration of deceased relatives. I also discovered that Eames, like me, was an inveterate collector.

He had assembled a tremendous collection of toys from different cultures all over the world. Prime amongst these was a large number of trains – and we then discussed the film he was currently engaged upon, *Toy Trains*. Each train was to be given a different personality – like our *Thomas the Tank Engine!* He enjoyed making things work – rather as Alexander Calder worked his famous sculptured circus. When I showed Ray Eames a large piece of Mackintosh silk, printed in the Mackintosh black and white check, she asked if she could make a small cushion; so the cloth was divided and now 'Mackintosh' resides both in the Eames' house in California and here in my apartment. Charles was a truly creative man and he later became a regular visitor to my students in Toronto. He was a great teacher. His aim, and my aim, was to stimulate thought and creativity but his starting points were usually more radical than mine. In one of his films, called *The Powers of Ten*, he photographed, from a vertical position, two people lying on a rug in a Chicago garden; then he raised the camera ten times the original distance and photographed the same subject – again, and again and again... The figures soon become indistinguishable from the garden – then the garden is lost in the city, then the city is lost in the continent of North America, which then becomes a segment of the earth seen from space, until, finally, the world becomes one of millions of stars in the Milky Way... Today, in an age of digital television, space travel, computer graphics and every kind of virtual reality, Eames' film may seem small beer, but Eames was a true originator and his work was not so much clever as philosophical. Once he had transported his audience out into the universe he rapidly reversed the movement of the camera and zoomed back in onto the couple in the garden, on their rug. Then, he zoomed closer still, onto the hand of the man, and over his skin, closer and closer until his pores filled the screen and once more we seemed to enter boundless space... It was a film that could raise 10,000 thoughts and ideas – about measure and perspective and proportion – numerical calculation and poetical dreams – Oscar Kokoscar's great painting of cosmic lovers – impermanence and timelessness.

Both Charles and Ray Eames were interested in my Mackintosh research and keen to see the Mackintosh collection I had brought with me. They suggested I mount a small exhibition and give an accompanying 'private' lecture. He told me he knew an Englishman, called Huntsman Trout, who would be delighted to host the exhibition and lecture. Trout had a grand house with spectacular gardens in Mandeville Canyon, beautifully landscaped with scarlet hibiscus and bougainvillea cascading everywhere, and, very appropriately, the house had a large living space with a black boot-polished floor – for my exhibition! This fact stimulated me to relate how Mackintosh had, especially, ordered a black ceiling for Walter Blackie's sitting room in the Hill House, Helensburgh. Thus it was with pleasure and anticipation that I set up my exhibition. All the free-standing artefacts were placed on the black floor. The mounted drawings were hung on the walls or rested on the windowsills. The cutlery and Cranston china, I set out on small tables, and other things were given chairs.

Evening arrived, a large, elegant audience gathered, champagne was served by beautiful waiters. The weather was glorious, the garden perfect. To my surprise Mr Huntsman Trout suddenly announced that my lecture would be preceded by a live programme of eighteenth-century music played on a harpsichord and flute. It was beautiful and provided a perfect introduction to me and my talk on 'The Art of Charles Rennie Mackintosh'. The evening was a great success. One of the most memorable of my life. This was life – this was culture of the kind that Margaret Macdonald had given her life to nurture. Afterwards, my only regret was that Richard Neutra, in his own way a pioneer like Mackintosh, was not there to savour the delights of the evening. He was to have been one of the special guests but illness prevented his attendance. 'Ah – in the very temple of delight/veiled melancholy has her sovereign shrine!'

Driving me back, next day, towards Carmel, Allan Siple took me to see the Greene brothers' Thorson House, a splendid building with excellent interior wood and stained glass. These architects had practised at the turn of the century and originated what became known as the Bay Region Style. They mainly built timber houses with high-pitched shingle roofs and wide overhangs. They were influenced by the British Arts and Crafts tradition, particularly through *The Studio*, launched in London in 1893. An American edition followed in 1896. Thus it seems probable that the Greenes were aware of The Glasgow Four and their British contemporaries. This gave me a special reason for wanting to view and study their work – then little known outside California. Because of the danger of earthquakes in the Bay region the Greene brothers developed a system of building which was unique – at once functional and aesthetically dynamic. All major timber joints at the Thorson House – roof trusses, beams and pillars – were bound together by metal straps and wedges. Climbing into the roof spaces I was surprised and delighted to find the roof members, the queen and king posts, beautifully finished and all constructed of high-grade timber: everything in that house was finished to the best Arts and Crafts standards – the standards of a different and now lost age! The combination of good timbers with this high-quality strapping meant that, after an earth tremor, the stability of the timber joints could be simply re-established by re-hammering the metal wedges tight into the metal straps. It was an adaptation to circumstance similar to certain mediaeval practices in Europe's earthquake zones but a rare sophistication in the land of the clapboard house! The Greenes also recognised screws and bolts as structurally inappropriate items and only used them where fracture was unlikely or a break would be of no structural consequence. The architecture of these Californian brothers can be seen as exemplary – structurally, aesthetically, socially and in the field of environmental architecture. I was delighted to have made their acquaintance.

My 'statutory' Mackintosh lecture was not a total success in Berkeley, mainly because an enormous projector that looked like a machine gun and had been brought in to show my old-fashioned 3x3 glass slides, exploded! After a long delay, a normal sized projector was found and I continued – greatly deflated. Events can disturb the best-laid plans. Host institutions are usually solicitous with regards to the needs and status of visiting lecturers but there are, occasionally, individuals who like to see a lecturer exposed at the dais – reduced to size – struggling with dimmer switches that refuse to dim and microphones that don't work or howl like dogs! Sometimes a callous or resentful professor will use subtle, psychological tools to undermine a visitor. I remember being introduced at UCLA by Arthur Gallion with these words. 'Dr Howarth is going to speak to us on the subject of housing and schools in the UK; I don't know anything about him; I've not met him before; but here he is!' It was a deliberately belittling introduction. I might have responded in kind – with cutting, or defensive, or non-explanatory remarks but I just turned from him – to the students – and, after a pause, said 'Hi'. It is a greeting that has now become almost universal but at that time was still very American and very fresh to me. It was direct and informal and it broke the ice with the students. They didn't expect this bespectacled Englishman to be so colloquial. As in the theatre, the atmosphere in a lecture hall can be crucial to the success of a lecture and the relationship between a lecturer and his audience can dramatically elevate or diminish the information and ideas he is there to deliver.

One fruitful consequence of my time in California was a Mackintosh lampshade. Some days after my 'explosive' lecture a senior member of staff introduced himself to me saying, 'I come from Scotland', and he asked me if I would like a Charles Rennie Mackintosh lampshade! I said, of course I would. Whereupon he delved into a bag and brought out a brown paper parcel and unwrapped one of the superb lampshades Mackintosh had designed for his apartment at Mains Street, Glasgow, in 1900. It was a wedding present for Margaret – a beautiful addition to the newly-weds new home. I was thrilled beyond words. 'You're welcome to take it', he said 'my wife doesn't like it. She won't have it in the house – it's been in the basement for years. If it stays there it'll get damaged, or forgotten. I'd like it to go where I know it'll be valued. It's yours to take home.' It was a gift of great generosity. His wife didn't know what she was casting out and I don't think he knew how much that lampshade would come to mean to me: it has illumined every home I have been in since and is 'a conversation piece' of surpassing merit. I thank him from the bottom of my heart – particularly because I can't now remember his name.

From Carmel we travelled north towards British Columbia, through the Redwoods to Seattle; there I detoured to see the Tacoma Narrows, where the famous suspension bridge 'flapped itself' into oblivion. The Director of the School of Architecture in Vancouver was Fred Lassere. He had designed the school himself and it was spacious and well-equipped. My one question concerned his placement of all the staff offices on the top floor. They provide great views over the campus to the mountains but the staff were thereby permanently physically cut-off from their students. I told him I didn't think this was a good idea. Because internal movement was mainly by elevators, staff could enter and leave the school with minimal contact with students. The nature of the circulation of people within buildings is an often-overlooked factor in architecture. Later Lassere designed the university's athletics entrance, with its elegant and much used swimming pool, and a charming graduate building on a magnificent oceanfront site.

In the school at Vancouver I met two of those 'artists' who have frequently, but too rarely, provided a necessary yeast in the bread of architectural education; their names were Bert Binning and Lionel Thomas. Binning was a painter and sculptor of powerful imagination, and Thomas an etcher and sculptor. Vancouver's architectural bias towards the Arts and Crafts seems to have existed over many years and it has played a significant part in shaping the form of this great modern city. For example the outstanding building designed in Vancouver, in the mid-fifties, was the British Columbia Electricity Building: its designer was Ron Thom, a man who trained as an artist before moving into architecture and, like Frank Lloyd Wright, Thom's ability to 'paint with forms' shows itself. I also made contact with Arthur Erickson. He had been building a series of houses on steeply sloping rocky sites, the kind most architects would seek to avoid like the plague, but Erickson was a brilliant designer and problems stimulated much of his best work. His office was later responsible for the Law Courts and the Anthropological Museum in Vancouver. He is generally recognised as the outstanding Canadian architect of his generation and he did a good deal of work in the United States and the Middle East; unfortunately, in the early nineties, his firm collapsed as a result of the global downturn in the economy and financial mismanagement. It was a great career that terminated very sadly.

Leaving Canada, we drove south to Aspen, Colorado, then east to Pittsburgh where I received two awards for my book on Mackintosh. They had both been awarded in 1953, following publication, but were held over for my arrival, in person. One was the annual Book Prize of the American Society of Architectural Historians, the other was the Alice Davis Hitchcock Medal. This medal had been commissioned from the Wedgwood factory and was a handsome white on black bust of James Stuart, the first British architect-historian. It is enclosed in an oval stainless steel frame. I was fêted in Aspen in a way that I had never been at home.

I then returned to Princeton, where Joseph Albers was teaching in the design section. He was one of the last survivors of the Bauhaus. I attended a lecture/demonstration he was conducting. He was a gentle, quiet spoken person but in complete command of himself and his students. The students were making montages with autumn leaves – then falling outside in great numbers and very beautiful. They had been asked to form the leaves into patterns, which could be representational or abstract, by gluing them to sheets of paper. On one level it could be seen as a primary school activity, on another, an extremely sophisticated creative exercise. After a while Albers, with his wife, gave a public criticism of the work and that simple exercise provoked a marvellous exploration of ideas – about colour, form, space and the theories of architecture that have shaped building over the centuries. I was greatly impressed by the Albers.

After that, leaving the family, I flew to Charleston, South Carolina but ended up, by mistake, in Charleston, West Virginia! A blizzard was blowing and I was kept awake half the night by the annual celebrations of the local Chamber of Commerce. Wandering downstairs to find out what the hell was going on – I suddenly found myself being 'celebrated' for coming all the way from England! I was royally entertained – treated to drinks, burgers, speeches, dances and a couple of old-style fist-fights. Waking up next morning I found that whole grimy, run-down place transformed – deep snow had fallen. No wind. Perfect peace. As I stood at my window, John Ruskin's words, referring to J.M.W. Turner's procedure as a painter, came into my mind: 'never lose an accident'. And the snows of West Virginia have always stayed with me – in a way that nothing I experienced in Charleston, South Carolina, my real destination, has.

One of my final calls was to the School of Architecture in the University of Toronto. I had been advised to make contact with two lecturers who had done research relevant to mine. Gordon Stephenson, who had studied architecture in Liverpool and Paris and worked for two years in the office of Le Corbusier; and Eric Ross Arthur, a New Zealander who was editor of the journal of the Royal Architectural Institute of Canada and knew my historical work well. To my surprise, when I tried to make contact by telephone – I got short shrift! Arthur told me he was far too busy to see me, and Gordon Stephenson was nowhere to be found. Someone later told me 'Gordon Stephenson is a busy man – with his office on the train! He views with pleasure the university within which he teaches – every time it passes through Toronto!'

Thus I arrived in Toronto in a slightly disorganised state and things immediately got worse. At the School of Architecture I was, unceremoniously, told to enquire about lodgings at the student accommodation centre. There, I was handed a long list of 'rooming houses'. Driving around I saw that most were in a very dilapidated condition and I couldn't help but contrast the open welcome we had received in almost every American city with the hard coming we were getting in Toronto. I refused to leave my family in any of the 'rooming houses' suggested and I returned to the university where a member of the architecture staff was pointed out to me. His feet were on a table and he was slouched back reading a book. Introducing myself as a visitor from the School of Architecture in Manchester, on a tour of North American schools of architecture, I politely asked whether anyone in the school might be available to show me round Toronto and the school's educational facilities. He lowered his book, looked me in the eye, and said, 'you visitors are all alike! No one can possibly view or appreciate the architecture of Toronto in two or three days, and, certainly, I haven't got the time to show you.' And he went on reading his book! That young man was William Goulding. He was shortly to become one of my members of staff. I never mentioned this incident to him, I don't know whether he ever connected it to me, but I have never forgotten the studied insolence of his remarks or the shabby introduction to Toronto he, and his colleagues, gave me.

Fortunately, I finally met Stanley Kent – a responsible member of staff. He agreed to give up a planned afternoon's golf to show me round the school and some of Toronto's more modern buildings. We visited the extension to the Plaza Hotel, which was undistinguished; then drove to the headquarters of the Ontario Association of Architects, a genuinely distinguished and memorable building by John C. Parkin. There we had lunch, specially prepared by the caretaker and his wife but by evening I was pleased to shake the dust of Toronto off my feet, and head for the more invigorating sound of Niagara Falls! After that it was south to Buffalo to view Sullivan's Guarantee Building and the Martin House by Frank Lloyd Wright. Both more than came up to my high expectations.

Driving towards Albany, I was moved by the functional simplicity of the numerous old buildings that dotted the agricultural landscape. They reminded me of the Pennine barns of home and the wood barns of East Anglia. They had a 'Shaker' functional simplicity about them. Not all were of the marvellous aesthetic standard that was the norm amongst the Shakers, but many were fine buildings worthy of architectural analysis. I had seen an excellent display of Shaker furniture at Cornell University and became an enthusiast. Everything produced by the Shakers had a formal simplicity, an elegance of proportion, and a dramatic clarity of outline that is simple and surprising. Their design and craftsmanship struck me with the same kind of exhilaration and joy I had felt on first looking at Mackintosh's furniture fifteen years earlier. And, later, I was interested to learn that the founder of the Shaker Movement was Mother Anne, a fellow Lancastrian – who left England with a small band of followers in 1774, the year that the American Revolution started, to establish her New Jerusalem in the New World.

The Shakers were a hardworking, practical, thrifty, health conscious, sexually chaste group who believed in the equality of people beyond race, colour, and creed, long before most other groups. They were pacifists who emerged out of Quakerism. They were spiritual enthusiasts; they danced, sang and deliberately sought visions and prophecies. They took in runaway slaves, they tilled their communal lands, and their quality seed was in demand all over America. Their craft products have similarities to those produced by the Arts and Crafts movement but the Shakers never aspired to be 'artists', they were always workers and craftsmen. Once established, they gathered distinguished admirers – from Thomas Jefferson to Abraham Lincoln. Abroad, they inspired many of the world's most influential nineteenth-century thinkers, Ruskin, Tolstoy, Gandhi, and political philosophers like Marx and Engels. Mother Ann Lee was illiterate, the daughter and wife of uneducated blacksmiths. In England she had suffered the loss of all her four children and spells of imprisonment. She went to America in search of renewal, and to expiate the pain of her losses and her gross ill-treatment. Ann Lee had undoubted charisma, and she released in her followers a combination of aesthetic and religious enthusiasm that suggests she had genius.

Mother Ann was not interested in art: 'Labour to make the way of God your own. Let it be your inheritance, your treasure, your occupation, your daily calling.' She was not egocentric: 'don't kneel to me. Kneel to God. I am but your fellow servant.' And, she had the wisdom to delegate the overseeing of making and building to men of managerial competence and proven architectural knowledge. She described her chosen successor, Joseph Meacher, as 'the wisest man born of a woman in 600 years'. He established the rules – of art and social behaviour – that were to govern the communities which, subsequently sprang up all over Eastern America. A unique society developed, directed by elders with sensibilities shaped by the neo-classical architectural tradition and Georgian craftsmanship. Work was understood to be natural and satisfying. The Shaker communities produced ordinary artefacts of exemplary worth and usefulness. Driving through those north-eastern States, I felt strangely proud that Mother Ann had come to America, carrying her gospel of Hardwork, Service and Praise, from the same dark Lancashire to which I was returning. 'Hands to work; hearts to God' was her clarion call.

In Boston we unloaded our bulging Dodge, sold it, and boarded a cargo-vessel for Manchester. It made call at St John, New Brunswick, Halifax, Nova Scotia and finally, St John's, Newfoundland, picking up cargo and people as we went. At each port we had time ashore and it was fitting that we should finish our American odyssey – viewing the settlements and architecture of the Maritime Provinces, through which so many British emigrants had moved into Canada over the centuries. Our ship was far from grand but proved much more fun than the luxurious Cunarder that had borne us across, the year before. After all the space, grandeur and gaudy newness of America this well-rusted hulk gave us a strange feeling of security: and that little ship took us right up the Manchester Ship Canal to deliver us, with gritty precision almost to our door. The lines of John Masefield often came into my mind:

> Dirty British coaster with a salt-caked smoke stack
> Chugging up the channel with a cargo of pig iron...

But America had been welcoming and grand and given me far more than I had expected, planned or dreamed. I came back hugely stimulated and determined to use the knowledge I had gained. I had established contacts with many of the world's leading architects, I had made myself familiar with the strengths and weaknesses of architectural education in the wealthiest, most powerful and most open society in the world. I had seen many of the world's great modern buildings and my family had had an unforgettable adventure. We had tramped almost every state in America at a benign moment in American history. The American people showed me the ways in which individual effort and personal vision are the keys to personal and artistic success and happiness, at least in a capitalist world. No one in America demonstrated this more clearly than Mackintosh's still living contemporary, Frank Lloyd Wright.

I first met Mr Wright in New York, at the start of my year. He had a suite in the Plaza Hotel. I went to meet the great man in some trepidation. His rooms were a surprise – all decorated in scarlet and gold. Like an eastern potentate, Mr Wright held audience. He greeted me warmly. I informed him of my Mackintosh research, my educational programme in America, and my hope to visit his desert school at Taliesin West. He said he would be delighted to welcome me to Arizona and we immediately made outline plans for my visit. I told him I would bring a selection of works from my Mackintosh collection and suggested we discuss the ways in which the Arts and Crafts movement and traditional architectural forms had influenced his architecture and, what his relationship with his fellow Celt, Mackintosh, was. He was warm, kind, grand and endearing. I left the Plaza Hotel in high excitement. I felt that the bond between Wright and

Drawing of a tree at Chideock, Dorset (Mackintosh 1895). ©Christie's Images Ltd. 2002

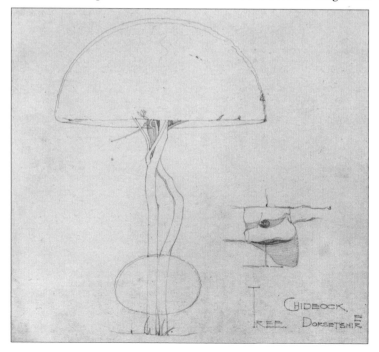

Plan for International
Exhibition, Glasgow
(Mackintosh 1901).
Competition design
for buildings.

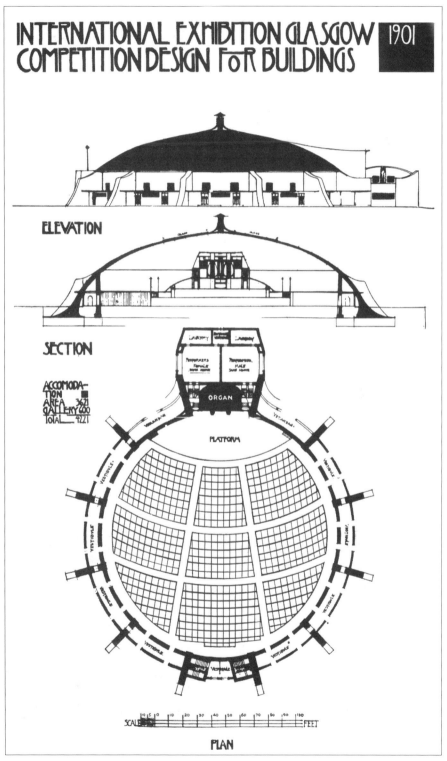

Mackintosh was not just architectural and poetical but also personal and that I, somehow, was the living link between those two great artists.

Wright was brought up, almost a Welshman, amidst the fertile, rolling hills of Wisconsin but he later developed a love of the arid deserts of the south-western states – where any life or growth seemed like a miracle, or a determined creative act. In 1937 he had purchased eight hundred acres of the southern slopes of the McDowell range, overlooking Paradise Valley, at a cost of three and a half dollars an acre! There was no water until, like Moses, a rock was struck and out it poured. He knew it was there! Wright had the character and presence of a prophet; he cultivated his powers as a magician just as surely as he cultivated his skills as an architect. He created Taliesin West as his winter home and what might be called a permanent architectural research centre. It was designed on the spot and built frontier style in 'desert concrete'. It still carried a sense of being a 'spontaneous design' when I visited it nineteen years later. On arrival, I was thrilled by an extraordinary combination of archetypal landscape, Wild West lifestyle, and high modern culture.

Top. Greek Orthodox Church, Milwaukee (Lloyd Wright 1956).

Bottom. Marin County Civic Centre (Lloyd Wright 1957).

Wright was a man who had always enjoyed journeying. He normally made the run from Taliesin East to Taliesin West by car, with a great convoy of followers and, I think, our arrival in a battered, dust-covered Dodge, somehow, impressed him. He made us very welcome and we settled into our quarters. I was given an extensive tour of the studios and he gave me his interview. I set out my exhibition of Mackintosh and the students told me that this, as far as they knew, was the first time that any work by an architect, other than Mr Wright himself, had ever been displayed in Taliesin. Various of the Mackintosh pieces raised great interest. I kept an eye on Mr Wright and noticed the special attention he paid to a photograph of Mackintosh's competition design for an International Exhibition Centre for Glasgow in 1901.

On the day I was leaving I called into Mr Wright's office, where he was working, to say goodbye. He was bent over his desk, deeply absorbed in what he was doing. I waited a short while, then called out at a distance, 'Goodbye, Mr Wright, we have to go now.' He looked up. 'Don't go,' he said, 'don't go yet – I've something to show you.' He beckoned me over and pointed to his drawing board. He had just begun work on the Greek Orthodox Church that was to be completed after his death, at Milwaukee. 'Look at this,' he said, 'You've never seen anything like this before – its Wright Byzantine!' And he stood back and raised his hands to shoulder height, his elbows bent. He was ablaze with creative excitement but I was, immediately, embarrassed –I didn't know what to say – because the emerging design was so like the Mackintosh International Exhibition design that he had been studying over the preceding days. I wondered, should I say what I am thinking, or keep silent? But, even whilst I thought, I found myself saying, 'it's a great drawing, it has Byzantine features but it's also remarkably like Mackintosh's Exhibition Hall!' He looked at me, gave a little cough into his hand, looked at the drawing; then sat down and got on with his work. As I turned away he smiled and raised his hand slightly. He came to the door with us. He was very gracious to Edna and the children and wished us all well and the last I saw of him was his white suit passing the huge Welsh harp in the studio on his way back to his desk. He didn't change the basic design he conceived that morning, and the Milwaukee Greek Orthodox Church retains, to this day, many of the forms originally conceived by Charles Rennie Mackintosh in 1901. My observations were meant then, as they are meant now, not to deflate the reputation of a man of amazing genius but to recognise facts and to show the many-faceted sources of creativity, to show 'Truth against the World' as Frank Lloyd Wright would say.

PROFESSORSHIP 7

Drink of this and take thy fill ANON

For the water falls by the Wizard's will.

The return from America provided Howarth with both welcome stability and a culture shock. Lancashire was damp, grey and fitfully beautiful; Manchester impoverished, noisy, overcrowded and its School of Architecture sometimes seemed an inhibited and provincial place compared to the extravagantly confident institutions he had encountered in America. But, coming back, Howarth felt 'at home' and he couldn't help but feel pride in the resilience and character of the Lancashire people. He listened with fresh ears to the vigour of the local dialects; he enjoyed again the Turneresque drama of the smoke red sunsets; he drove out into the Pennines to re-establish communion with the hills of his boyhood. At the university, Professor Cordingley was delighted to have his trusted lieutenant back at his side and, almost immediately, the Howarth family was offered a large apartment in a splendid country house, Firwood, at Alderley Edge, in Cheshire.

It was still occupied by descendants of the original owners – two spinster sisters in late middle-age, Margaret and Dorothy Pilkington. Their wealth was the product of

Pilkington Tiles, a company renowned for avant-garde ceramics. Margaret Pilkington worked as a curator at the Whitworth Art Gallery in Manchester, and she seems to have been pleased to offer a fellow historian accommodation: the arrangement provided her with companionship and the house with increased security. Firwood also gave Howarth entrée to a wide circle of cultured associates and for the next two years the Howarths lived 'the life of the landed gentry'. Notable visitors included Lord James, High Master of Manchester Grammar School, and Charles Sewter, then engaged in the preparation of a major book on the stained glass of William Morris. Howarth used Sewter's knowledge to clarify his own theories about the connections between the English Arts and Crafts Movement and the Modernism of Mackintosh. Margaret Pilkington also encouraged Howarth to take his architectural students to the Whitworth Art Gallery which contained first-rate Pre-Raphaelite paintings and the world's most complete collection of work by William Blake. She allowed him access to works in storage and, in the basement, Howarth was thrilled by a splendid collection of African tribal sculpture.

> I thought such treasures should come out of the darkness – be made available to the public and critically assessed. I proposed that I mount a major exhibition that would also be a useful design exercise for my students. It would cost very little and not involve the Whitworth in significant work. Surprisingly, I suddenly found it no end of a task to persuade Miss Pilkington to let anything happen And, it was only after I had obtained large quantities of bamboo and rattan, via personal contact with business people in the city of Manchester, that I was given the go ahead. The bamboo was used to create an exciting exhibition space. A variety of splendid tribal artefacts were then brought out of storage, cleaned, catalogued, and displayed and the exhibition proved to be a major public, educational and artistic success. The students designed all aspects of the exhibition stands, divisions, notices, lettering and organised the overall display. Herbert Read, and my old friend Margaret Bulley, had been articulating the formal and dramatic power of such 'primitive' art to British audiences for many years, but most museum directors remained stuck in the mud of their institutionalised perceptions and many fine things were never seen. I was pleased to throw a little light into the black cellars of the Whitworth and that exhibition stimulated my lifelong enthusiasm for the dynamic realities of African, Oceanic and Inuit art. I began to build my own 'primitive' collections. I also became convinced of the educational and cultural importance of exhibitions. And, since those grim post-war days, I am pleased to say, exhibitions have now become one of the great 'art-forms of our time'.

By chance, I almost immediately organised another even more unusual

exhibition. Asked to evaluate the 'redevelopment' possibilities of a university building that was part of the School of Dentistry, I began digging and delving and found, in a locked cupboard, several large boxes filled with mathematical models made of plaster. They were of simple, abstract shapes and very beautiful. I recognised them as various kinds of hyperbolic paraboloids – examples of complex geometric forms which, at that very moment, were beginning to be used by some of the world's leading architects. The Manchester dentists had apparently been using these forms for years! More than that, some of these 'dental' paraboloids included formal and structural use of 'strings', of the kind being used by contemporary sculptors like Naum Gabo, Henry Moore and Barbara Hepworth and I thought – these strange plasters – linking medicine, science, architecture and the fine arts – are worth serious examination and exhibition! So, once more, I got my students involved and we created a small but important, public exhibition.

The models had in fact been made relatively recently, by the engineering department, to demonstrate certain principles about structures and structural strength. They were not totally original inventions. The real advances had been made in Switzerland and Mexico in the early fifties and I soon remembered a cosmic-ray laboratory, designed by Felix Candela, that I had seen in Mexico City in 1956. It was a tiny, elegant and remarkable building – with its parabolic, concrete-shell roof just three-eights of an inch thick and reinforced by piano wire. Candela and I had become friends and I was, later, to invite him to lecture in Toronto... Whatever, it was with great pleasure that I dusted down those noble parabolas, stored in that soon-to-be-demolished adjunct to the Manchester Dental School, and displayed them – in a small but stunning exhibition. My aim was to focus interdisciplinary attention on a new technology of great interest to engineers and architects – worldwide – and the exhibition was a remarkable success on its many levels.

There were, I think, twenty different paraboloid plaster models. My first priority was to dramatically present these very pure forms. We removed twenty bookcases from the walls of a library that was to be demolished. Each bookcase was four feet by four feet, just the right size to accommodate the models. We painted each bookcase – terracotta on the inside and white on the outside. Then, we laid these twenty bookcases, symmetrically, across the floor – with one paraboloid in each bookcase, and all lighted from above. When visitors entered the exhibition room they got an immediate and strong aesthetic impression – our dental library had been transformed into a modern, minimalist art gallery. Each visitor then felt propelled to move forward to view each different paraboloid, in each identical box. After that, they could read the information we had assembled and begin to think about the structural, architectural and artistic uses of the paraboloid form. Student seminars were conducted and school groups visited whilst staff explained why the paraboloid is such an economical form of construction. It uses straight reinforcing rods – to build curved and complex structures. The principle could be explained by simply taking a handful of drinking straws, holding them in the centre, and twisting them slightly. It was, I think, a ground-breaking exhibition and ahead of its time.

Another visitor to Firwood House was Margaret Pilkington's niece Noel and her husband, Basil Williams. They lived in a handsome Regency-

style house at Bowden, Cheshire. After we became friends they consulted me about their plans to redecorate their home, then they invited me to design furniture. Basil had originally worked for Pilkingtons but soon moved sideways to become a salesman for the Exide Battery Company, He did not, however, sell batteries. He sold factories for the manufacture of batteries! He was a brilliant linguist and his work took him frequently to the Soviet Union and the then rapidly industrialising countries of the Eastern Block. We became travelling companions. I never visited behind the Iron Curtain but we drove to various parts of England and once to Copenhagan – where a strange incident occurred. It sticks in my memory, like a scene from a film. We were dining in the Tivoli Gardens, in Copenhagan, after looking at various of the best buildings in the city. Basil was greatly enjoying himself and already speaking Danish like a native. He informed me that the Danes were a remarkably friendly, informal and liberal minded of people. He pointed out a very attractive girl sitting at a table with, we presumed, her parents. Basil said, 'In Denmark, the girls are just like the men, you can go up to a stranger – and ask them to dance. They don't say "no" – you watch!' He straightened his tie, walked over and began a conversation that went on for some time. They were serious, they laughed, but – the girl did not rise and no dancing occurred. After a while, Basil returned to say, a little crest-fallen, 'Some Danes are more formal than others!' And that was the end of that. In retrospect, I sometimes wonder whether that 'film' I remember was really about Danish girls dancing – or espionage! Those were the years of Harry Lime – Philby, Burgess and Maclean!

At home, the Williams asked me to redesign their house garden. It was a south facing but awkward site – very long, very thin. I decided to turn it into a series of narrow, stepped terraces which would tier down through lawns and flower beds to a small orchard – with a vegetable garden at the bottom. Before beginning work I suggested to Basil that we visit Sonning, on the Thames, to see Edwin Lutyen's Deanery Garden. It is, I think, a domestic masterpiece, with a superb garden designed by the landscape architect Gertrude Jekyll. By showing Basil a great Arts and Crafts garden I knew I could stimulate his imagination – and gather slides and knowledge for my own researches. I was then avidly building up my collection of slides and was increasingly excited by the idea of 'architecture' within its wider environment.

The visit to Sonning was a great success. It was spring but the trees were hardly in leaf, so we were able to see unobstructed views of the house – rising above a carpet of daffodils. One enters through a heavy door into a small vestibule. Beyond this is another door which leads into the entrance hall proper, and one then passes into the great hall. It is a modern space but it grows absolutely out of mediaeval tradition and mediaeval lifestyle – when life was communal, not private. Lutyens used half-timbering freely. Everywhere the brickwork is of exceptional quality. On the garden side of the house, a series of arched openings have elegant tiled voussoirs that are carried high into the wall and are beautifully formed. Like Mackintosh, Lutyens works with nature, he orchestrates spatial and tactile surprises, he works with traditional materials. In America, I had been pleased to hear Gropius repeat his famous dictat, 'We start from Zero!' But there, in the south of England, I was reminded of the importance of continuity and tradition. And knowing that I was likely to be returning to America, I was keen, to imbue myself with the best of Europe's long heritage of vernacular empiricism: the three vernacular unities – of the architect with his craftsman, of that of the craftsman with his place of habitation, and of both with the tested traditions they inherit.

I remember my visit to Sonning for one other reason. That evening at dinner, after our inspiring wanderings in Miss Jekyll's garden, I drank and enjoyed red Burgundy. Basil Williams was a bon viveur who knew his wines even better than the ladies of Copenhagan, and he persuaded me to part-share a bottle he had ordered. My single previous experience of wine had been that very cheap glass I had tried in Italy in 1937. It failed to convert me and I happily returned to my teetotal ways – to Methodist propriety. My family, on both sides remained teetotal, Edna's family were teetotal. Tea fuelled the rational mind, hard work and serious endeavour but the more I had learned of the world, the more I felt the spiritual inhibitions such blanket prohibitions engendered. I had begun to see that whilst 'the Pledge' could be a material necessity to families threatened by poverty and degeneration – it was becoming, for me, in the mid-fifties, culturally and artistically, a negative and unnecessary constriction. I began to see that wine was one of the pleasures of life that artists, like Lutyens and Mackintosh, had released into the world. Good conversation and communality are nurtured by wine and creative insights engendered by pure pleasure in life. So there, in Sonning, by the soft flowing Thames, I sipped the wine that Basil poured me and 'I found that it was good'. I was forty-three, exactly halfway through my life.

Subsequently, Howarth was delighted to be asked to become godfather to Basil's youngest daughter, Julia and the families remained close for almost fifty years, Just before Howarth died, Julia sent this message by fax:

Dearest Tom,

So you're packing your case… I hope this catches you before your train leaves. Or are you flying? What a remarkable phone call – a most unusual message. A brave and helpful one. Thank you. You'll always be with us in our conversations – whenever C.R.M. is mentioned. And for me – you're there whenever 'treacle tart' is mentioned! It always makes me smile when I remember how much you enjoyed your slice at the Old Crown in Skirmett. I expect you remember our day in the Thames Valley villages. A lovely day – and I now lead walks there – to share it with others.

And now its time to go. Thank you for making it easier for me, for us perhaps. And thank you for being my Godfather… Bon voyage, traveller – till the next rendezvous.

With love, Julia.

Left. Marsh Court, Stockbridge, Hampshire. Sir Edwin Lutyens; Arts and Crafts movement.

Right. Blackwell House, English Lake District. M.H. Baillie-Scott, 1897; a building Howarth knew well from his youth.

The village of Alderley Edge gets its name from a serrated outcrop of rock which dominates the largely flat landscape of Cheshire. At weekends Edna and I would often climb to the summit with the children. From the north side of the rocks a spring wells from the mouth of a sculpted, bearded face of the prophet Merlin, bardic source of the Arthurian legends. Beneath the water these words are inscribed:

> Drink of this and take thy fill
> For the water falls by the Wizard's will.

For some reason those words always reminded me of Frank Lloyd Wright and America – and each time I read them I felt the hand of destiny on my shoulder. I felt 'here is good' but, perhaps, I should be somewhere else. Winters in Manchester sapped not only one's physical well-being but also one's spiritual and psychological resources. Coming home on the bus from Manchester I used to think hard and long about the future. Sitting with Edna around a good log fire we would reminisce about the blue skies and sunshine of America and it seemed the best and the natural thing – to return. Merlin was daring me to imagine something else, something other than the life we had.

During my American tour, two universities had approached me with offers of a position as director of new postgraduate research departments. At the time, I was contracted to return to Manchester but I showed interest in the offers and kept my options open.

Once back in Manchester I informed Professor Cordingley and the Chancellor of the University, Professor Mansfield-Cooper, of the offers I had received and asked for their advice. To my surprise both of them advised me not to accept either position. They suggested that something better would be sure to come my way. Consequently, in the autumn of 1957, after long consideration, I wrote letters to the directors of the two institutions, refusing them both. I vividly remember walking, on a cold, damp Cheshire evening to the letterbox in the lane outside Firwood and hesitating – with the two letters balanced on the lip of the slot. I thought of the aphorism, 'a bird in the hand is worth two in the bush'. But I also felt strangely confident and with the words, 'What the hell!' I thrust them in and walked home, strangely euphoric. That act of refusal precipitated another of those 'magical moments' that have articulated my life. The very next morning, the postman delivered a letter from Canada – asking if I would allow my name to go forward as a candidate for the headship of the School of Architecture at the University of Toronto. I told no one for several days – then I arranged a joint meeting with Cordingly and Professor Mansfield-Cooper. They were delighted at the invitation and said that Toronto was a place of exciting new developments. I told them that, during the whole of my year in America, the only place that had seemed to me cold, unresponsive and academically restricted – was Toronto! This, they said, showed how much someone with vision and leadership was needed! They, unconditionally, encouraged me to accept the offer to let my name go forward – which I did.

To what extent these two distinguished gentlemen were aware, or involved in the situation that had developed, I do not know, and I have never attempted to discover. I do know, however, that the then President of the R.I.B.A., Colonel Graham Henderson, who was a partner in Mackintosh's old firm, had recently visited Toronto; and it is likely that he was consulted by the architectural profession in Ontario with regard to their search for a new director of the School of Architecture. For various reasons he might have spoken well of me. It was also true that the Universities of Toronto and Manchester had an exceptionally good and close relationship at that time, before the so-called 'French Fact' negated all direct Anglo-Canadian contact. The lingering colonial relationship can be questioned, but today's 'flat playing field' has reduced much of what I would call 'genuine cultural exchange' to a bureaucratic horse-trading that has little to do with culture and too much to do with reconditioned nationalism and institutional mediocrity. So, my name went out and things moved quickly.

Because of financial stringencies, the University of Toronto was not able to invite me for a personal interview but it was soon arranged that I should meet with the University's Vice-president, Murray Ross, when he visited London. He was a genuine Canadian, open, sincere and friendly; he greeted me in the lobby of his hotel in grey trousers, a sports coat and a bright red sweater: a Scots Canadian. Murray Ross arranged that I meet Bill Morris, one of Canada's leading architects, who was also in London – to receive the Royal Gold Medal of the R.I.B.A. This award had provoked fierce controversy on both sides of the Atlantic. Bill Morris was senior partner at Morani & Morris, a well-known Canadian company which had produced numerous buildings recognised as superbly constructed and beautifully detailed but which were, also, indelibly conservative and showed little of the imagination, or genius, normally associated with the work of the recipients of this most prestigious award. That the name of a good but ordinary architect should be engraved on the RIBA's marble roll of honour, alongside names like Frank Lloyd Wright, Le Corbusier, Mies van der Rohe and the Saarinens, seemed incongruous – to me and to many others. However, that first meeting was not one of those occasions when my honesty outshone my discretion; I needed to be diplomatic and I was.

Bill Morris invited me to his hotel and, on meeting, I congratulated him warmly on the award, saying that it was a great honour – not just for himself and his firm, but for Canada. In fact, what I said – was true – and Bill Morris and I, immediately, got on very well. It quickly became obvious that he would support my appointment. We spoke about many issues and the ways in which he and his partner, Ferdinand Marani, would support the new policies I advocated if I took over direction of the School of Architecture. My fears – that Toronto's architectural community was a nest of vipers – began to evaporate. Both Bill and his wife were charming. We spent many hours together in London and, when I arrived in Canada, we re-established a friendship which was to last till the end of his life

Another coincidence occurred at this time. A competition was announced for the design of a new city hall for Toronto and, amongst hundreds of others, my old friend George Grenfell Baines decided to enter. When he heard that I was being considered for the professorship in Toronto, he asked me to join him as a design consultant. Town halls were my forte! By the mid-fifties, George had established a successful practice based in Preston, known as the Grenfell Baines Group. It included several distinguished young architects, notably Tom Mellor, John Ashworth and Tom Hargraves, and we all got involved. Our building consisted of twin

hexagonal towers rising above a pool. The all-important council chamber was placed on the roof, as an exciting sculptural feature, following the example of Oscar Niemayer in Brasilia. I remember the creative excitement the competition engendered – in particular I remember George Grenfell Baines bursting in, each evening, to review what we had done. He was full of ideas and he had the confidence to change things – even at the last moment. Our only major disagreement concerned his wish to create a formal French garden as part of the design. To me it seemed a gesture rather than an integrated necessity but – someone has to take final decisions.

The competition jury was chaired by Eric Arthur, a senior member of staff in the Toronto School of Architecture. One excellent idea he had come up with was the commissioning of a large model of the central section of the city of Toronto, with an empty space, eighteen inches square, where the new city hall was to stand. All competitors were informed that they must submit a scale model of their design, on a base eighteen inches square, which could be slotted into the jury's model. Thus, each proposal could be judged in its environmental context as well as on its purely formal architectural merits. Over 700 submissions came in from around the world. I later heard that the jury's task was so complex that wheelchairs were needed to trundle the more elderly jurors around the mass of material submitted! The winner was Viljo Revel. Interestingly, his design turned out to be surprisingly like that submitted by the Grenfell Baines partnership, but whereas we suggested hexagonal towers, he proposed aerofoil shaped towers. We had, however, no reason to complain – our design was disqualified before evaluations started! Our model was destroyed in transit. I had supervised the building of a superb balsa-wood model. I saw it neatly and very securely packaged. I took it, personally, to Preston Head Post Office. I ensured I had a record of the postage time and date but, to our great disappointment many months later, we learned that our model, like many others, arrived in Toronto damaged beyond repair.

This incident is interesting because it is one, of a series, of unusual 'accidents' that impinged on Howarth's professional life and one wonders whether there wasn't some pattern or psychological reason for them. For example, when studying for the compulsory Italian component of his PhD in Glasgow, Howarth missed a crucial examination by turning up just when all the other examinees were leaving the building. He had misread the timetable. He informed his lecturers that he thought the exam began at the moment it ended! Was this a genuine mistake, a Freudian slip, or was it a conscious act that resulted in Howarth having to resit the exam a year later – and passing – when he knew he had the knowledge to succeed? Was the breaking of the Grenfell Baines city hall model a genuine disaster, outwith the control of Howarth, or a convenient end to a project that had already served its purpose? His main purpose, at that time, being to secure the post of Director of the School of Architecture in Toronto. For all his Victorian probity, Howarth was never above showmanship, and, by another strange coincidence, within weeks of being approached about the Toronto headship, Howarth was asked by his brother, Jay Howarth, to design new facilities for the joint medical practice he ran in Orlando.

I was delighted to accept this invitation but made the proviso that I must see the site before being commissioned and, in due course, an airline ticket from Manchester to Orlando, via London and New York, arrived. I then informed the University of Toronto that I was, shortly, to visit North America on business. They responded with an invitation that I should come north for an informal interview; and they agreed to cover my expenses and airfare from New York.

I, immediately, did some research into small-scale hospital architecture and carefully prepared my itinerary. I also had the idea that the thought of two young neuro-surgeons inviting an English architect to design new premises in Florida would be a big story in the American media and I decided to create an appropriate and memorable impression. I saw myself stepping off an airplane – straight into cinema newsreels all across America! It was early autumn but I set off from Manchester in a magnificent winter overcoat with a huge, turn-up collar that my grandfather had given me, a long university scarf, black leather gloves and a fedora of the type Sir Anthony Eden had worn during the Suez Crisis. For some reason we flew via Iceland and my choice of clothes turned out to be perfect – there. It also proved relatively sensible in New York. I arrived at night and was ushered aboard a Helicopter Link-Service that took me from Idlewild Airport to Newark, New Jersey. The views of Manhattan were truly spectacular: such night flights have now been banned but as we rose and sank between those brilliantly illuminated skyscrapers I had a tremendous feeling of arrival and the possibilities of life in that vast, booming continent. We dropped down onto various roof-pads, discarding and picking-up passengers, then surged forward through a metropolitan fairyland which still has no equal on earth. This fantastic, elevating experience increased the hubris I was to feel on landing in Florida.

I had phoned my brother to tell him the exact time of my arrival. As we came into land at Orlando, I donned my greatcoat and fedora, took down my umbrella and tucked a large roll of architectural drawings under my arm. I gathered myself at the exit door of the aircraft, paused whilst I selected the right moment to stride purposefully down the steps – ready to be snapped by the assembled throng of photographers... I was in for a double surprise – first, the heat of Florida hit me with palpable force – second, the crowd was non-existent, there was nobody there! I trotted onto empty tarmac, the place was deserted but for a single airhostess and a refuelling wagon! I was brought down-to-earth with a bang! I walked into the air-cooled terminal building where my brother stood in shirtsleeves and splendid isolation! I told him I'd expected some photographers. The sweat was running off me. He said he had informed the press but that my plane was late and the photographers must have given up waiting! It was a farce. Imagination and ambition had run away with me. It was a salutary lesson that I have not forgotten. Over the next few days I discussed the building my brother wanted, I viewed the proposed site and met a local architect who, it was proposed, would control developments on site. Then I flew north for Toronto.

In common with most schools of architecture in America, the Toronto School had developed within a faculty of engineering. It had been established in 1892 by C.H.C. Wright and, with the School of Architecture at the Massachusetts Institute of Technology, could claim to have inaugurated architectural teaching in North America. I was given a conducted tour of the campus. The architectural facilities were spread over three separate locations – centred on the library, an administrative block, and studio spaces. The Search Committee was comprised of Moffat Woodside, a university Vice-president; Roland McLaughlan, Dean of the Faculty of Engineering; and two architects, Shy Mathers and Gordon S. Adamson. A very Scottish-sounding group! My interview went well. But I expressed doubts about the long-term future, if the school continued to function on its disparate sites. I explained that I had had experience of administering a similar split-site in Manchester but would not wish to take responsibility for a similar school – if there was no prospect of such a fundamental problem being remedied. They told me that plans were already afoot to unify the school by transferring the whole operation to the Victoria Curling Rink in Huron Street. I was taken to view it – and was more than delighted. The rink was a fine stone building, built in the Romanesque style in 1887; a style I prefer to call 'Canadian Robust'. The floor space of the ice rink was covered by a great timbered arch with an eighty-seven foot span. There were balconies on two sides, space for a library, workshops, offices, even an underground bowling alley! I was greatly impressed and informed my interviewers that, I believed, I could create a first-rate school, given appropriate resources, within such an exciting building.

I was then invited to meet Sidney Smith, the President of the University. Our discussions were less about whether I was the man for the job and more about the processes by which I could create a rejuvenated school. He informed me that the university and the architectural profession were very concerned about the administrative state of the school, its educational policies and interminable problems with staff, and students. He said no research work of any significance had ever been produced within the school and that there was a total lack of cultural exchange between the school and the university as a whole. The school had become a 'training place' for the architectural profession; it was not a seat of enlightened cultural and intellectual enquiry. He also stated that, he believed, too many of the current staff had external architectural commitments that constricted their abilities to fulfil their teaching responsibilities. It was a list of woes that was at once intimidating but also challenging. I left Toronto in high spirits, confident that I would be offered the post and confident that I could do the job that so obviously needed to be done.

On my return to Manchester, I was greeted by a letter offering me the position of Director of School of Architecture at the University of Toronto. The salary was 12,500 dollars a year, not high. I queried the amount, and Murray Ross advised me, confidentially, that the figure would be increased, substantially, once I was in post. Within days, news came in – that the project to design the Medical Centre in Orlando was to be abandoned, because my brother's medical partner had died, suddenly, from a heart attack. The abandonment of this project was a loss but my colleagues and family were delighted to hear of my appointment. We were soon working hard to tie up loose ends in Manchester. Edna did a great deal to see our parents happily settled before we left – perhaps for ever. Her father still ran two large cotton mills in the Preston area but he showed no interest in visiting Canada saying he was more than happy to live out his life in England. My mother and grandparents were keen to 'cross the pond' for a visit but, they too, were content to stay put in the family home at Mayfield. As a farewell present, I designed them new interiors in a contemporary, Mackintosh style. In addition, flushed with the prospect of my professorial salary, I sent Edna to Glasgow to bid for a set of eight Mackintosh chairs which came up for auction. They had been made for the Argyle Street Tearooms, two tall ladder-backs and six squarish chairs, all in excellent condition and made of fine stained oak. They were beautiful, historical works of art but also functional dining-room chairs that we would need in Canada and she got them for a remarkably low figure.

It was on the 18th of July 1958 that we arrived in Toronto. At first we took temporary furnished accommodation in Moor Park. Then, we moved permanently to a new apartment block on Glen Elm Avenue, north of St Clair Avenue and East of Yonge Street - still 1,500 miles long. Glen Elm gave us access to good shops, the subway, and bedrooms that looked out over the green parklands of the Mount Pleasant Cemetery. The children were almost as free to wander there – as they had been in Cheshire. They chased butterflies, racoons, chipmunks, squirrels and skunks. John was ten and Katharine was seven. To enjoy, fully, the freedoms of North America all families need a car so I selected a grand old Chevrolet, banana yellow with a green roof. I thought it had panache but the children named it 'Trusty Rusty'! Which is what it became over the years.

Education is something that does not keep and Murray Ross was just one of several people who advised us to send the children to private

Toronto skyline from the
Royal Canadian Yatch Club.
Thomas Howarth

schools. Katharine was enrolled at Havergal, one of the principal girls' schools in Canada, and John went into the Junior School of Upper Canada College. Both were accelerated a year beyond their natural ages but settled in tolerably. The fees were high but so were the academic standards, and so were the cultural and sporting expectations placed on the children and we have always felt our money was well spent. Thus, as a warm, late-summer turned into a golden autumn we felt deeply content and excited by the new life before us. When winter arrived, we bought snowshoes and skies. Edna had always been the sporty type and she handled the Blue Mountains with all the aplomb of a native. I was never naturally sporty, and on sloping ice and snow I tend to feel insecure; I tried joining in but, after a fall that damaged my hip, I gave up skiing – for the pains of arthritis! In 1971 I had hip-replacement surgery but a great deal had happened meantime: The children had become Canadians, the School of Architecture had become part of a Faculty of Environmental Design and Edna and I were living separate lives.

8 THE UNIVERSITY OF TORONTO

THOMAS HOWARTH

Any lingering doubts about why I had been 'head-hunted' for this appointment had, by this time, vanished and I felt I could make Toronto one of the outstanding schools of architecture not just in North America but the world.

Arriving at the University of Toronto I was astonished by the administrative formality. The contrast with my alma mater was striking. In Manchester we had one professor who was head of school. In Toronto I found sixteen professors, a school council and umpteen standing committees. In Manchester, Professor Cordingley was a member of the Faculty of Fine Arts to which he reported on behalf of the School of Architecture. When departmental decisions had to be made he called a staff meeting, which would often take place over coffee, in the Faculty Club. Cordingley disliked any unnecessary formality. Views and opinions would be expressed, discussion would take place, then he would sum everything up. Decisions were made and documented only when, he thought, appropriate. Was this tyranny? I think not. During twelve years of intimate work with Cordingley I cannot remember one occasion when his colleagues disputed his decision, and subsequent action. We might frequently disagree amongst ourselves – about future developments and policy – but once argued through at a staff meeting, Cordingley's codifications of the decisions reached were always respected. He was not a manipulator or interested in the personal assertion of power; he sought ideas and opinions, orchestrated a consensus, and then implemented it with bold disinterest. Cordingley is safe, with my grandfather, in my Pantheon of Heroes.

The situation in Canada was very different. The school council met four times each year in the university's Senate Chamber. This was a room with a vast, rectangular oak table with circumferential seating for thirty

Thomas Howarth (1972), Toronto. *Robert Lansdale*

203

people and space for another 350 'senators' ranked in rows around in parliamentary style. There was a raised dais at one end with a high-backed chair – a throne – for the President of the University. As Director of the School of Architecture I was given a substantial typewritten document bound in blue paper which contained 'the rules of conduct' for the Federal House of Commons in Ottawa – this was the coda that governed our school! We had a permanent teaching staff of twenty; I glanced at the book and put it away, unread in the central drawer of my desk where, in the rare likelihood of trouble, it would be available.

I chaired our first school council meeting. I was a little nervous but everyone was on their best behaviour and it went extremely well. Anyone wishing to speak would rise from their seat and address the council – through me, as chairman. I had participated in similarly formal proceedings at committee meetings of the R.I.B.A. in London and I performed my duties with due gravity. In fact I quickly learned to enjoy and appreciate the administrative advantages of such formality and, today, I lament the loss of the discipline that ensured good and efficient governance in those days. The chairman is now, in the year 2000, a unisex 'speaker', and the council has been greatly enlarged by student representatives and others from the profession and elsewhere. This democratic improvement has been undermined by ever increasing structural informality; no one rises to speak through the chair, uncontrolled discussion now takes place across a table. Such spontaneity and emotional 'expression' are not conducive to the clarification of issues, nor to positive decision-making. In 1958, however, my induction proved a pleasure and I decided that I would exercise my authority as little as possible until I had assessed the requirements of the university, my staff and students. Within six months I began to make serious changes.

The work of students on the first four years of our courses was satisfactory although I saw no outstanding submissions. The presentation of theses by fifth-year students, however, was generally shoddy and unsatisfactory. They tended to be carelessly drawn on tracing paper and mounted, if at all, on brown card that confused interpretation and reduced aesthetic impact. I did not express my criticisms directly but wrote to Michael McKinnell, who had been one of my top graduate students at Manchester, and asked him to send me copies of the splendid thesis presentation he had made the previous year. It had been inspired by Eero Saarinen's T.W.A. Terminal at Idlewild (now Kennedy) Airport, New York. His drawings were four or five feet long, brilliantly executed in black and white ink, and lucidly defined his concepts. They had been strongly influenced by the artistry of Paul Rudolf and I still consider them to be exemplary student work. A small exhibition was mounted and it caused a great deal of interest. I then suggested to staff and students that these drawings should represent the standard towards which we should aim – not just with regard to presentation but all aspects of our architectural thinking. It has always seemed to me evident that the hand can lead both the eye and the mind; most great architects have been draughtsmen of the first rank – from Michelangelo to Mackintosh. There is no doubt that Michael McKinnell's work stimulated a good deal of debate in Toronto and was responsible for a marked improvement in student work over several generations, though none, I think, ever produced work like McKinnell's! He was exceptional, and soon left Manchester to pursue a highly successful career. He was a founder partner in the firm of Kalman and McKinnell of Boston, and became an outstanding teacher at Harvard.

Until the computer made artistic skills semi-redundant to the practice of architecture I was a strong believer in the importance of students of architecture developing their artistic talents. And I remain proud of the ways in which we continued to develop the drawing and sketching skills of the students in Toronto. Colour theory, watercolour painting and sketching were all taught by associate professor W.E. Carswell. He was a trained architect but had never practiced. He was, however, a diligent and excellent teacher and a most valuable member of staff. He worked with an assistant, John A. Hall, a practising artist. Together they had established a little 'school of art' within the School of Architecture and an annual 'sketch camp' had became a required programme for all second, third and fourth-year students. I was delighted to endorse it. The 'sketching camp' had been established near Dorset, a small village about 200 miles north of Toronto, amidst 30,000 acres of forest wilderness gifted to the university's Faculty of Forestry. It consisted of dormitories, basic classrooms and offices, a good assembly hall with a stage, a large dining room and kitchen, a boathouse with canoes, etc. It provided an ideal environment within which students could explore nature, make art and develop a communal sense of togetherness. For many students their weeks at Dorset became the outstanding highlight of their university experience. Talk on graduation days would often turn to reminiscence – 'Do you remember such and such at Dorset camp?'

The students spent most of their time sketching in the field but visiting lecturers organised special projects and mini-courses. Christopher Chapman, the filmmaker, would show films and lead discussions. The sculptor Ronald Baird would oversee the production of three-dimensional works I would go up to lecture, and play the piano. Friday nights would see drawings exhibited and informal criticism. Each Saturday a semi-formal dinner was laid on, with a head table for staff and visitors. Huge steaks were barbecued and afterwards a ceilidh-type entertainment would be presented – music, song, poems; skits and playlets – some were naïve, some powerfully dramatic. Scurrilous verses describing events during the week might be recited – in the style of poets like Robert Burns, Dylan Thomas or Bob Dylan – to cheers or derision. And out of all this much good would come; staff would recognise unsuspected creativity, qualities

Students from the University of Toronto (c. 1960) at Summer Camp, Dorset, Ontario.
Thomas Howarth

of leadership, outstanding practical skills. New friendships were cemented, new ideas nurtured, new frameworks for research set in train. Saturday nights were times for fun and games, walks in the moonlight, long discussions around the pine logs blazing in the assembly hall. It was exhilarating and liberating.

Sunday was still the 'quiet' day. The students would set out in canoes loaded with picnics. Visitors, university administrators or practising architects, might follow to gather at a distant spot where a giant cast-iron cauldron was used to boil water and make tea 'frontier style'. The lake was deep enough and warm enough to swim in with pleasure and in those idyllic surroundings I had my first experience of 'skinny dipping'! Nude bathing. The water was crystal clear, cold and invigorating; the sense of being beyond the bounds of convention made the camaraderie doubly enjoyable. Sun, water, earth, and air showered their beneficence on us. Light, colour, tone, textures, growing plants and decaying trees, flowers, birds, bees and insects – all there for our delight.

It was always difficult to quantify the 'architectural' benefit of the two weeks our students spent at the Dorset camp but they, undoubtedly, promoted good staff-student relationships and the spiritual sustenance those camps provided was beyond measure. For example, a young Cree Indian was working as a general factotum in the school office. His name was Gus, and it suddenly occurred to me that Carswell and Hall should take him up to Dorset to help with general duties round the camp. Imagine my surprise when John Hall reported that Gus had no idea how to light a camp fire! His lack of knowledge told me something about the nature/nurture debate, as did the alacrity with which Gus then adapted to life in the north. His character and confidence bloomed up at Dorset and as a speaker of several Indian languages, he soon found employment as an interpreter for the Provincial Government.

One thing I quickly learned in Canada was that whilst most Canadian youngsters were lively and charming, few had much knowledge of world affairs or any culture outside their own. Thus, as a 'bookend' to our rural camp, I insisted that all first-year students also spent at least one week in New York, and that the upper years had field trips to Chicago, Boston or Philadelphia. Toronto still had strong anti-liquor laws in the 1950s! It was a very British city, known either as 'Toronto the Good' or 'Hogtown'. It needed to be internationalised and today's cosmopolitan, multicultural Toronto would be unthinkable without the changes that were set in train during the fifties and sixties.

One intellectual problem I faced on becoming director of a school of architecture was that I arrived at the moment in history when the 'warts' in Modernism were beginning to show themselves. All revolutionary movements throw up new problems as well as new solutions and I decided that teachers and students must address the serious problems, as well as the great possibilities of the Modern aesthetic and the new technologies. Numerous of the great modern buildings were beginning to show not just minor 'teething' problems but 'physical flaws' that were dangerous. As the airplane industry was forced to face the problem of metal fatigue, architecture had to face several similar technological problems. I believed it crucial that the new generation of architects should become thoroughly versed in 'the physics of building'. Consequently courses were arranged that explored the nature and function of new materials and new structural forms: even basic things, like the characteristics of wind and weather, had to be studied afresh. How did the untested products of our synthetic age react to years of ice and sun? New materials and working practices meant new responsibilities – for the craftsman, the building contractor, the architect and the engineer. New divisions of labour necessitated new methods of organisation and administration. New buildings might be brilliant, innovative and visually stunning but all buildings must function according to human need, and not just for months but many years.

Some extraordinary errors of judgement were already apparent: the rapid deterioration of the stain glass windows in Sir Frederick Gibberd's Roman Catholic cathedral in Liverpool; the repeated shattering of windows in Ming Pei's skyscraper office block in Boston; the springing of leaks in the roof of Saarinen's segmental, spherical chapel at the Massachusetts Institute of Technology. When Le Corbusier designed the United Nations building in New York he seems not to have realised that strong winds on large sheets of glass or metal can force rain sideward and upwards! Great damage was being done where damage was never traditionally expected. The details of sills, window bars and joints needed to be designed to accommodate new circumstances. Non-load bearing walls of glass and steel had become very popular since the early Bauhaus experiments, usually suspended beyond the structural frame of the building, but this created new problems with regard to condensation, moisture penetration, summer heat and winter cold. Such issues needed to be confronted by architects, by engineers and manufacturers, and by the schools of architecture.

One of the specialists I brought to Toronto to lecture on this subject was William Allan, formerly head of the Architectural Association School in London. His London office had a section devoted to building restoration. He informed us that the oldest of the British buildings then needing urgent repair by his company had been built just twelve years previously. He was a consultant to the Church of England, at that time responsible for about 7,000 churches, some dating back 1,400 years but even its most dangerous buildings had been built after 1945. One statistic he mentioned sticks in my memory: exposed external concrete takes seven years to stabilise chemically. It was these kinds of facts, squarely addressed, that allowed us to encourage our students to be imaginative and innovative because we worked from the technology outwards. We worked to see students designing, unblinkered, for the real world.

On the professional front, I quickly realised that many of Canada's leading architects wanted to know where the new Director of Architecture at the University of Toronto stood; what I planned with regard to the teaching of the new generation, how I saw the future of their profession and the booming city of Toronto. I soon found myself invited to address the annual banquet of the Ontario Association of Architects Convention, in February 1959. This provided me with a major intellectual challenge, equal to that issued in 1940 when I was asked to lecture on Mackintosh before the Lord Provost of Glasgow. By strange coincidence, one of the other speakers invited to the Ontario Convention was Nikolaus Pevsner, with whom I had jousted when asked to 'share' my research on Mackintosh! I had every reason to make a good presentation and began to formulate my thoughts well in advance. Then things began to go wrong. My two children, John and Katharine, went down with chicken pox. Then I, too, contracted the disease which, in an adult, can be serious. The doctor confined me to my bed for two weeks, a period that ended on the day of my lecture. For ten days I felt bad but my confinement was also a blessing: without the distraction of teaching or administration, I was able to really concentrate on planning my lecture. Edna, as well as looking after her three invalids, typed out my notes. All was completed by the evening of the 6th February. But, during the night, Edna began to suffer terrible pains in the stomach and, at four in the morning, she was rushed to hospital with acute appendicitis. She was operated on immediately. Reports came back suggesting all was well but I passed a disturbed day dozing and worrying and rehearsing my speech. I rose at five, for the first time in two weeks, to dress and be driven by friends to the York Hotel, where the banquet was to be held. My address was the last thing on the programme so, whilst the delegates dined, I rested in one of the hotel bedrooms and fell fast asleep. At the appointed hour my friends returned. Seeing me asleep they were just deciding that my address should be cancelled when I awoke and stood up, 'as white as a ghost' they said. I said I was ready and they more or less carried me to the banqueting hall, where I was propped up on a high stool, on a cushion, in front of the lectern. It was a dramatic entrance.

Most of the audience already knew something about my condition and family circumstances but, after being introduced, I was pleased to announce that Edna was well and I was no longer infectious! This broke the ice. And, with the audience behind me, I began to speak with an almost transcendental confidence, like the ascetic who has starved himself into knowledge! I felt I knew why the old Celtic bards would gorge themselves sick with pork and alcohol and lock themselves away in the darkness for days before coming out into the light to prophesy the future. I wished Frank Lloyd Wright were there to hear me. It was as if I was on auto-pilot but I also consciously addressed my lecture directly towards two particular members of the audience Dr Murray Ross, the Vice-president of the University, and his wife. It is good to address a particular person rather than an amorphous mass. And, because the address was an after-dinner speech, not a lecture, I was able to range widely in subject and add humour without cheapening my performance. Thus, chance and propitious circum-stance combined and I experienced one of the most compelling and influential nights of my life. The speech was a success and I was given a standing ovation.

I started by using my experience 'on the road' in the United States as a vehicle for exploring differences between the Old World and the New. First I played with the problems of our 'single' language. In North America, a car's bonnet becomes its hood, its hood is a soft-top, its boot a trunk, and a bumper – that part of a child's anatomy designed by providence for spanking! I also suggested that concepts of space and time on our two continents differ considerably. In Britain the vast majority of students then graduated from the universities they enrolled in. In America, even then, 60 percent of students graduated from institutions different to those in which they commenced their studies. I detailed the history of one student who had enrolled at Stanford, California, but changed her mind and spent her first year at Columbia, New York, her second year at the Sorbonne in Paris, her third year in Edinburgh and she was return to Columbia for her finals. But, because she would end up where she began she would not, statistically, be described as a 'mobile' student. Statistics and damned lies!

I quoted statistics affirming the fact that the average North American was then moving house once every five years. It's much less today! Such facts affect architecture. Unfortunately, almost wholly for the worse –

encouraging speculation, shoddiness, the quick fix and unedifying sprawl. I was able to quote a recent statement by an 'unnamed' local architect in the *Toronto Globe and Mail*: 'It is up to us to make the consumer so dissatisfied with his house that he is going to go out and buy a new one more quickly than he would have. I am not recommending that we cut quality, but that we should temper it with realism.' Realism! This architect had substantial interests in a speculative building firm and he personified an aspect of modern life that I, I informed my audience, stood firmly against. Architecture always reflects the spirit of the age. Our age is an age of disposability, novelty, materialism, early marriages and frequent divorces but we must not forget the enduring values of permanence, quality, harmony, beauty and repose. These things must continue to inform our lives and our architecture.

Coming from industrial Lancashire I was able to speak from experience about the value of wild nature and the importance of environmental protection. 'The vast open spaces of North America give the illusion that there is plenty of land for everybody and that plenty will be left when the last lot is sold! Freedoms can destroy as well as create.' I spoke of some of the savage, sprawling development projects I had seen in Florida and California. I assaulted the revolting network of overhead cables and junction boxes that benight the urban landscape of North America. Then, I changed gear and mentioned the subjects on which Professor Pevsner had been lecturing: The art of the Renaissance, Sir Christopher Wren, trends in modern architecture and the staircase; and I suggested that it would be truly ironic if the architects of Ontario were to view his beautiful slides, listen to his highly civilised ideas and then go out to despoil their native landscape and our nascent Canadian cities. If, however, they took his exemplars as models on which to base new work in a young country, future ages would remember them with honour.

I then spoke about Toronto and its great potential, stating that Toronto's new city hall about to be built by Viljo Ravell of Finland, might not, in itself, make Toronto a Mecca for visitors interested in architecture but that it could provide a key to future developments and, in time, Toronto could become a great city – drawing visitors from all over the world. I suggested that an imaginative city plan should be created and that a combination of civic and commercial buildings should be first envisioned, then developed in an orderly and systematic way.

I stated my belief that the architect must be a central figure in modern society and that the influence of architects must extend far beyond their responsibilities with regard to the erection of individual buildings. I suggested that the architect must be a man, or woman, of many parts – artist, technologist, philosopher, designer, administrator – but, at the same time, we should never deny that 'individuality' that makes each of us unique and which, so crucially, nurtures the human spirit. I suggested that architects must move confidently into the world of public relations and be a little less modest and introverted. 'Toronto: The Turbulent City' was the umbrella title under which we had gathered. I stated that we should involve ourselves fully in public discussions in the media and in the political arena, about the future of all our towns and cities. At that time newspapers, radio and television were only minimally concerned with architectural affairs. Such involvement should be informed, constructive, witty, exciting, as well as intellectually coherent.

I made a special plea to the leaders of the profession not to turn their backs on the less prestigious zones of architecture like domestic housing and low-cost urban housing. The uncontrolled, essentially unplanned, expansion of the great cities of Canada left us in danger of creating, in the New World, all the problems that unplanned industrial expansion had created in nineteenth-century Britain. I asked them to think fresh and be contemporary but also to look hard at the best precedents from the past mentioning Charleston in South Carolina, the great squares of London and Edinburgh and the vernacular farmhouses of the Mid-West and Canada. I commended the sense of 'place' those names engender. I mentioned Frank Lloyd Wright, Edwin Lutyens and Mackintosh.

Turning to my own hopes for the School of Architecture, I informed the profession that the University of Toronto was giving us new and unprecedented support, particularly in the field of graduate research. I expected many more of our undergraduate students to become postgraduates and, I expected all my colleagues to engage in serious research. I contrasted the extent to which scholarships and grant-aid supported undergraduate education in Britain, and in Canada – where only thirty percent of students received any kind of external financial support. I said I would fight to improve this unsatisfactory situation. I also outlined plans to reduce the student dropout rate. New, more creative and opened-ended systems of evaluating the applicants coming from school to university were needed. Standards in my school would be rigorous but if students proved themselves over the first three years, there would be no relegations during the final two years, except in the most extraordinary circumstances. I stated my wish for a closer liaison between the profession and the school of architecture, suggesting various ways in which we could help the profession and it could help us. The school's educational philosophy would be founded on the highest ideals of Western civilisation and my commitment to the noble profession of architecture. I concluded with a quotation that I had noted down whilst listening to the B.B.C. Foreign Service: 'the teacher's horizon must be far beyond the immediate demands of the next lesson or the particular level at which he teaches his subject; the teacher's ultimate command is not 'Look at me', but 'look at the way I am looking!'

Although my speech had been written out and Edna's typed text was on the lectern before me, a mixture of memory and inspiration allowed me to deliver the whole lecture as an extemporary performance off the cuff. And, when I sat down, the response was electric, the whole audience rose to applaud 'their' new Head of School and I was warmly congratulated by all around me. Nikolaus Pevsner pushed forward to offer generous praise and, to my great surprise, asked for a copy of my speech, to take back to London. Exhausted, I was helped back to my hotel bedroom where I again fell asleep. I was confident that my address had secured my entrance into the cultural and educational life of Canada.

Shortly after this, I was invited to direct the academic sessions of the next annual convention of the Royal Architectural Institute of Canada at the Banff Springs Hotel in Alberta. It provides a stunning setting, especially in wintertime, with the magnificent Rocky Mountains all around. I gathered together a brilliant series of speakers and asked John Burchard of Harvard to give the keynote address. He was seriously controversial and we had a week of highly stimulating architectural enquiry. In retrospect, I can see that most of the major issues we confronted remain the major issues facing architects today. Recreational facilities were marvellous and the hospitality of the Western Canadians was like that of the Scots. An external swimming pool was fed by hot springs which steamed in the freezing temperatures. There was a notice, 'Please do not throw snowballs into the swimming pool!' If one's hair got wet, it quickly froze and the sight of various grand ladies swimming round with spiked coiffures reminded me of *The Beano* and the Bash Street Kids in Britain's popular comics!

Each night bedroom drinking parties went on long into the night but on the last night a farewell dance was organised. Unfortunately it proved a great disappointment. For the first few hours the company was unsociably compartmentalised – the men at one end of a big room, talking and drinking – the women at the other end, talking and drinking – but many of them were obviously very keen to dance. I had done enough talking by this time! So I decided to dance and I had a wonderful time dancing with a select group of beautiful women who were, almost without exception, excellent dancers. I had learned to dance well in the ballrooms of Blackpool and, it seems to me, that formal dancing is one of the few genuinely civilised forms of entertainment left in the Western World. Slowly a few other men joined me but most of the evening I swept around that room in splendid isolation. Later one of the ladies was invited to sing. She sang a number of very ordinary popular songs but it was obvious she had a trained and gorgeous soprano voice. I went across to compliment her and I asked her why she was singing such ordinary songs when she had such an extraordinary voice. She replied that she had sung what she thought was wanted but she had various musical scores with her, if I could find her an accompanist.

We quietly slipped out of the dance hall and into the main auditorium. When I drew back the canvas cover of the grand piano I was delighted to find it unlocked and in perfect tune. And so, I played and she sang. We had an exquisite private recital of some of the most beautiful music in the world. For two hours she sang and as her voice carried out into that great auditorium, and beyond, a small gathering of listeners became quite a crowd. It was a wonderful experience and I shall never forget how, at about half past two in the morning, she sang 'I Know that my Redeemer Liveth', from Handel's *Messiah*. Thinking of that, even now, brings tears to my eyes. And next morning one of the architectural roughnecks asked me, 'Where were you last night?' There was censor in his question, so I paused before answering, whereupon he butted in to tell me he'd got blitzed at a bedroom party that went on till dawn! 'I couldn't match that', I said.

That same year, 1960, I was invited to work on two major architectural developments. The vice-president of the University of Toronto, my good friend Dr Murray Ross, had been appointed President of the city's second university, the University of York. He wanted me to prepare the master plan of its first, purpose-built campus, Glendon College. It was a thrilling invitation but I had already been invited to collaborate on the design of a master plan for the New Town of Bramalea, working with Howard V. Lobb and John B. Parkin Associates. It was clear things were moving fast, and I had to very quickly decide what my responsibilities were, what my commitments would be. Should I should set up a professional practice in Toronto and chase commissions, like most of my colleagues, or concentrate my energies on the school of architecture? After much private agonising I decided to be a full-time educator. It is better to do one thing well than several badly. However, I did accept the offer to oversee the planning of Glendon College, it was an educational project of exactly the kind I had long hoped for, but, beyond that I decided to give absolute priority to my work as Director of the School of Architecture.

Once in post, in Toronto, I had begun to see that I really was well-qualified to be head of the school. Any lingering doubts about why I had been 'head-hunted' for this appointment vanished and I became determined to make Toronto one of the outstanding schools of architecture not just in North America but the world. For a number of years certain colleagues remained sceptical of me, and my plans for the school, but I recognised that one way in which I could encourage their commitment to the school and their loyalty to me, was to offer them not just exciting educational possibilities but also any private work that might come to me. I do not regret my decision. A great head of school, like Fra Newbery in Glasgow, has to subordinate some of their personal creativity in order to fully serve their students. Although it is also a fact that some heads of schools use 'busy-ness' as a cover for the lazy complacency that executive power too often engenders. Golden Means must be found in teaching as in building.

Within two months of my arrival in Toronto, the School of Architecture began the move from its four separate buildings to the great Victoria Curling Rink at 177 Huron Street. Oversight of the conversion and occupation of this building took up a good deal of my time. The architects were Marani and Morris. Their chief associate was Michael Barstow, an Englishman with an impeccable military background. He proved to be a most congenial person to work with and the ice rink soon provided us with our own 'Canadian' Bauhaus! The great, clear floor-space of the rink was a marvellous place within which to teach, and to mount exhibitions. Our 'Dorset Nights' were memorable occasions with our students exhibiting their work – in the great tradition of The Group of Seven! Over a thousand visitors could be comfortably accommodated. The ice rink also provided a marvellous arena for the students 'Fall Ball' – a fancy dress extravaganza, and the 'Spring Fling' – a more formal occasion with a head table, black ties and a plethora of speeches. Such formalities are, I believe, good training for professional architects.

Our school in the ice rink was a triumph. Unfortunately, by the mid 1950s, an ever-increasing number of students were putting intolerable strains on the building fabric of universities across Canada and a huge educational expansion was underway. The province of Ontario decided to build nine new universities and to hugely expand the University of Toronto. I became a member of the President's Advisory Committee on Accommodation and Facilities. Ad hoc solutions had resulted in

educational sprawl, so they now proposed the demolition of our beautiful school in the ice rink! I pleaded for planned long-term developments and I made it clear that the Victoria Ice Rink was both an architectural treasure and a resource of great educational value. All to no avail. Ad hoc opinion gathered further momentum and I was informed of three possible sites where the School of Architecture might be rehoused. Each in my opinion, were unsatisfactory. By this time, however, I knew the fabric of the university extremely well, and I had come to realise that 'necessary deceit' is a tool used in education, just as it is in almost every other form of organisation. Thus, I decided to play the game being used against me.

I examined all the university buildings earmarked for change of use and, it occurred to me, that the former school of dentistry at 230 College Street, would make the most satisfactory school of architecture. It was 'designated' as the future accommodation of the Faculty of Pharmacy. The building dated from the 1920s and was very substantial, U-shaped in plan and five storeys high, with plenty of basement space. I carefully surveyed the building and was rather pleased to find it 'in very poor condition'; partly because the architects, Mathers and Haldenby, had carried out a savage structural examination that left various holes in walls, floors and ceilings. The place was, I noted, 'a dust-encaked shambles'. Reconstruction of such a building as a pharmaceutical laboratory would have been

Howarth with students (1965). *Jack Marshall*

'horrendously expensive'. Consequently, I outlined all the problems this building presented and suggested that the faculty of pharmacy needed an entirely new, purpose-built, building. This would be not only the best option but, in the long run, much the cheapest. I informed the committee that the former dental school could, relatively cheaply, be transformed to accommodate a non-scientific teaching department but its current assignation as the home for a science faculty was dangerously mistaken. To my surprise, at the next meeting of the P.A.C.A.F., my suggestion was accepted! And the chairman then enquired as to whether I would consider the School of Dentistry as a new home for the school of architecture. I said I would examine the possibilities. I felt like Brer Rabbit after Brer Fox had flung him into the bramble bush! Mighty relieved!

Things then moved quickly. Mathers and Haldenby were appointed to effect the transformation and I established an excellent working relationship with their senior partner, Basil Ludlow. The building was well supplied with elevators, one of which had been designed to carry cadavers, kept in cold storage in the basement, up to a splendid operating theatre on the ground floor! This theatre had a ceiling sixteen feet high and an enormous north-facing glass wall – specially designed to cast a pure north light into the mouths of the cadavers being examined. I, immediately, earmarked this room as a future 'artists' studio'.

Since my early days in Glasgow, where Mackintosh's building so practically affirms the poetic relationship between all the arts, I had planned to employ 'resident artists' as members of any school of architecture that I might, one day, direct. This was my golden opportunity. Within months I had established an annual 'residence' that brought practising artists into the school allowing all our students, during their five-year courses, close contact with a painter, a sculptor, a ceramicist, and a weaver or craft specialist. It proved a great success. My first choice of artist was Lyn Chadwick, a leading British sculptor, who had just been commissioned to create a work for a wealthy patron in Toronto and was temporarily resident in Canada. Unfortunately the commission fell through and Chadwick withdrew from the residency but, over the next decade, a series of distinguished artists used the studio to great effect. They received no payment but had full use of the studio and in return they gave informal tutorials to interested students. By the mid-seventies, however, as pressure on work spaces increased and the demand for technological solutions in architecture became overwhelming this experiment with living artists was discontinued. The cadavers' theatre then became a photography and visual aids centre.

I decided to use white paint throughout the interior of the new school. White provides maximum illumination and a maximum feeling of spaciousness. I have always found white the best colour for older properties – even when your aim, longer term, is to introduce colour. Experience of the white space gives you 'a get acquainted period' during which you can begin to 'feel' what colours will work best where, what textures are needed, what patterns will best humanise the environment. About some things it is good to take your time. Other things can and should be instantly decided. For example, one day, the buildings superintendent arrived with a lorry-load of the most appalling lecture room chairs. As soon as I saw them I asked him to remove them. Immediately! And I insisted that I be consulted about all future furnishings for the school of architecture. I then skimmed through various current catalogues and was delighted to find a rather fine chair for sixteen dollars. It was a heavy-duty chair modelled on a wonderfully light, fibreglass chair designed by Charles Eames. The metal frame was rather clumsily designed, the moulded plyboard seat less than elegant but it was strong and practical and in no way an 'insult' to a school committed to visual education.

My office was at the south-west corner of the building and Basil Ludlow redesigned it exactly to my liking. There was space for a conference table as well as my desk, and the Frank Lloyd Wright table which I had found, grossly neglected, when I arrived at the school in 1958. It had been salvaged by a group of Toronto students, in Chicago on a field trip, when the Larkin Building was being demolished. My desk came from its basement. The students brought it back to the school as a momento and, when I saw it, I got it repaired by our lab technician, Fred Bolduan. Its still there and I like to think that that table, if sold today would reimburse the university for the whole of my professorial salary! Basil Ludlow designed an excellent suite of bookcases and cupboards for the south wall leaving an arched recess in the north wall into which he built a low cupboard with a black arborite top. The whole alcove was then painted black which, I believe, is the best background for any coloured work of art. Here I placed various items from my Mackintosh collection including high-back chairs, paintings and designs for fabrics. These provided a most stimulating environment within which to have small-scale meetings. My conference table was also black, an Art Deco extending dining table with matching eight chairs. The floor was covered wall to wall in Naugahide, a rubber-backed, rather hairy fabric with a good range of colour. I got this as a free offer, the company insisting that it sought no advertising return, only the honour of carpeting the office of the Director of the 'best' school of architecture in Canada. How we all succumb to flattery!

The student studios also turned out well and, over the years, we had no reason to regret moving into the building providence gave us. However, even today, the thought of the loss of the Victoria Ice Rink causes me pain. I can still see it – half railway terminal, half Grand Palais; the students vitalised by the great space, their dark desks set out between classical mouldings, column capitals, Michelangelo's *David* and the *Venus de Milo* – the white plaster casts I'd salvaged during the chaos of our first removal! Such remnants of the classical tradition have long been out of fashion in schools of art but there is no doubt that the education of the eye is a slow process best nurtured over years, rather than one or two slide lectures – as the art of the Mediterranean world has proved over millennia. Shortly after we left the ice rink, the University of Toronto ordered its demolition and, in it's place, Allward and Gouinlock designed a big, undistinguished building which still serves the faculty of chemistry.

To establish the tone of our new school building I immediately organised two very different exhibitions. The first presented 'Locks and Keys through History', and was supported by the Yale and Town Manufacturing Company of St Catherine's, Ontario. Such items have importance in the history of architecture; attention to detail and the unity of design, the happy marriage of microcosm and macrocosm, have marked all the great periods of architecture. A second exhibition presenting 'The Visual Arts of Japan', was organised and designed by Professors Hall and Grooms. It was an early acknowledgement of the Oriental World's importance to modern Canada and it complemented my lectures on Mackintosh, to whom I was introducing the students at that time. Japan and Mackintosh – there is an unfathomable connection. As the old, mad Ruskin used to say as he wondered around Brentwood House, 'everything black, everything white'!

My years as director and dean, 1958–78, were the great years of demolition and urban renewal in Toronto and across the world. New cities and new environments were being created and recreated, some of them splendid, too many of them ugly, draughty and inhuman. At such a moment, it was doubly important that schools of architecture should oversee the creation of the best possible new buildings whilst encouraging architects, and society to conserve the best of the old. Three of my staff, Eric Arthur, Acland and Goulding took leading rolls in the architectural conservancy of Toronto and although the city fathers and property developers got their way too often, their work achieved notable successes including the preservation of the old city hall which, in the early seventies, was to be demolished to facilitate an extension to the Eatons store! Academic research into conservation was one of the many areas of research I encouraged amongst the School's permanent staff. I made it clear that I would support any staff engaged in serious and innovative design work and in technological experimentation but I was not in favour of staff using their employment at the University merely as a economic safety net to help weather ups and downs in the economic cycle. I stated my belief that the creation of an important building was at least as admirable as the publication of a major book but because they were architects who had chosen to work at a university, I did expect them to keep abreast of academic developments and to pursue knowledge of the kind that was not for sale in the architectural market place. Not all of them did, but the university itself was partly at fault; at that time no member of staff was allowed to read for a higher degree within their own university. To counter that short-sighted restriction, I offered leave of absence to any staff willing to pursue courses, and research, overseas and, over the years, the school reaped significant rewards.

Stanley Kent took a master's degree at Liverpool University and Fraser Watts gained an M.L.A. from Harvard. Professor Raymore produced a much-needed book on architectural specification and supervision; Professor Acland travelled to Central and Eastern Europe to collect material for a book on Gothic vaulting; Irving Grossman went to India to compare the relationship of painting and sculpture to architecture in Oriental and Western societies. Professor Arthur took a year's leave of absence to complete his book on the architecture of the city of Toronto; a project he had been working on, fitfully, for twenty years. It was published to acclaim in 1964 as *Toronto: No Mean City*, and resulted in a Canada Council grant for a similar survey of buildings in the Maritime Provinces. It was partly as a result of Arthur's work that I was able to launch our collaboration with the city of Milan, which led in 1976 to the creation of the brilliantly successful symposium – 'Due Culture, Due Citta.'

One postgraduate research project of which I remain particularly proud was carried out by Thomas Ibronyi and entitled, 'Building in the North'. I had been surprised by the lack of interest, both in university and government circles, in the problems and potentialities of Canada's vast northern hinterland. It was a huge issue and I felt that architects must get involved. Ibronyi spent a long period in the Mackenzie River area and produced a master's thesis in 1960. A string of subsequent research projects followed. Outstanding amongst these was an Arctic Dome –

designed by Peter Favot. It was planned to house a community of 2,000 people and was to be serviced, internally, by a submarine! This design provoked a great deal of interdisciplinary enthusiasm and representatives of Montreal's Expo 1967 visited Toronto to enquire about using it as a centrepiece attraction. Their enquiries came to nothing but the ramifications of Favot's research are still being felt.

Since my Glasgow days I have been a strong believer in 'competitions' as a means of stimulating students, they can be yeast to the dough of hard study. In Toronto, I encouraged sponsorship for numerous competitions and awards. I remember Peter Hamilton winning a competition to design an aluminium light fixture for the lofty entrance hall to 230 College Street. It still looks good. Taivo Kapsi, a brilliant young architect, won a fabric design competition – having devised a dramatic pattern of Toronto buildings and printed them black on heavy white cotton. I like to think this was one of the high points of his short life. He was murdered by a group of young thugs trespassing on his country property outside Toronto.

Research work of various kinds slowly gathered momentum in Toronto, but even today, I contrast the extraordinary scholarship that Professor Cordingley was able to generate in post-war Manchester with what I managed to generate in Toronto in the prosperous sixties and seventies. Almost all his staff gained master's degrees or PhDs – at a time when such qualifications were genuine tests of academic achievement. He himself was immersed in a long-term plan to visually document all the farmhouses and 'lesser' homes of England, county by county! When I was at Manchester he was working on Cheshire, Lancashire, Northumberland and the whole of the Lake District. It was a prodigious task that preceded, and possibly stimulated, Sir Nikolaus Pevsner's monumental survey of *The Buildings of England*. (How often my tracks and those of Nikolaus Pevsner seem to have crossed!) I used these exemplary projects by Cordingley and Pevsner, to try to stimulate my staff to take a similar interest in Canadian vernacular architecture but my success was limited.

As an adjunct to departmental research I invited many prestigious lecturers, including Pevsner, to Toronto. Serge Chermayeff of Harvard, one of the last survivors of Early Modernism came, and the two leading American art historians Henry-Russell Hitchcock and Hugh Scully. Sir Basil Spence came to talk about his New Coventry Cathedral; I was particularly interested to hear him discuss the ways in which he had integrated the bombed shell of the original cathedral into the fabric of his contemporary building; I was also interested in the ways in which he used leading artists and craftsmen. Public lectures of this kind were also grand social events which took place in Convocation Hall before audiences of up to 1,700 people. They raised the profile of the School and the city's architectural profession. The impact of such lectures is often long-term, almost subterranean. Who knows when and how a student will be inspired by direct contact with a great mind? Who knows how nascent genius is nurtured into growth? Certainly history would seem to validate the resonance of such a 'laying on of hands'.

One unusual lecture was presented by William Zeckendorf, a multimillionaire American, who, in the early sixties, was recognised as one of the great entrepreneurs of the post-war period. To get him to come to Toronto was a major achievement. He had never lectured at a school of architecture. His life was carefully controlled by assistants, secretaries and minders of various kinds. I was briefed in great detail as to how the great man was to be received and asked to set out exactly what his programme would be. He arrived, to the second, in the middle car of a small convoy of Cadillacs, and he moved everywhere surrounded by an entourage of seven or eight people like presidents since the assassination of Kennedy, though Zeckendorf's visit was a year or two earlier. He swept through the School, looked appreciatively at an exhibition of original Frank Lloyd Wright drawings and then, exactly to the second, entered the lecture theatre where a capacity audience was packed, hungry to hear the secret of acquiring great wealth! Zeckendorf spoke with a surprisingly self-deprecating humour about how he worked and how his business functioned. His listeners were attentive, a congenial atmosphere was engendered and, surprised by his reception, Zeckendorf rearranged his schedule to partake of refreshments at the Faculty Club. He then left us, a little wiser about the ways of the world and in strangely good humour!

One research project that I helped initiate proved a failure. Professor Llewlyn Thomas, a colleague at the university, had invented what he described as a 'head camera': a movie camera mounted on a helmet which, by the use of mirrors and micro lenses, recorded the movements of the eyes of the wearer. These movements were then codified as spots of light that traversed the moving film. The instrument thus recorded the eye movements of people in movement – a pedestrian, a car driver, a pilot. Thomas believed that his invention could provide important safety information for all concerned with the development of high-speed transport. I saw that it might also provide interesting optical and psychological information of use to architects and planners designing freeways, road junctions, airports, pleasure parks and the general urban environment.

To this end I applied for and obtained a research grant and bought one of his cameras – at a cost of 6,000 dollars! That was a lot of money forty years ago! I then allocated the camera to the Division of Town and Regional Planning and awaited significant developments. Years passed and nothing happened. Perhaps it was a dud idea but, more likely, it was an idea well ahead of its time. It certainly showed the ways in which a great deal of public money can be wasted.

Much more constructive was my early commitment to the use of computers in architectural design. Computers did not come to me as a surprise in Canada. The University of Manchester was the original home of modern computing. I was appointed lecturer there at the same time as Tom Kilburn, the mathematician, who with Professor Sir Freddie Williams, created the world's first stored-programme computer, on 21st June 1948. I knew them both and I remember that date very clearly. Their invention engendered great excitement within the University. Alun Turing was also there. He was a most brilliant man who, during the Second World War, made the crucial breakthroughs that allowed Britain to decipher the secret codes of the German High Command. He shortened the length of the war by many months, if not years, and then found himself hounded by the British Secret Service, because of his homosexual leanings. He committed suicide. It was a tragedy and it occurred during my time in Manchester, and I have never forgotten it. Today they've named a roundabout, on an industrial estate on the outskirts of the city – the Turing Roundabout! In 1964, I was pleased to hear that his colleague, Tom Kilburn, had been appointed the first Professor of Manchester's Department of Computer Science. During the same year, I went off to M.I.T. in Boston to attend a major conference on computers in architectural design. I was greatly impressed by the conference and the potential uses of computers in the field of architecture. On the spot, I invited all the most important conference speakers to Toronto, and computer technology became an integrated part of our teaching from that time on.

Computers are important tools but it is people, and direct human contact, that have always guided my life. One of the most telling relationships I established in Toronto was with Fred Coates, a technician and model-maker who managed the school's architectural workshop. Fred was also a true artist-craftsman who carried a living Art Nouveau tradition into the mid-twentieth century. He was also unique creative personality who gave Canada something immeasurable and valuable. Fred Coates was born in Nottingham, England, in 1890. After a short spell at the local school of art he spent a year in Paris, then enrolled at the Royal College of Art in

London. In 1913 he emigrated to Toronto, to establish a practice as a sculptor and model-maker. In 1916, he enlisted in the Canadian Army Medical Corps. After basic training he was selected to work as a 'medical sculptor'; it was his job to help surgeons remodel the heads and faces of soldiers disfigured in battle. This greatly interested me because my own brother, Jay, had worked as a surgeon in Italy and Austria during the Second World War. Facial reconstruction has become one of the necessary 'arts' of our time and it reminds us why the patron saint of artists and doctors is the same man, St Luke. Medicine and art both grow from the same ancient root when healing, divination and artistic expression were one.

Fred Coates worked with the Canadian war-wounded at military hospitals in the south of England. His remodelled 'heads' were produced after he had studied photographs taken before injury was inflicted. He also worked from life and from imagination; the surgeons then 'twisted human flesh into new noses and jaws. Dozens of operations were often required on one man and, for all of them, Fred Coates acted as the "facial architect". The doctors knew how to graft flesh and bone: Coates knew what a remodelled face should look like.' That report comes from the *Toronto Star Weekly*, 18th April 1934.

When on leave, Coates used to travel around England viewing art galleries and sights of architectural interest. He admired Rossetti, G.F. Watts, Lord Leighton, Beardsley, and Rodin. He copied precious textiles in the British Museum and the Victoria and Albert, and avidly read back numbers of the arts magazine *The Studio*. He also toured the great cathedrals and churches of the battlefields, Amiens, Arras, Mons, Reims, Peronne, and Boulogne. Amidst the devastation of war he continued, as it were, his artistic apprenticeship – filling his mind with the imagery that would feed his art for a lifetime. He was discharged from the army in August 1919. He

Fred Coates with plaster casts of injured heads.

Left. The Coates' 'ideal' house, Sherwood, at Scarborough Bluffs, Ontario.

Right. Louise Coates.

returned to Canada determined, like so many of his fellows, to live close to the beauties of nature and to serve his fellow man. He fell in love with Louise Brown, a talented young artist who had been brought up in the Whitby Township, Ontario. Both struggled to find work but, out of the blue, they were offered a small wooded lot, overlooking the Scarborough Bluffs, by a landscape painter George Gieseke and they started to plan an 'ideal' house, hidden amongst the pines. They determined to destroy no trees other than those where their house would stand. They were ecological enthusiasts fifty years before that enthusiasm became fashionable. They built the house themselves with limited help from a carpenter, a stonemason, blacksmiths and various friends. It is an excellent late example of the Arts and Crafts movement in Canada. In 1922 they got married and they lived in that house until the end of their lives.

Many years after their deaths, I helped Paul Makovsky curate an exhibition of the Coates' work for the University of Toronto and it, very beautifully, presented the art and the lives of this exemplary couple. They imbued all they touched with poetic charm and vitality and their hand-built house reflected their values. It was functional and very much part of nature but it was also mystical and communal, as many mediaeval buildings were. One journalist described their house as amongst 'the most romantic in Canada. It might be called a magic house, for if the exterior is changeless, the interior is as flexible as Mr Coates' accomplishments and stage-settings.' Fred named the house 'Sherwood'. And, just as in the Greenwood of England, Robin Hood lived a life in which lifestyle, culture and social values could not be separated, so Fred Coates and Louise lived lives in which lifestyle and culture became one unified whole. Work and leisure, the pleasures of the country and the civilised delights of the city, were seamlessly integrated as one. Some people would describe them as an

eccentric pair but, for me, their lives illustrated what Christ meant when he said, 'in my house are many mansions'.

During the 1920s they worked mainly as stage-set designers and became crucial figures in the theatrical life of Toronto. Over the years they also practised weaving, basketry, jewellery-making, pottery, and bookbinding; they designed and block-printed textiles; they worked in linoleum, they sketched, painted and sculpted; they were excellent photographers; they enjoyed the recitation of poetry; and they organised masques and musical entertainments of various kinds. Fred had designed a memorable production of Shakespeare's *The Tempest*, at the Hart Theatre in 1922 and, perhaps as a reaction against the terrors of war, he decided to live out his life like a Prospero. His paintings seem to embody the dream worlds of both Caliban and Miranda. As hosts, the Coates loved to surprise their guests with the delights of their 'island' in the woods of Scarborough. Their private rooms were quite small because their studio, their mediaeval hall, was huge. It provided them with a marvellous work-space and a communal 'theatre', with stage and minstrels gallery which they would transform into a circus ring, a cowboy camp, an Elizabethan hall, a den for Ali Baba or the drawing room of a Spanish grandee!

This was the man who was our technician and model-maker at the school of architecture! I was hugely impressed by Fred's talents and the strange world that he and Louise continued to inhabit. With the artist Ed Carswell I became a frequent visitor to their house and every visit to Sherwood was always a genuine experience of what I call 'the artistic enterprise'.

Fred died in 1965, just three years after his retirement, after thirty-two years in the school. Louise lived on till 1975 and I was later moved to learn that she had bequeathed 'Sherwood' to the school of architecture. They had had no children and they saw architecture as a key to humanity's future well-being. The house contents were to be sold but I was given first option to purchase any items I wished before the sale. Their archives were of real artistic and historical importance and, although most of the furniture and fittings were ordinary, I felt strongly that the whole collection should be preserved together. The library, for example, contained superb books by Beardsley, Arthur Rackham, Dulac and many others. I suggested that Hart House and the university should acquire the bulk of this fascinating and valuable material. They decided to only take Fred's personal papers and diaries so I determined to form my own Fred Coates Collection. I have never regretted buying what I did: books, various stage designs, two large gesso panels of exotic flowers, and a huge linoleum panel – a paradisal scene that 'Le Douanier' Rousseau would have been pleased to envision – with a nude female figure reclining in a forest surrounded by flowers, peacocks and brilliantly coloured birds in flight through the trees. All these things are gifted, in my will, to Hart House. Thus they will go where I originally planned. Meantime they have given me quite extraordinary pleasure.

One general disappointment I experienced in coming to Toronto was to find how many Canadian academics, at that time, were habitual backbiters, wilfully provincial and politically manipulative. I had grown up to assume higher education was the disinterested pursuit of knowledge and that architecture, 'the Mother of the Arts', was the exemplary custodian of all civilisation's best qualities. For sometime I assumed the infighting and vindictiveness in Toronto sprang from my advent as a foreigner. The truth was that a sour and inbred defensiveness pervaded the whole university. Nearly all staff were Toronto graduates. Once in, they made sure they stayed in for life. The school of architecture, for instance, had had only two directors in the sixty-eight years of its existence before my arrival in 1958. 'Daddy Wright', C.H.C. Wright, was a solid engineer, a traditionalist who laid good foundations. His successor, H.H. Madill was a Toronto architect who was a skilled administrator but a weak personality who became the plaything of his deputy, Eric Arthur, in 1923. In 1958 he became mine!

Eric Arthur was a raconteur of the first order, a bully and a natural politician. He had a powerful network of friends and acquaintances, many of them in local government and educational administration. During the Second World War he served in the Merchant Navy. I believe it a pity he did not serve in the Royal Canadian Navy where he would have encountered men and inhaled a discipline that might have brought something better out of him. As it was, he returned to Toronto with his original personality intact, and his propensity for bullying stronger than ever. He could be a bitter, caustic critic of student work and of his architectural colleagues. By nurturing his political contacts in Toronto he alienated many of the city's practising architects and, to his chagrin but no architect's surprise, when Madill retired in 1957 and an interim director of the School of Architecture was appointed – it was not him! The University's Board of Governors draughted in Milton Osborne, from Manitoba, a complete outsider, to be director pro tem. During this interregnum the staff split into three factions: the design team gathered around Eric Arthur, the technologists around Raymore and Ed Carswell provided a natural focus for staff teaching the arts and humanities.

Thus, in the autumn of 1958, I entered a lion's den. Staff were at each other's throats and all outstanding staff appointments had, unfortunately, been filled shortly before my appointment (largely dictated by Arthur). I had very little room within which to manoeuvre. I had to work with the resources in place but, risking further segmentation, I recommended that Raymore and Carswell be promoted to become full professors and I removed responsibility for design from Eric Arthur's professorship (which he kept). I informed all three that I had been shocked to learn that many architectural firms within Toronto preferred to hire their graduates from the Ryerson Institute of Technology rather than from our school of architecture. It was a situation that I asked be changed, by us working together.

Ryerson ran sound courses in the teaching of draughting skills, problems of structure, and building technology but they did not even presume to teach architectural design. We had complimentary responsibilities yet our two institutions had no formal or creative contact. It was a disgrace and I was determined to improve the situation. I invited C.R. Worsely, Head of the Ryerson Department, to visit the school to discuss matters of mutual interest. In particular I was keen to facilitate student exchange, suggesting that, on graduation, a selection of his best students should consider transfer to the School of Architecture where they could complete fully professional qualifications. I also suggested that some of our more technologically minded students might wish to transfer to Ryerson. Productive contact was established and over the years numerous students crossed the city to the School of Architecture though, I'm proud to say, none of our students ever went over to Ryerson. I was appointed to their advisory committee, which met twice a year, and I agreed to give their students an annual lecture, a tradition that continued long after I retired.

One of my fellow board members at Ryerson was S. H. Mathers, who, like most Canadian architects of that time, had a very empirical and eclectic attitude towards modern architecture. I remember visiting Mathers' office and being taken into his inner sanctum where he had a row of three or four drawing boards. On the first was a fine drawing, in the neo-Gothic style, for the Royal Canadian Air Force chapel he was designing for a clifftop site overlooking the St Lawrence River, adjacent to Parliament Hill, Ottawa. The chapel was beautifully detailed and harmonised well with the nearby Château Laurier. I admired it, but I asked him why he was perpetuating the Gothic style; had he ever considered designing in the Modern manner? He laughed and removed the dust sheet from the next drawing board and said, 'What do you think of this?' 'This' was a sleek, modern design in steel and concrete for a Coca Cola stand and roadside service station. 'This sort of thing,' said Mathers, 'is dead easy, but you have to really understand architectural design and materials to design in the traditional ways.' His comments underline the extent to which Victorian values underlay most aspects of Canadian life well into the second half of the twentieth century but one has to ask, was such continuance so wrong? Time has shown us that third-rate Modernism is a poisoned chalice – traditional materials, natural building methods and historical 'styles' usually have redeeming features. Modernism lives or dies in the hands of the designer; it has few redeeming features when in insensitive hands or is a mere excuse for a cheap fix.

Modern Architecture in Contemporary Canada was the subject of three television programmes I made for C.B.C. in the fall of 1961. I worked in collaboration with Vincent Tovell. The programmes were entitled *Architecture for Worship*, *Architecture for Learning*, and *Architecture for Recreation*. They were wide-ranging, but all revolved around the Modernist aesthetic. The programmes were well received and led on to a second series entitled *A Future for the Past*. These allowed me to place Modernism in context with the great traditions of the past, and also to plant the importance of 'the principle of conservation' in the minds of the Canadian public.

As master-planner of the York University campus I was able to put theory into practise and 'the whole environment' became my prime concern. As I worked on this commission I became ever more determined to unify our separate study of architecture, planning and landscape at the university beneath some kind of environmental studies umbrella. My aim was not fired by personal ambition, it was not ideological or purely 'educational' – I saw it as practical common sense, precipitated by the nature of Canadian society and its rapid expansion.

Throughout the early sixties, I gradually strengthened our planning unit by appointing new members of staff and inviting international environmental specialists like Professors Hideo Sasaki of Harvard, Christopher Tunnard of Yale, and my good friend Sir Hugh Casson in London. Things went well and by the spring of 1964, I thought the moment right to establish a department of landscape architecture within the school of architecture. I asked the University President if I could give a short slide lecture to the University Senate to show them the nature and importance of this neglected subject. It was the first time the university's academic governors had been addressed in this particular way. I illustrated my talk with a superb collection of slides built up over twenty years showing cultured and wild landscape from Europe, Britain and North America; Capability Brown, Ormstead, Robert Adam, Gertrude Jekyll; great boulevards and national parks. Who would not be persuaded of the importance of such a subject and the necessity of training professionals to confront the issues the future must address? The senate agreed to set up a four-year undergraduate programme leading to a bachelor's degree in landscape architecture. I was delighted and, in 1967, the School of Architecture became an independent faculty with three departments: Architecture, Planning, and Landscape Architecture – all, I believe, of genuinely international status.

Whilst determinedly pursuing these kinds of strategic targets, I remained, perhaps unwisely, open to chance and serendipity. One day at work in my office, I became aware of a figure standing in the open door. No knock, no word. When I looked up a young man was walking towards me. 'I am John Andrews and I'm looking for a job', he said. I had no knowledge of any John Andrews but I asked him to sit down and tell me about himself. He announced that he had been one of the finalists in the Toronto City Hall competition and had worked with John Parkin Associates. Following a disagreement he had just thrown in his job. He planned to go home to Australia in the fall but would be pleased to stay on in Toronto if I was willing to give him a job. He was brash and excitable but we had a very amicable chat and I said I'd speak to the Parkins about him. That evening John B. Parkin came round to College Street and drove me home, talking all the way. Andrews was, he said, an outstanding designer, but difficult to work with, and Australian to his boots! I should be prepared for the odd clash and administrative grumbles but the man had talent and a rare energy. I was persuaded and I gave John Andrews an open-ended, part-time contract. That decision was to have dramatic long-term consequences on the School of Architecture.

I decided to put Andrews in joint charge of students doing their fifth-year thesis projects, with Frank Jenkins, another new appointee. Frank was quiet and introverted but a brilliant scholar and excellent teacher. John Andrews was a showman who 'damn-blasted' and 'bloody exploded' at the least provocation. He was a good teacher, too, but students had to be resilient and prepared to defend themselves. Andrews would suddenly, and dramatically, tear student proposals apart. Fortunately, he and Jenkins brought the best out in each other and, jointly, they brought a great deal out of the students. Their fifth year produced work that stood as the measure of the high quality I expected, throughout the years of my directorship. Some students found Andrews a little too unpredictable but everyone got experience of what is called 'the rough school of life'.

Deep down, John Andrews was a man of high sensibility and, as he

began to enjoy his time at the school, he consciously tried to control the wilder side in himself. He came to me one day to ask my advice about his natural compulsion to swear, and throw his weight around; he knew it wasn't appropriate to 'a university situation', he almost shouted! He explained how much he admired Frank Jenkins' ability to get at the root without flinging mud! I told him that 'many roads lead to Rome' and that he shouldn't worry about his 'damn-blasting' provided it was justified and supported by critical insight. I said time and experience would, probably, mellow him and that just as an athlete responds to a flow of adrenalin so does the artist and teacher. I said that I believed him to be an able and sincere teacher and, even more important, an architect who really knew what he was talking about.

So, John Andrews stayed on and gradually became more like the rest of us but there was a flaw in his character and just as much as his enthusiasms were uncontrolled, his choice of friends was highly suspect. One day, he told me about a friend of his, Jack Diamond from the University of Pennsylvania, a brilliant architect. John recommended I employ him as a teacher in Toronto. I met Diamond and found him to be a product of the *atelier* of Louis Kahn, one of America's truly original Modern architects. He had achieved great success as a student in Natal, at Oxford, and at the University of Pennsylvania. I invited him to join our part-time staff and shortly afterwards, he and John Andrews became design partners in Toronto. The trouble was that both had such strong and wilful characters – their partnership was not a team and soon became a conflagration! I remember, one day, watching John Andrews as he observed Jack Diamond coming into the staff room, I saw first dark depression then fuming anger pass over his face and I knew that their partnership was doomed. At the same time I had a premonition of a threat to the future of the school of architecture. Shortly after this, Jack Diamond returned to work in the United States. That was in 1967. Nothing untoward happened in the school but John Andrews' next friend was another kettle of fish altogether. His name was Peter Prangnell.

Looking back, 1967 was the high point of my whole career. The School of Architecture had grown significantly and, after nine years, I was genuinely proud of what we had achieved. There was a palpable, creative buzz amongst students, staff and the architectural profession in Ontario. That year the School of Architecture was formally integrated into what became the new Faculty of Environmental Design. It was my creation and I was honoured to be its first Dean. I liked the name dean; it seemed less prosaic and more approachable than director. Faculty status gave me increased authority when debating issues in the University Senate, the body that controlled all aspects of the University's academic life. It comprised about 360 people and in general this university senate worked well, partly I suspect, because of the existence of an informal group that met 'post senatum'. I had been invited to join this select group of about a dozen of the university's senior academics, almost immediately after my appointment, in 1958. Meetings took place in the house of a senior colleague and there was always an attractive spread of food, wine and good strong coffee. The atmosphere was relaxed, friendships were established and future policies discussed. In a way, it acted like a Cabinet in a parliamentary democracy but it was unofficial, and almost invisible, and it caused resentments and charges of elitism.

University finances and public policy were controlled by the board of governors; a body dominated by businessmen, industrialists and public figures. Thus the university had a tried and tested, bicameral, system of governance that worked. The orderly systems of debate and decision-taking was generally enjoyable to the participants, however, such formality and its associated 'officer corps mentality' was beginning to run out of sync. With the times and as the student radicalism of the sixties gathered pace, it came under attack. Perhaps Toronto's proximity to the United States was part of the problem; the Vietnam War spilling its poisons north into Canada. In retrospect, however, it seems amazing that such a flaccid and ill-disciplined movement, as the student movement was, should have so profoundly influenced events – local, national and international – as it did. In Toronto, the very being of the university seemed to change; the University Senate was disbanded and the Board of Governors removed. A joint body called the Governing Council was created. It, undoubtedly, represented a wider range of interests and pursued a more 'open' administrative policy; it was much more 'politically' correct than its predecessor, but its form and constitution often nurtured confusion not clarity; debates became woolly, subjective and open-ended, and decisions were often equally muddled. In my opinion, the termination of bicameral responsibilities was a great loss, and the University of Toronto remains, to this day, chained to a cumbersome system that it embraced without due forethought, and which, mindlessly helped undermine all I had achieved for the School of Architecture and the Faculty of Environmental Design.

Once our new faculty was established we needed chairmen for each of the three separate departments. After a long debate and advice from various quarters, John Andrews was offered the chair of the Department of Architecture. He said he would be delighted to accept but only on the condition that a new member of staff be appointed to administer the department. He stated 'I am a designer, an architect, a teacher not an administrator. If you want to get the best out me, I suggest you allow me to concentrate on what I am best at and find someone else, with administrative skills, to oversee the day-to-day management of the department. In fact, I insist that you do.' At the time it seemed a reasonable and sensible proposal and our committee, under my chairmanship, accepted it. It was the worst decision I made in my life. It had huge unforeseen consequences, not just for the Department of Architecture but for the new faculty. John Andrews' nominee was soon appointed – an energetic Englishman called Peter Prangnell. John had known him since his student days at Harvard and Prangnell proved to be a radical amongst radicals. For some years, things went well enough – but steadily downhill. Various members of staff began to become alienated by John Andrews' brusque manners and methods and, outwith the university, Prangnell infuriated a large section of the profession by his outspoken criticism of contemporary architectural practice. These working architects began to see how Prangnell was influencing the minds of a whole generation of students, and they feared the consequences. My efforts to apply the brakes on a whole raft of changes that were beginning to run out of control had little effect. My powers as Dean were far more limited than I had presumed.

Then in early January 1971, out of the blue, John Andrews announced that he was returning to Australia! He asked for leave of absence but had already booked his flight: 'two weeks to the day, I'll be gone.' And, he said he was unable to specify the date of his return. I informed him that such an arrangement by a departmental chairman, without discussion, was most irregular. He insisted on his demands. I said I would have to discuss the situation with the University President. Consequently, I informed John Andrews that he could visit Australia but must agree to return to the school by 1st February or tender his resignation. To my disappointment, he resigned. He said he had to put his private practice and his personal needs ahead of his school responsibilities, and that was that. I was to miss him badly. He had managed to keep Peter Prangnell's excessive 'political' enthusiasms under control but now all hell broke loose. Prangnell became acting head of the Department of Architecture and applied for the now vacant post of chairman.

A shortlist of candidates was drawn up: a Hungarian architect teaching at Columbia University, New York; the head of the Bartlett School of Architecture at London University; the head of the School of Architecture at Portsmouth Polytechnic; and Peter Prangnell, our internal candidate. Over the years Prangnell had built up considerable support within the student body and such bodies could by this time assert real power – through a mixture of direct protest, administrative involvement, and the sewing of what can only be described as 'corporate fear'. Through the sixties many of the staff in Toronto had gradually 'gone casual', dressing in jeans and sporting beards and sandals. By the early seventies, many had gone 'native' and become uncritical supporters of student radicalism; acquiescent to every madcap request and demand. Had John Andrews seen the writing on the wall? Or was it just a quirk of fate that saw our chairmanship vacated at the very moment when student radicalism was at its height? Either way, the consequences for the Department of Architecture were bad.

All four candidates attended formal interviews but the students also demanded and got separate, public, face to face question and answer sessions. I had strong suspicions as to what was likely to happen but not to have concurred would have precipitated a small riot. The Hungarian suffered first. He returned, indignant and very angry. He told me he had been ushered into a staff room packed with students who sat him on a table and insolently harangued him. Their questions, statements and demands were not about architecture, or education, but Hungarian politics and the Soviet Union. A number of students deliberately tried to disorientate and provoke him. He informed me that he held a senior position at Columbia University, he had an excellent architectural practice in New York, that he was not begging for a job and he had no intention of coming to Toronto to try to educate such an ill-disciplined, ill-mannered, biased, politically-motivated group of thoroughly unpleasant student hooligans!

When my friend Geoffrey Broadbent, from Portsmouth Polytechnic, entered the fray he was greeted with chants and slogans. 'Why are you here? We don't want you! We already have a chairman!' He described half a dozen bearded, be-jeaned men sitting on the left side of the room barking questions on behalf of some architectural 'Red Guard'. Four female activists had sat at the front, one with a large dog – all with their legs spread wide, lolling together and apart. Broadbent told me that he never encountered such an uncouth or disturbed group of students and under no circumstances would he consider accepting the post. I thought of Yeats:

> Mere anarchy is loosed upon the world
> The blood-dimmed tide is loosed, and everywhere
> The ceremony of innocence is drowned;
> The best lacked all conviction while the worst;
> Are full of passionate intensity.'

The candidate from the Bartlett suffered a similar fate. Prangnell was not called before the students because he and his opinions were well-known. My responsibility was then to call our selection committee together to reach a final decision about the appointment. We met in my office with about fifty students assembled on the staircase immediately outside. The door was locked. As our meeting began, the students started to hiss, slogans were shouted and the hissing continued for the duration of our meeting. We decided to decide nothing.

A second meeting was planned for the following week at Hart House, but time and place was not announced. However, within minutes of our meeting convening, the corridor was, once more, filled with students hissing and grunting. Once more we deferred making a final decision. Before our third and final meeting all members of the selection committee, except myself, received letters from the students demanding the appointment of Peter Prangnell. I knew nothing of these letters until our meeting was well under way and despite being chairman of that appointment committee and Head of the Faculty, I was unable to neutralise the momentum for Prangnell and the powerful effect those letters seemed to have. It was claimed that they were signed by a substantial percentage of students from the Department of Architecture and, as the meeting proceeded, the majority of the committee swung powerfully behind Prangnell. In the end I felt bound to agree to his appointment. Thus was set in train, a long-term and disastrous series of consequences. The rigorous, disciplined, creative school that I had worked so hard to build, quite quickly became a softheaded, sociologically-based 'educational institution' deeply interested in the 'philosophy' of architecture. Such a change was typical of the period but all the worse for being so. Although nominally in charge I found that, as Dean, I had lost the 'constituency', the specific powers I had had as Director of the School of Architecture. Over the next four years the Faculty of Environmental Design devoured itself.

It took me some time to realise how invasive and permanent the changes that gathered pace around Peter Prangnell were to become. But, by 1976, I was sixty-two and after eighteen years in Toronto, I began to think about a new phase and new directions in my life. New generations have new ideals; I had a certain sympathy with the best of the radical's values and no wish to destroy myself in a battle that I knew I could not win.

Change is inevitable, life adaptable. I retired.

ARCHITECTURE AND PLANNING 9

In shaping our future we must use our minds and imaginations, and look to the past for the best of precedents. Architects and architecture always exists in a historical context.

THOMAS HOWARTH

The one major problem Howarth encountered as a teacher of architecture flowed from student perception that their professor was not sufficiently an architect; that he was a man who rarely practised what he preached, a man with no outstanding buildings to his name. During the 1960s, however, Howarth was centrally involved in two major architectural projects: the creation of York University in Toronto, and Laurentian University in rural Ontario. Both of these two very different campuses have, admirably, stood the test of time and are worth serious historical and critical estimation.

As the twentieth century advanced most of the world's great cities have demanded not just one university but two, or three, or four. Toronto was no exception and, during the 1950s, plans slowly evolved to create a second university. For the first ten years York remained affiliated to the University of Toronto but it is, today, a huge independent university with 80,000 students. My friend and colleague, Murray Ross, was appointed as the first President of York in 1960 and, over the next decade, I was closely associated with the new university – most significantly I oversaw the master plan of first phase development – at the Glendon Campus, off Keele Street. I greatly enjoyed my involvement in this project and it remains, I think, my most notable architectural and environmental achievement. Murray Ross got things started at a memorable meeting. On the dot of four o'clock, the door opened and an exquisite young lady walked in carrying a tray with tea and cookies. She stood at a table and very sedately, very grandly, poured tea and brought it to each one of us. Then, leaving the cookies and taking the tray, she left the room. It was a 'happening'. As we sipped our teas, Murray Ross, called for order to state, mixing gravitas with a boyish wickedness that this girl, and her service, represented the kind of standards to which the new university should aspire and that he was determined that such aspirations would be realised. Murray Ross was a delightful man, with a warm sense of humour, and I felt that no new university could be in better hands. On the 21st June 1960 he addressed a large gathering: 'By 1970, we hope to have at Glendon Hall a liberal arts college for 1,200 to 1,500 students, most of whom will live in residence on the campus, and its buildings will reflect, in their design and structure, the ideal of the contemplative life.'

The new college would house a department of humanities, a department of social sciences, a department of physical sciences, plus a major library, and a creative arts centre for theatre, music and painting. Students would be housed in residence blocks of 200 rooms, each with its own dean, or senior don, living in. Each residence would have a senior common room, and a dining room with a high table. Murray Ross believed that 'dignified and proper dining is an essential aspect of "the whole man" towards which we aim. We seek to encourage serious study, contemplation and good discussion.' And he was more than willing to sacrifice so-called efficiency and size to gain the unique features that would support these grand old-fashioned ideals. 'We want buildings with grace and dignity; we will leave open spaces in mid campus, we want to take advantage of the view provided by the valley. Our model is "the enclosed campus" that provides a distinctive atmosphere, separate from the noise and pressure of urban life, the Harvard Yard, Dartmouth College, the Brown University Campus – these are the examples we wish to follow.'

With these plans and ideals in mind, President Murray Ross asked me to design a master plan for the whole Glendon property and to 'comment' on the style of architecture for the campus buildings. Various teams of architects had already been appointed to design the various individual buildings but Murray Ross wanted me to unify their contributions and oversee the whole. Canada, with its vast landscape and natural resources, had, up till then, rarely felt the need to build in harmony with nature and the opportunity to plan the Glendon Campus not only presented me with a wonderful opportunity to work creatively in the field I knew best and loved most – education in the liberal arts – but it also gave me the chance to set new 'environmental' standards, a new philosophical framework, for the future of building and architecture in Canada.

The schedule Murray Ross gave me was extremely tight. It was already mid-summer and the master plan was wanted for the 15th August, final design proposals were to be ready by the 15th September, and the first units habitable within one year on the 1st September 1961. Fortunately we

Dr Murray Ross being
installed as President of York
University, Toronto.

had arranged a holiday in a cabin, in the Algonquin National Park, with a small studio room attached, and there, whilst Edna, John and Katharine explored, fished and canoed, I set to work with a will. Each morning I worked and each afternoon I walked and relaxed with Edna. In the evenings I remember us reading, together, Ernest Hemingway's *The Old man and the Sea*. The cabin belonged to one of my Toronto colleagues, Jim Murray, and his children were with us. It was a great moment in our lives.

I designed with one major principle before me – that the physical characteristics of the very beautiful site should *dominate* any buildings the architects chose to construct. That principle immediately necessitated two confrontations. In my first discussion with the architects I learned that Marani, Morris & Allan had already proposed a high-rise academic block in the centre of one of the great lawns opposite Glendon Hall! They would have to climb down. And, in my discussions with the City of Toronto Highways Department I learned that a huge clover-leaf road crossing was to be built immediately in front of Glendon's main gate at the intersection of Lawrence and Bayview Avenues. Such a plan would have to be stopped! The planned junction would destroy a large proportion of Glendon's handsome, ancient woodland and permanently blight the entrance to our 'contemplative' campus. Fortunately, I won both battles.

Simple food is often the best and taste in food has architectural equivalents. I like simplicity and clarity, and the building committee agreed with my wish for a 'limited palette' at Glendon. With several different architectural firms already promised involvement I was determined that whatever brick and concrete we used should be unified and complimentary. A variegated red brick of delightful colour and texture was especially produced for us and later marketed as York Bricks. The concrete was also 'tuned' to my demand by the addition of certain aggregates. In addition, all cables were housed underground so that the wires and junction boxes that disfigure so much of urban America, would not besmirch Glendon. It was initially expensive, but maintenance costs, particularly winter costs, were reduced long-term. Because I came from a wet and equitable climate I was very aware of the vicissitudes of temperature and the biting cold of continental Canada, thus, I was determined to make the physical movement of people on campus as easy, pleasing and sheltered as possible. My plans allowed passage from classroom to classroom, to dining room, to common room without the necessity of going outside. I also arranged that there should be plenty of storage space for coats and boots and all the accoutrements of students pursuing active sporting lives. I greatly enjoy this kind of attention to detail and I revelled in the attempt to create the timeless 'collegiate' atmosphere that Murray Ross wanted to leave as his memorial to Canada – by keeping all the great trees, by keeping the rose garden, by orchestrating the placement of buildings in concert with the lawns and green vistas that make Glendon unique.

The three major architectural companies involved at Glendon were Marani, Morris & Allan, Mathers & Haldenby, and Allward & Gouinlock. They controlled designing and building but all worked to my master plan. I directly encouraged Marani and Morris to articulate two of the lecture theatres in such a way as to provide a large south-facing curved wall on which a major relief sculpture could be placed. I also got them to provided large glazed doors to all the dining rooms so that students would, in summertime, be encouraged out onto the paved patio and grass, where tables and chairs could be easily placed. I wanted light, open, clean, modern spaces – responsive to the human scale. When I recommended that we should allocate half a percent of our budget to works of art, our building committee enthusiastically accepted the proposal. This enabled me to commission three eminent Canadian artists to create site-specific works for Glendon: Lionel Thomas, Eldred Cox, and Trapenier. Their work created a precedent and an excellent collection of contemporary art was accumulated at York over subsequent years.

Once the various architectural firms started work I left them to get on with it but I did take a direct interest in the interior design. The unity and quality of furnishings might have been lost if each firm of architects had chosen what they liked, was cheapest, or was just readily available. Furnishing in Canada lagged behind architectural advances. For example, all the main stores in Toronto still sold heavy, dull, post-Victorian furniture. And such stores could wield political and economic clout! I insisted on modernity and chose fabrics with turquoise-blue, green, and brown stripes for the chairs and settees.

One idea that proved impossible to realise concerned the college library. It was to be built adjacent to the rose garden and I hoped that this delicious formal space would provide a *hortus secludus* into which students could wander for rest and relaxation, direct from the library, as the spirit moved them. But the new age of pilfering and vandalism was just beginning to gather force and it was decided that open access between the garden and the library would create insurmountable security dangers. I had to accept access to the library through a single main entrance door and a concrete moat now separates the library from the garden. This moat filters good light direct into the library basement and I like to think of it as a modern version

John Howarth (1961).

Glendon College, York
University, Toronto,
2000. Thomas Howarth
master planner.
Timothy Neat

of the eighteenth-century, ha-ha. But is it not an indictment of our society that a university library needs to be fortified like a prison?

Throughout the sixties, the various stages of Glendon College opened on schedule and a splendid new university got off to an excellent start. In fact York University expanded so rapidly that Glendon College soon became little more than an annexe to the main university campus in North West Toronto, a 200-hectare site with 80,000 students. This huge development has left the Glendon campus looking and feeling a little 'provincial', but none the worse for that and Glendon now has the reputation of being one of a select band of small collegiate campuses where natural beauty and scholastic quiet collude for the good of mankind. Glendon has become a special place, its students enjoy what they have and it attracts numerous visiting scholars and conference organisers.

When the first stage of Glendon was completed I was asked, by the *Journal of the Royal Architectural Institute of Canada*, to write an illustrated article about the project. One consequence was that I was, invited by Dr Doherty, on behalf of the Board of Governors of Laurentian University at Sudbury in Northern Ontario, to prepare a similar master plan for the Laurentian site. It too was embarking on major expansion and I acquired

a new set of major planning responsibilities that were to recurrently engross my attention for almost twenty-five years.

Laurentian University was founded by the Jesuit Order. The site was dramatic, beautiful and spacious, set amidst a wilderness that had been denuded of trees and natural greenness by the fallout of sulphuric acid from the nearby I.N.C.O. factories. Laurentian University, like Glendon, offered me a great planning opportunity but the two sites could hardly have been more different. This was a barren region of sparse population and great mineral wealth – discovered by a rail labourer working on the Canadian Pacific Railway in the 1880s. In 1901 the population of the main town, Sudbury, was 2,027; in 1930 it was 20,000, and in 1966 it was 84,586. It was an unlovely sprawling town. Today, partly as a result of the development of Laurentian University, some fine modern architecture has turned Sudbury into a modern conurbation of real potential.

A written description of my master plan appeared in Laurentian University's yearbook in 1964 and it quite accurately documents my major interests and responsibilities.

The Board of Governors agreed to a limitation of materials. The dominant material used in phase one is pre-cast concrete with a near white aggregate, local stone and brick for small controlled areas. Thus, Laurentian University stands out white and pristine against the landscape, its recessed windows and strong modelling giving a powerful surface texture that will throw the buildings into dramatic relief when the landscape is covered with winter snow. I was very keen not only to articulate the buildings within the landscape but also to orchestrate the vehicular experience of visitors as they approached the university by road or walked about the campus.

Our next site project is to drive a road through the south valley to link up with Loach Road. This will only give us a useful south approach to the campus and allow for the planning of new faculty residences above Trout Lake. We are also working on a scheme for transforming the marshy area on Ramsay Lake Road into landscaped lawn that will provide a dignified approach to the campus after the drama of wild nature. This road will give the visitor a panoramic view of all the major buildings as he leaves Ramsay Lake Road, then all are suddenly lost to view as one ascends the hill until, Trout Lake appears beyond the golf course. Turning south, the buildings now reappear close-up and dramatically grouped together. When the site has matured the landscape architecture of Laurentian university should be a continual source of pleasure for future generations.

Thinking back on my architectural career and the nature of creative achievement various questions arise. Of course I would like to have been involved more directly in more building and planning but definitions as to what is creative work and what is not, are sometimes difficult to define. A great deal of teaching demands creativity and it can be creatively exhausting. Even administration and management can be creatively pursued. Lecturing, research, even conference organisation can be creative – a real conference 'event' can be as thrilling as a great theatre performance and, on occasion, more important. During my professorship, four international conferences I attended stand out in my memory: one in Paris, one in Denver, one in Prague and one in Greece – all beautiful places – three of them centres of great historical interests to architects.

The annual assembly of the International Union of Architects met in Paris in 1965. I was invited to give a paper entitled 'Architectural Education in Canada'. It was an opportunity to draw together a raft of little known historical facts and present a summary of my educational and architectural philosophy. The language problem encouraged me to be to the point and practical. Having set out my Canadian table, I addressed a very practical problem. I asked the question 'what is the best proportion of architects to the proportion of non-architects in the best architectural offices?' Research we had carried out in Canada had persuaded me that the best ratio was one architect to ten technological specialists. Such a balance produced the greatest efficiency in designing, in the oversight of

Models of Laurentian
University, Sudbury, Ontario,
c.1965. Thomas Howarth,
master planner.

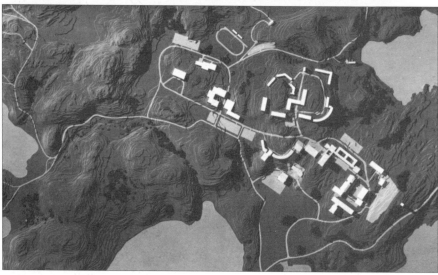

Top. North facade,
Laurentian University.
H.R. Jowett

Bottom. The library
podium, Laurentian
University. *H.R. Jowett*

construction, and economic return. At that time, many countries had plenty of trained architects but most had a big shortage of well-trained technologists ready and able to work with the architects: compounding the problem, most technological education was physically separate from the schools of architecture. I suggested a good solution would be 'satellite colleges' and courses that worked in 'twinned' relationships with the major architectural institutions. I explained how the relationship I had established between the University of Toronto and Ryerson Institute of Technology might be viewed as a pilot project. In a way I was advocating a return to Renaissance values, when great achievements sprang from the happy relationship between the master-designers and an array of skilled artists, craftsmen and technologists, willing to serve the master-builders – and the civilisation their vision embodied. Our twentieth-century civilisation, I stated, must be the product of 'unified sensibilities' and embrace the whole environment. We must always be open to technological change but honour the timeless values that tradition has handed down.

In 1966 I became Vice-president of the American Association of Collegiate Schools of Architecture and immediately went off to a major conference at the Mile High Centre in Denver, Colorado. The work was interesting but the reason that Denver remains indelibly and pleasurably in my mind, has nothing to do with architecture or education, or 'the mile-high club!' It was there that I discovered a particularly beautiful jewel. Denver has a remarkable climate and clear, thin air which encouraged me to walk and to explore the city and the country round about. I also wandered the back streets, where the Indians had stores. Browsing in one, I found a magnificent necklace which embodied much silver and fine turquoise. The price was 500 dollars. I couldn't afford it but I handled it with great pleasure and, I hungered for it. Shortly afterwards I bumped into John B. Parkin, the distinguished Toronto architect, who was also attending the conference and whom I knew well. I said, 'John, this is going to be an expensive conference for you.' He was with his wife – a tall, dignified and elegant lady with jet-black hair and fine dark skin that would glow beneath silver and blue. I told him that I'd just come from a small Indian store that had a necklace of a quality that one might not see again in a lifetime! I guided the two of them back down the streets I had come and, without being asked, the proprietor of the shop took out the necklace I had been admiring just ten minutes before. He put it gently round Mrs Parkin's neck. The effect was electrifying! She tried on a whole drawer-full before, in her own time, she came back to the first that I had chosen, and John B. Parkin signed the cheque without further ado.

In Prague, in 1967, I presented an ambitious conference paper, of which I am still proud. It was entitled 'Man and the Landscape'. This was another conference organised by the International Union of Architects. I wanted to make a hard-hitting statement that would stimulate political as well as architectural responses. I began by exploring man's destructive nature; youth's urge to desecrate and sloganise (the word 'graffiti' had not emerged then); the general lack of respect for 'public' property (in communist as well as capitalist societies); the general willingness to litter the countryside (not just with rubbish but unnecessary ribbon-developments); the short-termism that nurtures acceptance of industrial despoliation, the public vandalism (too often perpetrated in the name of social improvement and governmental needs); the insatiable appetite of the citizens of the Free World for advertising and growth. I articulated the visual 'illiteracy' of modern man: how we calmly accept visual disorder, whilst responding passionately to anything that assaults our sense of smell, or taste, or hearing. We curtail the pig farmer spraying his spring fields with slurry but accept the permanent disfigurement of fine streets and squares with wires, hoardings, bins and ugly signs. How can such invasions of our favourite places, our civilised values be countered? First, I suggested, by the general education of children, and the public, towards an intolerance of that which reduces their lives; and second, by the greater professional involvement of educated and cultured people in our communal and political lives. Laws are not the answer to all problems. 'Trust your own eye, even crooked.' I said they should go out and become more involved in the big decisions, in the political process.

Finally, I remember a great conference in Greece, in 1971. This remains, for me, the measure of what a conference can be – and do. It was a unique event. It was advertised as DELOS 9 and was the ninth in an annual series of conferences funded, largely, by the Ford Foundation. The whole event was co-ordinated by Constantinos Doxiadis, Director of the Ekistics School in Athens. About sixty scholars and specialists from all over the world gathered, by personal invitation, in Athens – that most perfect of the various 'cradles' of world civilisation. Our conference title was *Man's Buildings and Shells* but the 'declaration' that concluded our conference more precisely describes the subjects we explored. It was, 'A Declaration on the State of Emergency in Human Settlements'. Exploration of such a subject, in such company, in such a place, was a privilege I have never forgotten.

First, we were given the opportunity to explore the Acropolis – that fortress-like rock on which the most famous group of buildings on the face of the earth stand in their ruined glory. I had long waited for the moment and each building came up to my high expectation. With a strange mixture of intellectual excitement and pure aesthetic pleasure I moved through that marvellous complex close to a physical ecstasy. Classical perfection. I went up twice in the mornings when the crowds were thin and I returned for a third time, to circle the Parthenon in moonlight, almost alone. The marble took on an insubstantial, ethereal quality and dramatic force – that made the whole site powerfully romantic. One could feel the history of Athens substantial in the air. A dog trotted out from between two columns and all around him was shining proportion. Here, at once, was the most lucid measure of human being and a fantastic painted stage by De Chirico or the Belgian surrealist, Delvaux. I walked through those moonlit spaces feeling the press of priests, acolytes and heroes and, looking down 'saw' the panathenaic procession winding up the rock towards us! I thought of the vase that had inspired Keats:

> What men or Gods are these? What maidens loth?
> What mad pursuit? What struggle to escape?
> What pipes and timbrels? What wild ecstasy?…

> Thou silent form, dost tease us out of thought
> As doth eternity: Cold pastoral!
> When old age shall this generation waste,
> Thou shall remain in midst of other woe
> Than ours, a friend to man, to whom thou sayest,
> 'Beauty is truth, truth beauty,' – that is all
> Ye know on earth, and all ye need to know.

It was truly marvellous. After that, we went down to Piraeus to board a splendid small cruise ship that was to be our home, our floating conference centre, for the next seven days. A handsome Greek crew saw to all our physical needs, beautifully mannered young students took care of conference arrangements and all our secretarial requirements. Thus we set sail on Homer's wine-dark sea to discuss *Land Use and Building in the Late Twentieth Century*. I felt inspired and committed myself to contribute something to the better-being of the world. Buckminster Fuller was there. I knew his birthday was imminent, and surprised him at breakfast with the gift of a special tie from my collection – a vivid, strongly patterned tie appropriate for the man who had invented the geodesic dome! He was very pleased. Margaret Mead, the anthropologist was there – Curator Emeritus

Howarth with Pete Bynoe of Grenada (1969) at the Commonwealth Association of Architects conference.

of Ethnology at the American Museum of Natural History. Her reputation has declined in recent years but I found her an imposing and very interesting woman. Jonas E. Salk was there, using our conference as a cover for his honeymoon. He had just married François Gilot, one of Picasso's later mistresses. A decade earlier, Salk had discovered the vaccine which has gradually eliminated poliomyelitis from the world and we felt greatly honoured to have him aboard. His Salk Institute, designed by Louis Kahn, is, I think, one of the finest institutional buildings in the world. It stands on a magnificent cliff-top site in California, looking out over the Pacific.

There was also a fine array of academics, mainly from the English-speaking world, including Gerald Dix, an old student of mine from Manchester and Director of the Institute of Planning Studies at Nottingham University; Lawrence Halpin, a landscape architect from the University of Berkeley, Robert Hastings, President of the American Institute of Architects; Peter Shepherd, President of the R.I.B.A. in London; Patrick Nuttgens, the Arts and Crafts specialist, then Director of Architecture at Leeds Polytechnic; Sir Robert Matthew from the University of Edinburgh, Paul T. Hellyer from the Federal Parliament of Canada; Amos Rapoport from Australia. We were a distinguished gathering and we took our work deeply seriously: none more so than Lady Jackson, then Albert Schweitzer Professor of International Economic Development at Columbia University. She had a deserved reputation as a brilliant public speaker but she was also an opinionated and self-centred woman too used to getting her own way. The symposium, however, was almost well enough organised to keep her in check and I, along with various others, was able to challenge her interpretation not just of the world but of what, SHE thought, WE ought to be saying!

Our ship sailed each evening and each morning we found ourselves moored off another beautiful island brimming with archaeological and architectural treasures – it was Paradise and most of us were happy to look, to think and wander at leisure – but such small things were not enough for Margaret Mead. At each landfall, she strode forward in her voluminous drab clothes with a long, forked 'adder stick', loudly addressing a group of acolytes who scrambled along behind endeavouring to keep up with the wisdom hurtling from her lips. She reminded me of a new-age John the Baptist, though I'm sure she would have challenged such a description; she being confident there was no greater prophet, than herself. Her megalomania made me conscious of how important our discussions and subject matter really were.

Through the Corinth Canal we sailed, past the island of Zakynthos, then around Sparta and through the Cyclades. I remember waking to find ourselves anchored off Skala on Santorini, 'The Wild Island', with cliffs rising, crystal clear, to over a 1,000 feet above us. I rode up the 600 steps to Thera on the back of a pony. Thera was an absolute delight; its whitewashed houses, small squares, winding lanes and sudden vistas were inspirational and one could appreciate the magical effect settlements like these had had on Josef Hoffman, Le Corbusier, and Brancusi, in those years of discovery before the First World War. Such splendid days were complimented by the reading of 'papers' and chaired meetings which, each evening, attempted to draw the day's investigations to some kind of conclusion. Then, like magic, each morning, the previous days papers and the conclusions reached, were waiting for us in tidy piles outside our cabin doors – having been typed up by the students overnight.

From Rhodes we moved to Patmos, the island of St John the Divine who, we believe, wrote The Book of Revelations. I went up to the Monastery of the Apocalypse. There is a chapel, built into a cave, where St John is said to have set down the visions he had seen. I was alone and the whole place had an air of neglect, very appropriate for an island of exile. I was deeply moved. Then, as I came out into the sunshine above the cobalt waters of that placid, beautiful bay, the stillness and then the silence was broken by the inrush, around the headland, of two powerful speedboats with water-skiers weaving behind them. This violent intrusion struck me like an act of sacrilege and I sat down, greatly deflated. Then I began making notes that I integrated into my 'paper', to be delivered the following day, on noise pollution and environmental desecration. There can be a wisdom in anger that only anger knows. A charge of adrenalin can affect the thinker just as much as the athlete.

And then we came to Delos, birthplace of Apollo and Artemis, protected by its great circle of islands, the Cyclades. It was in honour of this island that our host, Constantos Doxiadis, had named his annual conferences. It was an appropriate choice: a place beautiful and sacred; a place ravished by pirates and nations; a place, mercifully, not developed for tourists – yet. Our last formal seminar was held in the open-air theatre. I walked through the famous avenue of marble lions and sat on a cool marble seat to watch the sun go down whilst listening to the 'Declaration' that concluded our week's deliberations. The acoustics were superb. Doxiadis read the statement. It had been originally prepared by Lady Jackson and Margaret Mead but some of us had, the previous evening, disputed their interpretation of events. I was one of a group who finalised a document with which we were all, in the end, well pleased.

DECLARATION ON THE STATE OF EMERGENCY IN HUMAN SETTLEMENTS, JULY 19TH 1971.

The vast increase and migration of people (today) represents the largest single cause of misery, insecurity and communal upheaval ever experienced by the human race; despite this, 200 billion dollars a year is being spent on armaments. All individuals and groups need water, clear air, adequate sanitation – pollution of all kinds should be controlled – local peoples should be involved in the evolution of their particular economic and architectural needs; cultural diversity is a positive fact of world culture and should be encouraged not negated; massive high-rise buildings sterilise city life; suburban development must not be allowed to cushion the few whilst ruining the long-term use of land which is, increasingly, in short supply. The problem of the automobile must be addressed – useable housing stock should be upgraded rather than torn down. Home-ownership and co-operative development are both to be encouraged; development must be seen and co-ordinated within the international context…

On our return to Athens, Doxiadis had arranged that I should do a week's teaching at his School of Ekistics. This too proved an illuminating experience. Mackintosh was royally welcomed into the Greek Pantheon and Doxiades informed me in detail about his master plan for *Land Development across the World*. He had codified twelve fundamental approaches to land use into four groups: land that should remain undeveloped (because it exists as wilderness, or as a space of cultural or spiritual importance); land reserved for cultivation and agricultural production; land for human settlement and urban development; and land for industry and industrial development. I was greatly impressed.

During my stay in Athens I was handsomely entertained by Constantinos and his wife and, when I left, I was pleased to give them an Inuit painting which showed Eskimo family life within an igloo seen in cross-section. Poetically, it embodied the title he had chosen for his conference, *Man's Buildings and Shells* and he was, I think, genuinely delighted by it. I left Athens feeling that I had been in close contact with the ancient and continuing genius of the Greek people and returned to Canada with renewed interest in the importance of environmental planning and the philosophy behind it. It seemed significant that the ancient nations of the Mediterranean World were at the centre of the new environmental analysis and later when a group of Italian architects from Sicily and Milan brought a proposal to Toronto, aiming to stimulate architectural contacts between our two countries, I was delighted to set in train a great symposium entitled *Two Cultures: Two Cities – Toronto and Milano*.

Two satisfactions of my declining years have been watching the city of Toronto expand to become one of the great international cities of the world, and seeing the career of Norman Foster reach recurrent new heights. Norman was one of my most brilliant students at Manchester. Now, he is one of the half dozen outstanding architects in the world, and I like to see a direct link between Mackintosh, my teaching, and his achievements.

It was Norman Foster's former partner, Sir Richard Rogers, who designed the Millennium Dome in London. The Dome Exhibition may have been a colossal failure but the building itself is a triumph, and, I would claim, it marvellously updates the dome Mackintosh designed for the great Glasgow Exhibition of 1901 which inspired Frank Lloyd Wright to design his domed Greek Orthodox Church, for Illinois in 1956. The circles of these things never close. Further up the Thames, Norman Foster, himself, designed the Millennium Bridge. It seems to have proved to be one of his very few failures. The millennium brought out hubris in certain politicians but Foster's concept was great and the bridge looks good. It was the structure that was faulty: people walking made it oscillate so dangerously that it had to be closed. 'The best laid plans of mice and men...'

Thomas Howarth (back left) at the meeting of the Board of Architectural Education, Commonwealth Association of Architects, London 1966. *Marilyn Stafford*

10 APRIL IN THE FALL

TIMOTHY NEAT

| *The end of the human race will be that it will eventually die of civilisation… The hero is he who is immovably centred.*

When Tom Howarth phoned to say his last goodbyes, adding, 'I'll try to stay alive till Friday!' it was obvious he was still his old self and intellectually alert. Four days later, there he was, propped up in bed and very much alive. We, immediately, re-established a very close relationship, almost like father and son but as always, he remained, the teacher:

> *Remember [he said] what John Ruskin wrote, 'That art is greatest which, by any means whatsoever, conveys to the mind of the spectator the greatest number of the greatest ideas.' That's what this biography should do; present ideas, through me, through Mackintosh, through you. Don't step back; face the reality of what I have been. My life may be, even now, a pleasure and a teaching tool. My body goes to the medical students: you can have my warts and soul. Be specific.*

All his life Howarth was a stickler for exactitude. For example, trying to recall events and conversations when he left Frank Lloyd Wright for the last time, he paused and said, 'Tim, wait! Let me see it in my mind again, so that I can get it right…' (There was always a vase of roses on his windowsill and he would look at it for sustenance.) And over that week he gave me vignette after vignette from a long life's experience. I told him I was honoured to be writing the book, and pleased to be being drawn back into the Mackintosh field after five years of work on other projects. Our last afternoon together was memorable for two very different reasons. After speaking with him and reading to him, I decided to say my final goodbye some time before the taxi, already ordered, arrived. Something triggered me to quote the first words of the hymn, 'Immortal, invisible…' Immediately, he responded with the next line, 'God only wise…' His eyes sparkled in appreciation of his continuing sharpness, and years of the pleasure of music-making passed over his face. That great hymn seemed to finalise our being together: I rose and said, 'Tom, we will make something of this book.' He held up his right hand from the bed and I went forward to take it. 'Goodbye Tom,' I said, 'dear man.' I bent and kissed him on the

257

forehead. Howarth was not a man to cry but, as I stood back from him, tears came down his face. 'God bless you, Tim,' he said.

I sat in the living room, awaiting the taxi. Gilli McDermott made a pot of tea. I looked at the magnificent silvered wall-plaques by Margaret and Frances Macdonald on each side of the window. I read the words beaten out, in Greek, in Margaret's hand: 'A great purple wave rose up, equal to a mountain'. I thought of Mackintosh, to whom the words were addressed. I thought of Highland Scotland where death is referred to as 'The Day of the Mountain'. I thought of the Rose, and of Life as a Great Purple Wave. In the distance I could see the waters of Lake Ontario beyond the hard-edged silhouette of downtown Toronto. Suddenly, a less than feeble voice called out from the other room, 'Tim, can you come through?' I was loath to return, aware that whatever was to pass was likely to be an anticlimax. However, when the call came a second time, more insistent, I felt impelled to respond. Howarth was lying, propped on his pillows, with a large white flannel on his head and a piece of paper fluttering in his hand. He looked, exactly, like Samual Jonson's *Volpone* with his night-cap askew. He waved the paper and said, 'Tim. I've been looking at your expenses. I've got the airline receipt but there's no receipt for the taxi, from the airport!' We had just experienced a strange, uniquely human moment, and now this noble, dying man was querying a taxi bill! He must have seen my annoyance and qualified his statement. 'Tim, it's not for me, it's my accountant. He needs receipts for everything.' I replied, 'Tom, I've written out my expenses, I've signed them. You've already given me a cheque; I'm not, now, going to open my suitcase and start hunting for a taxi bill!' He looked slightly ashamed, then said, 'I would have phoned him, but he's on vacation till Tuesday, in the Bahamas!' It was laughable.

Painkillers and imminent death do peculiar things to the human mind but there was more to the incident than that. This conjunction of the sublime and the ridiculous, this trivial commercialisation of a sacred moment epitomized a persistently wilful and destructive side in Howarth's character. 'I expect this'll do' he said, 'your note.' And so our friendship of twelve years, ended with a whimper and in deflated confusion. It may be true that 'if you look after the pennies, the pounds will look after themselves', but it is also, undoubtedly, true that here was a man who recurrently traded in letdowns. Here was a man various, generous and loving, here was a man touched by greatness; but here, too, was a man, spoilt, mean, reductive, manipulative and emotionally destructive despite his high ideals, perhaps destructive to spite himself. Was this the reason why Howarth thought to call his *Memoirs*, 'Dreams, Visions and Nightmares'?

The older Howarth got the more he was tempted, like a small boy, to test situations and people to breaking point. It was a personality defect that had substantial consequences for the people, and the society, around him. It affected his marriage and it affected his work at the University of Toronto. Indeed, it may provide the clue to the 'mystery' that surrounds Howarth's last years as Dean of the Faculty of Environmental Design – when a decade of outstanding success was followed by a decade of 'inexplicable' failure. It would be unjust to suggest that Howarth deliberately undermined his early success as Director of the School of Architecture in Toronto, by presiding over its collapse when it became just one of three departments within the Faculty of Environmental Design, but some parallels can be drawn between the ways in which Howarth sabotaged moments of personal happiness and the manner in which he 'oversaw' the disintegration of architectural education in his beloved school of architecture. The dispersal at auction of Howarth's unique Mackintosh Collection might, possibly, also be interpreted as another instance of this syndrome in action. These are serious charges but they touch important issues that should not be ignored. They raise questions about Howarth's personality and professional achievement that any serious biographer must address.

Why did the school of architecture, that Howarth led so successfully in the 1960s, fall apart in the 1970s and 1980s? Was Howarth himself a prime cause of this failure or were he and the school victims of external pressures that nothing, or no one, could have prevented? The short answer must be that Howarth was to blame, at least partly. He was *Director* of the School of Architecture from 1958 to 1966 and *Dean* of the Faculty of Environmental Design from 1967 until 1976 two years before his formal retirement in 1978. He was the man in charge throughout the crucial years. The new Faculty of Environmental Design was his idea, for eight years he worked hard to create it. And, initially, he saw this new Faculty as his crowning professional achievement, the educational embodiment of his environmental and artistic vision. Unfortunately, almost immediately, what he had created began to run out of control and neither Howarth, nor anyone else, was able to bring it back on track. Even today, forty years later, the three departments that make up the faculty – Architecture, Planning, and Landscape Architecture are still struggling to regain the reputations they enjoyed in the late 1960s. Why did the Toronto School of Architecture, once an internationally-recognised centre of excellence, become, for a generation, an architectural black hole?

Worldwide, the 1960s were years of radical educational change. In Toronto, change gathered with particular ferocity around the School of Architecture. Why? At first, the 'winds of change' were liberal, centrifugal and exciting but, quite suddenly, they became dangerously destructive. International historical forces and a uniquely idiosyncratic group of individuals came together in Toronto to create a poisonous cocktail which ruptured the lives of many people. The prime ingredients of the minor tragedy that unfolded were: the sexual and materialistic revolutions that the sixties unleashed; the politicised student radicalism that demanded 'free expression'; the confrontational history of architectural education in Toronto; and most importantly the personalities of Thomas Howarth and the men he appointed.

As a teacher of architecture and a critic, Howarth was a progressive Modernist but he was, at the same time, a conservative in politics and educational philosophy. He was a traditionalist who was genuinely shocked by the anarchic radicalism that erupted within the hallowed realms of higher education. His students grew their hair and went hip, and many of his staff took to beards and jeans: Howarth resolutely stuck to his collar and tie.

More importantly, Howarth had always worked within clear external perimeters, with defined responsibilities and the presumption of good manners and orderly behaviour. Once these bounds were breached, he found himself clinging to straws. He became a classic example of the 'paper tiger' denounced by Maoist theorists. His professional career, which had for thirty years run so smoothly, now hit the buffers. From the moment Howarth began his architectural studies in Manchester he had been driven by clear scholastic goals and a conscious professional ambition. Every challenge was followed by an appropriate response and he successfully leapfrogged along a well-marked professional path. By the mid-1960s, Howarth had realised all his major professional ambitions: he was Dean of an internationally-respected faculty of environmental design; he was recognised as *the* world authority on Charles Rennie Mackintosh; his health had greatly improved; the 'New World' lay before him. Thus, it was a huge shock to Howarth, and to those around him, when things began to go wrong both at work and at home.

In retrospect, however, one can see that behind the façade of success and external conformity, Howarth did undergo various personality changes during his first decade in Canada and these had a direct influence on both his work and his marriage. His commitment to Methodism had gradually waned and, in Canada, Howarth set aside the faith that had sustained him for so long. Also, for the first time in his life, Howarth found himself without 'a master'. Since boyhood, Howarth had always been susceptible to strong personalities and willingly played the role of 'disciple'. He was a man of determined character, but deep down he was, by nature, more the ideal servant than the propelled leader. Throughout his life Howarth was proud to acknowledge his dependence on a series of mentors: first his grandfather, then George Grenfell Baines, Professor Cordingley in Manchester and Professor Hughes in Glasgow. He was prone to hero-worship and ever eager to take up a cause be it that of Charles Rennie Mackintosh, Jesus Christ, John Wesley or a disabled student. Psychologically, Howarth was a man who needed parameters. He prospered most when using his skills to advance other people's ideas and art; he was always more of a teacher than a commander.

When Howarth became Director of the School of Architecture in Toronto, his responsibilities were clearly defined within the great institution of the University of Toronto but, in 1967, when he became Dean of the Faculty of Environmental Design, he found himself, essentially, autonomous and, for the first time in his life, in a powerful, but vague, executive position. When the going got rough, Howarth drifted in an uncontrollable sea. In the face of the storm that erupted around him, he retreated to port to shelter amongst the securities he had known in his youth and search for those pleasures he had missed. The ideal of service was not abandoned but, by the late sixties, Howarth was content to leave confrontation to others: he would enjoy life whilst he had it.

He began to behave like 'the Englishman abroad'. With great civility, he threw off the inhibitions that had so strongly shaped the first half of his life: the constraints of family and sexual denial; Methodist Christianity and the sense that public respectability must extend to one's private behaviour. Howarth faced a classic mid-life crisis: 'Who am I, where do I come from, where am I going?' Canada liberated Howarth rather as Tahiti had liberated Paul Gauguin, seventy years earlier. And, like Gauguin, Howarth found 'liberation' affected all aspects of life: what he did and where he did it; what he ate and what he drank; where he travelled and to what end. The framework within which he sought personal fulfilment was reconstructed. His absolute dedication to teaching and scholarship was modified and he began to feel a little above the vulgar machinations of disputatious students and politically ambitious young lecturers. Bob Dylan's, *The times they are a changin'* was the song of the moment. In England, the inhibited poet-librarian, Philip Larkin, announced that 'sexual intercourse began in 1963!' It was a tongue-in-cheek 'call to arms' that went out across the generations. Few wanted to be left behind and Tom Howarth was not one of them. As 'the consumer revolution' gathered pace, the personal trajectory of Howarth's life followed the general trajectory of Western life in the twentieth century; forty years of war and depression, followed by forty years of peace and prosperity; forty years of sacrifice and heroic endeavour followed by forty years of well-being, and indulgence.

Howarth's diaries document these changing attitudes and, for the first time in his life, he began to write poetry. The first poems emerging during a trip to the Caribbean, where he worked as an advisor to the University of the West Indies. He usually stayed at Middlemist, the home of the Jamaican architect Donald Brown and his German wife, Dorette. In this new, strange, tropical environment he luxuriated, for the first time in his life. He began to feel at ease amidst a world of plenty: an Indian summer was upon him. One of his most notable early poems is entitled 'April in the Fall.'

> If there is magic
> > And music
> > > In a word
>
> If there is sweetness
> > And promise
> > > In a name
>
> If there is hope
> > And love
> > > In a phrase
>
> It is April
> It is April
> It is April
> It is April in the Fall

> An enigma is
> April in October
> And a conundrum
> Is April
> Is April
> Is April
> Is April in the Fall.

Howarth's birthday was on 1st May. The poem revels in the idea of rebirth symbolised by the sudden springs and colourful autumns for which Canada is famous. Out of the blue, Howarth sees his late middle-age bursting into an 'Eternal Springtime' of the kind Rodin had made substantial in clay and bronze and which Howarth felt he had missed out on during the emotionally constricted years of his youth. Now, realising afresh that all life is chanceful, unfathomable, beautiful, he decides he *will* enjoy and engage with the world – Carpe Diem. 'The moment is, the living is', as Fra Newbery had written seventy-three years before.

Howarth was fifty in 1964 and, after that date, his determination to enjoy the comforts of female love, the excitements and satisfactions of physical sexuality, good food and good wine, become increasingly evident. In the spring of 1965 for example, his diary notes what would seem to have been his first marital indiscretion. Returning by air from another consultancy trip to Jamaica, Howarth went straight to the Grand Ball of the School of Architecture and records his weekend thus:

> *With the Edmond family at the Inn in the Park. Replied to the toast 'The Staff'. Used the Jamaica trip as a starter. O.K. Very enjoyable affair. Straight to bedroom party after. Long argument with Edna.*

In the autumn of the same year Howarth visited London and Venice. On 27 October he mentions, for the first time, a particular lady companion with whom he was to travel extensively and maintain close contact till the end of his life. She was a vibrant, humorous woman of great energy, but Howarth introduces her on a very downbeat note

> *X as saturnine as ever. To Brenda Jones for dinner. Took Liebfraumilch. Margaret and eighteen-year old guests talk of parties and happiness. 'Depends on who you're with!' Cat and allergy...*

These are cryptic notes but their thrust seems clear. By the end of 1965, Howarth was living apart from Edna Howarth and their two children and, despite guilt and regrets, he was enjoying himself. He was also working obsessively hard: founding his Faculty of Environmental Design, planning the Laurentian University campus, and ambitiously involving himself in the politics of architectural education across North America. His diaries reveal little, but occasionally things slip his guard. For example, he regularly appended newspaper clippings, advertisements and astrological predictions loose-leaf in his diaries, and these clippings often carry important psychological messages concerning Howarth's thinking. They set down what he chose or dared not write himself. Here is a selection of examples:

You should never meet someone whose work you admire. Their work is always much better than they are.

Life is short. The sooner a man begins to enjoy his wealth the better.

'Marriage' declares Jose Ferrer, 'is like a very dull dinner, with the dessert at the beginning.'

'Sorrow is a calamity but brooding over it is a disaster.' W. Russell

Ambition: 'By that sin angels fell.' Shakespeare

Ambition: 'All may have, if they dare try, a glorious life or grave.' Herbert

'What happens to us doesn't really matter. The only thing that matters is our reaction to what happens to us.' Leslie Weatherhead

Genius = extraordinary and exceptional intellect.

Pavlova, on being asked the meaning of one of her dances replied, 'If I could have said it, do you think I would have danced it?'

Le Corbusier and De Pierrefeu Francois were convinced of the power of the home to colour man's character with the three essential joys of life: sun, space and verdure.

'Flattery is all right – if you don't inhale.' Adlai Stevenson

The sheik's son went into the harem. He said, 'I know why I'm here but I don't know where to begin.'

Give me ten days and ten nights and I can guarantee to cure any man of any hang-ups, from impotence to premature ejaculation...

A study of navy pilots taken prisoner by the North Vietnamese has found that they are much healthier today than a similar group of non-captured fliers. The Navy's explanation is that the former POW's are now reaping the benefits of an austere diet, little drinking or smoking and vigorous fitness programmes during their confinement – which averaged five years. The ex POW's also seemed to survive their confinement emotionally but experienced a divorce rate two or three times higher than the control group...

Leo Tolstoy, 'Remember that there is only one important time, and that is now. The present moment is the only one over which we have dominion. The most important person is always the person you are with, who is right before you; for who knows if you will have any dealings with anyone in the future? The most important pursuit is making the person standing at your side happy, for that alone is the pursuit of life.'

If you educate a devil – you just get an educated devil.

One *risqué* thing Howarth writes out himself is a joke, told at a party, by one of his lady friends: 'Liberace was stopped at the Golden Gates. St Peter said, "You can't enter here – you kissed a parrot!" Liberace replies, "I've never kissed a parrot! I only kissed a cockatoo!" And with that Liberace was ushered into Paradise'. Such jokes are normal in modern educated society but they would not have been told at Howarth's parents' table, nor at the table of his in-laws. A story told by Howarth's long-time friend, Leslie Rebanks, illustrates how much Howarth's social behaviour changed over the years: 'He had a party-piece, that I witnessed more than once at dinner parties, Howarth would suddenly bring out from his pocket, a cartoon – showing a woman meeting a man – she leading a completely shaven cat, saying, "Well, you told me to shave my pussy!"' This ribaldry may demonstrate a Falstaffian vitality in the elderly Howarth, but it contrasts strongly with the ideas that excited his admiration in young manhood. For example in 1942, Howarth stuck into his diary a newspaper article on John Wesley, the founder of Methodism, and one can almost feel the young scholar's identification with the values of a man he considered a true dissident hero.

A Methodist is one who has the love of God shed abroad in his heart by the Holy Ghost with all his heart and soul and mind and strength. He rejoices evermore, prays without ceasing, and in everything gives thanks. His heart is full of love to all mankind and is purified from envy, wrath, malice, and every unkind affection. His one desire and the one design of his life is not to do his own will but the will of Him whom sent him. He keeps all God's commandments from the least to the greatest. He follows not the custom of the world, for vice does not lose its nature by becoming fashionable. He fares not sumptuously every day. He cannot lay up treasures on earth, nor can he adorn himself with gold and costly apparel. He cannot join in any diversion that has the least tendency to evil. He cannot speak evil of his neighbour any more than he can lie. He cannot utter unkind or evil words. He does good with all men, unto neighbours, strangers, friends and enemies. These are the principles and practices of our sect. These are the marks of a true Methodist. By these alone do Methodists desire to be distinguished from all other men.

In retirement, Howarth's long interest in cosmology and superstition was restimulated by the prospect of his own death. Superstitious beliefs are frequently strong amongst individuals and groups whose lives appear to lie in the lap of the gods: fishermen, gypsies, soldiers, gamblers, the sick and disabled – and maybe it was Howarth's chronic ill-health that nurtured in him a susceptibility to superstitious enthusiasms and astrological predictions. His diaries are littered with appended predictions; the most notable comes very early via a film, *The Clairvoyant*, which he watched at the New Victoria in Preston on Monday 6 January 1932. All members of the audience were given free horoscopes compiled by 'the famous Psychologist Dr Leopold Thoma, 24 Harrington Square, London. NW1' Howarth took his astrological chart home, and preserved it for sixty-eight years.

> TAURUS – GENERAL CHARACTERISTICS: people born under this sign have power of brain and concentration, the natural gift of endurance and determination to persist in any pursuit. They are able to take over leadership with responsibility, and when given a chance they will use it to the utmost, going straight ahead. They do not like quarrels and they do not like giving presents to anyone. They are not afraid of any risks and cost to reach their goal. Full of vitality and perseverance they are representatives of the type; the man who knows what he wants. Originality is sometimes lacking but they have the talent for quick understanding and carrying out the ideas and orders of others. A slight inclination to self-indulgence and indolence; ardently hating to find obstacles in their way or enemies. They are able to hate without remorse, nevertheless they are real good friends, willing to make any sacrifice to help people for whom they feel affection. Therefore they are generally good building stones for society and the state with a special flair for a comfortable and quiet life.
>
> PROFESSION: No particular inclination for any special kind of profession, these people are in all kinds of business where reliable, steady and energetic work is needed. The women make excellent nurses, housewives and cooks, very often gifted with musical talent. Also fond of dancing but never neglecting their duties.
>
> MARRIAGE: People born under this sign must be careful with regard to marriage because of their tendency to take their affections very seriously and if they do not find the right partner they suffer intensely as their sense of duty urges them to carry on in spite of sorrow or heartache. They are fond of homelife and a large circle of friends.
>
> HEALTH: Disposition for colds and throat troubles often inborn. They must take care of their hearts and not overstrain them, a thing they are especially inclined to do, having so much zeal for their duties.

SPECIAL CHARACTERISTICS: Particular attention for all details. Interest for anything however small and things that another would throw away. Personality becoming of the highest efficiency between thiry-five and forty years. Idealistic nature, always ready to help others. Not fond of speeches, prefer actions. If they have to speak on some occasions they ponder over what they shall say. Good listeners to others. Not able to earn a fortune through adventures. Keep only on the straight path. Important to learn self-government. Often playing with the idea of making a fortune overseas but the carrying out of this would be wrong. Disposed to be led to decisions by the influence of anyone. Important to build up firmness in life. Deeply affected through adversity which is inevitable as there are many obstacles, especially in youth. Talent for sport of any kind. In general these Taurus people are deeply religious and not at all lascivious. Nevertheless gifted with much joy of life, carrying gaiety with you and distributing joy to those with whom you come in contact. Many Taurus people earn wealth but not in youth. Governed by Jupiter and Venus, the general prediction for these people is happiness in life.

That chart describes the habits, life and attributes of Thomas Howarth with remarkable accuracy. Whether this is due to coincidence, chance, destiny, the impress of cosmic forces, or whether Howarth 'became' what was predicted, it is impossible to say, but there can be no doubt that Dr Thoma's prediction struck a cord in the young Tom Howarth and excited an interest that lasted a lifetime. Did this prediction nurture in Howarth the idea that by his mid-forties his major achievements would be behind him, thus justifying the casualness of his actions as Dean in Toronto? Did this prediction justify the increasing frustration Howarth felt within his marriage? Did it encourage him to make sexual hay whilst the sun still shone? It is certainly possible. But whilst Howarth was always susceptible to mystical forces, he was also a factual rationalist and in the same diary in which he appended the psychic wisdom of Dr Thoma, he sets down the facts of his own physical measurements: size in gloves 7, size in boots 7, size in collar 14½, size in hats 7. Weight 8 stones 2¼ lbs, height 5 feet 10 inches… And he carefully writes out 'a good spelling test': 'In the vicinity of a cemetery, a harassed cobbler and embarrassed peddler were gauging, with unparalleled ecstasy, the symmetry of a lady's ankle.' Like a magpie and 'the chameleon poet', Howarth was attracted by whatever shone brightly.

Howarth was not a betting man but he always enjoyed a gamble and the risk of consequences. Many psychologists suggest that amongst gamblers the excitements and fears engendered by 'loss' are just as addictive as the thrill of winning, and that deep inside every gambler there is a compulsive wish to lose, an unfathomable desire for dissolution. There was certainly something of this 'death-wish' in the personality of Thomas Howarth and various events in his life conditioned him to the idea of the normality of loss, of existence as a sequence of letdowns. Howarth's own body and physical health continually 'let him down'. His father had died young and let his family down. His first love, Isabel Kent, had left him. Beyond the domestic circle, the three men whom Howarth admired most, C. R. Mackintosh, Jesus Christ, and Fra Newbery had been 'let down' and perhaps 'let themselves down'. Their failures, of course, raise the question as to what failure and success are. And, if we are to look for a golden lining, that may explain Howarth's failure to fight boldly to prevent the collapse of the Faculty of Environmental Design in Toronto and justify his gradual retreat into ideological privacy, it is towards the precedents set by his heroes, Mackintosh, Newbery and Jesus Christ, that we should look.

Mackintosh was a great artist who 'created a civilisation' but he was also a difficult individual who was forced into non-employment, dependence on his wife's private income; a man who lived out his time in exile, his great achievements unrecognised or forgotten. Jesus Christ created a new religious, philosophical and social framework within which men and women have redeemed their lives over two millennia, but he, too, was denied and brought low. Howarth knew that both Mackintosh and Christ had been vanquished by 'Mammon'; that each became victims of the world they stood against. And he also knew that if either had sought to destroy those who stood against them, they would have become like their enemies and invalidated the essence of their vision and their lives. Yet their visions, their perceptions, and their realised idealism did not die, rather they prospered in the minds, the eyes, the hearts of followers across many generations. In worldly failure the seeds of their immortality were sown.

Thus, in the late 1960s, when Howarth began to find himself confronted by hostile forces surprisingly similar to those that had brought down the men he most honoured in the world, he seems, to have decided it would be wrong, as well as useless, to resist. Why batter his head against a brick wall or seek martyrdom? He would leave the dead to bury the dead; he would stand by his own standards and principles. And he retreated into a more private world, within which he could maintain his personal equilibrium and, almost invisibly, disseminate the ideas and values he believed to be of real importance. Why should he break himself on the wheel of institutional authority, student radicalism, or petit bourgeois respectability? He would grasp the possibilities of life. 'Truth against the world': he would embrace the rose.

Whatever the reason, or whatever the motive, it is a fact that, after 1968, Howarth increasingly withdrew from the fractious convolutions of university politics and sought fulfilment in gathering a close circle of 'private' students and associates around him. He travelled the world advancing his highly personal Anglo-Christian ideals through the Commonwealth Architectural Association, lecturing on Mackintosh, on architecture and the environment (his own version of the Gaia ecological hypothesis), on the importance of art, education and democracy. Like a latter-day John Wesley he would either house with friends or be put up in the best hotels. To help finance these trips he began to sell selected items from his collections. He started to invest in new works and start new collections. As a rule he bought straight from the artists and craftsmen themselves, in the streets of West Africa, New Guinea, New Mexico. He had grown tired of the politics of education and also began to recognise that saintly ambitions can co-exist with wine, women and song. Such frameworks opened up new directions in Howarth's life but, before exploring life in the pleasure dome that Howarth constructed around himself, it is important to analyse in some detail, the circumstances that caused the Faculty of Environmental Design at the University of Toronto to implode as it did.

Howarth had been appointed Director of the School of Architecture because he was a Modernist, a scholar, a historian and a successful, didactic teacher. By the late sixties and seventies, these qualities were seen by many to have become unfashionable liabilities. A new generation of students was eager to reject the rigorous intellectuality that Howarth demanded. Howarth's methods suddenly became too traditional, academic and techno-logical. Students became impatient with rules; they wanted to express themselves and they rejected everything that smacked of hard grind. They wanted a new political and socially dynamic architecture that related to changing times. Howarth was deeply opposed to the vagaries of the new 'sociological, arty architecture' but always tried hard to accommodate his students' changing demands. However, whatever he gave was never enough, and he quickly found himself in a cleft stick. And the more he gave the students and their more radical lecturers, the more he ran foul of the architectural profession in Toronto which had always demanded competence and skills above creativity. By the mid-seventies Toronto's professional architects began to reject students 'from their own university' as architecturally illiterate. A booming profession, building a new, urban Canada, did not want 'ideological designers' impatient with the mechanics of building, the needs of clients, the reality of the marketplace. It wanted competent, practical architects. Howarth thus found his faculty attacked from two sides: by a significant section of his own students and staff, and by much of the Canadian architectural profession.

In addition, worldwide, attitudes to criticism and the methodology of history were changing. These were the two areas of scholarship with which Howarth had been most closely and successfully associated. In 1970, John Wain, the literary critic, wrote in *The Listener*,

> In the literature of the English-speaking world, one thing has been clear for some time: no matter which side of the Atlantic, or which hemisphere, one looks at, the literary critic no longer occupies the centre of the stage. The age of criticism is over: that age when a handful of critics, mostly employed at universities, formed and cultivated a landscape within which young imaginative talent could grow and measure its growth.
>
> In an interview with the *Paris Review*, Robert Lowell recalled, 'When I was twenty and learning to write Allen Tate, Eliot, Blackmuir and Winters and all those

people were very much news. You waited for their essays, and when a good critical
essay came out it had the excitement of a new imaginative work'. Between 1945
and 1960 a body of literary criticism, written mostly by middle-aged men had a
profound effect on 'people under thirty'. Now no such phenomenon exists. What
was it about the young then that made them so interested in criticism? And what
is it about the young today that makes them no longer interested?

    Since we have to start somewhere, let us begin with the fact that the young
in the fifties were much less politicised than they are now. The energies which
now go into 'direct action' went, then, into other things...

What was true of literary criticism was equally true of architectural criticism. After two
generations of heroic revolutionary endeavour in art, architecture, music, literature,
science and technology (1885–1935), a creative pause had become artistically, and
educationally, necessary. The great ideas and achievements of International Modernism
needed to be digested and developed: critics and teachers were desperately needed to help
students, and society, come to terms with the facts and possibilities of the new
technologies and the new aesthetics. Thus, between 1940 and 1965, Howarth taught
during a golden age in which the New Architecture was, historically and critically, systematically addressed for the first time. Howarth found himself responsible for disseminating
new ideas and technological possibilities to a generation of students hungry for a clarity
he was able to bring. It was a crucial historical moment. In different schools, different
architects brought different emphases to their teaching: Howarth brought Mackintosh;
a philosophical vision of environmental wholeness; a restrained, very English vision of
International Modernism and a love of the achievements of the Arts and Crafts
movement. In the mid-fifties, in Manchester, Howarth's ideas had electrified brilliant
students like Norman Foster. By the mid-seventies in Toronto, he was being lampooned
as 'Uncle Tom'. And, the more Howarth found himself under attack the more he retreated
onto a 'high horse' of *values* stamped not by contemporary Canadian needs but what he
had known in the Old Country. As the years went by, far too many of the specialist
lecturers Howarth invited to Toronto were old friends and associates from Britain,
brought in to 'validate' *his* position and values. If architectural education in Toronto was
in 'meltdown', the one thing that wouldn't restore its rationale and vitality was fair-
minded preaching about the gardens of England.

    It may be chance that Lord Norman Foster came from Manchester and was a protégé
of Howarth; it may have been chance that drew Howarth to start his great study of
Mackintosh, but the end result, in both cases, was of great cultural significance.
Howarth's appointment as Dean of the Faculty of Environmental Design in Toronto
might have been another equally significant cultural moment, but it was not to be. Man-
management and political manipulation were not his forte. After 1968, having achieved
high executive office, Howarth, for the first time in his life, let his focus drift sideward

from his prime responsibility. His actions can be explained but not excused. In retrospect, it seems clear that Howarth should either have efficiently addressed the academic problems that confronted him or resigned from office long before he did.

One man who can speak with authority about Howarth, as both a teacher and architectural force in Canada and Britain, is the architect Leslie Rebanks of Rebanks Associates, Toronto. Rebanks was brought up at Lytham St Annes in North Lancashire, the son of a chief of police. In 1944, at the age of seventeen, he joined the Grenadier Guards. He was soon commissioned as an officer and joined his local Lancashire regiment, the Loyals. He saw action in Europe, in Eritrea and in Palestine. Rebanks is a tall, handsome man with bardic gifts that were much appreciated in the officer's mess. In 1947, asked by his commanding officer to prepare his troops for Civvy Street, Rebanks decided to give a series of lectures on 'The Importance of Eating a Healthy Diet'. His first lecture led to such a rash of complaints about army food that the course was immediately terminated! Ordered to pursue other subjects, Rebanks discovered a set of army aptitude tests. These proved entertaining and so useful to the soldiers that Rebanks decided to take one himself and the result declared that he should be an architect. Thus, on leaving the army in 1948, Rebanks started architectural studies at Blackpool Technical College. It was a low-grade institution and things proceeded with frustrating slowness until a lecturer from the University of Manchester arrived as a visiting design critic. His name was Dr Tom Howarth. Rebanks remembers:

Suddenly, the wool dropped from my eyes. Suddenly, instead of being asked to follow some 'pattern book' telling me how to design a 'Georgian House' for a residential area of Morecombe, I was confronted by a man with a developed and coherent intellect who saw architecture within a clear, contemporary, framework. My chance contact with Howarth was a moment of revelation. In the army I had been used to clarity and to getting things done, it was Howarth who showed me such things were possible in civilian life. I had felt, for months, that my teachers in Blackpool were inadequate and that architecture was bigger than they conceived it to be – now I knew I had to get out! With Howarth's direct encouragement I abandoned the technical college and went to work for the architects Tom Mellors and James Arthur Morrison Bell, in Preston. They were closely associated with Howarth's old friend George Grenfell Baines. I became, as it were, an old-fashioned apprentice working in an office through the day, imbibing the thoughts and habits of two estimable masters then going off to night classes. I later won a scholarship to continue my studies at Oxford University, where I did my dissertation on military architecture – very conscious that Scottish castles had inspired Mackintosh and that the Atlantic Wall had inspired Le Corbusier.

Left. The Weston Centre,
Toronto (Leslie Rebanks).

Right. Interiors of the
Weston Centre, showing
various Mackintosh
characteristics.
(Leslie Rebanks).

I came to work in Canada in 1957 before Howarth did, but I returned to England between 1961 and 1965. I got unmarried, then I remarried a Canadian girl. When we returned we came to Toronto – to find the School of Architecture was on a real high. Howarth had established an excellent school, there was a buzz of excitement about the place. I was delighted to renew personal contact with Howarth and I was soon keen to employ his students in my practice. In 1975 I designed the Weston Centre, here at St Clair, off Yonge Street. It is a modern, high tech, hexagonal building, with certain features influenced by Mackintosh: its use of glass, space and artworks has been much commented on and it established my reputation in North America. Consequently, I was employing large numbers of architects, but gradually, as the seventies progressed Howarth's students became unemployable! They weren't, of course, really Tom's students at all but they were products of the school of which he had been director and for which he was still responsible as Dean of Environmental Design. By 1980, as a matter of principle, no Toronto students were accepted into this practice.

They seemed to have had minimal technical and structural training but were full of every kind of political, sociological and ideological conceit! They *might* have been artistic but *I definitely know* they were useless. I remember one student arriving for an interview, with a great roll of drawing paper which he unrolled to cover the whole of a very large office floor, then he announced that this was his plan for a linear city! I had no interest in linear cities. One Yonge Street is quite long enough. What we needed to know, was whether an applicant was capable of designing a building and overseeing its construction. Radical educational experiments might be all right in the fields of sociology and psychoanalysis but in architecture they tend to be counterproductive, as they would be in nuclear physics. Looking back, one can see that few, if any, of those students were architectural radicals, they were amateurs, dilettantes, playing on the backs of earlier generations who had worked and died for their freedoms.

Tom Howarth was away from the University of Toronto by the time things reached their nadir but he must bear some responsibility with regard to what happened to the Faculty he established and the school of architecture of which he was formerly director. It was a man called Peter Prangnell, who replaced Howarth as Chairman of the School of Architecture, who started the rot. That man presided over a tragedy, not just for education and architecture in Toronto but for Tom Howarth himself. Prangnell was a rebel, proud to describe himself as 'a pedagogue'. He became committed to the educational ideals of teachers like Montessori and A.S. Neill but, as far as I know, Prangnell never built a single building. For twenty years what students learned at the School of Architecture in Toronto had to be, largely, unlearned before they could begin serious work as architects. Whilst trendy professors, and a fair proportion of their students, luxuriated in their ideological and sexual freedom, small firms of architecture, across Canada, had to pick up the bill.

The tragedy for Tom Howarth was that, by appointing Peter Prangnell as Director of Architecture, he promoted someone whose limited skills exaggerated all the worst aspects of his own weaknesses. What Howarth needed, as Dean of the Faculty of the Environment, was a chairman of architecture who was a reputable, dedicated, *practical* architect, who complimented his own skills as a historian, a critic, a scholar and academic administrator. What he got was a charming, abrasive, compulsive educator who saw architecture as just part of his wider, political vision. Prangnell was determined to stimulate minds, to make students question everything around them, and he did this with messianic fervour. Under Prangnell, anarchic educational 'enquiry' replaced 'architectural training' and Howarth was totally incapable of controlling the situation; worst of all whilst the reputation of his School of Architecture fell slowly to tatters, Howarth was gallivanting around the world representing Canada as Vice-president of the Commonwealth Architectural Association! To look back and contrast this with the determined vision of the young man who inspired me, is salutary.

Having said all that, we remained close friends. I wrote a review of his Mackintosh book when it was published here in North America. I thought it was great and I said so and afterwards Tom announced, 'Leslie, it was worth writing the book, just for your critique!' We liked to try to fathom the connections between Mackintosh and Frank Lloyd Wright and we both tried to follow Wright's dictum, 'Do not copy an effect that you admire; look for the principle behind the effect; apply that principle to your own problem and you will own your own effect.' There was a big dinner organised by Corey Keeble at the Royal Ontario Museum, in honour of Tom; he was always giving them a Mackintosh chair or selling them furniture designed by Frank Lloyd Wright at a special low price, so I made up a poem. This was just after the big Christies sale so I spoke in the guise of C.R.M.

> I'm Charles Rennie Mackintosh
> And I was One Hot Cookie.
> I liked to drink my whisky neat
> And – I liked my Nookie.

But as time went by
I became an old Soak
- I shouted at Clients
And I died broke.

Then – along came Tom
And that lady from Christies
And what they did
Will make your eyes Misty.

They sized up the Market
And they worked without stint.
They sold all my stuff
And they made a Mint.

Well! I don't need the money
And I don't want to taunt you
But – keep Rebanks in whisky
Or I'll come back to haunt you!

A second valuable source of contemporary information about the problems experienced within Howarth's Faculty of Environmental Design is an article, by Adele Freedman, published in *The Globe and Mail,* 19 February 1983. The fact that Howarth's name is not mentioned is highly revealing.

The Department of Architecture at the University of Toronto is fighting for its life. Ostensibly, this has to do with budget cuts and administrative reshuffling, but the problem goes deeper than that. It is the story of a revolution that began in a revolutionary decade, only to create a groundswell of frustration and hostility. It is the story of one man and his passion for buildings, education and togetherness – Peter Prangnell. Fifteen years after the revolution, Prangnell's vision of a school rooted in mutual trust and the 'patient exploration through examination of each other's reactions, feelings and ideas' is simply known as Prangnellism. His followers are known as Prangnellites, or Prangnellians, or believers... He is the picture of his belief that 'everything I see of importance is struggle'.

The staff functioned as advisors, resource people, critics, co-ordinators. Letter grades were abolished. Prangnell established a department council with staff-student parity to advise on staff appointments, incoming students and curriculum. The council was instrumental in overwhelming the department's old guard so the new program could get rolling. Prangnell maintains, 'Any school

worth its salt would be in trouble with the profession. Otherwise we'd be simply
maintaining the status quo. I don't believe it's necessary to be interested in all
points of view, in the same way I don't go to see many new buildings. They're like
fliers people hand out to you in the street. One tries to save one's energy...'

In the mid 1990s, Eb Zeibler, a distinguished architect and university teacher, was
brought in to lead yet another attempt to sort out continuing problems. His committee
advocated that the department of architecture be made autonomous again (as it was when
Howarth was first appointed), so that it could pursue its architectural responsibilities to
the profession of architecture uncluttered by related environmental interests. The Zeibler
proposals attracted widespread support but were finally vetoed by the university because
such 'departmental independence' might trigger the collapse of the whole faculty system.

It is not surprising that Howarth almost entirely expunges the Prangnell episode from
his memoirs. He lamely concludes:

> My position was difficult since I had established the three departments and
> given them a high degree of autonomy within the faculty's structure. I was
> approached by several members of staff urging me to fire the chairman
> and several of his followers. Tempting as this proposal was I had to
> recognise the academic qualities of the people involved and I was reluctant
> to take such a dramatic step.

Some aspects of Prangnell's vision were undoubtedly fashionable and some major
thinkers were involved in exploration of the kind of ideas he advocated. One was Ivan
Illych whose book, *Deschooling Society,* had a profound influence on liberal thinking during
the early seventies. Illych was a Catholic priest who worked in rural Mexico. Illych
believed traditional conviviality was being fatally eroded by Western materialism and
technological dominance, and his practical, non-technological vision, his support for
native peoples, struck home in Canada. Many students were genuinely alarmed by the
nuclear threat, the Vietnam War, the burgeoning materialism of modern Toronto, but,
whatever the problems, Prangnellism was not the solution and Howarth, by allowing
Prangnell his freedom threw his own baby out with the bathwater. It is to Howarth's
discredit that he never mustered the courage to cut 'the Gordian knot' with which
Prangnell suffocated the nascent Faculty of Environmental Design in Toronto.

If one compares the confused and incoherent statements made by Prangnell in the
newspaper article above, with the heroic precision of the statements made by the young
Mackintosh one has to ask why Howarth allowed his school to be deconstructed by such
a well-meaning non-entity? The fact that Howarth always loved Mackintosh, whereas he
distrusted Prangnell from the moment they met, is no excuse. Howarth seems to have
become transfixed by Prangnell like a rabbit in the eye of a snake, or a hare on the

highway. Listen to Mackintosh:

> The day is happily passing when architecture may be deemed a thing of quantities of dilettantism and drains... The other is passed – and well it is – for its aim was to crush life. The new, the future, is to aid life – and to train it – 'so that beauty may flow into the soul like a breeze.'... The power the artist has of representing objects to himself explains the hallucinatory character of his work, the poetry that pervades it and the tendency towards symbolism... Symbols must be thoroughly understood and appreciated before you can interpret the true meaning of architecture and all the arts... And still you ask what is the connection between architecture and painting – everything... Architecture and building are quite clear and distinct ideas – the soul and the body... Old art lived because it had purpose. Modern architecture, to be real, must not be an envelope without contents... Artists – and I mean architects – must be as selective in those whom they desire to please as in those they desire to imitate.
>
> The man with no convictions – no ideals in art – no desire to do something personal, something his own, no longing to leave the world richer, his fellows happier – is no artist. The artist who sinks his convictions is no man... All artists know that the pleasure derivable from their works is their life's pleasure – the very spirit and soul of their existence. But you must be independent, independent – don't talk so much but do more – go your own way and let your neighbour go his... Shake off the props – the props tradition and authority give you – and go alone – crawl – stumble – stagger – but go alone... Art is the flower. Life is the Green Leaf. Let every artist strive to make his flower a beautiful living thing, something that will convince the world that there may be, there are, things more precious – more beautiful – more lasting – than life itself...

If one compares the 'wisdom' of Mackintosh with the 'philosophy' of Peter Prangnell, one feels a contrast like that made by Hamlet between his father and the self-serving corruption of his murderous uncle Claudius: 'Look upon this and this, the counterfeit impression of two brothers – Hyperion to a satyr.' But, year after year, as Dean of the Faculty of Environmental Design, Howarth displayed irresolution like that for which Hamlet is famed: 'Conscience doth make cowards of us all.'

He seems to have been determined not to become a disapproving authority figure like the hard-nosed John Keppie who broke Mackintosh; he wanted to be, and be seen to be, a generous, nurturing leader like Fra Newbery. Unfortunately, such ambitions are hard to realise, and, as the years passed, Howarth became in many ways, a vain and silly old man, who was terrified by Prangnell as King Lear was fooled by his two elder daughters.

Externall Howarth's experience of his disintegrating educational domain can be seen to have parallels with the experience of many other 'traditional' educators – for example his academic contemporary, Robert Lowell. Much of the poetry Lowell wrote in New

England in the late sixties describes a world remarkably similar to that Howarth was inhabiting. These quotations come from two shorts poems published in 1970: 'In Dreams begin responsibilities'; and 'Secondary Sex'.

> The dream is off, the sun tears stars in the shade,
> the heater starts snoring, but the cold is inside –
> a hundred breasts inside the same black sweater,
> like and unlike as the stars in many snowflakes.
> My headache is to keep the movie running...

> ... When I am happy I try to make the hour
> an hour or half an hour sooner than it is;
> orphaned, I wake at four and pray for day –
> lovely ladies have helped me through the day;
> man retreats, and its the same old story.

After his retiral, in 1978, Howarth's diaries gradually become increasingly confessional. That year he cut out this astrological prediction: 'If 1st May is your birthday – you are creative, independent and have been accused of having a one-track mind. Leo and Aquarius persons play important roles in your life. You make valuable contacts in June. The year features marvellous opportunities, a chance to erase past mistakes and find life happier, more productive...'

He was delighted to throw off the weight of his university commitments, but immediately flung himself into organising a major exhibition of his Mackintosh collection at the Art Gallery of Ontario. 'Mackintosh' was his signature tune and he was determined to 'sign off' with a flourish. He also tried to renew close contact with his family. On 1 December 1978, he took his daughter Katharine out to lunch at the A.G.O. It was their first meeting for three or four years and on the 17th she attended the opening.

> *'C.R.M. exhibition – Katharine and fiancé, Eric, turn up unexpectedly – first meeting. He seems a good person – they are to be married on 21st June, Ottawa.'*

The exhibition was a major success and on 8 January 1979, Howarth celebrated by catching a British Airways Concorde from New York to London. He lodged at the Savoy Hotel and then flew on to Abu Dhabi: a new, hedonistic pattern to his life was being established. In May he was in Japan. Shortly afterwards he was in Calgary, Alberta, with his son John, then in California where he stayed with his brother, Jay. The distant, resentful, yet still affectionate relationship with Edna continued, measured out in 'dutiful gifts' and dollar bills. On 8 February 1980, Howarth's diary, punctiliously notes, 'Edna's birthday – sent daffodils. $12.75... X came and left in a huff. Olga came with a letter and a catalogue for the Decorative Arts Society...'

A decade of professional difficulties was now replaced by a decade of domestic difficulties as a series of 'lovely ladies' began to play an increasingly important part in his life. The Canadian Society of Decorative Arts was the product of an initiative, jointly developed, by Howarth and a former student, Olga Williams. Olga, a strikingly beautiful woman, originally from Cheshire, had first met Howarth when she was a student at the school of architecture in Manchester in the early fifties. Olga later married a fellow student and, after the marriage collapsed, followed Howarth to Toronto where she established a successful career and renewed their friendship: it lasted for the rest of Howarth's life. Today, after twenty years, The Canadian Society for the Decorative Arts remains a small but prestigious organisation. It has functioned as a national 'arts society' for over twenty years, but runs more as a club than as a dynamic cultural force and thus reflects the general tenor of Howarth's later life.

In the early 1980s, as Howarth travelled the world, he began, for the first time, to try to make money out of his Mackintosh collection – by making the occasional sale, and by collaborating in a venture to manufacture high-quality Mackintosh reproductions. His partner was a brilliant Toronto craftsman, Walter Putzer. This led to a commission from the Toronto-based television entrepreneur Moses Znaimer and the actress Marilyn Lightstone, for Howarth to redesign their Arts and Crafts house in the 'Mackintosh' style. Its transformation emerged slowly over almost two decades with an extensive cast of artists and craftspeople involved. During the first decade, Howarth oversaw design and construction. During the second, Marilyn assumed prime responsibility. The final result is a remarkable Mackintoshesque interior in which individual craftsmanship and personal vision (Mackintosh's, Howarth's, Marilyn's and various craftworkers) have combined to make something new. This project was, however, the only large-scale commission overseen by Howarth during his retirement and the business venture with Walter Putzer never did more than 'tick-over'. All furniture produced was of the highest quality and, to the centimetre, as Mackintosh originally designed it, but Putzer was neither a good salesman, nor a businessman and the project declined into bankruptcy. At a certain point Howarth decided to curtail the funds he was committing. Since then, all his tools sequestered by creditors, Putzer has worked privately and heroically, on a commissioned basis. His 'Mackintosh flower holders' stand comparison with some of the best sculpture produced in the twentieth century.

Howarth now lived alone in a relatively small but beautifully lighted Bloor Street apartment. It was a prestigious address close to the university, the Royal Ontario Museum, excellent shops and various facilities. He was financially comfortable but not wealthy. He had an established circle of friends but he was very conscious of being alone, and he sought to alleviate his loneliness in a series of domestic and sexual relationships with beautiful, charming and, occasionally, acquisitive women. Over the years these relationships seem to have become of addictive importance to Howarth: he liked to be noticed as 'the meticulously dressed gentleman with the lovely lady on his arm'. He liked

Olga Williams at a Mackintosh exhibition booth designed by Thomas Howath, Toronto, 1984.

Interior of Thomas
Howarth's apartment
in Toronto.
Mark Shapiro

Interior of Thomas
Howarth's apartment
in Toronto.
Mark Shapiro

Below left. *Rome, Arch of Titus* (Mackintosh 1891); pencil, watercolour.

Below right. *Certosa di Pavia, Studies of the Ceiling Decorations* (Mackintosh undated); pencil, watercolour.

Bottom left. *Orvieto Cathedral: A Sheet of Studies of Mosaic Bands* (Mackintosh 1891); pencil, watercolour.

Bottom right. *Certosa di Pavia, Intersia* (sic) *Panel Study;* (Mackintosh undated); pencil, watercolour.

CRM. 1891.

MOSAIC BANDS.

ORVIETO CATHEDRAL. INTERIOR.

Below left. Fabric design (Mackintosh c. 1916); pencil, bodycolour, on tracing paper.

Below right. Fabric Design (Mackintosh c. 1916); pencil, watercolour, on oiled tracing paper.

Bottom. *The White Cockade* (Margaret Macdonald Mackintosh undated); illustration for a menu; lithographic print, poster colour on white paper.

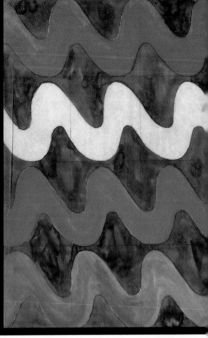

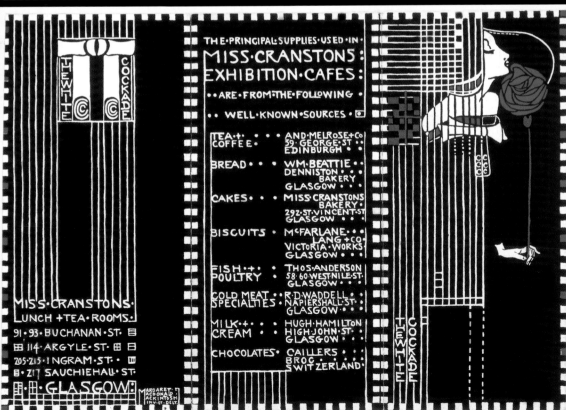

Left. Fabric Design (Mackintosh 1916); pencil, bodycolour, on oiled tracing paper.

Right, top. Design (Mackintosh 1916); pencil, bodycolour, on oiled tracing paper.

Right, middle. Design for an exhibition stand (Mackintosh 1901); pencil, grey wash, watercolour.

Right, bottom. Design for ceramic plates (Mackintosh 1916/18); pencil, bodycolour, on oiled tracing paper.

Elevation to Cheyne House Garden.

Below. Two dark-stained oak armchairs (Mackintosh 1898–99); designed for the Billiards and Smoking Rooms at Miss Cranston's Argyle Street Tea Rooms.

Bottom. Two rare dark-stained oak high ladder-back chairs (Mackintosh 1898–99) designed for the Billiards and Smoking Rooms at Miss Cranston's Argyle Street Tea Rooms.

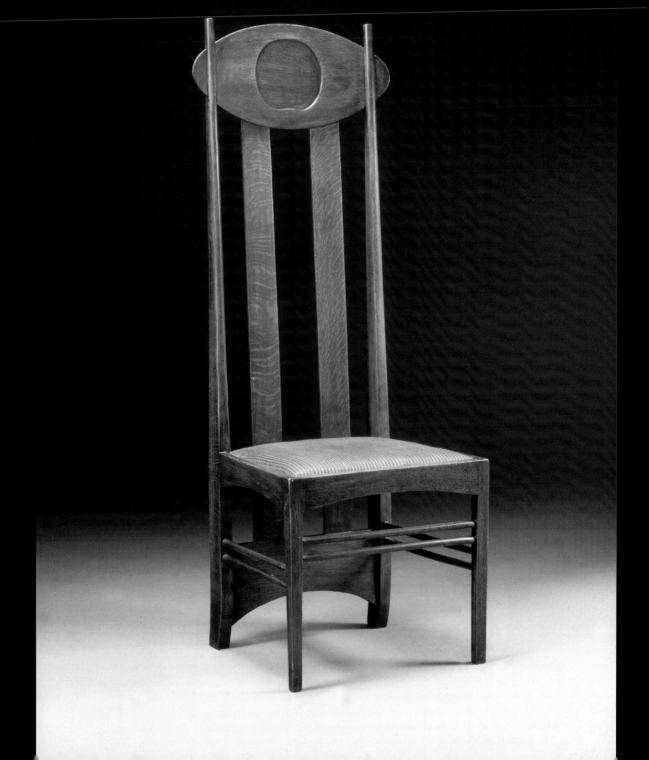

Left. High-backed oak chair
Mackintosh c. 1898–99)

Below. Pair of dark-stained ash bed-
ends (Mackintosh 1910); designed for
Fra Newbery.

Bottom. Painted settle (Mackintosh
1917); designed for the Dug-Out at
Miss Cranston's Willow Tea Rooms.

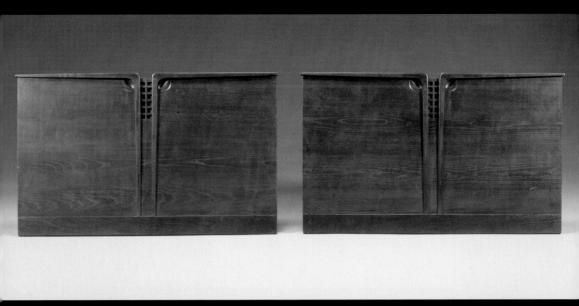

CHRISTIE'S

A highly important ebonized mahogany writing cabinet
Designed by Charles Rennie Mackintosh for The Hill House, 1904
44⅜ in. (112.6 cm.) high, 37 in. (94 cm.) wide, 18¾ in. (46.7 cm.) deep

**Sold in the sale of The Dr. Thomas Howarth Collection
on 17 February 1994 for £793,500**

Auctions   Valuations   Private Sales
Important 20th Century Decorative Arts

London
Adam Chadwick
achadwick@christies.com
+44 (0)207 389 2141

Paris
Sonja Ganne
sganne@christies.com
+33 (0)1 40768354

New York
Peggy Gilges
pgilges@christies.com
+1 212 636 2240

www.christies.com

to be 'in love', and he craved care and attention. He became rather Edwardian, slightly Frank Lloyd Wright, very Thomas Mann. Living a modern, civilised life amongst successful and moneyed people Howarth wanted and needed to keep up appearances. He also knew that his financial and intellectual capital were invested in one and the same thing – his Mackintosh collection and, after 1980, he began to think, seriously, about what he should do with it. Should he keep it? Should he gift it as a collection to a single gallery or museum? Should he sell it as a collection or piecemeal at auction? Should he give it away to relations and friends? It was already far too large to be safely kept or displayed in his apartment, and after a plumbing disaster, in the late 1980s most of the collection was stored, for safekeeping, at the Royal Ontario Museum, whilst his long-running debate with himself, his family and his friends, rumbled on and on.

As old age approached, Howarth's feelings of vulnerability increased. His university pension was satisfactory but his health remained poor. He had the prospect of good Canadian state medical care at no direct cost but, despite the fact that his 'glorious art objects' had become hugely valuable, he still felt financially insecure. His collections had always given him kudos, now they began to offer him the prospect of financial freedom and an old age without money worries. The prospect was both alluring and liberating – and this was, presumably, the reason why he spent fifteen years toying with his options! Howarth's collection was the source of real personal and emotional power and he became, increasingly, 'possessed' by what he had. He was never a miser but he undoubtedly enjoyed the same pleasures that misers enjoy. Over the years, he wrote will after will, all in extended longhand, each subtly modified according to changing likes, dislikes, situations and people. And he, recurrently, subtly, vicariously played possible recipients off one against another. It is not a seemly story.

The first institution involved was the Art Gallery of Ontario which, in the seventies, had been gifted the magnificent Henry Moore Bequest. The second, was the Royal Ontario Museum, where his friend Corey Keeble was a curator. A third possibility was opened up by a Glaswegian friend of Howarth's, Harry Ferguson. After emigrating to Toronto in 1956, Ferguson had become an extremely successful businessman and closely involved with the development of the School of Scottish Studies at the University of Guelph. On 8 August 1987, Howarth wrote in his diary, 'Harry Ferguson is convinced I should give my C.R.M. collection to Guelph – the centre for Scottish Studies in Canada. He said he would press for me to be invited to design and build a C.R.M. style museum for the collection – and me as lifetime curator! Harry considers me to be a very important historical figure – flattering but mistaken...'

This interesting offer from Ferguson did not progress far, mainly because of a lack of funds, but the proposal gave Howarth new ideas with regard to what he might expect to get out of the A.G.O., or the R.O.M., or any other interested party. Subsequent negoti-ations with all parties seem to have been conducted with a tantalising wilfulness and, not surprisingly, the various individuals and institutions involved became deeply frustrated.

On all issues, it became more and more difficult to know what Howarth wanted and where he stood and Howarth put himself under considerable unnecessary pressure. Shortly after initiating discussions with the University of Guelph, he fell badly in Bloor Street, cut his head and was taken to hospital where he received fifteen stitches. His emotional adventures were affecting his physical and intellectual life, and as in the Prangnell days, things began to run slightly out of control.

Mackintosh reproduction furniture produced by the Putzer/Howarth company.
Thomas Howarth

In addition to discussing gifting the collection to the various Canadian institutions, Howarth considered various institutions in Glasgow: the School of Art, the Hunterian Museum, the City Art Gallery and Museum, and the C.R.M. Society. He also trawled for possibilities in England, in Australia and in Japan. He wanted the collection to stay together, he wanted to be assured the collection would be permanently on show, he wanted some financial return for his gift and he insisted that it would be known as either 'The Howarth Mackintosh Collection' or 'The Mackintosh Howarth Bequest'. Negotiations meandered on and none advanced near to contractual conclusion. In retrospect, it is clear that one reason for this is the fact, documented in Howarth's diary, that before beginning formal discussions with any of the great art institutions, Howarth discussed disbursement of the collection with his children, in the early 1980s. Their suggestion seems to have been that Howarth should sell it and use the proceeds to make the rest of his life comfortable. They saw the collection as a family collection and they believed that their mother, who had played a very definite part in acquisition of the collection, should benefit from any sales that might take place. Thus, it may be that whilst Howarth seriously tested the possibilities of gifting the collection as a collection to various museums, deep down, he always presumed to sell the bulk of his collection for the benefit of himself and his family. Although Howarth was estranged from Edna and, at times, from his children, there is no doubt that all three continued to mean a great deal to him. He wanted to be loved and recognised in their eyes and he felt a deep and genuine responsibility for them as a husband and father.

The facts of the disbursement of the Howarth collections are outlined in the next chapter but, for the moment, it is important to return to Howarth's 'Indian summer' when, as a man in his sixties, the ascetic and stylish professor remodelled himself as a temperate but hedonistic *bon viveur*. As usual, Howarth was in tune with the zeitgeist and his 'blossoming' reflects something of the extraordinary changes that reshaped Western society in the second half of the twentieth century. Externally, Howarth remained much as he was, but internally, intellectual hunger and professional ambition were now replaced by sexual striving and a search for holistic, personal satisfaction. Set against his Christian youth, these years of well-being and indulgence can be seen either as decadence and betrayal, or as a natural urge to embrace life's riches. Many of Howarth's friends were unhappy about his change of attitude and behaviour but others would ask, 'Why shouldn't an old man enjoy his life? Why should the old be excluded from the pursuit of happiness – as they see it, as they feel it and want it?' As usual, it is probable that Howarth sought confirmation of his behaviour in that of Mackintosh who, in his last years, sought and found a marvellous physical and spiritual contentment travelling in France, Spain, England and Italy with his beloved Margaret Macdonald. Why should he not, in his different circumstances, follow suit? He had often referred to Madame de Stael's description of architecture as frozen music, now he began to agree with the French courtesan who stated that 'the only aim in life is to seek pleasant sensations'. His diary of 1970 carries an incongruous jotting: 'C.R.M. described as recht dekadent – by L. Abels, *Das Interiors*, 1901'

After 1980, Howarth's diaries create a portrait of a man who seems to have moved beyond the concept of bodily sin, a man who obsessively seeks female companionship and redemption through love. In the Calvinist sense Howarth becomes another Justified Sinner. He began to embrace life in the manner of Mary Magdalene, or a Titian.

DECEMBER 8TH 1984. Glorious Day. RCYC pool 8.00 a.m. Twenty lengths. Breakfast of muffins and tea. Laundry 10.15. D. came and we shared laundry and spent an hour afterwards. Very Good. But life is complicated. Leave for Niagara – on the lake – for New Year's Eve. So I shall be done and X and family are now out of bounds.

JANUARY 5TH 1987. Sad Monday. John's thirty-eighth birthday. D. left a message on tape saying she would call me after 6.00 p.m. She called from the library at 6.45 to say that I could not pick her up and she thought it best that we did not see each other again. This was quite incomprehensible – she is still overworking at the university and her full-time job and claims the strain of our relationship complicates her life with her live-in manfriend too much. Apparently she has decided she cannot come to live with me as I have suggested. Sad, very sad but maybe the best of a bad job. This leaves me high and dry and the future seems bleak without her. But we'll see – she's changed her mind before.

JAN 12TH. 3,000 dollars from York University. Unpleasant indigestion. Worried about York in retrospect. Why the Golden Handshake?

JAN 23RD. D. at El Toro Filet – excellent – complimentary Drambuie. D. uptight as usual – quite unresponsive and cool – seems to have lost all interest in our relationship – except where food is concerned. A very strange and disconcerting time. Says she's applied for another job, but would not say where – department head of some school. Wants $45,000, is getting 40. Ambitious, ruthless in getting her own way. Yet she has wonderful human qualities I can encourage.

FEBRUARY 21ST. E.Y. – to movie, *Decline of the American Empire*, an extraordinarily explicit study of human sexual mores. Four couples. French

Canadian. Superbly done. Frank discussion of the attitudes of the sexes. Surprised that the 'innocent' E. (19) wanted to see it but she, like most of her generation have little to learn in this area of human activity. Had dinner afterwards.

FEBRUARY 27TH. Edna's birthday. Sent card.

MARCH 14TH. RCYC Dinner Dance with X [mother of E.Y., above]. Excellent and afterwards to her apartment for a rest – she proved to be charming and affectionate. Her mastectomy was no hardship and she soon overcame her inhibitions and timidness. This was a heart-warming and delightful experience after months of uncertainty and denial.

MARCH 16TH. 7.30 pm. Z. Came to dinner – a delightful person – vastly entertaining and attractive. We became firm friends. I cooked her steak. She brought two bottles of red wine – Montebar – V.G. We talked of life and love and labour (and lovers). A most enjoyable and disturbing evening. She says she will cook dinner for me next Monday. We will see!

MARCH 24TH. D. came to see me from the French Department – after two glasses of wine and a hot dog she relaxed and became more human. I told her I would be happy to resurrect our amoretto – she went over a lot of old ground, including her desire to have a child before she was forty – she's thirty-eight. I said I didn't think that would be a problem and maybe we should get to work! This was an old joke and she went through all her evasive tricks – including probing about X, whom she saw me with in the courtyard last week… And so it goes on.

APRIL 14TH. D called. Had beer and appetisers – Seafood Café – V.G. scallops wrapped in bacon. Long talk about the future. She seems to have no concept of the human art of living together. She may never learn. She is fed up with her school and is seeking other opportunities… I have given her a week to decide whether to join me in the U.K.

APRIL 17TH. E.Y. called about arrangements to meet her in Hamilton. She would like me to go to the Lynwood auction on Saturday – but I may be spending Saturday night with D – if she decides we get together. Interesting and critical situation. Three women all eager.

SUNDAY 22ND MAY 1988. Timothy Neat from Dundee to discuss C.R.M. A bearded swarthy, Jewish looking individual and an extraordinary extrovert who talked all day. He brought slides and files and proceeded to give a lecture on CRM and The Four's watercolours. He teaches at Dundee University and his interpretations of the watercolours were quite startling.

He related them to cosmic life and emotional problems and used them to illuminate many issues that have puzzled us for years… Katharine and Eric came as arranged at five – and we all went to Tim Neat's room at the Sheraton Hotel to watch my C.R.M. programme on City TV. They thought it good. I had reservations. At 7.30 we came home and had a cold roast beef supper. V.G.

FEBRUARY 10TH 1989. 4.00 X came early from work so that we could go to the 4.15 showing of *Little Dorrit* – unfortunately, D. came in with two friends and, on the way out, X said, 'That's your slut!' At which I left her, and walked out to get a taxi home. [This followed an incident in which X, who had a key to Howarth's apartment, had entered to find him in bed with D.]

FEBRUARY 23RD. Very disturbed night – worried about clash of times for Monday evening – V.S. and E.Y., unfortunate overlap. Can't change E.'s time so must try V.'s.

APRIL 10TH. V. brought sandwiches for lunch and we spent a fascinating afternoon unpacking C.R.M. and other artefacts. V. enthralled by the number and variety of things – favourite exclamation – 'O My!' As we open each package. It's a joy being with her. She is an acute observer and shares my sensitivity to beauty and craftsmanship. She handles artefacts well, infinite care and appreciation. We have very much in common. Later to bed – very tired.

APRIL 12TH. Late start, V. leapt up at 9.00 a.m. for work. Unpacked more treasures from my closets for display in living room (first visit from Christies re planned Mackintosh Sale).

APRIL 14TH. Began repacking collection after Sotheby's visit [they, too, were offered the sale]. Wendy Rebanks came to see C.R.M. and other things. She, like everyone else, was greatly impressed. They are so familiar to me that even when displayed I cannot get too enthusiastic about them…

APRIL 15TH. Drove to see Ed Hasselfeldt, jeweller and silversmith, about a ring mount for the Australian black opal in my collection which I have promised V. Ed was as friendly as ever and displayed a magnificent collection of semi-precious stones he had cut. We agreed on a gold mount for my piece. And among the stones viewed, V. was greatly impressed by an Ametrine – a combination of Amethyst and Citrine – a beautiful delicate purple stone about 1 inch long and five-eights of an inch wide, carved by himself. Twenty-three carats at twenty dollars a carat. Ed offered it to me at $300, so I bought it for V. Great joy. So I owe Ed $550 cash. [Howarth's version of events here is absolutely contradicted by V. who states that she that was never given this ring.]

APRIL 18TH. Love in the afternoon – unpremeditated can be delightful – write poem on this theme.

APRIL 21ST. V. arrived at 4.30. Went to see new dress I had noticed in the window. It looked splendid… Shopping for groceries – surprised by the cost of providing for two!

APRIL 23RD. To Ed Hasselfeldt's. For diplomatic reasons V. may decide to wear neither ring at the wedding – but we will see – the situation vis-à-vis her parents is delicate… V. is clever, loving and affectionate and she says she is going to look after me – which is and will be a very happy experience. Thus we will await developments. My task is to help her with her education in my field, in life generally and love-life in particular. She is an apt pupil! She herself is determined to lose weight and attain maximum advantage for her natural beauty and charm and character – what a girl!

JUNE 1ST. V. opened up the problem of our relationship, which is at breaking point. I cannot understand her attitude. She said that she, and her parents, had discovered that she was only thirty-two years of age, thirty-three on 29th June! She looks seventeen!

JUNE 3RD. V. stayed. Incidentally we were both very tired. The usual argument about our relationship.

JUNE 4TH. V. came. We spent an enjoyable half hour with U.K. maps exploring possibilities for our holiday in July.

JUNE 6TH. Went with V. to 2nd Baseball Game at the Skydome. Game as confusing and futile as ever. Skydome spectacular – 60,000 spectators – ripple motion and applauding spectators – blue seats colourful. An engaging aesthetic experience.

JUNE 7TH. Visit from Bill Hardie [of Hardie Fine Art, Glasgow]. Phyllis Lambert tells me that Bill has panel from the Willow, also project drawings.

JUNE 16TH. V. has changed completely from the loving, caring companion to a cold withdrawn friend.

JUNE 24TH. Until V. and I got together, in February this year, she had never been to a symphony concert or choral work. Her taste was largely formed by records and popular song and rock bands. I have educated her by taking her to major concerts. She is good company but immature. She has a menagerie of stuffed animals and, even at thirty-three, sleeps with her teddy bear which she treats as a human. I am just realising that she is remarkably insecure, childlike, and charming. I have made the mistake of treating her like an adult. She said we had better talk about our relationship. She made the following points: she is not comfortable with sexual aspects; I am not satisfied with simple affection; she wants to marry and have a family; and she can't give me what I need in terms of home and affection.

JULY 2ND. To London with V.

JULY 9TH. 5.00 p.m. – abortive dinner with Hugh Casson, Indian – requested by H.C. – Noisy and pretty dreadful.

Thus a life of heroic scholarship was replaced by a life in which Howarth seems to play a bit part in his own 'soap opera'. As his physical health declined he, more and more, desperately sought refuge in female care and consumer comforts. Indeed, Howarth's lifestyle might be described as a demonstration of Arnold Toynbee's theory of why civilisation collapses. Toynbee, for many years a distant neighbour of Howarth's up the Vale of Lune in Lancashire describes in his great *Study of History* how collapse is predictable when 'the dominant minority within an established civilisation begins to, increasingly, imitate the behaviour and life-values of the mass at the bottom of society.' Toynbee's theory was coloured by his own Imperial Age but carries self-evident truths. Great civilisations have, necessarily, always depended on the differentiation of values. And, whilst Howarth's external 'eye' remained as perceptive as ever, his chameleon being took its colour from the patchwork of life around him. Cultural, national and personal decline are always sad spectacles but often accompanied by compulsive vitality as, unfettered, humanity luxuriates in clover. This energy can engender renewal and a new order but, usually, once established such declines are rarely arrested.

Howarth and V. spent July 1989 touring Britain, sometimes together, sometimes apart. Together they toured the Lake District, Howarth rejoicing in Coleridge's description of this 'great camp of mountains... a non-stop theatrical performance', and acknowledging Wordsworth as 'the first man to insist that scenery was a common heritage that all nations should treasure'. The beauty of landscape and its importance to man was a fundamental cultural premise that Howarth had always tried to integrate into his architectural teaching and he continued to believe that however beautiful or useful architecture is, it must always exist and be seen within its wider environmental context. He reread and applauded Wordsworth's 1810, *Guide to the Lakes,* in which the poet describes certain landscapes as being 'a sort of national property, in which every man has a right and an interest who has an eye to perceive and a heart to enjoy'.

Annual visits to Britain were now personal and intellectual reprises of all Howarth held dear – and he used them as grist for his *Memoirs*. Without compunction, Howarth arranged that old friends and former students drive him from place to place as he found convenient. Close to Heathrow lived John Griffiths, another of Howarth's Manchester students and he, and his wife Helen, regularly went to great lengths to accommodate Howarth's needs for a dust-proof room and a comfortable car. In Toronto, Marina Winters and Josette Banz, were always 'on-call' as chauffeurs and companions and seem never to have grumbled at the demands put upon them. Howarth commanded quite extraordinary loyalties: but whilst he took a great deal from a great many people, he also gave a great deal back. In the North of England, Sid Tasker was one of several people drawn into Howarth's retinue. Tasker was a distinguished architect who studied in Manchester, then quickly rose to become a partner in the Grenfell Baines Group. After forty years of minimal contact, Sid came out of retirement – to become 'a driver for Dr Howarth'.

> I drove him around Kirkham in the Fylde and I think he startled the occupants of more than one of his family's homes, which were all very modest terraced houses, by knocking unannounced. But he was always invited in whilst I remained in the car. When he had exhausted all his old Kirkham haunts he said he would like me to drive him along the Golden Mile at Blackpool and, in particular, he wanted to see the 'Big Mac' – the enormous and very new Big Dipper. He insisted on getting out of the car and wandering along the pavement gazing up at the thing, apparently fascinated. I then took him home for tea before delivering him to a rendezvous at a motorway service station on the M6 with a young lady from Wigan (he had met her somewhere on his travels) and she took over my escort duties for the next part of his trip.
>
> Although I am very fond of Mackintosh's work it was forty years before I got round to buying a copy of Tom's book. And before he left I got him to sign it. He wrote, 'to Sidney Tasker an excellent student of mine at Manchester University, long ago, and now a valued friend, with best wishes, Tom Howarth.' I'm rather proud of that. By my judgement, Howarth was the best lecturer on the architecture staff in Manchester. He was completing the writing of his Mackintosh book at that time and I recall he had the best draughtsman in the Second Year do all the line drawings of plans and sections. Those that had to be redrawn for publication. I hope he got a good mark! Tom later photographed drawings I made and hung them in his study – next to Mackintosh.

There is no doubt that Howarth, like many artists and individuals of high energy, 'took things unto himself'. His boyhood magpie instinct remained with him all his life; he was always attracted by the brilliant and beautiful, he retrieved and hoarded and nothing was forgotten. Thus, Howarth returned to England to show his Lakeland mountains to V., and, in other years, to other lady friends. His pleasure was doubled by the fact that these were the hills he had climbed as a boy on chapel outings, these were the hills he wandered with Isabel Kent; these were the mountains he had climbed on honeymoon with his wife...

From the Lake District Howarth went, alone, to Glasgow to meet various old friends – Bill Hardie, Julian Spalding, Patricia Douglas, and Andy Macmillan, professor at the Mackintosh School of Architecture. He describes Macmillan as 'a compulsive talker and a strange personality but vastly entertaining with his coarse Glasgow accent – which he cultivates.' Returning south, Howarth rejoined V. and the two of them drove to view the Iron Bridge at Coalbrookdale in Shropshire, the Georgian splendours of Bath, the great Gothic cathedral at Wells. In London, Howarth bought some fine Art Deco silver that V. had admired in a window and generally flaunted his taste like a Regency buck but, immediately this holiday was over, this briefly passionate relationship fades into oblivion and various of the presents bought were set aside to tempt the next lady who might enter his life. One of Howarth's short poems, 'The Lissom Blond' affirms the voyeuristic sexual energies that infused many of these friendships:

> I saw her in a bar
>> Where else indeed would one expect
> To view so fair a sight
>> From such an angle?
>
> She was sitting cross-legged
>> On a stool
> And now I know
>> Why stools in bars
> Are high
>> And seats are low.

In another poem, 'Parties', he recoils from the inanity and noisy confusion that is the norm at so many modern parties but, as usual, Howarth seems totally unable to break free from a social framework that he finds, highly distasteful:

> ... Hour after early hour
>> Insufferable fascinating hypnotic
> Human frailty exemplified
>> Yet there is maybe
> A curious logic to it all
>> For at a point in time

Sometime may be sublime
>If the gods so will
All maybe transformed.
>As one becomes aware
Of a new presence there
>Through the din steals silence
Electrifying silence
>An island of dynamic solitude
Created in a moment of time
>As eyes glance
Connect by chance
>As spirits interweave
As words flow tentatively
>Then gathering momentum
Cascade bubble and sparkle
>Challenge and caress
Provoke and stimulate
>As ideas clash
And smash through constraining walls
>Of convention
While ectoplasmic bonds twine
>And interwine
Softly seductively irrevocably
>Linking together
For ever and ever
>The isolated few who care
For life and truth
>Or they who are prepared to wait
And wait
>Until just one
The only one
>Is there to share
An island
>Of dynamic solitude
In a sea of sound.

Howarth's poetry is interesting but it further encourages one to contrast the sophisticated experiential world of his maturity with the innocence and idealism of his youth. Diary jottings, from seventy years before his book of poems was published, clearly document the fundamental change that has occurred:

JANUARY 2ND. 1929. Stayed in all morning. Went collecting for the Church Missionary Society in the afternoon. Stayed in at night.

JANUARY 15TH. Stayed in all morning. Went to John's all afternoon and to concert at night – Kirkham Grammar School.

FEBRUARY 3RD. Chapel in morn, Sunday School in afternoon, chapel at night – had to come out at 7.00 – very ill.

MARCH 4TH. Thus endeth my second week in bed. Made the aeroplane given free with *Modern Boy*, in afternoon with John. Asthma very bad.

DECEMBER 31ST. New Year's Eve Party. Had a great time. We all listened to the Grand Goodnight on the wireless.

JANUARY 13TH 1930. After tea went to see *Journey's End* at Kirkham with Mr Laithwaite.

JANUARY 15TH. Busy all day. At night to the Senior Guild. Discussion on legacy of £65,000.

JANUARY 17TH. All afternoon and evening at Chapel, 1.30–10.00 p.m. Concert a great success. Made £5.

JANUARY 29TH. Walk in afternoon. Wesley Guild in the evening. Talk by Mr Middleton on Gilbert and Sullivan.

FEBRUARY 1ST. Chapel in morn. Sunday School in afternoon. Mrs Laithwaite's at night. Had to break into home – after being locked out!

APRIL 27TH. STARTED WORK TODAY AT KIRKHAM P.O. Finished at 7.50. Chapel Meeting at 8.00.

APRIL 28TH. Worked all day. Came home at 7.15 – straight to bed. Had doctor – terrible stomach pains.

MAY 12TH. Very ill all day. Off work – never been so ill before. Called doctor. He gave me a hypodermic injection.

MAY 21ST. Lovely day. Much better – walk with John. Got reed warbler's eggs.

JUNE 13TH. Saturday. Clubday. Walked in afternoon. Blackpool at night. Saw *Dracula* at the Palace. Other films recently seen: *Just Imagine*, *The Grande Parade* (rotten), *Hell's Island* (VG), *Raffles* (VG), *Trader Horn*, *Up for the Cup* (VG), *Strangers May Kiss*, *Down the River*, and *Daddy Long Legs* with

Janet Gaynor. Also *A Dangerous Affair, Condemned to death, Daughter of the Dragon, Cuban Love Song, A Lady's Man, Unfaithful* (a rotten show), and *My Sin* with Tallulah Bankhead.

SEPTEMBER 30TH. Still in bed. Nothing to eat for six days.

OCTOBER 2ND. Chicken broth for dinner. My it tastes good!

Howarth stopped work at Kirkham Post Office on 26 September 1931. This first job at the local post office is not mentioned in his *Memoirs*. It was obviously unstimulating and provoked a bad spell of ill-health. From this time, until he started his course at the University of Manchester in 1934, Howarth worked from home as a choirmaster, organist and music teacher. He also ran a small home-printing business, on the side:

JANUARY 8TH 1932. In morning called at Dr Haddow's with two proofs of printing I had done for him. After dinner called at chemist's with prescription for flu. Stayed in all evening with feet in mustard. Cold increases and I feel awful by bedtime.

JANUARY 9TH. Annual Tea and Concert. Bad as it is possible for me to be and, as usual, right at the time I should be up and doing...

FEBRUARY 27TH. Beautiful day, hardly a cloud in the sky. Grandma went to Preston before dinner (another cloud gone). John has gone to Blackpool with Jack Smith so I have been quiet all day. At least a minute bit quieter than if he had come – for John is not famed for his rowdiness.

APRIL 14TH. 'At Home' at chapel. G'dad presented with chair for fifty-five years service as Chapel organist.

APRIL 15TH. Up at 8.30, packed trunk and at 9.20 set of towards Matlock for a one-month holiday at Lilybank Hydro (with chapel). It should be a rest cure but I have a strong foreboding of evil.

APRIL 30TH. Received fourteen letters and two parcels this morning. Had breakfast in bed. Went to meet Big Joe at Preston at 3.00. Had ripping tea party at 4.00. After dinner had a dance that lasted till 11.30p.m. Wonderful time. Danced mostly with Doreen Guthrie.

MAY 1ST. My eighteenth birthday. Big Joe stayed in bed till 11.00. I went for a wonderful drive with Mr and Mrs Eldridge and Mrs Guthrie and Doreen, to Chatsworth. After lunch went for a walk with Doreen over High Tor and up to Riber Castle. Saw her off at 6.30p.m. and made Big Joe miss his train.

MAY 3RD. After lunch went with Mrs Guthrie to see painting at Elfin Chapel. Also saw a yew tree some 2,006 years old, and church interior at Durley Dale. After tea went to the Wishing Stone. Played cards after dinner. Won 2 out of 6.

JULY 23RD. After tea went with John and Uncle Fred to Preston Hippodrome and saw Professor Raymond 'Mind Reader and Hypnotist'. Jolly Good Show.

JULY 31ST. Chapel in morning and evening. Strange coincidence tonight at chapel. Last Sunday evening Corinthians 13th was read and this evening Isaiah 53rd – both of which I heard Isabel reciting two weeks ago...

DECEMBER 29TH. *Messiah* at Preston Public Hall. Black coffee at Booth's – nearly collapsed.

MAY 5TH 1933. After dinner Hughie, Isabel and I walked for two or three miles along the Morecambe Prom. and had some top-hole strawberry ices on our return.

MAY 6TH. Good times in evening with Isabel on the cricket field. Choir 7.45–9.00.

SEPTEMBER 6TH 1934. Tennis with George Grenfell Baines. Went to baths afterwards. Evening indoors. George left at 11.00.

SEPTEMBER 26TH. To Manchester. Rushed up George Ave at 5.45 and interviewed Professor Cordingley at the university at 6.00.

WEDNESDAY 3RD OCTOBER. THE DAY OF DAYS. Up at 6.30. Caught the 7.30 to Manchester and took Maths at the university, 9.30–11.30. After lunch in the refectory – English and General Knowledge until 5.50. Home 7.30.

OCTOBER 4TH. Sat French, 'made a hopeless mess of it'! Had lunch and made an unexpected start – on the course of architecture... Home 8.20.

OCTOBER 8TH. First real day of big adventure. Feelings of remorse predominate and everything seems strange – but start out the day and find new digs very good.

OCTOBER 9TH. Put in some good work. Things brighten up a little now. Seems years since I saw the home town! Two quotations: one for me, one for the future. Vitruvius, 'the true architect must not only understand drawing but music...' John Ruskin, 'No person who is not a great sculptor, or painter can be an architect; he can only be a builder.'

Four things stand out in that selection of quotations. First, Howarth mentions a legacy of £65,000, a huge sum of money in 1929. It is not clear whether the legacy is coming to the Howarth family, or to Kirkham Chapel, but it is certainly possible that it came to the Howarths. If so, this legacy may well account for the 'financial and psychological cushion' Howarth seems to have enjoyed during most of his professional life. In particular it might explain the availability of the funds that allowed Howarth to buy Mackintosh, because although he was given and found various pieces, some in dustbins, many were purchased. Second, it is clear that Howarth's first job was a humble appointment in a post office. Third, whilst Howarth's decision to pursue a career in architecture was the consequence of a tennis game, Howarth knew from the beginning that this decision was of the utmost importance. He marks it in capitals in his diary as 'THE DAY OF DAYS'. Fourth, with godlike conceit and boyish humour Howarth states that 'I interviewed Cordingley at six o'clock'!

11 CLOSING THE CIRCLE
TIMOTHY NEAT

LETTER TO HOWARTH
1994

It would have been wonderful if the collection could have stayed together, yes, but for me it is more wonderful that it should now, like seeds scattered in the wind and grow anew in new soil. My hope is that the objects will be well-spread across the world. World figures should pin-prick the globe with joy.

Most of Howarth's huge Mackintosh collection was sold, by auction, at Christie's in London on Thursday 17 February 1994. The sale raised over two million pounds. That evening, Howarth hosted an impressive after-sale party at the Royal Overseas League, St James Street. These twin events encapsulate the essence of Howarth's life in retirement: he had intellectual prestige and the money to enjoy a highly civilised, international lifestyle. He saw the ideal of a world commonwealth of nations as the best blueprint for mankind. News that he had cancer had been accepted with equanimity and, like a divine, or a man who knows he is to be hanged in the morning, Howarth began to dispense largesse far and wide. He was determined to say, and demand what he wanted for himself,

Thomas Howarth
(1998), St Ives.
Gillian McDermott

295

and mankind. He became a version of Bernard Shaw's Professor Higgins; an 'enabler' egging everyone to embrace the poetry of their lives and the pleasures of art. He reinvigorated old friendships, and slowly recovered his Christian faith. He glorified in the great collection he had dispersed and began, on a small scale, collecting anew.

What is it that makes a collector? The urge to collect springs from basic human instincts. It must have evolved from our animal need to think about the day after tomorrow. Squirrels gather nuts, dogs bury bones. In human beings the instinct can become an obsession that has nothing to do with the facts of survival, and such obsessions can become either noble or destructive compulsions akin to miserly gluttony. The urge to collect can be driven by various motives: aesthetic, scientific, a sense of historical responsibility, and by commercial interest. For most people collecting remains little more than a hobby but amongst a few collecting is a facet of genius, and a genuinely creative act. Great collectors become, in their own way, artists. The collector who recognises and preserves beauties and values that the world currently denies does something of creative and historical importance. Such collectors become remembrancers, custodians, and private archivists – the secretaries of mankind.

Thomas Howarth was a collector of genius and his Mackintosh collection, undoubtedly, plays a small part in the history of British civilisation though one would get no hint of this from reading his introduction to the Christie's sale catalogue of what is called 'The Dr Thomas Howarth Collection'. As was so often the public case, Howarth offers little and gives less away: 'Every collector, however modest, must have an objective or special interest. Mine has been Charles Rennie Mackintosh and his circle.'

And that's it. It is a statement that describes quite precisely what Howarth's prime interest was but it leaves a thousand questions unanswered. That, of course, is the nature of life; and why should Howarth reveal the answers *we* want? The questions, however, remain and they are worth exploration.

In the early sixties the English novelist John Fowles published a highly original murder novel, *The Collector*, in which the murderer is a repressed and inhibited collector of butterflies. Fowles later wrote the brilliant novel, *The French Lieutenant's Woman* which was turned into an equally exceptional film by Harold Pinter and Carel Reizs. A study of Fowles complete oeuvre clearly marks him as another man interested in Rosicrucian philosophy and who explores the ways in which our modern need for 'systems and possessions' can reduce and unman us. In *The Collector*, the murderer's future victim, a young and beautiful art student, speaks thus of her torturer,

> 'That sums him up. He's got to be correct, he's got to do whatever was "right" and "nice" before either of us was born.'
>
> I know its pathetic, I know he's a victim of a miserable nonconformist suburban world and a miserable social class, the horrid timid copycatting genteel class... It makes me sick, the blindness, deadness, out-of-dateness, stodginess,

and yes, sheer jealous malice of the great bulk of England... The feeling that England stifles and smothers and crushes like a steamroller over everything fresh and green and original. And that's what causes tragic failures like Matthew Smith and Augustus John – they've done the Paris rat and they live ever after in the shadow of Gauguin and Matisse or whoever it may be... The real saints are people like Moore and Sutherland who fight to be English artists in England. Like Constable, Palmer and Blake...

And, one might add, 'like Mackintosh in Scotland'. In another work, a novella entitled *The Enigma*, Fowles describes another man obsessed with preservation, with collecting, and with himself. He is a Conservative M.P., a successful lawyer, and a man of exactly Thomas Howarth's generation:

'He's like a fossil – while he's still alive...'
She tapped ash from her cigarette.
'Did you ever see his scrapbooks?'
'His what?'
'They're in the library down at Tetbury. All bound in blue Morocco. Gilt-tooled. His initials. Dates. All his press cuttings. Right down to the legal days. *Times* law reports, things like that. Tiniest things. Even little local rag clippings about opening bazaars and whatnot.'
'Is that so unusual?'
'It's just more typical of an actor. Or some writers are like that. An obsessive need to know... That they've been known?'
'Okay.'
'It's a kind of terror really. That they've failed, they haven't registered. Except that actors and writers are in far less predictable professions. They can have a sort of eternal optimism about themselves. Most of them. The next book will be fabulous. The next part will be a rave.'
She looked at him. Both persuading and estimating. 'And on the other hand they live in cynical open worlds. Bitchy ones. Where no one really believes anyone else's reputation – especially if they're successful. Which is rather healthy, in a way. But he isn't like that. Tories take success so seriously. They define it so exactly. So there's no escape. It has to be status. Title. Money...'

It is self-evident that Thomas Howarth shared many personality traits with John Fowles' fictional, West Country M.P.: Howarth was liberal, humane, isolated, and a committed Tory till the end of his days. Like the Fowles' politician Howarth continually sought status and personal recognition. In his last years he became almost desperate for public honours. He wanted a knighthood, like those enjoyed by so many of his friends and

associates Sir Hugh Casson, Sir George Grenfell Baines, Sir Harry Barnes, Sir Patrick
Nuttgens – he sought to no avail. In Toronto, Harry Ferguson went around collecting
names and recommendations that he hoped would lead to Howarth being properly
honoured by the British establishment. Ennoblement seemed possible. Nothing happened.
Off his own bat, with something close to undignified enthusiasm, Howarth made contact
with Prince Charles:

October 25th 1991

Your Royal Highness,
The third edition of my book on Mackintosh has been published recently in
paperback and I have taken the liberty of enclosing herewith a copy for you in the
hope that you will find it useful for reference. It is an amended version of the
second edition I presented to Her Majesty on the occasion of her Jubilee in 1977. I
respectfully suggest that you may find the two prefaces of special interest in
outlining the development of the fascinating Mackintosh story since I began my
research in 1940.

My friend, Sir Hugh Casson, introduced me to you at the memorable RIBA
Gala Evening at Hampton Court, and I look forward with great pleasure to
attending the panel discussion this afternoon at the Art Gallery of Toronto.

I have the honour to be, Sir,
Your Royal Highness's obedient servant –

Thomas Howarth

He wrote again on 18 November 1992

Your Royal Highness,
C. R. Mackintosh Collection. To supplement the information in my book on Charles
Rennie Mackintosh, I thought you might be interested in the short article on my
collection, Living with Legends *(editor's title), on pages 72–77 of the magazine*
City and Country Home *enclosed herewith.*

Incidentally, when you visited Toronto in October 1991, the two high-backed
chairs with the oval top-rail on which you and Princess Diana sat during the
welcoming service, were reproductions of Mackintosh pieces in my collection,
borrowed for the occasion.

Assuring you of my continuing loyalty and support in these difficult days,
I remain, Sir, yours very truly,

Thomas Howarth

By courting Prince Charles, Howarth shows both a childlike need for recognition and the nature of his old-fashioned high Toryism. He was also very conscious that he was a man who fell between stools, England did not see him as fully English, Scotland knew he was not a Scot, and Canadians never quite saw him as one of them. Thus, despite years of subtle effort, the plans to gain Howarth a major British honour ended in absolute failure. Why? Many lesser individuals have gathered MBEs, OBEs, Knighthoods and Dukedoms. Had the word gone round that this scholar was a womaniser? Was the academic elite in Canada unwilling to forgive Howarth's mistakes as Faculty Dean in Toronto? Harry Ferguson continues to think that it was the controversy surrounding Conrad Black, the Canadian newspaper tycoon, who was even more desperate for a major British honour, at the same time as Howarth! The precise reasons will never be known but, not for the first time, Scotland stepped into the breach that opened around Howarth and Scotland offered Howarth honour in his old age, just as she had offered him opportunity in his youth. In 1994 the University of Stirling awarded Howarth an honorary doctorate and, in 1999 the Lord Provost of Glasgow made Howarth 'Glasgow Citizen of the Year'. Although too ill to receive the award in Glasgow, Howarth was hugely appreciative and delighted when a major celebration was organised at the Royal Ontario Yacht Club at which David Mullane, director of the Mackintosh Society, presented the award on behalf of the Lord Provost. Even this recognition, however, only came *after* Howarth had written the cheque that enabled the Mackintosh Society to buy Queen's Cross Church and make it their permanent headquarters.

The big question remains – why should Howarth have so wanted official state honours? Throughout his life he wrote and lectured on the 'subversive power of art'; he knew that much of Mackintosh's genius sprang from his rebellious status as 'an outsider'. As an evangelical Christian he knew very well what usually happens to 'the man of the future'. To the last, Howarth remained a contradictory character and it may be that even whilst searching for public honours Howarth was secretly pleased that his failure was exactly the kind of failure that Christ and Mackintosh had endured? He knew very well that the essence of all 'classical tragedy' is 'the spectacle of a human being at the end of their tether' and heroic failure has long been the price of admission to those inner sanctums where immortality lives – both in the fictional world of Hamlet and the real world of Van Gogh.

Certainly Howarth hungered for love till the end of his life, the kind of love he so rarely got from his father, and all his life he sought succour in the strength of strong men. For example, during the penultimate week of his life, I helped Gillian McDermott lift Howarth's body up the bed so that his head could rest more comfortably on his pillow. We lifted him together – me for the first time, Gilli for the thousandth. And, as soon as he was settled, he turned with a smile to me and said, 'It's so good to have strong man to lift you.' The statement was generous to me, but also implied criticism of Gilli and the familiar, female world that she represented, and which he had so adroitly manipulated all his life. Despite Howarth's very real affection for Gilli, she frequently got minimal thanks for the selfless, loving service she rendered, daily, and over many years. And long after she had become the stable reference point in his life, it was still men and possessions, that gave him his real sense of personal identity and professional achievement. By choosing Mackintosh, Howarth believed he had played a crucial part in ensuring the continuance of cultural 'memes' of great importance to mankind, and it was his symbiotic relationship with high genius that continued to give the deepest satisfaction to Howarth's spiritual longings. It was Mackintosh who dramatised and justified Howarth's very existence yet, like his namesake St Thomas, Howarth remained a permanent doubter, desperate for his historic contribution to be affirmed by a visit to Buckingham Palace! 'Seek not artistic unity in character' as William Blake put it:

Thomas Howarth (middle back left) with Commonwealth Architectural Association Councillors (1987) at Buckingham Palace garden party.

> He who replies to words of Doubt
> Doth put the Light of Knowledge out.
> The Strongest Poison ever known
> Came from Caesar's Laurel Crown.
> Naught can deform the Human Race
> Like to the Armourer's iron brace.
> When Gold and Gems adorn the Plow
> To peaceful Arts shall Envy Bow.
> A Riddle or the Cricket's Cry
> Is to Doubt – a fit Reply.

In addition to his Mackintosh collection, Howarth accumulated several collections of lesser importance, including a good collection of sculptures from New Guinea.

Most of my objects come from the Sepik River valley and its coastal zone. Some of the pieces are relatively recent, but as with so much art the most interesting tends to be the oldest – even though, in New Guinea, old means fifty years. Rain, damp, termites and insects destroy most things of wood within two generations but a genuine tradition continues along the Sepik River and the simplicity of the wood carving process ensures that the 'professional' carvers are extremely prolific. My objects are all, I believe, genuine tribal artefacts, although trade had separated some of them from the villages in which they originated before I bought them. Tribal art is most valuable when the ethnological provenance and purpose of each particular piece is known and understood, but beyond that, most genuine, tribal art has a formal aesthetic energy that makes it Art in the modern Western sense of that term. And, in my opinion, it is invidious to suggest that Primitive Art has to be 'ethnographic' and judged by different criteria from the 'independent' artefacts of the civilised world. My collection had value on both these two levels.

I gave most of my New Guinea collection to the University of York, in 1976. It was exhibited, and then stored away never to reappear. I got a short formal note of thanks re the gift but that was all. It's very easy for men and horses to disappear without trace into the bowels of great institutions. That metaphor used to be used in England to describe the condition of the Great North Road! I often wish I had known as much about my New Guinea sculptures as I know about my Mackintosh pieces; context is always of huge importance in art and in life but I would never suggest that my two major collections were of equal importance in the history of mankind.

My other major 'folk' collection is of Balinese paintings from Penestanan on the island of Bali. I fell in love with the unique style and vitality of these paintings. Over the years I bought quite a number and they have delighted me and most of my visitors for twenty-five years. I also have smaller collections of Aztec and Inuit art and numerous glass, ceramic and metal objects from the Art Nouveau and Arts and Crafts periods.

Howarth first met Gilli McDermott in Dubai, in 1992, when they were both guests at the wedding of Heather Macfarlane, youngest daughter of one of Howarth's very old Toronto friends, Norma Macfarlane. Two years later, in London, whilst Howarth was completing arrangements for the Christies auction, he asked Gilli for professional assistance with the 'public relations' aspect of the sale and its aftermath. Almost immediately, he proposed that she should marry him. She later found out, he had, previously, made similar proposals to half a dozen other women during the previous decade – all whilst still married to Edna! Howarth had become a lonely, eccentric and sometimes tragic figure. Gilli, a well-travelled and cultivated young businesswoman from Cheshire was quite shocked. She refused and, over the subsequent months, tried to maintain their relationship as one based on shared interests and professional duty, however, Gilli had long sought an opportunity to enter the world of the arts and, after much soul searching, an informal, open-ended arrangement was entered into.

Thomas Howarth.
Gillian McDermott

In Toronto Gilli soon became deeply involved in collating and writing up Howarth's sprawling *Memoirs*. She also catalogued what remained of his collections and prepared his archives for the University of Toronto. It was interesting work that suited her career plans, but – Gilli McDermott's loyalty and commitment to Howarth's psychological and physical well-being must be described as nothing short of heroic. She came to Howarth, in the years of his decline, rather as Cordelia returned to King Lear in his extremity and it was she who enabled Howarth to make his exemplary exit from life.

Until Howarth's death in July 2000, Gilli McDermott brought order, stability, domestic comfort and remarkable happiness to a difficult, infirm old man whom many people would say, didn't deserve it.

The relationship was sometimes abrasive, often cantankerous and it had self-serving edges but this strange and unlikely meeting of an elderly man and a beautiful young woman made Howarth, consciously, know himself blessed. To his surprise and great satisfaction, he found himself drifting towards death content and in a manner that most human beings only dream of. The deep friendship and enhanced lifestyle this relationship

engendered quite naturally reawakened Howarth's intellectual and creative powers. Years of hedonistic escapism were replaced by visits and holidays planned with a view to serious study and the exploration of ideas relevant to the *Memoirs*. Howarth and Gilli visited galleries, houses, places, and people. Howarth again began to write poetry and Gilli oversaw the editing and publication of a handsome book he designed, *Poems – by Thomas Howarth*. He began to give more lectures, normally, proudly delivered from notes, not read. He aimed that his lectures should, like the best sermons he had heard in his boyhood, be inspired by the moment, the faces before him, the hand leading him forward.

One of the people whom he revisited during this time was Norman Foster. Howarth's diary of 21 February 1996 notes,

> *Norman Foster at office – splendid space – met Norman's wife of two years – a beautiful Pakistani woman. They were most affable – Norman and I reminisced about our Manchester days and I persuaded him to join us, at The Relita reunion of Manchester 1956 graduates. Lost my gloves – Norman's driver took me to Simpsons to buy new ones but they were absurdly expensive – so I bought four shirts instead at the Hansen shop... The room at The Relita was long, narrow, noisy and smoky. The graduates gathered slowly – very moving compliments paid to me. Altogether a delightful evening.*

Howarth got great pleasure from knowing that he had been one of the first to recognise the outstanding talents of this Mancunian student and had helped establish the frame within which Foster was to become one of the great architects of the late twentieth century. For sheer originality and poetic power, Foster does not match Mackintosh, but on every other level Foster's brilliant achievements already surpass Mackintosh's, and Howarth was delighted to be recognised as the bridge between the two great men who bestride modern British architecture. All his life Howarth remained a teacher – inspirational and habitually well-organised. After Howarth had left Manchester for Canada, a letter from Professor Cordingley states, 'the staff are working one-leggedly without you!'

As Foster's first-year tutor, Howarth photographed and carefully documented Foster's early architectural projects and George Grenfell Baines remembers how, in 1958, it was Foster whom Howarth selected to work with him on the City Hall Competition for Toronto. 'This was an office project in which I was leader and on which, at Tom's instigation, a student named Norman Foster worked... The model we sent to Canada was made by another of Howarth's students, Thomas Hargreaves. He later became my partner in *Grenfell Baines & Hargreaves*. Hargreaves was a brilliant draughtsman but not a good model maker, and I'm not surprised to hear that his model fell to pieces in transit!' In 1999, Norman Foster was one of the 'great names' Harry Ferguson enlisted in the quest for Howarth's knighthood. This is an extract from the letter Foster wrote:

Thomas Howarth with Hugh
Casson (1994), London.
Gillian McDermott

Dr Howarth is one of the world's leading architectural historians whose work as both a teacher and writer have brought the subject alive for generations of students. Uniquely, he was a champion of the work of Charles Rennie Mackintosh at a time when Mackintosh's work was held in low critical esteem. It is entirely due to Howarth's visionary efforts that Mackintosh is now popularly regarded as one of Britain's most important architects and lauded as one of the founders of European Modernism.

Another Mancunian who meant a great deal to Howarth was Neville Cardus, the cricket and music correspondent of *The Manchester Guardian*. 'For many years', he told me, 'we worked in the same street, Oxford Street – Cardus in his newspaper office, and me in the School of Architecture', and it was clear that Howarth felt a strange sense of identification with this brilliant, rogue journalist. Both men were orphans, and their different journeys towards high accomplishment in their very different artistic fields were remarkably similar. Cardus was the illegitimate son of a theatreland prostitute and hardly went to school at all. At the age of ten, he fell in love with music and cricket and decided to become a writer. After years of struggle, Cardus, suddenly, marvellously, found success and his great achievement was to raise cricket reportage and music journalism to the realms of high art. Unlike Cardus, Howarth was brought up within a loving and prosperous family but his life was never easy and both men were aesthetes who gave their lives to advancing the work of artists, whom they knew to have genius much greater than their own. Howarth had a brilliantly retentive visual memory and could recall every significant image he had seen in his life a painting, a building, a chair but Cardus was an even more extraordinary phenomenon; he could hold any music he heard in his head for ever. Frequently, after going to a concert, he would lie in bed and 'play' a whole symphony, fully orchestrated, back to himself before rising to

write his review for the next morning's paper. Both men had unique gifts, the kind of gifts that would, in pre-literary days, have marked them out for service as priests, genealogists or musicians. Such gifts can induce strong feelings of cultural or social responsibility, as they did in Michelangelo and the greatest of the saints. Such gifts certainly bestow senses of uniqueness and power that, over the centuries, have been used for great good, and ill, as they nurture genius, licence and megalomania in fairly equal proportions. The words with which Cardus sums up his autobiography, published in 1947, apply almost equally to Howarth:

> I did not, as I have shown, possess initiative, or the wish to, 'get on'. I had gifts that were very late to show themselves, and burdened by a timid disposition and ill-health, [but] I contrived in the end to get out of my bones some seventy per-cent of the assets granted me by the inscrutable gods. No man can hope to do more; I suspect that Shakespeare himself was conscious of at least ten per-cent of waste and frustration.
>
> It has been a different struggle to most of its kind. The rise of a Dickens from the underworld can be accounted for in terms of imaginative genius calling for no specialist education. In the England of my youth it was almost impossible for a poor boy to hear a note of good music, let alone find the means for a comprehensive study of music. No music education in the world – I am prepared to swear it with my last breath – has been earned harder than mine, or in a school more severely tested and proven by experience. Not abstract theory, but living contact out of sheer need and love.
>
> I have stored my heart and mind with good things; if I live for another fifty years there will not be enough time to explore and savour to the full this harvest. Such harvests need to be jealously preserved, and we should offer constant thanksgiving for them. I don't believe in the contemporary idea of taking the arts to the people; let them seek and work for them.
>
> For the Kingdom of Heaven is there; it is in the arts that I have found the only religion that is real and, once found, omnipresent. For years I was as dogmatic an atheist as could be. It was when I understood for the first time the later quartets of Beethoven that I began to doubt my rationalism. 'One cannot speak justly of the short idyllic movements of these later quartets,' wrote Samuel Langford, 'without regarding them as Elysian in their nature and removed by their ideality from every contamination of the world' – in this phrase there is illumination for us in the darkening corridors of existence. Without creative urge and imagination man would be less than the animals. There is for me no accounting in terms of evolution or survival value for the sense of beauty, for laughter and tears that come and go without material prompting, for the ache after the perfect form and the ineluctable vision. If I know that my Redeemer liveth it is not on the church's testimony, but because of what Handel affirms.

In his last years, Howarth, travelled to enjoy holidays at the McDermott house in Carbis Bay, St Ives, Cornwall. He drew his experience of these returns to his native Britain into his poetry, attempting to unite his individual life with the great cycles of evolutionary nature and cosmic fact. One poem that he rewrote in Cornwall was inspired by the view north up the coast from Carbis Bay. The same view inspired Virginia Wolfe's novel, *To the Lighthouse*. Howarth's poem, entitled 'Sand', embraces a particular moment and aeons of time, Hayle Towans and Barbados, the rolling Atlantic and the membrous caul within which he was born:

> As I look from my window
> > In the first light of day
> The sand
> > Curves away white sparkling
> Brilliant and virginal
> > Unmarred save my shells and seaweed
> Caressed
> > By the gentle ocean
> Soothed
> > By the whispering wind
> Perfumed
> > By a myriad flowers
> Seasoned
> > By the sea-salt scented breeze
> As irresistible
> > As Ulysses' sirens
> Calling
> > Softly, softly.
>
> As I step barefoot my toes
> > Press deeply
> Sinking as into a luxurious
> > Carpet and
> As I walk the sand speaks
> > Under duress
> Awakening primordial memories
> > Sea rhythms
> Ebb and flow through the fissures
> > Of the subconscious
> Recalling remote planktonic
> > Ancestors or

Reviving sensations of arboreal life
    Caught up again
In the rocking of a cradle.

As I walk
    My stride beats out
Th'eternal pulse
    Of wave and tide
A heartbeat of the universe
    Echoing
From the womb of time
    Caught
In the beat of seagull's wings
In the sway of tendrilled anemone
In the wash the endless wash of seaweed
On the breakwater's sheer sides.

It is good to be home
    Island-born returning to island
To the sea
To the wind
To the sun
The blue blue sky
… And the sand.

In this poem, Howarth recognises the fact of his own imminent death. But the imagery and symbolism owe a good deal to the paintings and philosophy of Margaret Macdonald as expressed in her late great paintings, like *The Opera of the Sea* of 1915, and *La Mort Parfumee* of 1921. 'Sand' is written to a thumping drum-like rhythm which recurrently dissolves into the rhythmic soaring of the best Methodist hymns. The Wesley brothers, who founded Methodism in the late eighteenth-century, were deeply affected by their missionary journeys to Cornwall and, in the sisterly company of Gilli McDermott, Cornwall brought archaic and archetypal satisfactions to Howarth. It had equally inspired the poet and architect Thomas Hardy in the previous century:

I mean to build a hall anon,
And shape two turrets there,
And a broad newelled stair,
And a cool well for crystal water;
Yes; I will build a hall anon,

> Plant roses love shall feed upon,
> And apple-trees and pear.

The far south-west has always drawn people interested in the elemental and the spiritual and many artists from further north have moved there during this century: Barbara Hepworth, Ben Nicolson, Patrick Heron, Sean O'Casey, Daphne du Maurier, Ted Hughes. Cornwall is also the subject of Howarth's Scottish contemporary Hamish Henderson's last poem, 'Under the earth I go'. Referring to the ancient fishing village of Padstow on May Day, Henderson writes:

> Under the earth I go
> On the oak-leaf I stand
> I ride on the filly that never was foaled
> And I carry the dead in my hand...
>
> Sun-showers over the estuary
> Cormorant black on the pale sands yonder
> Taste of dank earth on my tongue
> Trembling oak-leaves coortin' the Sun,
> And the twin dragons, Life and Death,
> Jousting thegither under the Maypole.

Another poet who spoke deeply to Howarth was W.H. Auden. Like Howarth, Auden spent a significant part of his life abroad, occasionally yearning for home and the Pennine landscape he had known in his youth. In 1999 I sent Howarth the following lines:

> Always my boy of wish returns
> To those peat-stained deserted burns
> That feed the Wear and Tyne and Tees...
> An English area comes to mind,
> I see the nature of my kind
> As a locality I love,
> Those limestone moors that stretch from Brough
> To Hexham and the Roman Wall,
> There is my symbol of us all.

A few days later he phoned back to read me extracts from Auden's 'In Praise of Limestone':

If it form the one landscape that we, the inconstant ones,
    Are consistently homesick for, this is chiefly
Because it dissolves in water. Mark these rounded slopes
    With their surface fragrance of thyme and, beneath,
A secret system of caves and conduits; hear the springs
    That spurt out everywhere with a chuckle,
Each filling a private pool for its fish and carving
    Its own little ravine whose cliffs entertain
The butterfly and the lizard; examine this region
    Of short distances and definite places:
What could be more like Mother or a fitter background
    For her son, the flirtatious male who lounges
Against a rock in the sunlight, never doubting
    That for all his faults he is loved; whose works are but
Extensions of his power to charm? From weathered outcrop
    To hill-top temple, from appearing waters to
Conspicuous fountains, from a wild to a formal vineyard...

Over nine decades, Howarth's artistic taste moved and changed: first he was enraptured by music, then architecture, then by Mackintosh and the process of scholarship but finally, it was poetry that brought him home to the English voices and the British landscape that he loved. Gilli McDermott became part of that landscape and Howarth treasured her voice: the timbre, the eloquent English, the gently North-Country vowels; he treasured her vitality, her spontaneity, her youthful gift to praise. One of the qualities that made Howarth such an outstanding teacher was his ability to praise. He could be a martinet, he would sometimes deliberately disorientate students and be destructively provocative; he liked to prick pretensions; but, always, he came back to praise as the best stimulant to new work. During his last years, Howarth deliberately sought to gather young people, particularly young artists around him. He wanted to be a patron; they gave him continued access to youth and creative joy. Notable amongst them were two couples whom he liked to think of as his own group of Four: four Toronto artists, Barbara Solowan and John Sapsford, Valerie Sinclair and Scott Gwilliams. He also established close relationships with four young Germans, Marena Arndt, Cornelia Kappler, Marion Jegan and Christiana Fogel.

Discussing the various people who had meant most to him, Howarth suddenly remembered the Austrian poet Rainer Maria Rilke and he compared the way in which Rilke had given his heart to the great, once-neglected, sculptor Rodin, to the way in which he had given his heart to Mackintosh. Both Howarth and Rilke were natural disciples who became first teachers, then poets. 'Give us teachers who will praise the present for us. You are such a teacher,' wrote Rilke in his *Young Workman's Letter*. When

Rilke attempted to describe the creative genius of Rodin he pinpointed the same 'impelled urgency' that Howarth was to later recognise in Mackintosh: 'His works could not wait; they had to be made. He long foresaw their homelessness. The only choice he had was to destroy them, while yet within him, or to win for them the sky which is about the mountain – and that was his work. He raised the immense arc of his world above us and made it part of nature.'

When Rilke writes of the innocent privacy of the poetic impulse – his words describe crucial aspects of Howarth's boyhood sensibility and experience:

> I attempt to describe the nature of a poet: that tremendous and childlike
> nature, which occurred (we do not understand how) not only in unsurpassingly
> great figures of earlier times, but which is here also, beside us, actually
> mobilizing; it may be, in the boy who lifts up his great eyes and does not see
> us, this nature which assails young hearts, at a time when they are still
> powerless to face, the slightest form of life, in order to fill them with capacities
> and relationships, which immediately exceed all that can be acquired in a
> whole existence; indeed who would be able to speak calmly of this nature…
> Nothing vouches for it but the coldness of a boy's hand, nothing but an upward
> glance terrifyingly withdrawn; nothing but the indifference of this young
> creature, who does not talk to his brothers and who rises, as soon as he can,
> from meals which expose him too long to the judgment of his family.

And when Rilke wrote of sex, he might have been speaking for Howarth, as age sharpened his interest in this much tabooed subject: 'My sex is not only directed towards posterity; it is the secret of my own life… The terrible untruthfulness and uncertainty of our age has its roots in the refusal to acknowledge the happiness of sex.'

The parallels between the sensibilities and careers of these two men are many, and in neither is it easy to separate their teaching from their art. In a general sense, most major artists are accepted as 'teachers' but few teachers, even great teachers, are recognised as artists: yet this is what the best must be as they make knowledge, and feelings permanent down the generations. One of the letters Howarth received, shortly before his death, says something both very personal and universal about this dynamic, almost invisible, phenomenon. It came from one of Howarth's old students, Professor Geoffrey Broadbent:

> *My Dear Tom,*
>
> *It's premature, I'm sure, to thank you for all your help; what a life you have had and how much good you have done, how many of us you have fired with your enthusiasms. I know of no other teacher, of anything, anywhere in the world who still maintains such contacts with his disciples after fifty years! For so it will be in October.*

The loyalty with which so many students and friends stuck by Howarth is remarkable. This frequently difficult man, teacher and ideologue, drew people to him with a strangely magnetic force. He nurtured and offended; he cut-through and built-up. People found something in Howarth and they found more in themselves after contact with him. One of his wartime students from Glasgow, David Scott, every week, brought him a copy of *The Sunday Times* within hours of its arrival in Canada. His masseur, Max Kothe, attended him for thirty years. He was paid a minimal, basic fee but he continued to visit till the last week of Howarth's life and, if he drifted off into sleep during a session, Max would always stay until his client awoke before leaving. Helgie Tiernmann, Howarth's Estonian domestic cleaner was equally loyal, year after year keeping her hypochondriac master's rooms spotless and free of the dust he railed at. Howarth was difficult but the concentrated attention he brought to everything his mind embraced was compelling to others: his love of beauty was infectious, his compulsive sense of focus sharpened the experience of all those with whom he came in contact, even those he alienated or revolted. He was a force and he remains a 'conundrum'.

The last poems I read Tom, were from Rilke's *Ten Sonnets to Orpheus*. The first begins,

> A tree is rising. What a pure growing!
> Orpheus is sing! A tree inside the ear!
> Silence, silence. Yet new buildings,
> signals, and changes went on in the silence.'

And the seventh sonnet is this:

> To praise is the whole thing! A man who can praise
> comes towards us like ore out of the silences
> of rock. His heart, that dies, presses out
> for others a wine that is fresh for ever.
>
> When the god's energy takes hold of him,
> his voice never collapses into dust.
> Everything turns to vineyards, everything turns to grapes,
> made ready for harvest by his powerful south.
>
> The mould in the catacomb of the king
> does not suggest that his praising is lies, nor
> the fact that the gods cast shadows.
>
> He is one of the servants who does not go away,
> who still holds through the doors
> of the tomb trays of shining fruit.

Howarth's ashes are now scattered in the graveyard of Kirkham Parish Church, and a new-planted rose tree grows from earth that holds the bones of generations of his ancestors. He arranged this, as he arranged everything else about his death carefully: first surgical dismemberment by medical students, then cremation, then entombment in his native soil. Having worried about his health for most of his life, Howarth approached his death with a Blakean joy and inquisitive excitement, not so much in hope of any kind of resurrection or heavenly abode but in celebration of the fact that he had come through against the odds, done so much, and been true to high personal values. Born on the eve of the Great War, bedevilled with asthma and shrouded by a good family of tight-laced respectability, he survived to find art, peace and a surprising happiness. Howarth nurtured joy and discernment in his fellow man and he was proud to have walked in the best of company, with Mackintosh and Margaret Macdonald, Fra Newbery and Herbert MacNair, William Moyes and Norman Foster, with Frank Lloyd Wright and Gilli McDermott, and thousands more. 'Tim,' he said, 'if I can sing as I die – I shall.'

> As I run
>> in the dark on the sand
> Tearing apart the membrane
>> that imagination stretches
> Smoothly over its surface
>> I create fantastic patterns in the moonlight
> With the sea phosphorescent
>> and layer on layer
> Of greys and blacks...
>
> And then she is here
>> distilled essence of a tropical night
> Materializing out of the darkness
>> stepping lightly
> From the shadows
>> onto the white white sand
> Beautiful graceful ethereal
>> the Spirit of Night itself.

T.H.